Programming Microsoft ASP.NET MVC, Third Edition

Dino Esposito

Published with the authorization of Microsoft Corporation by:
O'Reilly Media, Inc.
1005 Gravenstein Highway North
Sebastopol, California 95472

ISBN: 978-0-7356-8094-4

1 2 3 4 5 6 7 8 9 LSI 9 8 7 6 5 4

Printed and bound in the United States of America.

Microsoft Press books are available through booksellers and distributors worldwide. If you need support related to this book, email Microsoft Press Book Support at *mspinput@microsoft.com*. Please tell us what you think of this book at *http://www.microsoft.com/learning/booksurvey*.

Microsoft and the trademarks listed at *http://www.microsoft.com/about/legal/en/us/IntellectualProperty/Trademarks/EN-US.aspx* are trademarks of the Microsoft group of companies. All other marks are property of their respective owners.

The example companies, organizations, products, domain names, email addresses, logos, people, places, and events depicted herein are fictitious. No association with any real company, organization, product, domain name, email address, logo, person, place, or event is intended or should be inferred.

This book expresses the author's views and opinions. The information contained in this book is provided without any express, statutory, or implied warranties. Neither the author, O'Reilly Media, Inc., Microsoft Corporation, nor its resellers, or distributors will be held liable for any damages caused or alleged to be caused either directly or indirectly by this book.

Acquisitions and Developmental Editors: Russell Jones and Rachel Roumeliotis

Production Editor: Kristen Brown

Editorial Production: Dianne Russell, Octal Publishing, Inc.

Technical Reviewer: John Mueller

Copyeditor: Bob Russell, Octal Publishing, Inc.

Indexer: BIM Indexing Services

Cover Design: Twist Creative • Seattle and Joel Panchot

Cover Composition: Ellie Volckhausen

Illustrator: Rebecca Demarest

To Silvia, Francesco, Michela, and my back for sustaining me.

—Dino

Contents at a glance

Contents

PART III   MOBILE CLIENTS

Chapter 11 Effective JavaScript   367

Chapter 12 Making websites mobile-friendly   399

Chapter 13 Building sites for multiple devices   **439**

What do you think of this book? We want to hear from you!

Microsoft is interested in hearing your feedback so we can continually improve our
books and learning resources for you. To participate in a brief online survey, please visit:

microsoft.com/learning/booksurvey

Introduction

Get your facts first, and then you can distort them as much as you please.

—Mark Twain

ASP.NET was devised in the late 1990s at a time when many companies in various industry sectors were rapidly discovering the Internet. The primary goal of ASP.NET was to make it possible for developers to build applications quickly and effectively without having to deal with low-level details such as HTTP, HTML, and JavaScript intricacies. That was exactly what the community loudly demanded at that time. ASP.NET is what Microsoft delivered to address this request, exceeding expectations by a large extent.

Today, more than ten years later, ASP.NET is showing signs of age, and many started even questioning the real necessity of having a web framework at all. It's an amazing time, and several options exist. There are Web Forms and ASP.NET MVC applications, and then there are more JavaScript-intensive client applications (single-page applications) that just use a server-side back end for delivering the basic layout of the few pages they actually expose and for ad hoc services such as bundling.

Curiously, with the Web Forms paradigm, you can still write functional applications even though ASP.NET MVC addresses more closely the present needs of developers. The most common scenario of Web Forms is applications for which you focus on presenting data and use some third-party high-quality suite of controls for that. ASP.NET MVC is for everything else, including the scaffolding of client-side single-page applications.

The way web applications are changing proves that ASP.NET MVC probably failed to replace ASP.NET Web Forms in the heart of many developers, but it was the right choice and qualifies to be the ideal web platform for any application that needs a back end of some substance; in particular (as I see things), web applications that aim at being multi-device functional. And yes, that likely means all web applications in less than two years.

Switching to ASP.NET MVC is more than ever the natural follow-up for ASP.NET developers.

Who should read this book

Over the years, quite a few people have read quite a few books and articles of mine. These readers are already aware that I'm not good at writing step-by-step, reference-style books, in the similar manner that I'm unable to teach the same class twice, running topics in the same order and showing the same examples.

This book is not for absolute beginners; but I do feel it is a book for all the others, including those who are still fairly new to ASP.NET MVC. The higher your level of competency and expertise, the less you can expect to find here that adds value in your particular case. However, this book benefits from a few years of real-world practice; so I'm sure it has a lot of solutions that might also appeal to the experts, particularly with respect to mobile devices.

If you use ASP.NET MVC, I'm confident that you'll find something in this book that makes it worthwhile.

Assumptions

This book expects that you have at least a minimal understanding of ASP.NET development.

Who should not read this book

If you're looking for a step-by-step guide to ASP.NET MVC, this is not the ideal book for you.

Organization of this book

This book is divided into three sections. Part I, "ASP.NET MVC fundamentals," provides a quick overview of the foundation of ASP.NET and its core components. Part II, "ASP.NET MVC software design," focuses on common aspects of web applications and specific design patterns and best practices. Finally, Part III, "Mobile clients," is about JavaScript and mobile interfaces.

System requirements

You preferably have the following software installed in order to run the examples presented in this book:

- One of the following operating systems: Windows 8/8.1, Windows 7, Windows Vista with Service Pack 2 (except Starter Edition), Windows XP with Service Pack 3 (except Starter Edition), Windows Server 2008 with Service Pack 2, Windows Server 2003 with Service Pack 2, or Windows Server 2003 R2

- Microsoft Visual Studio 2013, any edition (multiple downloads might be required if you're using Express Edition products)

- Microsoft SQL Server 2012 Express Edition or higher, with SQL Server Management Studio 2012 Express or higher (included with Visual Studio; Express Editions require a separate download)

Depending on your Windows configuration, you might require Local Administrator rights to install or configure Visual Studio 2013 and SQL Server 2012 products.

Code samples

Most of the chapters in this book include exercises with which you can interactively try out new material learned in the main text. You can download all sample projects, in both their pre-exercise and post-exercise formats, from the following page:

> *http://aka.ms/programASP-NET_MVC/files*

Follow the instructions to download the asp-net-mvc-examples.zip file.

Installing the code samples

Perform the following steps to install the code samples on your computer so that you can use them with the exercises in this book.

1. Unzip the asp-net-mvc-examples.zip file that you downloaded from the book's website (name a specific directory along with directions to create it, if necessary).

2. If prompted, review the displayed end-user license agreement. If you accept the terms, select the Accept option, and then click Next.

Note If the license agreement doesn't appear, you can access it from the same webpage from which you downloaded the asp-net-mvc-examples.zip file.

Using the code samples

The folder created by the Setup.exe program contains one subfolder for each chapter. In turn, each chapter might contain additional subfolders. All examples are organized in a single Visual Studio 2013 solution. You open the solution file in Visual Studio 2013 and navigate through the examples.

Errata & book support

We've made every effort to ensure the accuracy of this book and its companion content. Any errors that have been reported since this book was published are listed on our Microsoft Press site:

http://aka.ms/programASP-NET_MVC/errata

If you find an error that is not already listed, you can report it to us through the same page.

If you need additional support, email Microsoft Press Book Support at *mspinput@ microsoft.com*.

Please note that product support for Microsoft software is not offered through the aforementioned addresses.

We want to hear from you

At Microsoft Press, your satisfaction is our top priority, and your feedback our most valuable asset. Please tell us what you think of this book at:

http://aka.ms/tellpress

The survey is short, and we read every one of your comments and ideas. Thanks in advance for your input!

Stay in touch

Let's keep the conversation going! We're on Twitter: *http://twitter.com/MicrosoftPress*

ASP.NET MVC fundamentals

CHAPTER 1

ASP.NET MVC controllers

They always say time changes things, but you actually have to change them yourself.

—Andy Warhol

I think ASP.NET Web Forms started getting old the day that Ajax conquered the masses. As some have said, Ajax has been the poisonous arrow shot in the heel of ASP.NET—another Achilles. Ajax made getting more and more control over HTML and client-side code a true necessity. Over time, this led to different architectures and made ASP.NET Web Forms a little less up to the task with each passing day.

Applied to the existing ASP.NET runtime, the MVC pattern produced a new framework—ASP.NET MVC—that aligns web development to the needs of developers today.

In ASP.NET MVC, each request results in the execution of an action—ultimately, a method on a specific class. The results of executing the action are passed down to the view subsystem along with a view template. The results and template are then used to build the final response for the browser. Users don't point the browser to a page, they just place a request. Doesn't that sound like a big change?

Unlike Web Forms, ASP.NET MVC is made of various layers of code connected together but not intertwined and not forming a single monolithic block. For this reason, it's easy to replace any of these layers with custom components that enhance the maintainability as well as the testability of the solution. With ASP.NET MVC, you gain total control over the markup and can apply styles and inject script code at will using the JavaScript frameworks that you like most.

Based on the same run-time environment as Web Forms, ASP.NET MVC pushes a web-adapted implementation of the classic Model-View-Controller pattern and makes developing web applications a significantly different experience. In this chapter, you'll discover the role and structure of the controller—the foundation of ASP.NET MVC applications—and how requests are routed to controllers.

Although you might decide to keep using Web Forms, for today's web development, ASP.NET MVC is a much better choice. You don't need to invest a huge amount of time, but you need to understand exactly what's going on and the philosophy behind MVC. If you do that, any investment you make will pay you back sooner than you expect.

> **Note** This book is based on ASP.NET MVC 5. This version of ASP.NET MVC is backward compatible with the previous versions. This means that you can install both versions side by side on the same computer and play with the new version without affecting any existing MVC code that you might have already.

Routing incoming requests

Originally, the entire ASP.NET platform was developed around the idea of serving requests for physical pages. It turns out that most URLs used within an ASP.NET application are made of two parts: the path to the physical webpage that contains the logic, and some data stuffed in the query string to provide parameters. This approach has worked for a few years, and it still works today. The ASP.NET run-time environment, however, doesn't limit you to just calling into resources identified by a specific location and file. By writing an ad hoc HTTP handler and binding it to a URL, you can use ASP.NET to execute code in response to a request regardless of the dependencies on physical files. This is just one of the aspects that most distinguishes ASP.NET MVC from ASP.NET Web Forms. Let's briefly see how to simulate the ASP.NET MVC behavior with an HTTP handler.

> **Note** In software, the term URI (which stands for *Uniform Resource Identifier*) is used to refer to a resource by location or a name. When the URI identifies the resource by location, it's called a *URL*, or *Uniform Resource Locator*. When the URI identifies a resource by name, it becomes a *URN*, or *Uniform Resource Name*. In this regard, ASP.NET MVC is designed to deal with more generic URIs, whereas ASP.NET Web Forms was designed to deal with location-aware physical resources.

Simulating the ASP.NET MVC runtime

Let's build a simple ASP.NET Web Forms application and use HTTP handlers to figure out the internal mechanics of ASP.NET MVC applications. You can start from the basic ASP.NET Web Forms application you get from your Microsoft Visual Studio project manager.

Defining the syntax of recognized URLs

In a world in which requested URLs don't necessarily match up with physical files on the web server, the first step to take is listing which URLs are meaningful for the application. To avoid being too specific, let's assume that you support only a few fixed URLs, each mapped to an HTTP handler component. The following code snippet shows the changes required to be made to the default *web.config* file:

```
<httpHandlers>
    <add verb="*"
        path="home/test/*"
        type="MvcEmule.Components.MvcEmuleHandler" />
</httpHandlers>
```

Whenever the application receives a request that matches the specified URL, it will pass it on to the specified handler.

Defining the behavior of the HTTP handler

In ASP.NET, an HTTP handler is a component that implements the *IHttpHandler* interface. The interface is simple and consists of two members, as shown here:

```
public class MvcEmuleHandler : IHttpHandler
{
    public void ProcessRequest(HttpContext context)
    {
        // Logic goes here
        ...
    }

    public Boolean IsReusable
    {
        get { return false; }
    }
}
```

Most of the time, an HTTP handler has a hardcoded behavior influenced only by some input data passed via the query string. However, nothing prevents us from using the handler as an abstract factory for adding one more level of indirection. The handler, in fact, can use information from the request to determine an external component to call to actually serve the request. In this way, a single HTTP handler can serve a variety of requests and just dispatch the call among a few more specialized components.

The HTTP handler could parse out the URL in tokens and use that information to identify the class and the method to invoke. Here's an example of how it could work:

```
public void ProcessRequest(HttpContext context)
{
    // Parse out the URL and extract controller, action, and parameter
    var segments = context.Request.Url.Segments;
    var controller = segments[1].TrimEnd('/');
    var action = segments[2].TrimEnd('/');
    var param1 = segments[3].TrimEnd('/');

    // Complete controller class name with suffix and (default) namespace
    var fullName = String.Format("{0}.{1}Controller",
                        this.GetType().Namespace, controller);
    var controllerType = Type.GetType(fullName, true, true);
```

```
// Get an instance of the controller
var instance = Activator.CreateInstance(controllerType);

// Invoke the action method on the controller instance
var methodInfo = controllerType.GetMethod(action,
        BindingFlags.Instance |
        BindingFlags.IgnoreCase |
        BindingFlags.Public);
var result = String.Empty;
if (methodInfo.GetParameters().Length == 0)
{
    result = methodInfo.Invoke(instance, null) as String;
}
else
{
    result = methodInfo.Invoke(instance, new Object[] { param1 }) as String;
}

// Write out results
context.Response.Write(result);
}
```

The preceding code assumes that the first token in the URL after the server name contains the key information to identify the specialized component that will serve the request. The second token refers to the name of the method to call on this component. Finally, the third token indicates a parameter to pass.

Invoking the HTTP handler

Given a URL such as *home/test/***, it turns out that home identifies the class, test identifies the methods, and whatever trails is the parameter. The name of the class is further worked out and extended to include a namespace and a suffix. According to the example, the final class name is *MvcEmule.Components.HomeController*. This class is expected to be available to the application. The class is also expected to expose a method named *Test*, as shown here:

```
namespace MvcEmule.Components
{
    public class HomeController
    {
        public String Test(Object param1)
        {
            var message = "<html><h1>Got it! You passed '{0}'</h1></html>";
            return String.Format(message, param1);
        }
    }
}
```

Figure 1-1 shows the effect of invoking a page-agnostic URL in an ASP.NET Web Forms application.

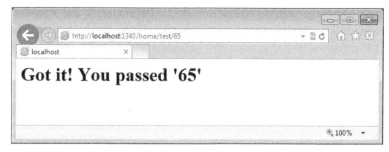

FIGURE 1-1 Processing page-agnostic URLs in ASP.NET Web Forms.

This simple example demonstrates the basic mechanics used by ASP.NET MVC. The specialized component that serves a request is the controller. The controller is a class with just methods and no state. A unique system-level HTTP handler takes care of dispatching incoming requests to a specific controller class so that the instance of the class executes a given action method and produces a response.

What about the scheme of URLs? In this example, you just use a hardcoded URL. In ASP.NET MVC, you have a very flexible syntax that you can use to express those URLs that the application recognizes. In addition, a new system component in the run-time pipeline intercepts requests, processes the URL, and triggers the ASP.NET MVC HTTP handler. This component is the URL Routing HTTP module.

The URL routing HTTP module

The URL routing HTTP module processes incoming requests by looking at the URLs and dispatching them to the most appropriate executor. The URL routing HTTP module supersedes the URL rewriting feature of older versions of ASP.NET. At its core, URL rewriting consists of hooking up a request, parsing the original URL, and instructing the HTTP run-time environment to serve a "possibly related but different" URL.

Superseding URL rewriting

URL rewriting comes into play if you need to make tradeoffs between needing human-readable and search engine optimization (SEO)-friendly URLs and needing to programmatically deal with tons of URLs. For example, consider the following URL:

```
http://northwind.com/news.aspx?id=1234
```

The *news.aspx* page incorporates any logic required to retrieve, format, and display any given news. The ID for the specific news to retrieve is provided via a parameter on the query string. As a developer, implementing the page couldn't be easier; you get the query string parameter, run the query, and create the HTML. As a user or for a search engine, by simply looking at the URL you can't really understand the intent of the page, and you aren't likely to remember the address easily enough to pass it around.

URL rewriting helps you in two ways. First, it makes it possible for developers to use a generic front-end page, such as *news.aspx*, to display related content. Second, it also makes it possible for users to request friendly URLs that will be programmatically mapped to less intuitive but easier-to-manage URLs. In a nutshell, URL rewriting exists to decouple the requested URL from the physical webpage that serves the requests.

In the latest version of ASP.NET 4 Web Forms, you can use URL routing to match incoming URLs to other URLs without incurring the costs of HTTP 302 redirects. Conversely, in ASP.NET MVC, URL routing serves the purpose of mapping incoming URLs to a controller class and an action method.

> **Note** Originally developed as an ASP.NET MVC component, the URL routing module is now a native part of the ASP.NET platform and, as mentioned, offers its services to both ASP.NET MVC and ASP.NET Web Forms applications, though through a slightly different API.

Routing the requests

What happens exactly when a request knocks at the Internet Information Services (IIS) gate? Figure 1-2 gives you an overall picture of the various steps involved and how things work differently in ASP.NET MVC and ASP.NET Web Forms applications.

The URL routing module intercepts any requests for the application that could not be served otherwise by IIS. If the URL refers to a physical file (for example, an ASPX file), the routing module ignores the request, unless it's otherwise configured. The request then falls down to the classic ASP.NET machinery to be processed as usual, in terms of a page handler.

Otherwise, the URL routing module attempts to match the URL of the request to any of the application-defined routes. If a match is found, the request goes into the ASP.NET MVC space to be processed in terms of a call to a controller class. If no match is found, the request will be served by the standard ASP.NET runtime in the best possible way and likely results in an HTTP 404 error.

In the end, only requests that match predefined URL patterns (also known as routes) are allowed to enjoy the ASP.NET MVC runtime. All such requests are routed to a common HTTP handler that instantiates a controller class and invokes a defined method on it. Next, the controller method, in turn, selects a view component to generate the actual response.

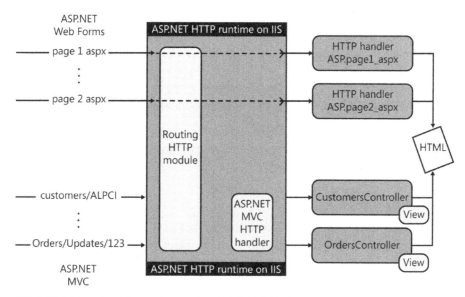

FIGURE 1-2 The role of the routing module in ASP.NET MVC.

The internal structure of the URL routing module

In terms of implementation, I should note that the URL routing engine is an HTTP module that wires up the *PostResolveRequestCache* event. The event fires right after checking that no response for the request is available in the ASP.NET cache.

The HTTP module matches the requested URL to one of the user-defined URL routes and sets the HTTP context to using the ASP.NET MVC standard HTTP handler to serve the request. As a developer, you're not likely to deal with the URL routing module directly. The module is provided by the system and you don't need to perform any specific form of configuration. Instead, you are responsible for providing the routes that your application supports and that the routing module will actually consume.

Application routes

By design, an ASP.NET MVC application is not forced to depend on physical pages. In ASP.NET MVC, users place requests for acting on resources. The framework, however, doesn't mandate the syntax for describing resources and actions. I'm aware that the expression "acting on resources" will likely make you think of Representational State Transfer (REST). And, of course, you will not be too far off the mark in thinking so.

Although you can definitely use a pure REST approach within an ASP.NET MVC application, I would rather say that ASP.NET MVC is loosely REST-oriented in that it does acknowledge concepts such as resource and action, but it leaves you free to use your own syntax to express and implement resources and actions. As an example, in a pure REST solution you would use HTTP verbs to express actions—GET, POST, PUT, and DELETE—and the URL to identify the resource. Implementing a pure REST solution in ASP.NET MVC is possible but requires some extra work on your part.

The default behavior in ASP.NET MVC is using custom URLs where you make yourself responsible for the syntax through which actions and resources are specified. This syntax is expressed through a collection of URL patterns, also known as routes.

URL patterns and routes

A route is a pattern-matching string that represents the absolute path of a URL—namely, the URL string without protocol, server, and port information. A route might be a constant string, but it will more likely contain a few placeholders. Here's a sample route:

```
/home/test
```

The route is a constant string and is matched only by URLs whose absolute path is /home/test. Most of the time, however, you deal with parametric routes that incorporate one or more placeholders. Here are a couple of examples:

```
/{resource}/{action}
/Customer/{action}
```

Both routes are matched by any URLs that contain exactly two segments. The latter, though, requires that the first segment equals the string "Customer". The former, instead, doesn't pose specific constraints on the content of the segments.

Often referred to as a *URL parameter*, a placeholder is a name enclosed in curly brackets { }. You can have multiple placeholders in a route as long as they are separated by a constant or delimiter. The forward slash (/) character acts as a delimiter between the various parts of the route. The name of the placeholder (for example, action) is the key that your code will use to programmatically retrieve the content of the corresponding segment from the actual URL.

Here's the default route for an ASP.NET MVC application:

```
{controller}/{action}/{id}
```

In this case, the sample route contains three placeholders separated by the delimiter. A URL that matches the preceding route is the following:

```
/Customers/Edit/ALFKI
```

You can add as many routes as you want with as many placeholders as appropriate. You can even remove the default route.

Defining application routes

Routes for an application are usually registered in the global.asax file, and they are processed at the application startup. Let's have a look at the section of the global.asax file that deals with routes:

```
public class MvcApplication : HttpApplication
{
    protected void Application_Start()
    {
        RouteConfig.RegisterRoutes(RouteTable.Routes);

        // Other code
        ...
    }
}
```

RegisterRoutes is a method on the *RouteConfig* class defined in a separate folder, usually named App_:Start. (You can rename the folder at will, though.) Here's the implementation of the class:

```
public class RouteConfig
{
    public static void RegisterRoutes(RouteCollection routes)
    {
        // Other code
        ...

        // Listing routes
        routes.MapRoute(
            "Default",
            "{controller}/{action}/{id}",
            new {
                    controller = "Home",
                    action = "Index",
                    id = UrlParameter.Optional
            });
    }
}
```

As you can see, the *Application_Start* event handler calls into a public static method named *RegisterRoutes* that lists all routes. Note that the name of the *RegisterRoutes* method as well as the prototype is arbitrary and you can change it if there's a valid reason.

Supported routes must be added to a static collection of *Route* objects managed by ASP.NET MVC. This collection is *RouteTable.Routes*. You typically use the handy *MapRoute* method to populate the collection. The *MapRoute* method offers a variety of overloads and works well most of the time. However, it doesn't let you configure every possible aspect of a route object. If there's something you need to set on a route that *MapRoute* doesn't support, you might want to resort to the following code:

```
// Create a new route and add it to the system collection
var route = new Route(...);
RouteTable.Routes.Add("NameOfTheRoute", route);
```

A route is characterized by a few attributes, such as name, URL pattern, default values, constraints, data tokens, and a route handler. The attributes you set most often are name, URL pattern, and default values. Let's expand on the code you get for the default route:

```
routes.MapRoute(
        "Default",
        "{controller}/{action}/{id}",
        new {
                controller = "Home",
                action = "Index",
                id = UrlParameter.Optional
        });
```

The first parameter is the name of the route; each route should have a unique name. The second parameter is the URL pattern. The third parameter is an object that specifies default values for the URL parameters.

Note that a URL can match the pattern even in an incomplete form. Let's consider the root URL—*http://yourserver.com*. At first sight, such a URL wouldn't match the route. However, if a default value is specified for a URL parameter, the segment is considered optional. As a result, for the preceding example, when you request the root URL, the request is resolved by invoking the method *Index* on the *Home* controller.

Processing routes

The ASP.NET URL routing module employs a number of rules when trying to match an incoming requested URL to a defined route. The most important rule is that routes must be checked in the order in which they were registered in global.asax.

To ensure that routes are processed in the correct order, you must list them from the most specific to the least specific. In any case, keep in mind that the search for a matching route always ends at the first match. This means that just adding a new route at the bottom of the list might not work and might also cause you a bit of trouble. In addition, be aware that placing a catch-all pattern at the top of the list will make any other patterns, no matter how specific, pass unnoticed.

Beyond order of appearance, other factors affect the process of matching URLs to routes. As mentioned, one is the set of default values that you might have provided for a route. Default values are simply values that are automatically assigned to defined placeholders in case the URL doesn't provide specific values. Consider the following two routes:

```
{Orders}/{Year}/{Month}
{Orders}/{Year}
```

If in the first route you assign default values for both *{Year}* and *{Month}*, the second route will never be evaluated because, thanks to the default values, the first route is always a match regardless of whether the URL specifies a year and a month.

A trailing forward slash (/) is also a pitfall. The routes *{Orders}/{Year}* and *{Orders}/{Year}/* are two very different things. One won't match to the other, even though logically, at least from a user's perspective, you'd expect them to.

Another factor that influences the URL-to-route match is the list of constraints that you optionally define for a route. A route constraint is an additional condition that a given URL parameter must fulfill to make the URL match the route. The URL not only should be compatible with the URL pattern, it also needs to contain compatible data. A constraint can be defined in various ways, including through a regular expression. Here's a sample route with constraints:

```
routes.MapRoute(
    "ProductInfo",
    "{controller}/{productId}/{locale}",
    new { controller = "Product", action = "Index", locale="en-us" },
    new { productId = @"\d{8}",
          locale = ""[a-z]{2}-[a-z]{2}" });
```

In particular, the route requires that the *productId* placeholder must be a numeric sequence of exactly eight digits, whereas the local placeholder must be a pair of two-letter strings separated by a dash. Constraints don't ensure that all invalid product IDs and locale codes are stopped at the gate, but at least they cut off a good deal of work.

Route handler

The route defines a bare-minimum set of rules, according to which the routing module decides whether the incoming request URL is acceptable to the application. The component that ultimately decides how to remap the requested URL is another one entirely. Precisely, it is the route handler. The route handler is the object that processes any requests that match a given route. Its sole purpose in life is returning the HTTP handler that will actually serve any matching request.

Technically speaking, a route handler is a class that implements the *IRouteHandler* interface. The interface is defined as shown here:

```
public interface IRouteHandler
{
    IHttpHandler GetHttpHandler(RequestContext requestContext);
}
```

Defined in the *System.Web.Routing* namespace, the *RequestContext* class encapsulates the HTTP context of the request plus any route-specific information available, such as the *Route* object itself, URL parameters, and constraints. This data is grouped into a *RouteData* object. Here's the signature of the *RequestContext* class:

```
public class RequestContext
{
    public RequestContext(HttpContextBase httpContext, RouteData routeData);

    // Properties
    public HttpContextBase HttpContext { get; set; }
    public RouteData RouteData { get; set; }
}
```

The ASP.NET MVC framework doesn't offer many built-in route handlers, and this is probably a sign that the need to use a custom route handler is not that common. Yet, the extensibility point exists and, in case of need, you can take advantage of it. I'll return to custom route handlers and provide an example later in the chapter.

Handling requests for physical files

Another configurable aspect of the routing system that contributes to a successful URL-to-route matching is whether the routing system has to handle requests that match a physical file.

By default, the ASP.NET routing system ignores requests whose URL can be mapped to a file that physically exists on the server. Note that if the server file exists, the routing system ignores the request even if the request matches a route.

If you need to, you can force the routing system to handle all requests by setting the *Route ExistingFiles* property of the *RouteCollection* object to *true*, as shown here:

```
// In global.asax.cs
public static void RegisterRoutes(RouteCollection routes)
{
    routes.RouteExistingFiles = true;
    ...
}
```

Note that having all requests handled via routing can create some issues in an ASP.NET MVC application. For example, if you add the preceding code to the global.asax.cs file of a sample ASP.NET MVC application and run it, you'll immediately face an HTTP 404 error when accessing default.aspx.

Preventing routing for defined URLs

The ASP.NET URL routing module doesn't limit you to maintaining a list of acceptable URL patterns; you can also keep certain URLs off the routing mechanism. You can prevent the routing system from handling certain URLs in two steps. First, you define a pattern for those URLs and save it to a route. Second, you link that route to a special route handler—the *StopRoutingHandler* class. All it does is throw a *NotSupported* exception when its *GetHttpHandler* method is invoked.

For example, the following code instructs the routing system to ignore any *.axd* requests:

```
// In global.asax.cs
public static void RegisterRoutes(RouteCollection routes)
{
    routes.IgnoreRoute("{resource}.axd/{*pathInfo}");
    ...
}
```

All that *IgnoreRoute* does is associate a *StopRoutingHandler* route handler to the route built around the specified URL pattern.

Finally, a little explanation is required for the *{*pathInfo}* placeholder in the URL. The token *pathInfo* simply represents a placeholder for any content following the *.axd* URL. The asterisk (*), though, indicates that the last parameter should match the rest of the URL. In other words, anything that follows the *.axd* extension goes into the *pathInfo* parameter. Such parameters are referred to as *catch-all parameters*.

Attribute routing

A popular NuGet package included in ASP.NET MVC 5 is AttributeRouting. (See *http:// attributerouting.net*.) Attribute routing is all about defining routes directly on controller actions by using attributes. As previously demonstrated, classic routing is based on the conventions established in global.asax, at the startup of the application.

Any time a request comes in, the URL is matched against the template of registered routes. If a match is found, the appropriate controller and action method to serve the request are determined. If not, the request is denied and the result is usually a 404 message. Now, in large applications, or even in medium-sized applications with a strong REST flavor, the number of routes can be quite large and could easily be in the order of hundreds. You might quickly find that classic routing becomes a bit overwhelming to handle. For this reason, the AttributeRouting project was started and is now integrated in ASP.NET MVC 5 and even in Web API, as is discussed in Chapter 10, "An executive guide to Web API."

```
[HttpGet("orders/{orderId}/show")]
public ActionResult GetOrderById(int orderId)
{
    ...
}
```

The code sets the method *GetOrderById* to be available over a HTTP GET call only if the URL template matches the specified pattern. The route parameter—the *orderId* token—must match one of the parameters defined in the method's signature. There are a few more attributes available (for each HTTP verb), but the gist of attribute routes is all here. For more information (for example, configuration), you can refer to *http://attributerouting.net* because the integration for ASP.NET MVC is a direct emanation of the existing NuGet package.

The controller class

In spite of the explicit reference to the Model-View-Controller pattern in the name, the ASP.NET MVC architecture is essentially centered on one pillar—the controller. The controller governs the processing of a request and orchestrates the back end of the system (for example, business layer, services, data access layer) to grab raw data for the response. Next, the controller wraps up raw data computed for the request into a valid response for the caller. When the response is a markup view, the controller relies on the view engine module to combine data and view templates and produce HTML.

Aspects of a controller

Any request that passes the URL routing filter is mapped to a controller class and served by executing a given method on the class. Therefore, the controller class is the place where developers write the actual code required to serve a request. Let's briefly explore some characterizing aspects of controllers.

Granularity of controllers

An ASP.NET MVC application usually comprises of a variety of controller classes. How many controllers should you have? The actual number is up to you and depends only on how you want to organize your application's actions. In fact, you could arrange an application around a single controller class that contains methods for any possible requests.

A common practice consists of having a controller class for each significant functionality your application implements. For example, you can have a *CustomerController* class that takes care of requests related to querying, deleting, updating, and inserting customers. Likewise, you can create a *ProductController* class for dealing with products, and so forth. Most of the time, these objects are directly related to items in the application's main menu.

In general, you can say that the granularity of the controller is a function of the granularity of the user interface. Plan to have a controller for each significant source of requests you have in the user interface.

Stateless components

A new instance of the selected controller class is instantiated for each request. Any state you might add to the class is bound to the same lifetime of the request. The controller class then must be able to retrieve any data it needs to work from the HTTP request stream and the HTTP context.

Further layering is up to you

Often, ASP.NET MVC and controller classes are presented as a magic wand that you wave to write layered code that is cleaner and easier to read and maintain. The stateless nature of the controller class helps a lot in this regard, but it is not enough.

In ASP.NET MVC, the controller is isolated from both the user interface that triggered the request and the engine that produces the view for the browser. The controller sits in between the view and the back end of the system. Although this sort of isolation from the view is welcome and fixes a weak point of ASP.NET Web Forms, it alone doesn't ensure that your code will be respectful of the venerable principle of Separation of Concerns (SoC).

The system gets you a minimal level of separation from the view—everything else is up to you. Keep in mind that nothing, not even in ASP.NET MVC, prevents you from using direct ADO.NET calls and plain Transact-SQL (T-SQL) statements directly in the controller class. The controller class is not the back end of the system, and it is not the business layer. Instead, it should be considered as the MVC counterpart of the code-behind class of Web Forms. As such, it definitely belongs to the presentation layer, not the business layer.

Highly testable

The inherent statelessness of the controller and its neat separation from the view make the controller class potentially easy to test. However, the real testability of the controller class should be measured against its effective layering. Let's have a look at Figure 1-3.

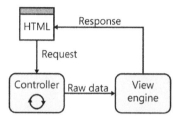

FIGURE 1-3 Controllers and views in ASP.NET MVC.

Although you can feed the controller class any fixed input you like and its output can be asserted without major issues, nothing can be said about the internal structure of action methods. The more the implementation of these methods is tightly bound to external resources (for example, databases, services, components), the less likely it is that testing a controller will be quick and easy.

Writing controller classes

The writing of a controller class can be summarized in two simple steps: creating a class that inherits (either directly or indirectly) from *Controller*, and adding a bunch of public methods. However, a couple of important details must be clarified: how the system gets to know the controller class to instantiate, and how it figures out the method to invoke.

From routing to controllers

Regardless of how you define your URL patterns, any request must always be resolved in terms of a controller name and an action name. This is one of the pillars of ASP.NET MVC. The controller name is automatically read from the URL if the URL includes a *{controller}* placeholder. The same happens for action names if the URL contains an *{action}* placeholder.

Having completely custom URLs devoid of such placeholders is still acceptable, though. In this case, however, it is your responsibility to indicate the controller and action through default values, as shown here:

```
routes.MapRoute(
    "SampleRoute",
    "about",
    new { controller = "Home", action = "About"}
);
```

If controller and action names can't be resolved in a static way, you might want to write a custom route handler, explore the details of the request, and figure out controller and action names. Then, you just store them in the *RouteData* collection, as shown here:

```
public class AboutRouteHandler : IRouteHandler
{
    public IHttpHandler GetHttpHandler(RequestContext requestContext)
    {
        if (requestContext.HttpContext.Request.Url.AbsolutePath == "/about")
        {
            requestContext.RouteData.Values["controller"] = "home";
            requestContext.RouteData.Values["action"] = "about";
        }
        return new MvcHandler(requestContext);
    }
}
```

For a route that requires a custom handler, the registration process is a bit different from what you saw earlier. Here's the code you need to have in *RegisterRoutes*:

```
public static void RegisterRoutes(RouteCollection routes)
{
    var aboutRoute = new Route("about", new AboutRouteHandler());
    routes.Add("SampleAboutRoute", aboutRoute);
    ...
}
```

Be sure to note that the controller name you obtain from the routing module doesn't match exactly the actual name of class that will be invoked. By default, the controller class is named after the controller name with a Controller suffix added. In the previous example, if *home* is the controller name, the class name is assumed to be *HomeController*. Note that conventions apply not just to the class name but also to the namespace. In particular, the class is expected to be scoped in the *Controllers* namespace under the default project namespace.

Note When you add a route based on a custom route handler that sets controller and action names programmatically, you might run into trouble with the links generated by the *Html.ActionLink* helper. You commonly use this helper to create route-based links for menus and other visual elements of the user interface. If you add a route with a custom handler, you might be surprised to see that the links you get from the helper are unexpectedly based on this route. To solve the issue, either you change *ActionLink* with *RouteLink* and expressly indicate which route you want the URL to be created after, or you specify in the custom route that controller and action are optional parameters.

From routing to actions

When the ASP.NET MVC run-time environment has a valid instance of the selected controller class, it yields to the action invoker component for the actual execution of the request. The action invoker gets the action name and attempts to match it to a public method on the controller class.

The action parameter indicates the name of the action to perform. Most of the time, the controller class just has a method with the same name. If this is the case, the invoker will execute it. Note, though, that you can associate an action name attribute to any public method, thus decoupling the method name from the action name. Here's an example:

```
public class HomeController : Controller
{
    // Implicit action name: Index
    public ActionResult Index()
    {
        ...
    }

    [NonAction]
    public ActionResult About()
    {
        ...
    }

    [ActionName("About")]
    public ActionResult LoveGermanShepherds()
    {
        ...
    }
}
```

The method *Index* is not decorated with attributes, so it is implicitly bound to an action with the same name. The third public method has a very fancy name, but it is explicitly bound to the action *About* via the *ActionName* attribute. Finally, note that to prevent a public controller method from being implicitly bound to an action name, you use the *NonAction* attribute. Therefore, given the previous code snippet when the user requests the about action, the method *LoveGermanShepherds* runs regardless of the HTTP verb used to place the request.

Actions and HTTP verbs

ASP.NET MVC is flexible enough to let you bind a method to an action for a specific HTTP verb. To associate a controller method with an HTTP verb, you either use the parametric *AcceptVerbs* attribute or direct attributes such as *HttpGet*, *HttpPost*, and *HttpPut*. Using the *AcceptVerbs* attribute, you can specify which HTTP verb is required to execute a given method. Let's consider the following example:

```
[AcceptVerbs(HttpVerbs.Post)]
public ActionResult Edit(Customer customer)
{
    ...
}
```

Given that code, it turns out that the *Edit* method can't be invoked by using a *GET*. Note also that you are not allowed to have multiple *AcceptVerbs* attributes on a single method. Your code won't compile if you add multiple *AcceptVerbs* attributes (or analogous direct HTTP verb attributes) to an action method.

The *AcceptVerbs* attribute takes any value from the *HttpVerbs* enum type:

```
public enum HttpVerbs
{
    Get = 1,
    Post = 2,
    Put = 4,
    Delete = 8,
    Head = 0x10
}
```

The *HttpVerbs* enum is decorated with the *Flags* attribute, so you can combine together multiple values from the enumeration by using the bitwise OR (|) operator and still obtain another *HttpVerbs* value.

```
[AcceptVerbs(HttpVerbs.Post|HttpVerbs.Put)]
public ActionResult Edit(Customer customer)
{
    ...
}
```

You perform an HTTP *GET* command when you follow a link or type the URL into the address bar. You perform an HTTP *POST* when you submit the content of an HTML form. You can perform any other HTTP command only via AJAX, or perhaps from a Windows client that sends requests to the ASP.NET MVC application.

The ability to assign a specific verb to a given action method naturally leads to duplicate method names. Two methods with the same name are acceptable in a controller class as long as they accept distinct HTTP verbs. Otherwise, an exception will be thrown because ASP.NET MVC doesn't know how to resolve the ambiguity.

 Note You can also use multiple individual attributes, one for each HTTP verb. Examples are *HttpGet* and *HttpPost*.

Action methods

Let's have a look at a sample controller class with a couple of simple but functional action methods:

```
public class HomeController : Controller
{
    public ActionResult Index()
    {
        // Process input data
        ...
```

```
    // Perform expected task
    ...

    // Generate the result of the action
    return View();
}

public ActionResult About()
{
    // Process input data
    ...

    // Perform expected task
    ...

    // Generate the result of the action
    return View();
}
}
```

An action method grabs available input data by using any standard HTTP channels. Next, it arranges for some action and possibly involves the middle tier of the application. We can summarize the template of an action method as follows:

- **Process input data** An action method gets input arguments from a couple of sources: route values and collections exposed by the *Request* object. ASP.NET MVC doesn't mandate a particular signature for action methods. However, for testability reasons, it's highly recommended that any input parameter is received through the signature. If you can, avoid methods that retrieve input data programmatically from *Request* or other sources. As you'll see later in this chapter, and even more thoroughly in Chapter 3, "The model-binding architecture," an entire subsystem exists—the model binding layer—to map HTTP parameters to action method arguments.

- **Perform the task** The action method does its job based on input arguments and attempts to obtain expected results. In doing so, the method likely needs to interact with the middle tier. As is discussed further in Chapter 7, "Design considerations for ASP.NET MVC controllers," it is recommended that any interaction takes places through ad hoc dedicated services. At the end of the task, any (computed or referenced) values that should be incorporated in the response are packaged as appropriate. If the method returns JavaScript Object Notation (JSON), data is composed into a JSON-serializable object. If the method returns HTML, data is packaged into a container object and sent to the view engine. The container object is often referred to as the view-model and can be a plain dictionary of name/value pairs or a view-specific, strongly typed class.

- **Generate the results** In ASP.NET MVC, a controller's method is not responsible for producing the response itself. However, it is responsible for triggering the process that will use a distinct object (often, a view object) to render content to the output stream. The method identifies the type of response (file, plain data, HTML, JavaScript, or JSON) and sets up an *ActionResult* object, as appropriate.

A controller's method is expected to return an *ActionResult* object or any object that inherits from the *ActionResult* class. Often, though, a controller's method doesn't directly instantiate an *Action Result* object. Instead, it uses an action helper—that is, an object that internally instantiates and returns an *ActionResult* object. The method *View* in the preceding example provides an excellent illustration of an action helper. Another great example of such a helper method is *Json*, which is used when the method needs to return a JSON string. I'll return to this point in just a moment.

Processing input data

Controller action methods can access any input data posted by using the HTTP request. Input data can be retrieved from a variety of sources, including form data, query strings, cookies, route values, and posted files.

The signature of a controller action method is free. If you define parameter-less methods, you make yourself responsible for programmatically retrieving any input data your code requires. If you add parameters to the method's signature, ASP.NET MVC will offer automatic parameter resolution. In particular, ASP.NET MVC will attempt to match the names of formal parameters to named members in a request-scoped dictionary that joins together values from the query string, route, posting form, and more.

In this chapter, I discuss how to manually retrieve input data from within a controller action method. Chapter 3 discusses automatic parameter resolution—the most common choice in ASP.NET MVC applications.

Getting input data from the *Request* object

When writing the body of an action method, you can certainly access any input data that comes through the familiar *Request* object and its child collections, such as *Form*, *Cookies*, *ServerVariables*, and *QueryString*. As you'll see later in the book, when it comes to input parameters of a controller method, ASP.NET MVC offers quite compelling facilities (for example, model binders) that you might want to use to keep your code cleaner, more compact, and easier to test. Having said that, though, nothing at all prevents you from writing old-style *Request*-based code, as shown here:

```
public ActionResult Echo()
{
    // Capture data in a manual way
    var data - Request.Params["today"] ?? String.Empty;
    ...
}
```

In ASP.NET, the Request.Params dictionary results from the combination of four distinct dictionaries: QueryString, Form, Cookies, and ServerVariables. You can also use the *Item* indexer property of the *Request* object, which provides the same capabilities and searches dictionaries for a matching entry in the following order: QueryString, Form, Cookies, and ServerVariables. The following code is fully equivalent to that just shown:

```
public ActionResult Echo()
{
    // Capture data in a manual way
    var data = Request["today"] ?? String.Empty;
    ...
}
```

Observe that the search for a matching entry is case insensitive.

Getting input data from the route

In ASP.NET MVC, you often provide input parameters through the URL. These values are captured by the routing module and made available to the application. Route values are not exposed to applications through the *Request* object. You have to use a slightly different approach to retrieve them programmatically, as demonstrated here:

```
public ActionResult Echo()
{
    // Capture data in a manual way
    var data = RouteData.Values["data"] ?? String.Empty;
    ...
}
```

Route data is exposed through the *RouteData* property of the *Controller* class. Also, in this case, the search for a matching entry is conducted in a case-insensitive manner.

The RouteData.Values dictionary is a String/Object dictionary. The dictionary contains only strings most of the time. However, if you populate this dictionary programmatically (for example, via a custom route handler), it can contain other types of values. In this case, you're responsible for any necessary type cast.

Getting input data from multiple sources

Of course, you can mix *RouteData* and *Request* calls in the same controller method. As an example, let's consider the following route:

```
routes.MapRoute(
        "EchoRoute",
        "echo/{data}",
        new { controller = "Home", action = "Echo", data = UrlParameter.Optional }
);
```

The following is a valid URL: http://yourserver/echo/Sunday. The code shown next will easily grab the value of the data parameter (Sunday). Here's a possible implementation of the *Echo* method in the *HomeController* class:

```
public ActionResult Echo()
{
    // Capture data in a manual way
    var data = RouteData.Values["data"];
    ...
}
```

What if you call the following URL, instead?

```
http://yourserver/echo?today=3/27/2011
```

The URL still matches the route pattern, but it doesn't provide a value for the data parameter. Still, the URL adds some input value in the query string for the controller action to consider. Here's the modified version of the *Echo* method that supports both scenarios:

```
public ActionResult Echo()
{
    // Capture data in a manual way
    var data = RouteData.Values["data"] ??
                (Request.Params["today"] ?? String.Empty);
    ...
}
```

The question is, "Should I plan to have a distinct branch of code for each possible input channel, such as form data, query string, routes, cookies, and so forth?" Enter the *ValueProvider* dictionary.

The ValueProvider dictionary

In the *Controller* class, the *ValueProvider* property just provides a single container for input data collected from a variety of sources. By default, the ValueProvider dictionary is fed by input values from the following sources (in the specified order):

1. **Child action values**   Input values are provided by child action method calls. A child action is a call to a controller method that originates from the view. A child action call takes place when the view calls back the controller to get additional data or to demand the execution of some special task that might affect the output being rendered. I discuss child actions in Chapter 2, "ASP.NET MVC views."

2. **Form data**   Input values are provided by the content of the input fields in a posting HTML form. The content is the same as you would get through *Request.Form*.

3. **Route data**   Input values are provided by the content associated with parameters defined in the currently selected route.

4. **Query string**   Input values are provided by the content of parameters specified in the query string of the current URL.

5. **Posted files**   Input values are represented by the file or files posted via HTTP in the context of the current request.

The ValueProvider dictionary offers a custom programming interface centered on the *GetValue* method. Here's an example:

```
var result = ValueProvider.GetValue("data");
```

Be aware that *GetValue* doesn't return a *String* or an *Object* type. Instead, it returns an instance of the *ValueProviderResult* type. The type has two properties to actually read the real parameter value:

RawValue and *AttemptedValue*. The former is of type *Object* and contains the raw value as provided by the source. The *AttemptedValue* property, on the other hand, is a string and represents the result of an attempted type cast to *String*. Here's how to implement the *Echo* method by using *ValueProvider*:

```
public ActionResult Echo()
{
    var data = ValueProvider.GetValue("data").AttemptedValue ??
                   (ValueProvider.GetValue("today").AttemptedValue ?? String.Empty);
    ...
}
```

ValueProvider is a bit more demanding than *Request* and *RouteData* when it comes to parameter names. If you mistype the case of a parameter, you'll get a null object back from *GetValue*. This leads to an exception if you then just read the value without checking the result object for nullness.

Finally, note that by default you won't get access to cookies through the ValueProvider dictionary. However, the list of value providers can be extended programmatically by defining a class that implements the *IValueProvider* interface.

Note The value-provider mechanism can be useful to retrieve some request data which is packed into a comfortable collection of values. Default value providers save you from the burden of looking into the *QueryString* or *Form* collection. What if you need to read data from a cookie or a request header? You can go the usual way and read the *Headers* or *Cookies* collection of the *Request* object and write the code that extracts individual values. However, if your application is extensively based on request headers or cookies, you might want to consider writing a custom value provider. It is not hard to find working examples of both from the community. You can find a good example of a value provider that exposes request headers at *http://blog.donnfelker.com/2011/02/16/asp-net-mvc-building-web-apis-with-headervalueprovider*.

Producing action results

An action method can produce a variety of results. For example, an action method can just act as a web service and return a plain string or a JSON string in response to a request. Likewise, an action method can determine that there's no content to return or that a redirect to another URL is required. In these two cases, the browser will just get an HTTP response with no significant body of content. This is to say that one thing is producing the raw result of the action (for example, collecting values from the middle tier); it is quite another case to process that raw result to generate the actual HTTP response for the browser. The *ActionResult* class just represents the ASP.NET MVC infrastructure for implementing this programming aspect.

Inside the *ActionResult* class

An action method typically returns an object of type *ActionResult*. The type *ActionResult* is not a data container, though. More precisely, it is an abstract class that offers a common programming interface to execute some further operations on behalf of the action method. Here's the definition of the *ActionResult* class:

```
public abstract class ActionResult
{
    protected ActionResult()
    {
    }

    public abstract void ExecuteResult(ControllerContext context);
}
```

By overriding the *ExecuteResult* method, a derived class gains access to any data produced by the execution of the action method and triggers some subsequent action. Generally, this subsequent action is related to the generation of some response for the browser.

Predefined action result types

Because *ActionResult* is an abstract type, every action method is actually required to return an instance of a more specific type. Table 1-1 lists all predefined action result types.

TABLE 1-1 Predefined *ActionResult* types in ASP.NET MVC

Type	Description
ContentResult	Sends raw content (not necessarily HTML) to the browser. The *ExecuteResult* method of this class serializes any content it receives.
EmptyResult	Sends no content to the browser. The *ExecuteResult* method of this class does nothing.
FileContentResult	Sends the content of a file to the browser. The content of the file is expressed as a byte array. The *ExecuteResult* method simply writes the array of bytes to the output stream.
FilePathResult	Sends the content of a file to the browser. The file is identified via its path and content type. The *ExecuteResult* method calls the *TransmitFile* method on *HttpResponse*.
FileStreamResult	Sends the content of a file to the browser. The content of the file is represented through a *Stream* object. The *ExecuteResult* method copies from the provided file stream to the output stream.
HttpNotFoundResult	Sends an HTTP 404 response code to the browser. The HTTP status code identifies a request that failed because the requested resource was not found.
HttpUnauthorizedResult	Sends an HTTP 401 response code to the browser. The HTTP status code identifies an unauthorized request.
JavaScriptResult	Sends JavaScript text to the browser. The *ExecuteResult* method of this class writes out the script and sets the content type accordingly.

Type	Description
JsonResult	Sends a JSON string to the browser. The *ExecuteResult* method of this class sets the content type to the application or JSON and invokes the *JavaScriptSerializer* class to serialize any provided managed object to JSON.
PartialViewResult	Sends HTML content to the browser that represents a fragment of the whole page view. A partial view in ASP.NET MVC is a concept very close to a user control in Web Forms.
RedirectResult	Sends an HTTP 302 response code to the browser to redirect the browser to the specified URL. The *ExecuteResult* method of this class just invokes Response.Redirect.
RedirectToRouteResult	Like *RedirectResult*, it sends an HTTP 302 code to the browser and the new URL to which to navigate. The difference is in the logic and input data employed to determine the target URL. In this case, the URL is built based on action/controller pairs or route names.
ViewResult	Sends HTML content to the browser that represents a full page view.

Note that *FileContentResult*, *FilePathResult*, and *FileStreamResult* derive from the same base class: *FileResult*. You use any of these action result objects if you want to reply to a request with the download of some file content or even some plain binary content expressed as a byte array. *PartialView Result* and *ViewResult* inherit from *ViewResultBase* and return HTML content. Finally, *HttpUnauthorized Result* and *HttpNotFoundResult* represent two common responses for unauthorized access and missing resources. Both derive from a further extensible class *HttpStatusCodeResult*.

The mechanics of executing action results

To better comprehend the mechanics of action result classes, let's dissect one of the predefined classes. I've chosen the *JavaScriptResult* class, which provides some meaningful behavior without being too complex. The *JavaScriptResult* class represents the action of returning some script to the browser. Here's a possible action method that serves up JavaScript code:

```
public JavaScriptResult GetScript()
{
    var script = "alert('Hello')";
    return JavaScript(script);
}
```

In the example, JavaScript is a helper method in the *Controller* class that acts as a factory for the *JavaScriptResult* object. The implementation looks like this:

```
protected JavaScriptResult JavaScript(string script)
{
    return new JavaScriptResult() { Script = script };
}
```

The *JavaScriptResult* class supplies a public property—the *Script* property—that contains the script code to write to the output stream. Here's its implementation:

```
public class JavaScriptResult : ActionResult
{
    public String Script { get; set; }

    public override void ExecuteResult(ControllerContext context)
    {
        if (context == null)
            throw new ArgumentNullException("context");

        // Prepare the response
        HttpResponseBase response = context.HttpContext.Response;
        response.ContentType = "application/x-javascript";
        if (Script != null)
            response.Write(Script);
    }
}
```

As you can see, the ultimate purpose of the *ActionResult* class is to prepare the *HttpResponse* object to return to the browser. This entails setting content type, expiration policies, and headers, as well as content.

Returning HTML markup

Most of the time, requests are served by sending back HTML markup. Composing the HTML for the browser is the core of a web framework. In ASP.NET Web Forms, the task of composing HTML is done through the page. Developers create ASPX pages as a mix of a view template and a code-behind class. Both the action to grab results and the production of the actual response are blurred in a single run-time environment. In ASP.NET MVC, the production of the results is the responsibility of the action method; managing for the response to be composed and served is the responsibility of the framework. Finally, composing the HTML markup is the responsibility of yet another system component—the view engine.

I discuss view engines in Chapter 2, but for now it suffices to say that a view engine knows how to retrieve a view template for a given action and how to process that to a plain HTML stream that mixes template information and raw data. The view engine dictates the syntax of the view template (ASPX, Razor, and Spark to name a few); the developer dictates the format of the raw data to be merged into the view. Let's consider a sample action method returning HTML:

```
public ActionResult Index()
{
    return View(); // same as View("index");
}
```

The *View* method is a helper method responsible for creating a *ViewResult* object. The *ViewResult* object needs to know about the view template, an optional master view, and the raw data to be incorporated into the final HTML. The fact that in the code snippet *View* has no parameters doesn't mean no data is actually passed on. Here's one of the signatures of the method:

```
protected ViewResult View(String viewName, String masterName, Object model)
```

By convention, the view template is a file named after the action name (*Index* in this case) and located in a specific folder. The exact location depends on the implementation of the currently selected view engine. By default, view templates are expected to be located in the Views folder in a directory that matches the name of the controller—for example, Views/Home. Be aware that you must maintain this directory structure when you deploy the site.

The extension of the view template file also depends on the implementation of the view engine. For the two predefined view engines you get with ASP.NET MVC, the extensions are *.aspx* if you opt for the ASPX view engine and *.cshtml* (or *.vbhtml*) if you opt for the Razor view engine. (I provide more details about this in Chapter 2.)

Returning JSON content

ASP.NET MVC lends itself very well to implementing simple web services to be called back from jQuery snippets in an Ajax context. All you need to do is set one or more action methods to return JSON strings instead of HTML. Here's an example:

```
public JsonResult GetCustomers()
{
    // Grab some data to return
    var customers = _customerRepository.GetAll();

    // Serialize to JSON and return
    return Json(customers);
}
```

The *Json* helper method gets a plain .NET object and serializes it to a string by using the built-in *JavaScriptSerializer* class.

> **Note** What if your controller action method doesn't return *ActionResult*? First and foremost, no exceptions are raised. Quite simply, ASP.NET MVC encapsulates any return value from the action method (numbers, strings, or custom objects) into a *ContentResult* object. The execution of a *ContentResult* object causes the plain serialization of the value to the browser. For example, an action that returns an integer or a string will get you a browser page that displays data as-is. On the other hand, returning a custom object displays any string resulting from the implementation of the object's *ToString* method. If the method returns an HTML string, any markup will not be automatically encoded and the browser will likely not properly parse it. Finally, a void return value is actually mapped to an *EmptyResult* object whose execution causes a no-op.

Asynchronous operations within a controller

The primary purpose of a controller is to serve the needs of the user interface. Any server-side functions you need to implement should be mapped to a controller method and triggered from the user interface. After performing its own task, a controller's method selects the next view, packs some data, and instructs it to render.

This is the essence of the controller's behavior. However, other characteristics are often required in a controller, especially when controllers are employed in large and complex applications with particular needs, such as long-running requests. In earlier versions of ASP.NET MVC, you had to follow a specific pattern to give controller methods an asynchronous behavior. Starting with the .NET Framework 4.5, you can take advantage of the new *async/await* language facilities and the underlying .NET machinery. Here's the way in which you write a controller class with one or more asynchronous methods:

```
public class HomeController : AsyncController
{
    public async Task<ActionResult> Rss()
    {
        // Run the potentially lengthy operation
        var client = new HttpClient();
        var rss = await client.GetStringAsync(someRssUrl);

        // Parse RSS and build the view model
        var model = new HomeIndexModel();
        model.News = ParseRssInternal(rss);
        return model;
    }
}
```

The code looks as if it were written to be synchronous—you don't care about callbacks. In the end, though, it is highly readable and runs asynchronously thanks to the syntactic sugar added by the C# compiler when you use *async/await* keywords.

Summary

Controllers are the heart of an ASP.NET MVC application. Controllers mediate between the user requests and the capabilities of the server system. Controllers are linked to user-interface actions and are in touch with the middle tier. Controllers order the rendering of the page but don't run any rendering tasks themselves. This is a key difference from ASP.NET Web Forms. In a controller, the processing of the request is neatly separated from the display. In Web Forms, on the other hand, the page-processing phase incorporates both the execution of some tasks and the rendering of the response.

Although based on a different syntax, controller methods are not much different from the post-back event handlers you have in ASP.NET Web Forms. In this regard, a controller class plays the same role of a code-behind class in Web Forms. The controller as well as a Web Forms code-behind class belongs to the presentation layer. For this reason, you should pay a lot of attention to how you code the behavior of the various action methods. Keep in mind that in ASP.NET MVC, any layering in the building of the solution is also up to you.

In this chapter, I skipped over all the details about how you add behavior to a controller method. I focused on an overview of what comes before and what comes after. In Chapter 2, I delve deeper into what comes after; therefore, the focus will be on views, view engines, and the generation of the markup. Then, in Chapter 3, I discuss model binding and what happens before the behavior of an action method comes into play. And in Chapter 7, I come back to this topic with some design considerations on how to structure methods in a controller class.

This has been just the first pass on controllers. A lot more must be said and learned.

CHAPTER 2

ASP.NET MVC views

Design is not just what it looks like and feels like. Design is how it works.

—Steve Jobs

In ASP.NET MVC, any request is resolved in terms of an action being executed on some controller. Even for a newcomer, this point is relatively easy to understand and figure out. But, there's another aspect of the request that the newcomer often has difficulty grasping—the generation of the HTML for the browser.

In ASP.NET Web Forms, you don't even think of an action—you think of a page, and a page incorporates both logic and view. In classic ASP.NET, you start with, say, a register.aspx page that the user reaches following a link. The page unfolds its user interface, which ends with a submit button. The button originates a POST to the same page that takes care of posted data, modifies the state of the application as appropriate, and prepares the expected thank-you screen. The entire process is rooted in the page resource.

However, in ASP.NET MVC, you set up a *Register* action on some controller class. When the action is invoked over a GET command, it results in the display of the user interface for the data entry. When invoked over a POST, the action performs the desired server-side tasks and then manages to serve back the thank-you screen. The entire workflow is similar to what you have in a nonweb scenario.

In ASP.NET MVC, you just deal with two main flavors of components. One is the controller, which is in charge of executing the request and producing raw results in return for raw input. The other is the view engine, which is in charge of generating any expected HTML response based on the results calculated by the controller. In this chapter, I'll first briefly discuss the internal architecture of the view engine and then move to more practical considerations on how you feed an engine with view templates and data.

 Note As is demonstrated in Chapter 1, "ASP.NET MVC controllers," a controller action doesn't necessarily produce some HTML. You can look upon an ASP.NET MVC application as a collection of components with the ability to serve various responses, including HTML, JavaScript, JavaScript Object Notation (JSON), and plain text. In this chapter, I'll restrict the discussion to considering the subsystem responsible for the production of HTML. Later in the book, I discuss other types of responses in more detail.

The structure and behavior of a view engine

The view engine is the component that physically builds the HTML output for the browser. The view engine engages for each request that returns HTML, and it prepares its output by mixing together a template for the view and any data the controller passes in. The template is expressed in an engine-specific markup language; the data is passed packaged in dictionaries or in strongly typed objects. Figure 2-1 shows the overall picture of how a view engine and controller work together.

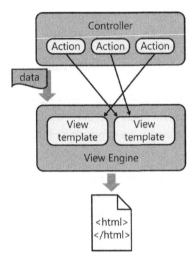

FIGURE 2-1 Controllers and view engines.

The mechanics of a view engine

In ASP.NET MVC, a view engine is merely a class that implements a fixed interface—the *IViewEngine* interface. Each application can have one or more view engines. In ASP.NET MVC 5, each application comes by default with two view engines. Let's find out more.

Detecting registered view engines

Until ASP.NET MVC 4, when you first created an ASP.NET MVC application, the Microsoft Visual Studio project wizard asked you to pick your favorite view engine—whether ASPX or Razor. Figure 2-2 shows the specific dialog box as it appears when ASP.NET MVC 5 is installed in Visual Studio 2013.

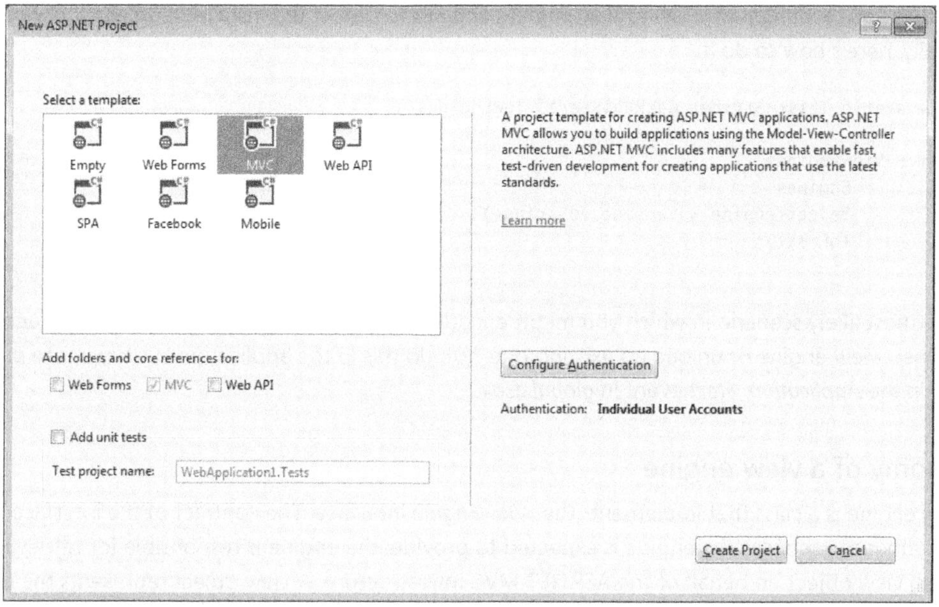

FIGURE 2-2 Choosing your favorite view engine.

As you can see, there's no choice between ASPX and Razor, and all view files are automatically created by using the Razor markup language. In spite of appearances, the choice you make here has a limited impact on the application. Your choice, in fact, influences only the content of the project files the wizard will create for you. By default, any ASP.NET MVC 5 application will always load two view engines: Razor and ASPX.

The *ViewEngines* class is the system repository that tracks the currently installed engines. The class is simple and exposes only a static collection member named *Engines*. The static member is initialized with the two default engines. Here's an excerpt from the class:

```
public static class ViewEngines
{
    private static readonly ViewEngineCollection _engines =
            new ViewEngineCollection {
                    new WebFormViewEngine(),
                    new RazorViewEngine()
            };

    public static ViewEngineCollection Engines
    {
        get { return _engines; }
    }
    ...
}
```

In case you're interested in using *ViewEngines.Engines* to detect the installed engines programmatically, here's how to do it:

```
private static IList<String> GetRegisteredViewEngines()
{
    return ViewEngines
            .Engines
            .Select(engine => engine.ToString())
            .ToList();
}
```

The most likely scenario in which you might encounter *ViewEngines.Engines* is when you need to add a new view engine or unload an existing one. You do this in the application startup, more precisely, in the *Application_Start* event in *global.asax*.

Anatomy of a view engine

A view engine is a class that implements the *IViewEngine* interface. The contract of the interface says it's all about the services the engine is expected to provide: the engine is responsible for retrieving a (partial) view object on behalf of the ASP.NET MVC infrastructure. A view object represents the container for any information that is needed to build a real HTML response in ASP.NET MVC. Here are the interface members:

```
public interface IViewEngine
{
    ViewEngineResult FindPartialView(
            ControllerContext controllerContext,
            String partialViewName,
            Boolean useCache);
    ViewEngineResult FindView(
            ControllerContext controllerContext,
            String viewName,
            String masterName,
            Boolean useCache);
    void ReleaseView(
            ControllerContext controllerContext,
            IView view);
}
```

Table 2-1 describes the behavior of the methods in the *IViewEngine* interface.

TABLE 2-1 Methods of the *IViewEngine* interface

Method	Description
FindPartialView	Creates and returns a view object that represents a fragment of HTML
FindView	Creates and returns a view object that represents an HTML page
ReleaseView	Releases the specified view object

Both *FindPartialView* and *FindView* return a *ViewEngineResult* object, which represents the results of locating a template for the view around the server directory tree and instantiating it. Here's the class signature:

```
public class ViewEngineResult
{
    ...

    // Members
    public IEnumerable<String> SearchedLocations { get; private set; }
    public IView View { get; private set; }
    public IViewEngine ViewEngine { get; private set; }
}
```

The *ViewEngineResult* type just aggregates three elements: the view object, the view engine object used to create it, and the list of locations searched to find the template of the view. The content of the *SearchedLocations* property depends on the structure and behavior of the selected view engine. The *ReleaseView* method is intended to dispose of any references that the view object has in use.

Who calls the view engine?

Although Figure 2-1 seems to show direct contact between controllers and view engines, the two components never communicate directly. Instead, the activity of both controllers and view engines is coordinated by an external manager object: the *action invoker*. The action invoker is triggered directly by the HTTP handler in charge of the request. The action invoker does two key things. First, it executes the controller's method and saves the action result. Next, it processes the action result. Figure 2-3 presents a sequence diagram.

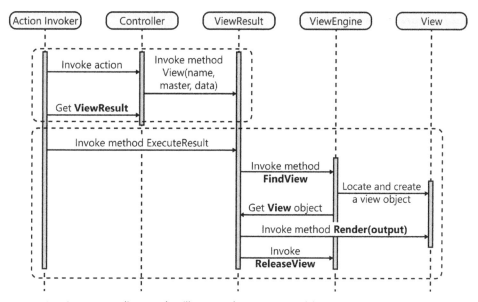

FIGURE 2-3 A sequence diagram that illustrates the request-servicing process.

Let's consider the typical code of a controller method as you saw it in Chapter 1.

```
public ActionResult Index()
{
    // Some significant code here
    ...

    // Order rendering of the next view
    return View();
}
```

The *View* method on the controller class packs a few pieces of data together in a single container: the *ViewResult* class. Information includes the name of the view template that the controller has selected as the next view to show to the user. An optional piece of data that goes into *ViewResult* is the name of the master view. Finally, the *ViewResult* container also incorporates the calculated data that will be displayed in the view. When the *View* method gets no parameters, as in the code snippet shown earlier, default values are provided. An instance of *ViewResult* object is delivered back to the action invoker.

Next, the action invoker invokes the *ExecuteResult* method on the *ViewResult* object. The method goes through the list of registered view engines to find one that can match the specified view and master view names. If no such view engine is found, an exception is thrown. Otherwise, the selected view engine is asked to create a view object based on the information provided.

Subsequently, the *ViewResult* object orders the view to render its content out to the provided stream—the actual response stream. Finally, the *ViewResult* object instructs the view engine to release the view.

The view object

The view object is an instance of a class that implements the *IView* interface. The only purpose of a view object is for writing some HTML response to a text writer. Each view is identified by name. The name of the view is also associated with some physical file that defines the HTML layout to render. Resolving the association between the view name and actual HTML layout is the responsibility of the view engine.

The name of the view is one of the parameters that the *View* method on the controller action is supposed to provide. If no such parameter is explicitly defined by the programmer, the system assumes by convention that the name of the view is the same as the action name. (As is demonstrated in Chapter 1, the action name doesn't necessarily match the method name.)

The *IView* interface is shown here:

```
public interface IView
{
    void Render(ViewContext viewContext, TextWriter writer);
}
```

Under the hood, a view object is a wrapper around an object that describes a visual layout devoid of data. Rendering the view means populating the layout with data and rendering it as HTML to some stream. Of the two default view engines in ASP.NET MVC, one—the ASPX view engine—just uses a derivative of the ASP.NET *Page* class to represent the visual layout. The other view engine—the Razor engine—is based on a different class designed around the same core idea. The Razor engine uses the *WebMatrix* counterpart of an ASP.NET *Page* class.

Definition of the view template

In ASP.NET MVC, everything being displayed to the user results from a view and is described in terms of a template file. The graphical layout is then transformed into HTML and styled via one or more cascading style sheet (CSS) files. The way in which the template file is written, however, depends on the view engine. Each view engine has its own markup language to define the template, and its own set of rules to resolve a view name into a template file.

Resolving the template

At the end of its job, the controller figures out the name of the next view to render to the user. However, the name of the view must be translated into some good HTML markup. This takes a couple more steps. First, the system needs to identify which view engine (if any) can successfully process the request for the view. Second, the view name must be matched to an HTML layout and a view object must be successfully created from there.

Starting from the point that the name of the view is known, the *ViewResult* object (shown earlier in Figure 2-3) queries through all the installed view engines in the order in which they appear in the *ViewEngines.Engines* collection. Each view engine is asked whether it is capable of rendering a view with the given name.

By convention, each ASP.NET MVC view engine uses its own algorithm to translate the view name into a resource name that references the final HTML markup. For the two predefined view engines, the search algorithm attempts to match the view name to a physical file in one of a few fixed disk locations.

A custom view engine, however, can release both constraints and employ a different set of conventions. For example, it can load the view layout from, for example, a database, or it can use a customized set of folders.

Default conventions and folders

Both the ASPX and Razor view engines use the same core conventions to resolve view names. Both match view names to file names, and both expect to find those files in the same set of predefined folders. The only difference between ASPX and Razor is the extension of the files that contain the view layout.

Unless you install a custom view engine, an ASP.NET MVC application finds its view templates in the Views folder. Figure 2-4 demonstrates that the Views folder has a number of subfolders, each named after an existing controller name. Finally, the controller folder contains physical files whose name is expected to match the view name and whose extension must be *.aspx* for the ASPX view engine and *.cshtml* for the Razor view engine. (If you're writing your ASP.NET MVC application in Microsoft Visual Basic, the extension will be *.vbhtml*.)

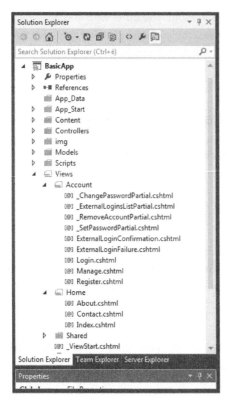

FIGURE 2-4 Locating view templates in an ASP.NET MVC application.

Although Figure 2-4 lists only *.cshtml* Razor view files, you are welcome to mix and match template files written according to different syntaxes.

 Important Having view templates written using different markup languages certainly doesn't increase the consistency of your source code, but it can be a viable solution for cases in which you have different skills within a team or when you need to incorporate some legacy code. Also, consider that when you have view templates for different engines, resolving the names can produce some surprises. View engines are called to claim the view in the order in which they are registered and, by default, the ASPX engine takes precedence over the Razor engine. To modify the order, you should clear the *Engines* collection during application startup and add engines again, in the order you prefer.

In general, ASP.NET MVC requires that you place each view template in the folder of the controller that uses it. When multiple controllers are expected to invoke the same view (or partial view), you should move the template file to the Shared folder.

Finally, note that the same hierarchy of directories that exists at the project level in the Views folder must be replicated on the production server. However, folders such as Controllers, App_Start, and ViewModels are plain namespace containers used to better organize the source files, and they can be ignored in production.

The template for the view

As mentioned, a view is nothing more than a template for the resulting HTML content. The following is valid content for a view template file to find in some Views subfolder. The view template targets the ASPX view engine.

```
<%@ Page Language="C#"
        MasterPageFile="~/Views/Shared/Site.Master"
        Inherits="System.Web.Mvc.ViewPage" %>

<asp:Content ID="aboutTitle" ContentPlaceHolderID="TitleContent" runat="server">
    About the book
</asp:Content>

<asp:Content ID="aboutContent" ContentPlaceHolderID="MainContent" runat="server">
    <h2><%: ViewBag.Message %></h2>
    <p>
        Put content here.
    </p>
</asp:Content>
```

Without beating around the bush, this looks nearly the same as an old, faithful ASP.NET Web Forms page. So, what's the point of ASP.NET MVC?

Admittedly, the syntax you see here is the same as in an ASP.NET Web Forms page; the role of this file, however, is radically different. In ASP.NET MVC, about.aspx is not a public resource you can request by following a link or typing it in the address bar of the browser. Rather, it's an internal resource file used to provide the template for a view. In particular, the about.aspx template is picked up only when the user makes a request that the system maps to a controller method which, in turn, selects the About view for display, as shown here:

```
public ActionResult About()
{
    ViewBag.Message = "Thank you for choosing this book!";

    // By default, the view name is the same as the action name.
    return View();
}
```

Another huge difference is the data you display through the template. In Web Forms, each page is made of server controls and, as a developer, you set properties on server controls to display any data. In ASP.NET MVC, you group the data that you want to pass to the view in a container object and pass the container object as an argument in the controller's call that selects the view.

ASP.NET MVC makes it possible for you to pass a container object directly in the call to the *View* method. In any case, two predefined dictionaries are available for the controller method to stuff data. They are the ViewData and ViewBag dictionaries.

A key point to remember is that ideally the view object doesn't need to retrieve data on its own; the only data it must deal with is the data it receives from the controller.

> **Important** The purpose of the view template is to produce HTML, but the source of the template doesn't need be HTML. The language used to write the template depends on the view engine. It can be nearly the same ASPX markup that you might know from ASP.NET Web Forms if you opt for the ASPX view engine; it will be something significantly different if you choose the Razor engine or another engine.

The master view

Just like in ASP.NET Web Forms, you need to decide whether you want to write the view template entirely from scratch or inherit some common markup from a master view. If you choose the latter option, you define the master template with respect to the syntax and constraints set by the view engine.

Specifying the master view is easy. You can use the conventions supported by the view engine, or you can just pass the name of the master view as an argument to the *View* method when you select the next view from the controller. Note that the master template might follow different conventions than plain views. For example, the ASPX view engine requires you to name it with a .master extension and place it in the Shared folder. The Razor view engine, instead, adds a .cshtml extension and requires you to specify the path in a special viewstart.cshtml file in the root of the Views folder.

I'll have more to say about the two default view engines in just a moment.

HTML helpers

Admittedly, the ASPX view engine is quite similar to ASP.NET Web Forms but doesn't support server controls in the same manner. This is not because of a partial implementation; there is a deeper explanation. Server controls are, in effect, too tightly coupled to the life cycle of a Web Forms page to be easily reworked in a request-processing model that breaks up action into neatly distinct phases, such as getting input data, processing the request, and selecting the next view.

On the other hand, server controls served a very important purpose in ASP.NET—favoring HTML-level code reuse. Even though ASP.NET MVC makes a point of letting developers gain control over every single HTML tag, a good deal of HTML can't be hard-coded in the view. It needs be built programmatically, based on dynamically discovered data. What's a technology equivalent to server controls in ASP.NET MVC? Enter HTML helpers.

Note HTML helpers certainly are not the same as server controls, but they are the closest you can get to HTML-level code reuse with a view engine. An HTML helper method has no view state, no postbacks, and no page life cycle and events. HTML helpers are simple HTML factories. Technically speaking, an HTML helper is an extension method defined on a system class—the *HtmlHelper* class—that outputs an HTML string based on the provided input data. In fact, internally an HTML helper simply accumulates text into a *StringBuilder* object.

Basic helpers

The ASP.NET MVC framework supplies a few HTML helpers out of the box, including *CheckBox*, *ActionLink*, and *RenderPartial*. The stock set of HTML helpers is presented in Table 2-2.

TABLE 2-2 The stock set of HTML helper methods

Method	Type	Description
BeginForm, BeginRouteForm	Form	Returns an internal object that represents an HTML form that the system uses to render the <form> tag
EndForm	Form	A void method, closes the pending </form> tag
CheckBox, CheckBoxFor	Input	Returns the HTML string for a check box input element
Hidden, HiddenFor	Input	Returns the HTML string for a hidden input element
Password, PasswordFor	Input	Returns the HTML string for a password input element
RadioButton, RadioButtonFor	Input	Returns the HTML string for a radio button input element
TextBox, TextBoxFor	Input	Returns the HTML string for a text input element
Label, LabelFor	Label	Returns the HTML string for an HTML label element
ActionLink, RouteLink	Link	Returns the HTML string for an HTML link
DropDownList, DropDownListFor	List	Returns the HTML string for a drop-down list
ListBox, ListBoxFor	List	Returns the HTML string for a list box
TextArea, TextAreaFor	TextArea	Returns the HTML string for a text area
Partial	Partial	Returns the HTML string incorporated in the specified user control
RenderPartial	Partial	Writes the HTML string incorporated in the specified user control to the output stream
ValidationMessage, ValidationMessageFor	Validation	Returns the HTML string for a validation message
ValidationSummary	Validation	Returns the HTML string for a validation summary message

As an example, let's see how to use an HTML helper to create a text box with programmatically determined text. You place the call in a code block if you're using the ASPX view engine:

```
<%: Html.TextBox("TextBox1", ViewBag.DefaultText) %>
```

Or, you prefix the call with the @ symbol if you're using Razor. (I'll say more about Razor in a moment and throughout the rest of the book.)

```
@Html.TextBox("TextBox1", ViewBag.DefaultText)
```

Note The *Html* in the code snippets refers to a built-in property of the base classes used by both view engines to refer to a rendered view. The class is *ViewPage* for the ASPX view engine and *WebPage* for the Razor view engine. In both cases, the property *Html* is an instance of *HtmlHelper*.

Each HTML helper has a bunch of overloads to let you specify attribute values and other relevant information. For example, here's how to style the text box by using the *class* attribute:

```
<%: Html.TextBox("TextBox1",
                 ViewBag.DefaultText,
                 new Dictionary<String, Object>{{"class", "coolTextBox"}}) %>
```

In Table 2-2, you see a lot of *xxxFor* helpers. In what way are they different from other helpers? An *xxxFor* helper differs from the base version because it accepts only a lambda expression, such as the one shown here:

```
<%: Html.TextBoxFor(model => model.FirstName,
                    new Dictionary<String, Object>{{"class", "coolTextBox"}}) %>
```

For a text box, the lambda expression indicates the text to display in the input field. The *xxxFor* variation is especially useful when the data to populate the view is grouped in a model object. In this case, your view results are clearer to read and strongly typed.

Let's see a few other examples of basic HTML helpers.

Rendering HTML forms

The unpleasant work of rendering a form in ASP.NET MVC occurs when you have to specify the target URL. The *BeginForm* and *BeginRouteForm* helpers can do the ugliest work for you. The following code snippet shows how to write a simple input form that presents user and password text boxes:

```
<% using (Html.BeginForm()) { %>
   <div>
     <fieldset>
        <legend>Account Information</legend>
        <p>
            <label for="userName">User name:</label>
            <%= Html.TextBox("userName") %>
            <%= Html.ValidationMessage("userName") %>
        </p>
        <p>
            <label for="password">Password:</label>
            <%= Html.Password("password") %>
            <%= Html.ValidationMessage("password") %>
        </p>
```

```
        ...
        <p>
            <input type="submit" value="Change Password" />
        </p>
    </fieldset>
</div>
<% } %>
```

The *BeginForm* helper takes care of the opening <form> tag. The *BeginForm* method, however, doesn't directly emit any markup. It's limited to creating an instance of the *MvcForm* class, which is then added to the control tree for the page and rendered later.

By default, *BeginForm* renders a form that posts back to the same URL and, subsequently, to the same controller action. Using other overloads on the *BeginForm* method, you can specify the target controller's name and action, any route values for the action, HTML attributes, and even whether you want the form to perform a GET or a POST. *BeginRouteForm* behaves like *BeginForm* except that it can generate a URL starting from an arbitrary set of route parameters. In other words, *BeginRouteForm* is not limited to the default route based on the controller name and action.

I believe that discussing HTML forms is the best scenario to showcase the added value of Razor over ASPX. Here's how you would rewrite the previous form with Razor syntax:

```
@using (Html.BeginForm())
{
    <div>
      <fieldset>
          <legend>Account Information</legend>
          <p>
              <label for="userName">User name:</label>
              @Html.TextBox("userName")
              @Html.ValidationMessage("userName")
          </p>
          <p>
              <label for="password">Password:</label>
              @Html.Password("password")
              @Html.ValidationMessage("password")
          </p>
          ...
          <p>
              <input type="submit" value="Change Password" />
          </p>
      </fieldset>
    </div>
}
```

In the rest of the book, I'll always be using Razor for views.

Note In HTML, when you use the form tag, you can't use anything other than the GET and POST verbs to submit some content. In ASP.NET MVC, a native method on the *HtmlHelper* class—*HttpMethodOverride*—comes to the rescue. The method emits a hidden field whose name is hard-coded to *X-HTTP-Method-Override* and whose value is *PUT*, *DELETE*, or *HEAD*. The content of the hidden field overrides the method set for the form, thus making it possible for you to invoke a REST API also from within the browser. You can also specify the override value in an HTTP header with the same *X-HTTP-Method-Override* name or in a query string value as a name/value pair. The override is valid only for POST requests.

Rendering input elements

All HTML elements that you can use within a form have an HTML helper to speed up development. Again, there's really no difference from a functional perspective between using helpers and using plain HTML. Here's an example of a check box element, initially set to true, but disabled:

```
@Html.CheckBox("ProductDiscontinued",
            true,
            new Dictionary<String, Object>() {{"disabled", "disabled"}}))
```

You also have facilities to associate a validation message with an input field. You use the *Html.ValidationMessage* helper to display a validation message if the specified field contains an error. The message can be indicated explicitly through an additional parameter in the helper. All validation messages are then aggregated and displayed via the *Html.ValidationSummary* helper.

You can find an expanded discussion of input forms and validation in Chapter 4, "Input forms."

Action links

As previously mentioned, creating URLs programmatically is a boring and error-prone task in ASP.NET MVC. For this reason, helpers are more than welcome, especially in this context. In fact, the *ActionLink* helper is one of the most frequently used in ASP.NET MVC views. Here's an example:

```
@Html.ActionLink("Home", "Index", "Home")
```

Typically, an action link requires the link text, the action name, and optionally the controller name. The HTML that results from the example is the following:

```
<a href="/Home/Index">Home</a>
```

In addition, you can specify route values, HTML attributes for the anchor tag, and even a protocol (for example, HTTPS), host, and fragment.

The *RouteLink* helper works in much the same way, except that it doesn't require you to specify an action. With *RouteLink*, you can use any registered route name to determine the pattern for the resulting URL.

The text emitted by *ActionLink* is automatically encoded. This means you can't use any HTML tag in the link text that the browser will be led to consider as HTML. In particular, you can't use *ActionLink* for image buttons and image links. However, to generate a link based on controller and action data, you can use the *UrlHelper* class.

An instance of the *UrlHelper* class is associated with the *Url* property on the *ViewPage* type. The code here shows the *Url* object in action:

```
<a href="@Url.Action("Edit")">
    <img src="editMemo.jpg" alt="Edit memo" />
</a>
```

The *UrlHelper* class has a couple of methods that behave nearly similar to *ActionLink* and *Route Link*. Their names are *Action* and *RouteUrl*.

> **Note** ASP.NET MVC routing is not aware of subdomains; it always assumes that you're in the application path. This means that if you want to use subdomains within a single applica-tion instead of virtual paths (for example, dino.blogs.com instead of www.blogs.com/dino), the extra work of figuring out which subapplication you're in is entirely up to you. You can address this in a number of ways. A simple approach consists in creating a custom route handler that would look at the host passed in the URL and decide which controller to set up. This solution, however, is limited to fixing incoming requests. It might not be enough for all of the helpers you have around to generate links to resources and actions. A more complete solution is creating a *Route* class that is aware of subdomains. You can find a good example at *http://blog.maartenballiauw.be/post/2009/05/20/ASPNET-MVC-Domain-Routing.aspx*.

Partial views

You use either the *Partial* or *RenderPartial* helper method to insert a partial view. Both methods take the name of the partial view as an argument. The only difference between the two is that *Partial* re-turns a string, whereas *RenderPartial* writes to the output stream and returns void. Because of this, the usage is slightly different, as demonstrated here:

```
@Html.Partial("login")
@Html.RenderPartial("login")
```

In ASP.NET MVC, a partial view is analogous to a user control in Web Forms. The typical loca-tion for a partial view is the Shared folder in Views. However, you can also store a partial view in the controller-specific folder. A partial view is contained in a view, but it will be treated as an entirely in-dependent entity. In fact, it is legitimate to have a view written for one view engine and a child partial view that requires another view engine.

The *HtmlHelper* class

The *HtmlHelper* class owes most of its popularity to its numerous extension methods, but it also has a number of useful native methods. Some of them are listed in Table 2-3.

TABLE 2-3 The most popular native methods on *HtmlHelper*

Method	Description
AntiForgeryToken	Returns the HTML string for a hidden input field stored with the anti-forgery token (see Chapter 4 for more details)
AttributeEncode	Encodes the value of the specified attribute using the rules of HTML encoding
EnableUnobtrusiveJavaScript	Sets the internal flag that enables helpers to generate JavaScript code in an unobtrusive way
EnableClientValidation	Sets the internal flag that enables helpers to generate code for client-side validation
Encode	Encodes the specified value using the rules of HTML encoding
HttpMethodOverride	Returns the HTML string for a hidden input field used to override the effective HTTP verb to indicate that a PUT or DELETE operation was requested
Raw	Returns the raw HTML string without encoding

In addition, the *HtmlHelper* class provides a number of public methods that are of little use from within a view but offer great support to developers writing custom HTML helper methods. A good example is *GenerateRouteLink*, which returns an anchor tag containing the virtual path for the specified route values.

Templated helpers

Writing HTML templates over and over again leads to repetitive, boring, and therefore error-prone code. Templated helpers help because they are created to take an instance of a C# class, read properties, and decide how to best render those values. By decorating the view-model objects with special attributes, you provide the helper further guidance regarding user-interface hints and validation.

With templated helpers, you are not losing control over the user interface; more simply, attributes in the model establish a number of conventions and save you from a number of repetitive tasks.

Flavors of a templated helper

In ASP.NET MVC, you have two essential templated helpers: *Editor* and *Display*. They work together to make the code for labeling, displaying, and editing data objects easy to write and maintain. The optimal scenario for using these helpers is that you are writing your lists or input forms around annotated objects. However, templated helpers can work with both scalar values and composite objects.

Templated helpers actually come with three overloads. Using the *Display* helper as an example, you have the following more specific helpers: *Display*, *DisplayFor*, and *DisplayForModel*. There's no functional difference between *Display*, *DisplayFor*, and *DisplayForModel*. They differ only in terms of the input parameters they can manage.

The *Display* helpers

The *Display* helper accepts a string indicating the name of the property in the *ViewData* dictionary, or on the view-model object, to be processed:

```
@Html.Display("FirstName")
```

The *DisplayFor* helper accepts a lambda expression and requires that a view-model object be passed to the view:

```
@Html.DisplayFor(model => model.FirstName)
```

Finally, *DisplayForModel* is a shortcut for *DisplayFor* getting the expression *model => model*:

```
@Html.DisplayForModel()
```

All flavors of templated helpers have the special ability to process metadata (if any) and adjust their rendering accordingly; for example, showing labels and adding validation. You can customize the display and editing capabilities by using templates, as will be discussed in a moment. The ability of using custom templates applies to all flavors of a templated helper.

> **Important** *ViewBag* is a property defined on the *ControllerBase* class defined to be of type *dynamic*. In .NET, the type *dynamic* indicates the site for dynamically interpreted code. In other words, whenever the compiler meets a reference to a dynamic object, it emits a chunk of code that checks at run time whether the code can be resolved and executed. Functionally speaking, this is similar to what happens with JavaScript objects.
>
> Lambda expressions don't support dynamic members and therefore can't be used with data passed into the *ViewBag* dictionary. Also note that to successfully use *ViewBag* content in HTML helpers, you must cast the expression to a valid type.

The *Editor* helpers

The purpose of the *Editor* helper is to let you edit the specified value or object. The editor recognizes the type of the value it gets and picks up a made-to-measure template for editing. Predefined templates exist for object, string, Boolean, and multiline text, whereas numbers, dates, and GUIDs fall back to the string editor. The Editor helper works great with complex types. It generically iterates over each public property and builds up a label and an editor for the child value. Here's how to display in an editor the value of the *FirstName* property on some object being passed to the view:

```
@Html.EditorFor(person => person.FirstName)
```

You can customize the editor (and the visualizer) by creating a few partial views in the *EditorTemplates* folder of the view. It can be in a controller-specific subfolder or in the Views\Shared folder, as well. The partial view is expressed as an .ascx template for the ASPX view engine and as a .cshtml template if you're using the Razor view engine. You can provide a custom template for each type that you expect to support. For example, in Figure 2-5 you see a datetime.cshtml template that will be used to modify the way dates are rendered in both editing and display. Likewise, you can provide a partial view for each type of property in the view-model object.

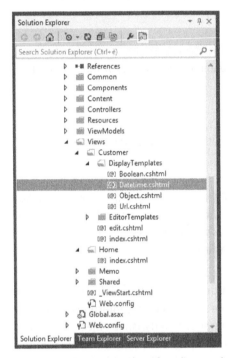

FIGURE 2-5 Custom templates for editors and visualizers.

If the name of the partial view matches the type name, the custom template is automatically picked up by the system.

You can also point the editor to your template by name and give the template the name you like. Here's an example that uses the date.ascx view to edit a *DateTime* property:

```
@Html.EditorFor(person => person.Birthdate, "date")
```

In the same ASP.NET MVC application, you can have views requiring different view engines. Note that ASP.NET MVC resolves each view and partial view independently. This means that if you're processing, for example, the about view, you end up with the Razor engine (as shown in Figure 2-5). However, if the about view requires an editor for dates and you have a matching .aspx template, it will be picked up anyway with no need for you to provide an analogous .cshtml template.

Finally, the Editor helper can recognize data annotation attributes on view-model objects and use that information to add special validation features, such as ensuring that a given value falls in the specified range or is not left empty.

> **Note** When you use *DisplayForModel* and *EditorForModel*, the system uses reflection to find all the properties on the specified object and then generates a label and visualizer or editor for each of those properties. The overall template of the resulting view is a vertical sequence of labels and visualizers/editors. Each emitted piece of HTML is bound to a CSS class and can be easily styled as you prefer. Furthermore, if you'd like to change the template of the view, you need to provide an object.aspx (or object.cshtml) template and use reflection, as well. I return to this topic with an example in Chapter 4.

Custom helpers

The native set of HTML helper methods is definitely a great benefit, but it's probably insufficient for many real-world applications. Native helpers, in fact, cover only the markup of basic HTML elements. In this regard, HTML helpers are significantly different from server controls because they completely lack abstraction over HTML. Extending the set of HTML helpers is easy, however. All that is required is an extension method for the *HtmlHelper* class or for the *AjaxHelper* class if you're interested in creating an HTML factory that does some Ajax work.

The structure of an HTML helper

An HTML helper is a plain method that is not tied to any forced prototype. You typically design the signature of an HTML helper method to make it receive just the data it needs. Having several overloads or optional parameters is common, too.

Internally, the helper processes input data and starts building the output HTML by accumulating text in a buffer. This is the most flexible approach, but it is also quite hard to manage when the logic to apply becomes complex. An alternate approach consists of generating the HTML by using the *TagBuilder* class, which offers an HTML-oriented, string-builder facility. The *TagBuilder* class generates for you the text for HTML tags, thus allowing you to build chunks of HTML by concatenating tags instead of plain strings.

An HTML helper is expected to return an encoded HTML string.

MvcHtmlString is better than just a string

What if you use the compact syntax on a piece of markup that is already encoded? Without countermeasures, the text inevitably will be double-encoded. For this reason, it is becoming a best practice to write HTML helpers that return an *MvcHtmlString* wrapper object instead of a plain string. In fact, all native HTML helpers have been refactored to return *MvcHtmlString*. The change is no big deal for developers. You can easily obtain an *MvcHtmlString* object from a string through the following code:

```
var html = GenerateHtmlAsString();
return MvcHtmlString.Create(html);
```

The *MvcHtmlString* type is a smart wrapper for a string that has HTML content, and it exposes the *IHtmlString* interface.

What's the purpose of *IHtmlString*? In ASP.NET an attempt to HTML-encode an object that implements *IHtmlString* results in a no-operation.

A sample HTML helper

Suppose that your view receives some text that can be optionally empty. You don't want to render the empty string; you'd rather display some default text such as N/A. How do you do that? You can brilliantly resolve everything with an *if* statement. However, nesting an *if* statement in ASPX markup doesn't particularly help to make your code clean; doing the same in Razor is only a little better.

An ad hoc helper can smooth things out because it encapsulates the *if* statement and preserves the required logic while delivering more compact and readable code. The following code demonstrates an HTML helper that replaces a given string with some default text if it's null or empty:

```
public static class OptionalTextHelpers
{
    public static MvcHtmlString OptionalText(this HtmlHelper helper,
        String text,
        String format="{0}",
        String alternateText="",
        String alternateFormat="{0}")
    {
        var actualText = text;
        var actualFormat = format;

        if (String.IsNullOrEmpty(actualText))
        {
            actualText = alternateText;
            actualFormat = alternateFormat;
        }

        return MvcHtmlString.Create(String.Format(actualFormat, actualText));
    }
}
```

The helper has up to four parameters, three of which are optional parameters. It takes the original text and its null replacement, plus a format string to embellish the text in both cases.

A sample Ajax helper

An Ajax helper differs from an HTML helper only because it is invoked in the context of an Ajax operation. For example, let's suppose that you want to use an image as a button. Clicking the image should automatically trigger an Ajax call to some application URL.

How is this different from just attaching a bit of JavaScript to the click event of the image and then using jQuery to carry the call? If you know the URL to pass to jQuery, you don't need this helper. If, however, you find it better to express the URL as a controller/action pair, you need this helper to generate a link that takes the user to wherever the pair controller/action pair points, as shown in the following:

```
public static class AjaxHelpers
{
    public static String ImgActionLink(this AjaxHelper ajaxHelper,
        String imageUrl,
        String imgAltText,
        String imgStyle,
        String actionName,
        String controllerName,
        Object routeValues,
        AjaxOptions ajaxOptions,
        Object htmlAttributes)
    {
        const String tag = "[xxx]";     // arbitrary string
        var markup = ajaxHelper.ActionLink(
            tag, actionName, controllerName, routeValues, ajaxOptions,
            htmlAttributes).ToString();

        // Replace text with IMG markup
        var urlHelper = new UrlHelper(ajaxHelper.ViewContext.RequestContext);
        var img = String.Format(
            "<img src='{0}' alt='{1}' title='{1}' style='{2}' />",
            urlHelper.Content(imageUrl),
            imgAltText,
            imgStyle);
        var modifiedMarkup = markup.Replace(tag, img);
        return modifiedMarkup;
    }
}
```

The helper first invokes the default *ActionLink* helper to get the URL as if it were to be a text-based hyperlink. In the first step, the hyperlink text is set to a known string acting as a placeholder. Next, when everything is ready to go, the helper strips off the placeholder string and replaces that with the URL of the image.

Why can't you just provide the <img> tag as the text of the original action link? Being a good citizen, *ActionLink* HTML-encodes everything, so you won't see any images, just the text of the URL.

The Razor view engine

The Web Forms view engine employs a syntax that on one hand is familiar to nearly all ASP.NET developers. On the other hand, the ASPX markup was devised as a way to support server controls, and it has severe limitations when used mostly with code blocks. Clearly, the major issue is lack of readability.

Introduced with ASP.NET MVC 3, the Razor view engine comes to the rescue, providing an alternate markup language to define the structure of view templates.

Inside the view engine

According to Razor, a view template is an HTML page with a few placeholders and code snippets. Overall, the readability of the view template is greatly improved, and by combining Razor code snippets with HTML helpers, you can arrange views to make them easier to read and maintain.

Search locations

The Razor view engine supports a bunch of interesting properties that are related to the locations of the view templates. Table 2-4 describes these properties.

TABLE 2-4 Properties to express desired location formats for view templates

Property	Description
AreaMasterLocationFormats	Locations where master views are searched in the case of area-based applications
AreaPartialViewLocationFormats	Locations where partial views are searched in the case of area-based applications
AreaViewLocationFormats	Locations where views are searched in the case of area-based applications
MasterLocationFormats	Locations where master views are searched
PartialViewLocationFormats	Locations where partial views are searched
ViewLocationFormats	Locations where views are searched
FileExtensions	List of extensions supported for views, partial views, and master views

Each property is implemented as an array of strings. Table 2-5 shows the default values for the properties.

TABLE 2-5 Default location formats

Property	Default location format
AreaMasterLocationFormats	~/Areas/{2}/Views/{1}/{0}.cshtml ~/Areas/{2}/Views/Shared/{0}.cshtml ~/Areas/{2}/Views/{1}/{0}.vbhtml ~/Areas/{2}/Views/Shared/{0}.vbhtml
AreaPartialViewLocationFormats	~/Areas/{2}/Views/{1}/{0}.cshtml ~/Areas/{2}/Views/{1}/{0}.vbhtml ~/Areas/{2}/Views/Shared/{0}.cshtml ~/Areas/{2}/Views/Shared/{0}.vbhtml
AreaViewLocationFormats	~/Areas/{2}/Views/{1}/{0}.cshtml ~/Areas/{2}/Views/{1}/{0}.vbhtml ~/Areas/{2}/Views/Shared/{0}.cshtml ~/Areas/{2}/Views/Shared/{0}.vbhtml
MasterLocationFormats	~/Views/{1}/{0}.cshtml ~/Views/Shared/{0}.cshtml ~/Views/{1}/{0}.vbhtml ~/Views/Shared/{0}.vbhtml
PartialViewLocationFormats	~/Views/{1}/{0}.cshtml ~/Views/{1}/{0}.vbhtml ~/Views/Shared/{0}.cshtml ~/Views/Shared/{0}.vbhtml
ViewLocationFormats	~/Views/{1}/{0}.cshtml ~/Views/{1}/{0}.vbhtml ~/Views/Shared/{0}.cshtml ~/Views/Shared/{0}.vbhtml
FileExtensions	.cshtml, .vbhtml

Pretty much everything works in the same way with the Web Forms engine. As far as the view is concerned, the only variation is the different file extension and, of course, the different syntax. Let's get familiar with it, then.

Code nuggets

A Razor view template is essentially an HTML page with a few code snippets, also known as code nuggets. Code nuggets are similar to ASP.NET code blocks, but they feature a simpler and terser syntax. You denote the start of a Razor code block by using the @ character. More important, you don't need to close those blocks explicitly. The Razor parser uses Visual Basic or C# parsing logic to figure out where a line of code finishes. Here's an example:

```
<html>
<head>
    <title>@ViewBag.Title</title>
    <link href="@Url.Content("~/Content/Site.css")" rel="stylesheet" type="text/css" />
    <script src="@Url.Content("~/Scripts/jquery.js")" type="text/javascript"></script>
</head>
...
</html>
```

You can mix any Razor code nugget with plain markup even when the code nugget contains control flow statements such as an if/else or for/foreach statement. The following code rewrites the page rendered in Figure 2-7 using code nuggets:

```
<body>
    <h2>@ViewBag.Header</h2>
    <hr />

    <table>
        <thead>
            <th>City</th>
            <th>Country</th>
            <th>Been there?</th>
        </thead>
    @foreach (var city in Model) {
        <tr>
            <td><%: city.Name %></td>
            <td><%: city.Country %></td>
            <td><%: city.Visited ?"Yes" :"No"%></td>
        </tr>
    }
    </table>
</body>
```

Note that the closing brace (}), which is placed in the middle of the source, is correctly recognized and interpreted by the parser.

Generally, you can use any C# (or Visual Basic) instructions in a Razor template as long as they are prefixed by @. Here's an example of how you import a namespace and create a form block:

```
@using YourApp.Extensions;
...
<body>
    @using (Html.BeginForm()) {
        <fieldset>
            <div class="editor-field">
                @Html.TextBox("TextBox1")
            </div>
        </fieldset>
    }
</body>
```

In the end, a Razor template is a plain HTML markup file intertwined with @ expressions that wrap executable statements and HTML helpers. However, a few shortcuts exist.

Special expressions of code nuggets

You can insert a full segment of code made of multiple lines anywhere by wrapping it within an @{ *code* } block like the one shown here:

```
@{
    var user = "Dino";
}
...
<p>@user</p>
```

You can retrieve any variable you create and use it later as if the code belonged to a single block. The content of an @{...} block can mix code and markup. It is essential, however, that the parser can figure out exactly where code ends and markup begins, and vice versa. Look at the following nugget:

```
@{
    var number = GetRandomNumber();
    if(number.IsEven())
      <p>Number is even</p>
    else
      <text>Number is odd</text>
}
```

If the markup content you're emitting is wrapped up by HTML tags, the parser will properly recognize it as markup. If it's plain text (for example, just a text string), you must wrap it in a Razor-specific <text> for the parser to handle it correctly.

A single statement that results from an expression can be combined in the same expression by using parentheses:

```
<p> @("Welcome, " + user) </p>
```

Parentheses also work when you intend to place a function call:

```
<p> @(YourMethod(1,2,3)) </p>
```

Any content being processed by Razor is automatically encoded, so you don't need to take care of that. If your code returns HTML markup that you want to emit as-is without being automatically encoded, you should resort to using the *Html.Raw* helper method presented here:

```
@Html.Raw(Strings.HtmlMessage)
```

Finally, when inside multiline code nuggets @{ ... }, you use the C# or Visual Basic language syntax to place comments. You can comment out an entire block of Razor code by using the @* ... *@ syntax, as shown here:

```
@*
<div> Some Razor markup </div>
*@
```

The Visual Studio toolbar buttons for commenting blocks in and out support the Razor syntax nicely.

Note Most of the time, the Razor parser is smart enough to determine from the context the reason why you're using the @ symbol, whether it's to denote a code nugget or perhaps a literal email address. If you hit a corner case that the parser can't successfully solve, using @@ makes it clear that you want the symbol @ to be taken literally and not as the start of a code nugget.

Conditional nuggets

Razor also supports conditional attributes that should be emitted only if the Razor expression is true or not null. Let's consider the following markup:

```
<div class="@yourCss">
   ...
</div>
```

The variable *yourCss* might be empty or null; in this case you ideally don't want the *class* attribute to be emitted. Up until ASP.NET MVC 4, you were forced to write some conditional logic yourself. Now, the conditional logic is built in to the Razor engine.

Be aware that the same happens if the Razor expression is Boolean: If it returns false or is null, the attribute is not emitted.

The Razor view object

When the Razor view engine is used, the resulting view object is an instance of the *WebViewPage* class defined in the System.Web.Mvc assembly. This class incorporates the logic to parse markup and render HTML. Public properties on this class are available to any code nuggets you might write in actual templates.

Table 2-6 provides a quick list of a few properties in which you might be interested.

TABLE 2-6 Commonly used properties and methods of a Razor view object

Property	Description
Ajax	Gets an instance of the *AjaxHelper* class used to reference Ajax HTML helpers around the template.
Culture	Gets and sets the ID of the culture associated with the current request. This setting influences culture-dependent aspects of a page, such as date, number, and currency formatting. The culture is expressed in xx-yy format, where xx indicates the language and yy the culture.
Href	Converts paths that you create in server code (which can include the ~ operator) to paths that the browser understands.
Html	Gets an instance of the *HtmlHelper* class used to reference HTML helpers in the template.
Context	Gets the central repository to gain access to various ASP.NET intrinsic objects: *Request, Response, Server, User,* and the like.
IsAjax	Returns true if the current request was initiated by the browser's *Ajax* object.

Property	Description
IsPost	Returns true if the current request was placed through an HTTP POST verb.
Layout	Gets and sets the path to the file containing the master view template.
Model	Gets a reference to the view model object (if any) containing data for the view. This property is of type dynamic.
UICulture	Gets and sets the ID of the user-interface culture associated with the current request. This setting determines which resources are loaded in multilingual applications. The culture is expressed in xx-yy format, where xx indicates the language and yy the culture.
ViewBag	Gets a reference to the *ViewBag* dictionary that might contain data the controller needs to pass to the view object.
ViewData	Gets a reference to the *ViewData* dictionary that might contain data the controller needs to pass to the view object.

Not all of these properties are effectively defined directly on the *WebViewPage* class. Many of them are actually defined on parent classes.

Designing a sample view

To create a Razor view of some reasonable complexity, you need to understand how to pass data to the view and how to define a master view.

Defining the model for the view

As previously mentioned, the controller can pass data down to the view in various ways. It can use global dictionaries such as *ViewBag* or *ViewData*. Better yet, the controller can use a strongly typed object tailor-made for the specific view. I'll discuss the pros and cons of the various approaches in a moment.

To use *ViewBag* or *ViewData* from within a code nugget, you don't need to take any special measures. You just write @ expressions that read or write into the dictionaries. To use a strongly typed view model, instead, you need to declare the actual type at the top of the template file, as shown here:

```
@model IList<GridDemo.Models.City>
```

The syntax you use to express the type is the same as the language you use throughout the template to write code nuggets. Next, you access properties in the view model object by using the *Model* property, as listed in Table 2-6. Here's an example:

```
@model IList<GridDemo.Models.City>

@{
    ViewBag.Title = ViewBag.Header;
}

<h2>@ViewBag.Header</h2>
<hr />
```

```
<table>
    <thead> ... </thead>
@foreach (var city in Model)
{
    <tr> ... </tr>
}
</table>
```

Of course, if *Model* references an object with child properties, you use *Model.Xxx* to reference each of them.

> **Note** In a Visual Basic–based Razor view, you define a view model object by using a different syntax. Instead of using the keyword @model, you go with the @ModelType keyword.

Defining a master view

In Razor, layout pages play the same role as master pages in Web Forms. A layout page is a standard Razor template that the view engine renders around any view you define, thus giving a uniform look and feel to sections of the site.

Each view can define its own layout page by simply setting the *Layout* property. The layout can be set to a hardcoded file or to any path that result from evaluating run-time conditions:

```
@{
    if (Request.Browser.IsMobileDevice) {
        Layout = "mobile.cshtml";
    }
}
```

You don't need to incorporate the code that determines the layout in each view file. With Razor, you can define a special file in the Views folder, which is processed before each view is built and rendered. This file, called *_ViewStart.cshtml*, is the ideal container of any view-related startup code, including the code that determines the layout to use. Here's a common implementation for the *_ViewStart.cshtml* file:

```
@{
    Layout = "~/Views/Shared/_Layout.cshtml";
}
```

According to the preceding code snippet, the file *_Layout.cshtml* defines the overall structure of each view in the site. (This is just the Razor counterpart to a master page.)

A layout page contains the usual mix of HTML and code nuggets and derives from *WebViewPage*. As such, it can access any properties on *WebViewPage*, including *ViewBag* and *ViewData*. The layout template must contain at least one placeholder for injecting the code of a specific view. The placeholder is expressed through a call to the *RenderBody* method (defined on *WebViewPage*), as demonstrated in the next example:

```
<html>
<head>
    <title>@ViewBag.Title</title>
    <link href="@Url.Content("~/Content/Site.css")" rel="stylesheet" type="text/css" />
    <script src="@Url.Content("~/Scripts/jquery-1.9.1.min.js")" type="text/javascript"></script>
</head>
<body>
    <div class="page">
    @RenderBody()
    </div>
</body>
</html>
```

Executing *RenderBody* causes any code in the actual view to flow into the layout template. The code within the actual view template is processed before the merging of the view and layout. This means that you can write view code that programmatically sets values in *ViewBag* which the layout can retrieve and consume. The typical example is the title of the page. Another good example is <meta> tags.

> **Important** In a view, it is recommended that you reference resources such as images, scripts, and stylesheets by using the tilde operator to refer to the root of the website. In earlier versions of ASP.NET MVC, you had to resort to the *Url.Content* method to ensure that the tilde was properly expanded in a URL. Starting with ASP.NET MVC 4, tilde is expanded automatically by the Razor engine, and using *Url.Content* is still supported but no longer necessary.

Defining sections

The *RenderBody* method defines a single point of injection within the layout. Although this is a common scenario, you might need to inject content into more than one location. In the layout template, you define an injection point by placing a call to *RenderSection* at the locations where you want those sections to appear:

```
<body>
    <div class="page">
    @RenderBody()
    </div>
    <div id="footer">
       @RenderSection("footer")
    </div>
</body>
```

Each section is identified by name and can be marked as optional. To declare a section optional, you do as follows:

```
<div id="footer">
   @RenderSection("footer", false)
</div>
```

The *RenderSection* method accepts an optional Boolean argument that denotes whether the section is required. The following code is functionally equivalent to the preceding code, but it's much better from a readability standpoint:

```
<div id="footer">
   @RenderSection("footer", required:false)
</div>
```

Observe that *required* is not a keyword; more simply, it is the name of the formal parameter defined on the *RenderSection* method. (Its name shows up nicely thanks to IntelliSense.)

If the view template doesn't include a required section, you get a run-time exception. Here's how to define content for a section in a view template:

```
@section footer {
    <p>Written by Dino Esposito</p>
}
```

You can define the content for a section anywhere in a Razor view template.

You can also use the *RenderPage* method if you need to send an entire view straight to the output stream. The *RenderPage* method takes the URL of the view to render. The overall behavior is nearly identical to the *RenderPartial* extension method that you might have used plenty of times in ASPX views.

Default content for sections

Master pages in the Web Forms view engine make it possible for you to specify some default content for a placeholder to use in case the actual page doesn't fill it in. This same feature is not natively supported in Razor, but you can arrange some quick workarounds. In particular, the *WebViewPage* class provides a handy *IsSectionDefined* method that you can use in a Razor template to determine whether a given section has been specified. Here's some code that you can use in a layout page to indicate default content for an optional section:

```
@* This code belongs to a layout page *@
<div id="footer">
    @if(IsSectionDefined("Copyright"))
    {
       @RenderSection("copyright")
    }
    else
    {
       <hr /><span>Rights reserved for a better use.</span>
    }
</div>
```

Keep in mind that section names are case insensitive.

Nested layouts

You can nest Razor layouts to any level you want. Suppose that you want to transform the About view created by the standard ASP.NET MVC application into something more sophisticated. The About view is based on the general site layout—the *_Layout.cshtml* file. Suppose further that you want it to accept contact information from an external view template. Here's the structure you expect:

```
@{
    ViewBag.Title = "About Us";
}
<h2>About</h2>
<p>
    @RenderBody()
</p>
```

You can't request a layout template—that is, any Razor template that calls *RenderBody*—directly; you get an exception if you try to do that. This means that you should rename the about.cshtml file, modified as shown in the preceding code, to something like aboutLayout.cshtml. In addition, you must explicitly mention the parent layout on which it is based:

```
@{
    Layout = "~/Views/Shared/_Layout.cshtml";
    ViewBag.Title = "About Us";
}
<h2>About</h2>
<p>
    @RenderBody()
</p>
```

Finally, you create the actual about.cshtml view, which is the view directly requested by the application:

```
@{
    Layout = "~/Views/Home/AboutLayout.cshtml";
}
<fieldset>
    <legend>Contact</legend>
    <p>Follow me on Twitter: @@despos</p>
</fieldset>
```

Declarative HTML helpers

As you saw earlier in the chapter, HTML helpers are a powerful tool to build reusable and parametric pieces of HTML. Written as extension methods for the *HtmlHelper* (or *AjaxHelper*) class, you can easily reference helpers in a Razor template without requiring even a single code change. This rule applies, for example, to all built-in HTML helpers, such as those used to emit a form or an action link.

The downside of writing HTML helpers as extension methods is the limited flexibility they offer for expressing the graphical layout. For example, to build an HTML table, you need to compose markup into a string builder. You can do it, but it's not really effective. In Razor, you have an alternate approach: *declarative helpers*.

You start by creating a .cshtml file in the App_Code folder of the project. The project wizard doesn't create this folder automatically, so you need to do it yourself. (Curiously, the folder is not even listed as an ASP.NET folder.) The name you choose for the .cshtml file is important because you'll be using it when making calls to the helpers. Think of this file as one of your helper repositories. A classic name for this file is something like MyHelpers.cshtml. Here's some content:

```
@using RazorEngine.Models;

@helper CityGrid(IList<City> cities)
{
    <table>
        <thead> ... </thead>
        @foreach (var city in cities)
        {
            <tr>
                <td>@city.Name</td>
                <td>@city.Country</td>
                <td>@(city.Visited ? "Yes" : "No")</td>
            </tr>
        }
    </table>
}

@helper ShowHeader()
{
    <h2>I'm a Razor declarative helper!</h2>
}
```

The *@helper* keyword begins the HTML declaration. The keyword is followed by the signature and implementation of the method. The body of the helper is just an embedded fragment of a Razor template. You can have multiple helpers in a single file. (Keep in mind that the helper repository won't be detected if it's placed outside the App_Code folder.)

To invoke a declarative Razor helper, you do as follows:

```
@using RazorEngine.Models;
@model IList<City>

@MyHelpers.ShowHeader()
<p>
    @MyHelpers.CityGrid(Model)
</p>
```

The name of the helper is composed of two parts: the repository name and the helper name.

Coding the view

In this final section of the chapter, I'll delve into a couple of important points that affect views and controllers: how to effectively pass data to a view, and how to add more flexibility to the view-rendering processing.

Modeling the view

Using Razor (or the ASPX engine), you define the graphical layout of a view. Sometimes, the view is just made of static content. More often, though, the view must incorporate real data resulting from some operation against the middle tier of the system or loaded from the application cache or session state. How would you make this data available to the view?

The golden rule of ASP.NET MVC design claims that the view receives but doesn't compute any data it has to display. You can pass data in three nonexclusive ways: via the *ViewData* dictionary, the *ViewBag* dictionary, and a tailor-made container object, often referred to as the *view model* object.

The ViewData dictionary

Exposed directly by the *Controller* class, the *ViewData* property is a name-value dictionary object. Its programming model is analogous to using *Session* or other ASP.NET intrinsic objects:

```
public ActionResult Index()
{
    ViewData["PageTitle"] = "Programming ASP.NET MVC";
    return View();
}
```

Any data you store in a dictionary is treated as an object and requires casting, boxing, or both for it to be worked on in the view. You can create as many entries as you like in the dictionary. The lifetime of the dictionary is the same as the request.

The ViewData dictionary is packed into the *view context*—an internal structure through which the ASP.NET MVC infrastructure moves data from the controller level to the view level—and made available to the view engine. The view objects—*ViewPage* for the ASPX engine and *WebViewPage* for Razor—expose the ViewData dictionary to any code in the view templates. Here's how you retrieve ViewData content from a view template:

```
<head>
    <title> @ViewData["PageTitle"] </title>
</head>
```

Keep in mind that you are not limited to storing strings in the ViewData dictionary.

Overall, the ViewData dictionary is straightforward to use and extremely flexible. In fact, it allows you to pass a new piece of data to the view by simply creating a new entry. At the same time, the name-based model forces you to use a lot of magic strings (plain-text strings such as *PageTitle* in the preceding example) and, more important, to match them between the controller and view code. By using constants, you can reduce some of the inherent brittleness of magic strings, but you still have no defense against the possibility of picking up the wrong name. If you happen to reference the wrong dictionary entry, you'll find out only at run time. The ViewData dictionary is well suited for simple solutions and applications with a relatively short lifetime. As the number of dictionary entries and the number of views grow, maintenance becomes an issue, and you should move away from ViewData when looking for other options.

The ViewBag dictionary

Also defined on the *Controller* class, the *ViewBag* property offers an even more flexible facility to pass data to the view. The property is defined as a *dynamic* type, as illustrated here:

```
public dynamic ViewBag { get; }
```

When a .NET compiler encounters a *dynamic* type, it emits a special chunk of code instead of simply evaluating the expression. Such a special chunk of code passes the expression to the Dynamic Language Runtime (DLR) for a run-time evaluation. In other words, any expression based on the *dynamic* type is compiled to be interpreted at run time. Any member set or read out of ViewBag is always accepted by compilers but not actually evaluated until execution. Here's an example that compares the usage of ViewData and ViewBag:

```
public ActionResult Index()
{
    // Using ViewData
    ViewData["PageTitle"] = "Programming ASP.NET MVC";

    // Using ViewBag
    ViewBag.PageTitle = "Programming ASP.NET MVC";

    return View();
}
```

The compiler doesn't care whether a property named *PageTitle* really exists on ViewBag. All it does is pack a call to the DLR interpreter, where it asks the DLR to try to assign a given string to a certain *PageTitle* property. Similarly, when *PageTitle* is read out of ViewBag, the compiler instructs the DLR to check whether such a property exists. If it doesn't exist, the compiler throws an exception. Here's how you consume content from ViewBag in a Razor view:

```
<head>
    <title> @ViewBag.PageTitle </title>
</head>
```

From a developer's perspective, which is better, ViewBag or ViewData?

The ViewBag syntax is terser than the ViewData syntax, but as I see things, that's the entire difference. Just as with ViewData, you won't have compile-time checking on properties. The dependency of the dynamic type on the DLR doesn't save you run-time exceptions if you mistype a property name. In the end, it's purely a matter of preference. Also, for what it matters, ViewBag requires at least ASP.NET MVC 3 and .NET 4, whereas ViewData works with any version of ASP.NET MVC and with .NET 2.0.

> **Note** Because the *dynamic* type is resolved at run time, Visual Studio IntelliSense can't indicate anything about its properties. IntelliSense treats a *dynamic* type like a plain *Object* type. Some tools—most noticeably JetBrains ReSharper—are a bit smarter. ReSharper tracks all the properties encountered along the way in the scope where the dynamic variable is used. For any properties used, an entry is added to the IntelliSense menu of members.

Strongly typed view models

When you have dozens of distinct values to pass to a view, the same flexibility that makes it possible for you to quickly add a new entry or rename an existing one becomes your worst enemy. You are left on your own to track item names and values; you get no help from IntelliSense and compilers.

The only proven way to deal with complexity in software is through appropriate design. So, defining an object model for each view helps you to track what that view really needs. I suggest that you define a view-model class for each view you add to the application:

```
public ActionResult Index()
{
    ...
    // Pack data for the view using a view-specific container object.
    var model = new YourViewModel();

    // Populate the model.
    ...

    // Trigger the view.
    return View(model);
}
```

Having a view-model class for each view also creates the problem of choosing an appropriate class name. You could use a combination of controller and view names. For example, the view-model object for a view named Index invoked from the Home controller might be named HomeIndexViewModel. Even better, you can create a subfolder named Home in the Models folder and host there an *IndexViewModel* class. In my applications, I often also rename Models to ViewModels. (This particular approach is just a suggestion, though; you should just feel free to choose meaningful names.)

How would you shape up a view-model class?

First and foremost, a view-model object is a plain data-transfer object with only data and (nearly) no behavior. Ideally, properties on a view-model object expose data exactly in the format the view expects it to be. For example, if the view is expected to display only the date and status of pending orders, you might not want to pass a plain collection of full-blown *Order* objects because they result from the middle tier. The following view-model class is a better choice for modeling data for the view. It helps keep the presentation layer and middle tier decoupled.

```
public class LatestOrderViewModel
{
    public DateTime OrderDate { get; set; }
    public String Status { get; set; }
}
```

The ASP.NET MVC infrastructure guarantees that ViewData and ViewBag collections are always made available to the view object without any developer intervention. The same is not true for custom view-model objects.

When you use a view model object, you must declare the view model type in the view template so that the actual view object can be created of type *ViewPage<T>* in the ASPX view engine and of type *WebViewPage<T>* if Razor is used. Here's what you need to have in an *.aspx* template if you use the ASPX Web Forms view engine:

```
<%@ Page Language="C#" MasterPageFile="~/Views/Shared/Site.Master"
        Inherits="System.Web.Mvc.ViewPage<LatestOrderViewModel>" %>
```

In the preceding code snippet, the type assigned to the *Inherits* attribute is not fully qualified. This means that you probably need to add an *@Import* directive to specify the namespace to import to locate the view-model type. If the view engine is Razor, here's what you need:

```
@model LatestOrderViewModel
```

To retrieve the view-model object in the view template, you use the *Model* property defined on both *WebViewPage* and *ViewPage*. Here's a Razor example:

```
<h2>
    Latest order placed
    <span class="highlight">@Model.OrderDate.ToString("dddd, dd MMM yyyy")</span>
    <br />
    Status is: <span class="highlight">@Model.Status</span>
</h2>
```

In this example, the format of the date is established in the view. It is also acceptable that the controller prepares the date as a string and passes it down to the view, ready for display. There's not a clear guideline on where this code belongs; it falls into a sort of gray area. My preference is to keep the view as simple as possible. If the format is fixed and not dependent on run-time conditions, it is acceptable for you to pass *DateTime* and let the view figure out the rest. When a bit of logic is required to format the date, in general I prefer to move it up to the controller.

Although each view should have its own model object, limiting the number of classes you deal with is always a good idea. To reuse model classes in multiple views, you typically build a hierarchy of classes. Here's an example of a view-model base class:

```
public class ViewModelBase
{
    public String Title { get; set; }
    public String Header { get; set; }
}
public class LatestOrderViewModel : ViewModelBase
{
    ...
}
```

Finally, it is always a good approach to devise the structure of the view model class around the view rather than around the data. In other words, I always prefer to have a view-model class designed as a container.

Suppose that you need to pass a list of orders to the view. The first option that springs to mind is using the following view-model class (in a Razor template):

```
@model IList<PendingOrder>
```

Functionally speaking, the approach is sound. But is it extensible? In my experience, you always end up stuffing a variety of heterogeneous data in a view. This might be required because of refactoring efforts, as well as new requirements that pop up. A more maintainable approach (one that will let you refactor without changing controller/view interfaces) is the following:

```
@model YourViewModel
```

In this case, *YourViewModel* is defined as shown here:

```
public class YourViewModel
{
    public IList<PendingOrder> PendingOrders {get; set;}
}
```

A view-model class ultimately models the view, not the data.

 Important I'm not sure if I stated it clearly enough, so let me rephrase it. Strongly typed view models are the only safe and sound solution for any ASP.NET MVC application of at least moderate complexity and duration. I do believe that using view models is a state of mind more than a way to fight complexity. However, if you can make it work with a couple of ViewData or ViewBag entries per view, and you'll be throwing the site away after a few months (for example, a site you set up for a specific event), by all means ignore view models.

Packaging the view-model classes

Where should you define the view-model classes? This mostly depends on the size of the project. In a large project with a good deal of reusability and an expected long lifetime, you probably should create a separate class library with all view-model classes you use.

In smaller projects, you might want to isolate all the classes in a specific folder. This can be the Models folder that the default Visual Studio project templates create for you. Personally, I tend to rename Models to ViewModels and group classes in controller-specific subfolders, as shown in Figure 2-6.

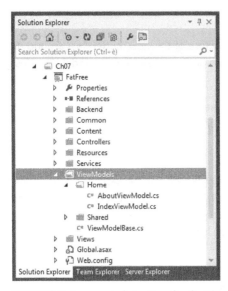

FIGURE 2-6 A suggested structure for the ViewModels folder.

Advanced features

ASP.NET MVC is built around the Convention-over-Configuration pattern. As is typical of frameworks, the pattern saves developers a lot of programming details as long as they adhere to a number of fixed rules and conventions. This is particularly evident with views.

The view engine works by retrieving and processing view templates. How does it know about templates? In general, it can happen in either of two ways: you register known views with the engine (configuration), or you place views in specific locations so that the engine can retrieve them (convention). What if you want to organize your views according to a different set of conventions? Quite simply, you need your own view engine.

Note The need for a custom view engine is more frequent than one might think at first. You might create a custom view engine for two main reasons: you want to express views in a new markup language, or you want to apply a set of personalized conventions. I'm not saying that every application should use a custom markup language, but most applications might benefit from views organized in a custom way.

Custom view engines

Most applications of mine employ their own view engine that just organize views in a slightly different way or need an extra layer of code to resolve view names to actual markup files. If you have reasons for using a different directory schema for some of your views, all you need to do is derive a simple class, as shown here:

```
public class MyViewEngine : RazorViewEngine
{
    public MyViewEngine()
    {
        this.MasterLocationFormats = base.MasterLocationFormats;
        this.ViewLocationFormats = new string[]
                                    {
                                        "~/Views/{1}/{0}.cshtml"
                                    };

        // Customize the location for partial views
        this.PartialViewLocationFormats = new string[]
                                    {
                                        "~/PartialViews/{1}/{0}.cshtml ",
                                        "~/PartialViews/{1}/{0}.vbhtml"
                                    };
    }
}
```

To use this class in lieu of the default view engine, you enter the following in global.asax:

```
protected void Application_Start()
{
    ...

    // Removes the default engines and adds the new one.
    ViewEngines.Engines.Clear();
    ViewEngines.Engines.Add(new MyViewEngine());
}
```

After you do this, your application will fail if any of the partial views is located outside a Partial Views subfolder.

Note While setting custom locations is a good reason for considering custom view engines, you should keep in mind that if all you need to do is set location format properties on one of the default engines, you might not need to create a custom view engine at all. It might suffice that you retrieve the current instance in *Application_Start* and set location format properties directly.

Important If you have a custom view engine that supports custom folders (for example, a PartialViews folder for grouping partial views) it is essential that you add a web.config file to it. You can copy the same web.config file you find in the Views folder by default. That file contains critical information for the ASP.NET MVC runtime to locate view classes correctly.

Render actions

Complex views result from the composition of a variety of child views. When a controller method triggers the rendering of a view, it must provide all data the view needs for the main structure and all of the parts. Sometimes, this requires the controller to know a lot of details about parts of the application with which the class itself is not directly involved. Want an example?

Suppose that you have a menu to render in many of your views. Whatever action you take in relation to your application, the menu must be rendered. Rendering the menu, therefore, is an action not directly related to the current ongoing request. How would you handle that? Render actions are a possible answer.

A render action is a controller method that is specifically designed to be called from within a view. A render action is therefore a regular method on the controller class that you invoke from the view by using one of the following HTML helpers: *Action* or *RenderAction*.

```
@Html.Action("action")
```

Action and *RenderAction* behave mostly in the same way; the only difference is that *Action* returns the markup as a string, whereas *RenderAction* writes directly to the output stream. Both methods support a variety of overloads through which you can specify multiple parameters, including route values, HTML attributes, and, of course, the controller's name. You define a render action as a regular method on a controller class and define it to be the renderer of some view-related action:

```
public ActionResult Menu()
{
    var options = new MenuOptionsViewModel();
    options.Items.Add(new MenuOption {Url="...", Image="..."});
    options.Items.Add(new MenuOption {Url="...", Image="..."});
    return PartialView(options);
}
```

The content of the menu's partial view is not relevant here; all it does is get the model object and render an appropriate piece of markup. Let's see the view source code for one of the pages you might have in the application:

```
<div>
   ...
   @Html.RenderAction("Menu")
   ...
</div>
```

The *RenderAction* helper method calls the *Menu* method on the specified controller (or on the controller that ordered the current view to be rendered) and directs any response to the output stream. In this way, the view incorporates some logic and calls back the controller. At the same time, your controller doesn't need to worry about passing the view information that is not strictly relevant to the current request it is handling.

Child actions

The execution of a render action is not simply a call made to a method via reflection. A lot more happens under the hood. In particular, a render action is a child request that originates within the boundaries of the main user request. The *RenderAction* method builds a new request context that contains the same HTTP context of the parent request and a different set of route values. This child request is forwarded to a specific HTTP handler—the *ChildActionMvcHandler* class—and is executed as if it came from the browser. The overall operation is similar to what happens when you call *Server. Execute* in general ASP.NET programming. There's no redirect and no roundtrip, but the child request goes through the usual pipeline of a regular ASP.NET MVC request and honors any action filters that it might encounter with just a few exceptions. The most illustrious examples of filters that won't work across child actions are *AuthorizeRequest* and *OutputCache*. (I'll say more about action filters later in the book.)

By default, any action method can be invoked from a URL and via a render action. However, any action methods marked with the *ChildActionOnly* attribute won't be available to public callers, and their usage is limited to rendering actions and child requests.

Summary

ASP.NET MVC doesn't match URLs to disk files; instead, it parses the URL to figure out the next requested action to take. Each action terminates with an action result. The most common type of action result is the view result, which consists of a chunk of HTML markup.

Generated by the controller method, a view result is made of a template and model. The view engine takes care of parsing the view template and filling it in with model data. ASP.NET MVC comes with two default view engines supporting different markup languages for expressing the template and different disk locations to discover templates. Today, Razor is the most commonly used view engine, and it superseded the old-fashioned ASPX syntax that reminds too much of classic ASP.NET but doesn't allow (reasonably) the use of server controls.

In this chapter, we first examined what it takes to process a view and then focused on development aspects, including using HTML helpers and templated helpers for the two default engines, ASPX and Razor. We also discussed best practices for modeling data and contrasted dictionaries with strongly typed view models.

I suggest that you take a look at the BasicApp examples that are in the companion source code to better understand what's been discussed in this chapter. In ASP.NET MVC 5, the default app built by the Visual Studio wizard is based on Twitter Bootstrap and offers a graphical template that is responsive to different screen sizes.

CHAPTER 3

The model-binding architecture

It does not matter how slowly you go, so long as you do not stop.

—Confucius

By default, the Microsoft Visual Studio standard project template for ASP.NET MVC applications includes a Models folder. If you look around for some guidance on how to use it and information about its intended role, you'll quickly reach the conclusion that the Models folder exists to store model classes. Fine, but which model is it for? Or, more precisely, what's the definition of a "model"?

I like to say that "model" is the most misunderstood idea in the history of software. As a concept, it needs to be expanded a bit to make sense in modern software. When the Model-View-Controller (MVC) pattern was introduced, software engineering was in its infancy, and applications were much simpler than today. Nobody really felt the need to break up the concept of model into smaller pieces. Such smaller pieces, however, existed.

In general, I find *at least* two distinct models: the *domain model* and the *view model*. The former describes the data you work with in the middle tier and is expected to provide a faithful representation of the entities and relationships that populate the business domain. These entities are typically persisted by the data-access layer and consumed by services that implement business processes. This domain model pushes a vision of data that is, in general, distinct and likely different from the vision of data you find in the presentation layer. The view model just describes the data that is being worked on in the presentation layer. A good example might be the canonical *Order* entity. There might be use-cases in which the application needs to present a collection of orders to users but not all properties are required. For example, you might need ID, date, and total, and likely a distinct container class—a data-transfer object (DTO).

Having said that, I agree with anyone who points out that not every application needs a neat separation between the object models used in the presentation and business layers. You might decide that for your own purposes the two models nearly coincide, but you should always recognize the existence of two distinct models that operate in two distinct layers.

This chapter introduces a third type of model that, although hidden for years in the folds of the ASP.NET Web Forms runtime, stands on its own in ASP.NET MVC: the *input model*. The input model refers to the model through which posted data is exposed to controllers and subsequently received by the application. The input model defines the DTOs the application uses to receive data from input forms.

Note Yet another flavor of model not mentioned here is the *data model* or the (mostly relational) model used to persist data.

The input model

Chapter 1, "ASP.NET MVC controllers," discusses request routing and the overall structure of controller methods. Chapter 2, "ASP.NET MVC views," explores views as the primary result of action processing. However, neither chapter thoroughly discusses how in ASP.NET MVC a controller method gets input data.

In ASP.NET Web Forms, we had server controls, view state, and the overall page life cycle working in the background to serve input data that was ready to use. With ASP.NET Web Forms, developers had no need to worry about an input model. Server controls in ASP.NET Web Forms provided a faithful server-side representation of the client user interface. Developers just needed to write C# code to read from input controls.

ASP.NET MVC makes a point of having controllers receive input data, not retrieve it. To pass input data to a controller, you need to package data in some way. This is precisely where the input model comes into play.

To better understand the importance and power of the new ASP.NET MVC input model, let's start from where ASP.NET Web Forms left us.

Evolving from the Web Forms input processing

An ASP.NET Web Forms application is based on pages, and each server page is based on server controls. The page has its own life cycle that spans from processing the raw request data to arranging the final response for the browser. The page life cycle is fed by raw request data such as HTTP headers, cookies, the URL, and the body, and it produces a raw HTTP response containing headers, cookies, the content type, and the body.

Inside the page life cycle, there are a few steps in which HTTP raw data is massaged into more easily programmable containers—server controls. In ASP.NET Web Forms, these "programmable containers" are never perceived as being part of an input object model. In ASP.NET Web Forms, the input model is just based on server controls and the view state.

Role of server controls

Suppose that you have a webpage with a couple of *TextBox* controls to capture a user name and password. When the user posts the content of the form, there is likely a piece of code to process the request similar to what is shown in the following code:

```
public void Button1_Click(Object sender, EventArgs e)
{
    // You're about to perform requested action using input data.
    CheckUserCredentials(TextBox1.Text, TextBox2.Text);
    ...
}
```

The overall idea behind the architecture of ASP.NET Web Forms is to keep the developer away from raw data. Any incoming request data is mapped to properties on server controls. When this is not possible, data is left parked in general-purpose containers such as *QueryString* or *Form*.

What would you expect from a method such as the *Button1_Click* just shown? That method is the Web Forms counterpart of a controller action. Here's how to refactor the previous code to use an explicit input model:

```
public void Button1_Click(Object sender, EventArgs e)
{
    // You're actually filling in the input model of the page.
    var model = new UserCredentialsInputModel();
    model.UserName = TextBox1.Text;
    model.Password = TextBox2.Text;

    // You're about to perform the requested action using input data.
    CheckUserCredentials(model);
    ...
}
```

The ASP.NET runtime environment breaks up raw HTTP request data into control properties, thus offering a control-centric approach to request processing.

Role of the view state

Speaking in terms of a programming paradigm, a key distinguishing characteristic between ASP.NET Web Forms and ASP.NET MVC is the view state. In Web Forms, the view state helps server controls to always be up to date. Because of the view state, as a developer you don't need to care about segments of the user interface that you don't touch in a postback. Suppose that you display a list of choices into which the user can drill down. When the request for details is made, in Web Forms all you need to do is display the details. The raw HTTP request, however, posted the list of choices as well as key information to find. The view state makes it unnecessary for you to deal with the list of choices.

The view state and server control build a thick abstraction layer on top of classic HTTP mechanics, and they make you think in terms of page sequences rather than successive requests. This is neither wrong nor right; it is just the paradigm behind Web Forms. In Web Forms, there's no need for clearly defining an input model. If you do that, it's only because you want to keep your code cleaner and more readable.

Input processing in ASP.NET MVC

Chapter 1, explains that a controller method can access input data through *Request* collections—such as *QueryString*, *Headers*, or *Form*—or value providers. Although it's functional, this approach is not ideal from a readability and maintenance perspective. You need an ad hoc model that exposes data to controllers.

The role of model binders

ASP.NET MVC provides an automatic binding layer that uses a built-in set of rules for mapping raw request data from any value providers to properties of input model classes. As a developer, you are largely responsible for the design of input model classes. The logic of the binding layer can be customized to a large extent, thus adding unprecedented heights of flexibility, as far as the processing of input data is concerned.

Flavors of a model

The ASP.NET MVC default project template offers just one Models folder, thus implicitly pushing the idea that "model" is just one thing: the model of the data the application is supposed to use. Generally speaking, this is a rather simplistic view, though it's effective in very simple sites.

If you look deeper into things, you can recognize three different types of "models" in ASP.NET MVC, as illustrated in Figure 3-1.

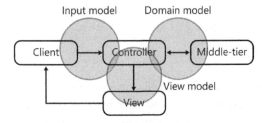

FIGURE 3-1 Types of models potentially involved in an ASP.NET MVC application.

The input model provides the representation of the data being posted to the controller. The view model provides the representation of the data being worked on in the view. Finally, the domain model is the representation of the domain-specific entities operating in the middle tier.

Note that the three models are not neatly separated, which Figure 3-1 shows to some extent. You might find overlap between the models. This means that classes in the domain model might be used in the view, and classes posted from the client might be used in the view. The final structure and diagram of classes is up to you.

Model binding

Model binding is the process of binding values posted over an HTTP request to the parameters used by the controller's methods. Let's find out more about the underlying infrastructure, mechanics, and components involved.

Model-binding infrastructure

The model-binding logic is encapsulated in a specific model-binder class. The binder works under the control of the action invoker and helps to figure out the parameters to pass to the selected controller method.

Analyzing the method's signature

Chapter 1 points out that each and every request passed to ASP.NET MVC is resolved in terms of a controller name and an action name. Armed with these two pieces of data, the action invoker—a native component of the ASP.NET MVC runtime shell—kicks in to actually serve the request. First, the invoker expands the controller name to a class name and resolves the action name to a method name on the controller class. If something goes wrong, an exception is thrown.

Next, the invoker attempts to collect all values required to make the method call. In doing so, it looks at the method's signature and attempts to find an input value for each parameter in the signature.

Getting the binder for the type

The action invoker knows the formal name and declared type of each parameter. (This information is obtained via reflection.) The action invoker also has access to the request context and to any data uploaded with the HTTP request—the query string, the form data, route parameters, cookies, headers, files, and so forth.

For each parameter, the invoker obtains a *model-binder* object. The model binder is a component that knows how to find values of a given type from the request context. The model binder applies its own algorithm, which includes the parameter name, parameter type, and request context available, and returns a value of the specified type. The details of the algorithm belong to the implementation of the model binder being used for the type.

ASP.NET MVC uses a built-in binder object that corresponds to the *DefaultModelBinder* class. The model binder is a class that implements the *IModelBinder* interface.

```
public interface IModelBinder
{
    Object BindModel(ControllerContext controllerContext, ModelBindingContext bindingContext);
}
```

Let's first explore the capabilities of the default binder and then see what it takes to write custom binders for specific types later.

The default model binder

The default model binder uses convention-based logic to match the names of posted values to parameter names in the controller's method. The *DefaultModelBinder* class knows how to deal with primitive and complex types as well as collections and dictionaries. In light of this, the default binder works just fine most of the time.

> **Note** If the default binder supports primitive and complex types and the collections thereof, will you ever feel the need to use something other than the default binder? You will hardly ever feel the need to replace the default binder with another general-purpose binder. However, the default binder can't apply your custom logic to massage request data into the properties of a given type. As you'll see later, a custom binder is helpful when the values being posted with the request don't exactly match the properties of the type you want the controller to use. In this case, a custom binder makes sense and helps keep the controller's code lean and mean.

Binding primitive types

Admittedly, it sounds a bit magical at first, but there's no actual wizardry behind model binding. The key fact about model binding is that it lets you focus exclusively on the data you want the controller method to receive. You completely ignore the details of how you retrieve that data, whether it comes from the query string or the route.

Suppose that you need a controller method to repeat a particular string a given number of times. Here's what you do:

```
public class BindingController : Controller
{
    public ActionResult Repeat(String text, Int32 number)
    {
        var model = new RepeatViewModel {Number = number, Text = text};
        return View(model);
    }
}
```

Designed in this way, the controller is highly testable and completely decoupled from the ASP.NET runtime environment. There's no need for you to access the *Request* object or the *Cookies* collection directly.

Where do the values for *text* and *number* come from? And, which component is actually reading them into text and number parameters?

The actual values are read from the request context, and the default model-binder object does the trick. In particular, the default binder attempts to match formal parameter names (*text* and *number* in the example) to named values posted with the request. In other words, if the request carries a form field, a query-string field, or a route parameter named text, the carried value is automatically bound to the text parameter. The mapping occurs successfully as long as the parameter type and actual value are compatible. If a conversion cannot be performed, an argument exception is thrown. The next URL works just fine:

```
http://server/binding/repeat?text=Dino&number=2
```

Conversely, the following URL causes an exception:

```
http://server/binding/repeat?text=Dino&number=true
```

The query-string field text contains *Dino*, and the mapping to the *String* parameter text on the method *Repeat* takes place successfully. The query-string field number, on the other hand, contains *true*, which can't be successfully mapped to an *Int32* parameter. The model binder returns a parameters dictionary in which the entry for *number* contains null. Because the parameter type is *Int32*—that is, a non-nullable type—the invoker throws an argument exception.

Dealing with optional values

An argument exception that occurs because invalid values are being passed is not detected at the controller level. The exception is fired before the execution flow reaches the controller. This means that you won't be able to catch it with try/catch blocks.

If the default model binder can't find a posted value that matches a required method parameter, it places a null value in the parameter dictionary returned to the action invoker. Again, if a value of null is not acceptable for the parameter type, an argument exception is thrown before the controller method is even called.

What if a method parameter must be considered optional?

A possible approach entails changing the parameter type to a nullable type, as shown here:

```
public ActionResult Repeat(String text, Nullable<Int32> number)
{
    var model = new RepeatViewModel {Number = number.GetValueOrDefault(), Text = text};
    return View(model);
}
```

Another approach consists of using a default value for the parameter:

```
public ActionResult Repeat(String text, Int32 number=4)
{
    var model = new RepeatViewModel {Number = number, Text = text};
    return View(model);
}
```

Any decisions about the controller method's signature are up to you. In general, you might want to use types that are very close to the real data being uploaded with the request. Using parameters of type *Object*, for example, will save you from argument exceptions, but it will make it hard to write clean code to process the input data.

The default binder can map all primitive types, such as String, integers, Double, Decimal, Boolean, DateTime, and related collections. To express a Boolean type in a URL, you resort to the true or false strings. These strings are parsed using .NET native Boolean parsing functions, which recognize true and false strings in a case-insensitive manner. If you use strings such as yes/no to mean a Boolean, the default binder won't understand your intentions and places a null value in the parameter dictionary, which might cause an argument exception.

Value providers and precedence

The default model binder uses all the registered value providers to find a match between posted values and method parameters. By default, value providers cover the collections listed in Table 3-1.

TABLE 3-1 Request collections for which a default value provider exists

Collection	Description
Form	Contains values posted from an HTML form, if any
RouteData	Contains values excerpted from the URL route
QueryString	Contains values specified as the URL's query string
Files	A value is the entire content of an uploaded file, if any

Table 3-1 lists request collections being considered in the exact order in which they are processed by the default binder. Suppose that you have the following route:

```
routes.MapRoute(
    "Test",
    "{controller}/{action}/test/{number}",
    new { controller = "Binding", action = "RepeatWithPrecedence", number = 5 }
);
```

As you can see, the route has a parameter named number. Now, consider this URL:

```
/Binding/RepeatWithPrecedence/test/10?text=Dino&number=2
```

The request uploads two values that are good candidates to set the value of the *number* parameter in the *RepeatWithPrecedence* method. The first value is 10 and is the value of a route parameter named *number*. The second value is 2 and is the value of the *QueryString* element named *number*. The method itself provides a default value for the *number* parameter:

```
public ActionResult RepeatWithPrecedence(String text, Int32 number=20)
{
    ...
}
```

Which value is actually picked up? As Table 3-1 suggests, the value that is actually passed to the method is 10, which is the value read from the route data collection.

Binding complex types

There's no limitation regarding the number of parameters you can list on a method's signature. How-ever, a container class is often better than a long list of individual parameters. For the default model binder, the result is nearly the same whether you list a sequence of parameters or just one parameter of a complex type. Both scenarios are fully supported. Here's an example:

```
public class ComplexController : Controller
{
    public ActionResult Repeat(RepeatText inputModel)
    {
        var model = new RepeatViewModel
                        {
                            Title = "Repeating text",
                            Text = inputModel.Text,
                            Number = inputModel.Number
                        };
        return View(model);
    }
}
```

The controller method receives an object of type *RepeatText*. The class is a plain data-transfer object, defined as follows:

```
public class RepeatText
{
    public String Text { get; set; }
    public Int32 Number { get; set; }
}
```

As you can see, the class just contains members for the same values you passed as individual parameters in the previous example. The model binder works with this complex type as well as it did with single values.

For each public property in the declared type—*RepeatText* in this case—the model binder looks for posted values whose key names match the property name. The match is case insensitive. Here's a sample URL that works with the *RepeatText* parameter type:

```
http://server/Complex/Repeat?text=ASP.NET%20MVC&number=5
```

Figure 3-2 shows the output that the URL might generate.

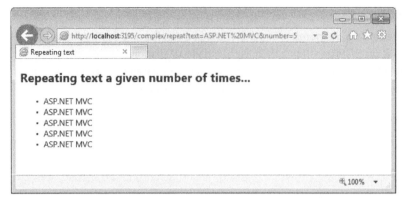

FIGURE 3-2 Repeating text with values extracted from a complex type.

Binding collections

What if the argument that a controller method expects is a collection? For example, can you bind the content of a posted form to an *IList<T>* parameter? The *DefaultModelBinder* class makes it possible, but doing so requires a bit of contrivance of your own. Have a look at Figure 3-3.

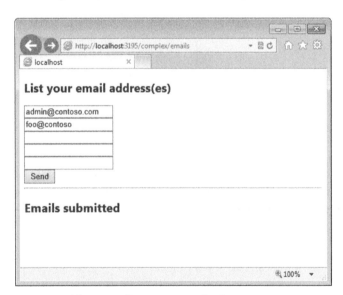

FIGURE 3-3 The page will post an array of strings.

When the user clicks the Send button, the form submits its content. Specifically, it sends out the content of the various text boxes. If the text boxes have different IDs, the posted content takes the following form:

```
TextBox1=admin@contoso.com&TextBox2=&TextBox3=&TextBox4=&TextBox5=
```

In classic ASP.NET, this is the only possible way of working because you can't just assign the same ID to multiple controls. However, if you manage the HTML yourself, nothing prevents you from assigning the five text boxes in the figure the same ID. The HTML DOM, in fact, fully supports this scenario (though it is not recommended). Therefore, the following markup is entirely legal in ASP.NET MVC and produces HTML that works on all browsers:

```
@using (Html.BeginForm())
{
    <h2>List your email address(es)</h2>
    foreach(var email in Model.Emails)
    {
        <input type="text" name="email" value="@email" />
        <br />
    }
    <input type="submit" value="Send" />
}
```

What's the expected signature of a controller method that has to process the email addresses typed in the form? Here it is:

```
public ActionResult Emails(IList<String> email)
{
    ...
}
```

Figure 3-4 shows that an array of strings is correctly passed to the method, thanks to the default binder class.

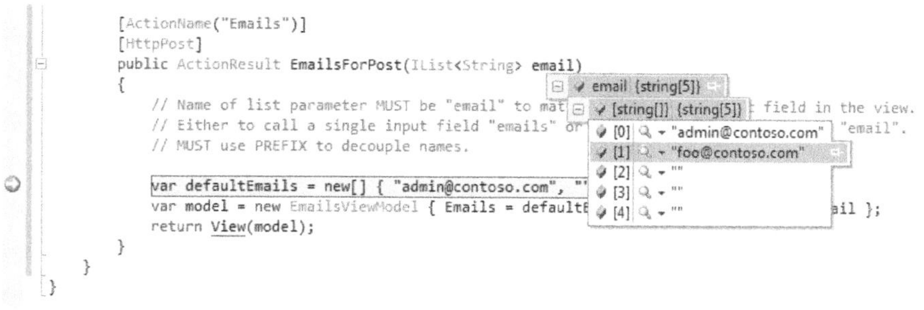

FIGURE 3-4 An array of strings has been posted.

As is dicussed in greater detail in Chapter 4, "Input forms," when you work with HTML forms, you likely need to have a pair of methods: one to handle the display of the view (the verb GET), and one to handle the scenario in which data is posted to the view. The *HttpPost* and *HttpGet* attributes make it possible for you to mark which scenario a given method is handling for the same action name. Here's the full implementation of the example, which uses two distinct methods to handle GET and POST scenarios:

```
[ActionName("Emails")]
[HttpGet]
public ActionResult EmailForGet(IList<String> emails)
```

```
{
    // Input parameters
    var defaultEmails = new[] { "admin@contoso.com", "", "", "", "" };
    if (emails == null)
        emails = defaultEmails;
    if (emails.Count == 0)
        emails = defaultEmails;
    var model = new EmailsViewModel {Emails = emails};
    return View(model);
}

[ActionName("Emails")]
[HttpPost]
public ActionResult EmailForPost(IList<String> email)
{
    var defaultEmails = new[] { "admin@contoso.com", "", "", "", "" };
    var model = new EmailsViewModel { Emails = defaultEmails, RegisteredEmails = email };
    return View(model);
}
```

Here's the full Razor markup for the view you see rendered in Figure 3-5:

```
@model BindingFun.ViewModels.Complex.EmailsViewModel

<h2>List your email address(es)</h2>
@using (Html.BeginForm())
{
    foreach(var email in Model.Emails)
    {
        <input type="text" name="email" value="@email" />
        <br />
    }
    <input type="submit" value="Send" />
}

<hr />
<h2>Emails submitted</h2>
<ul>
@foreach (var email in Model.RegisteredEmails)
{
    if (String.IsNullOrWhiteSpace(email))
    {
        continue;
    }
    <li>@email</li>
}
</ul>
```

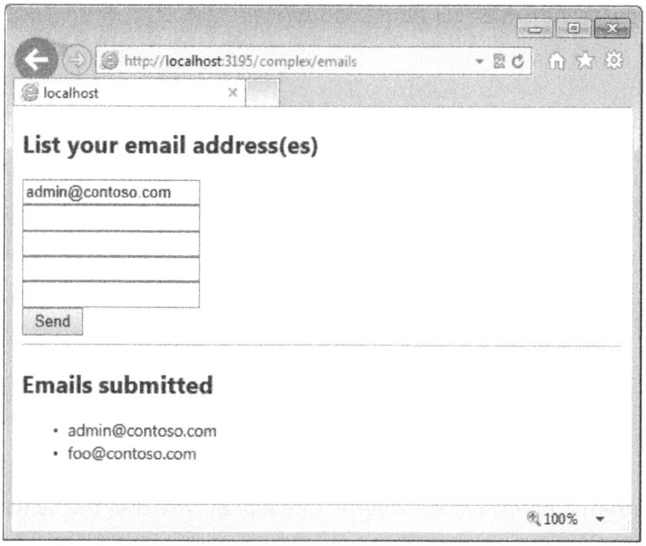

FIGURE 3-5 The page rendered after a POST.

In the end, to ensure that a collection of values is passed to a controller method, you need to ensure that elements with the same ID are emitted to the response stream. The ID, then, must match to the controller method's signature according to the normal rules of the binder.

In case of collections, the required match between names forces you to violate basic naming conventions. In the view, you have input fields and would like to call them, for instance, *email* using the singular. When you name the parameter in the controller, because you're getting a collection, you would like to name it, for instance, *emails*. Instead, you're forced to use either *email* or *emails* all the way through. The workaround comes in a moment when we move on to consider customizable aspects of model binders.

Binding collections of complex types

The default binder can also handle situations in which the collection contains complex types, even nested, as demonstrated here:

```
[ActionName("Countries")]
[HttpPost]
public ActionResult CountriesForPost(IList<Country> country)
{
    ...
}
```

As an example, consider the following definition for type *Country*:

```csharp
public class Country
{
    public Country()
    {
        Details = new CountryInfo();
    }
    public String Name { get; set; }
    public CountryInfo Details { get; set; }
}
public class CountryInfo
{
    public String Capital { get; set; }
    public String Continent { get; set; }
}
```

For model binding to occur successfully, all you really need to do is use a progressive index on the IDs in the markup. The resulting pattern is *prefix[index]*.Property, where *prefix* matches the name of the formal parameter in the controller method's signature:

```razor
@using (Html.BeginForm())
{
    <h2>Select your favorite countries</h2>
    var index = 0;
    foreach (var country in Model.CountryList)
    {
        <fieldset>
        <div>
            <b>Name</b><br />
            <input type="text"
                   name="countries[@index].Name"
                   value="@country.Name" /><br />
            <b>Capital</b><br />
            <input type="text"
                   name="country[@index].Details.Capital"
                   value="@country.Details.Capital" /><br />
            <b>Continent</b><br />
            @{
                var id = String.Format("country[{0}].Details.Continent", index++);
            }
            @Html.TextBox(id, country.Details.Continent)
            <br />
        </div>
        </fieldset>
    }
    <input type="submit" value="Send" />
}
```

The index is numeric, 0-based, and progressive. In this example, I'm building user interface blocks for each specified default country. If you have a fixed number of user interface blocks to render, you can use static indexes.

```
<input type="text"
       name="country[0].Name"
       value="@country.Name" />

<input type="text"
       name="country[1].Name"
       value="@country.Name" />
```

Be aware that holes in the series (for example, 0 and then 2) stop the parsing, and all you get back is the sequence of data types from 0 to the hole.

The posting of data works fine, as well. The POST method on the controller class will just receive the same hierarchy of data, as Figure 3-6 shows.

FIGURE 3-6 Complex and nested types posted to the method.

Rest assured that if you're having trouble mapping posted values to your expected hierarchy of types, it might be wise to consider a custom model binder.

Binding content from uploaded files

Table 3-1 indicates that uploaded files can also be subject to model binding. The default binder does the binding by matching the name of the input file element used to upload with the name of a parameter. The parameter (or the property on a parameter type), however, must be declared of type *HttpPostedFileBase*:

```
public class UserData
{
    public String Name { get; set; }
    public String Email { get; set; }
    public HttpPostedFileBase Picture { get; set; }
}
```

The following code shows a possible implementation of a controller action that saves the uploaded file somewhere on the server computer:

```
public ActionResult Add(UserData inputModel)
{
    var destinationFolder = Server.MapPath("/Users");
    var postedFile = inputModel.Picture;
    if (postedFile.ContentLength > 0)
    {
        var fileName = Path.GetFileName(postedFile.FileName);
        var path = Path.Combine(destinationFolder, fileName);
        postedFile.SaveAs(path);
    }

    return View();
}
```

By default, any ASP.NET request can't be longer than 4 MB. This amount should include any uploads, headers, body, and whatever is being transmitted. You can configure the value at various levels. You do that through the *maxRequestLength* entry in the *httpRuntime* section of the web.config file:

```
<system.web>
    <httpRuntime maxRequestLength="6000" />
</system.web>
```

Obviously, the larger a request is, the more room you potentially leave for hackers to prepare attacks on your site. Also keep in mind that in a hosting scenario your application-level settings might be ignored if the host has set a different limit at the domain level and locked down the *maxRequestLength* property at lower levels.

What about multiple file uploads? As long as the overall size of all uploads is compatible with the current maximum length of a request, you can upload multiple files within a single request. However, consider that web browsers just don't know how to upload multiple files. All a web browser can do is upload a single file, and only if you reference it through an input element of type *file*. To upload multiple files, you can resort to some client-side ad hoc component or place multiple <input> elements in the form. If you use multiple <input> elements that are properly named, a class like the one shown here will bind them all:

```
public class UserData
{
    public String Name { get; set; }
    public String Email { get; set; }
    public HttpPostedFileBase Picture { get; set; }
    public IList<HttpPostedFileBase> AlternatePictures { get; set; }
}
```

The class represents the data posted for a new user with a default picture and a list of alternate pictures. Here is the markup for the alternate pictures:

```
<input type="file" id="AlternatePictures[0]" name="AlternatePictures[0]" />
<input type="file" id="AlternatePictures[1]" name="AlternatePictures[1]" />
```

ASP.NET application account

Creating files on the web server is not usually an operation that can be accomplished relying on the default permission set. Any ASP.NET application runs under the account of the worker process serving the application pool to which the application belongs. Under normal circumstances, this account is NETWORK SERVICE, and it isn't granted the permission to create new files. This means that to save files, you must change the account behind the ASP.NET application or elevate the privileges of the default account.

For years, the identity of the application pool has been a fixed identity—the aforementioned NETWORK SERVICE account, which is a relatively low-privileged, built-in identity in Microsoft Windows. Originally welcomed as an excellent security measure, in the end the practice of using a single account for a potentially high number of concurrently running services created more problems than it helped to solve.

In a nutshell, services running under the same account could tamper with one another. For this reason, in Microsoft Internet Information Services 7.5, by default, worker processes run under unique identities that are automatically and transparently created for each newly created application pool. The underlying technology is known as *Virtual Accounts* and is currently supported by Windows Server 2008 R2 and Windows 7 and newer versions. For more information, have a look at *http://technet.microsoft.com/library/dd548356.aspx*.

Customizable aspects of the default binder

Automatic binding stems from a convention-over-configuration approach. Conventions, though, sometimes harbor bad surprises. If for some reason you lose control over the posted data (for example, in the case of data that has been tampered with), it can result in undesired binding; any posted key/value pair will, in fact, be bound. For this reason, you might want to consider using the *Bind* attribute to customize some aspects of the binding process.

The *Bind* attribute

The *Bind* attribute comes with three properties, which are described in Table 3-2.

TABLE 3-2 Properties for the *BindAttribute* class

Property	Description
Prefix	String property. It indicates the prefix that must be found in the name of the posted value for the binder to resolve it. The default value is the empty string.
Exclude	Gets or sets a comma-delimited list of property names for which binding is not allowed.
Include	Gets or sets a comma-delimited list of property names for which binding is permitted.

You apply the *Bind* attribute to parameters on a method signature.

Creating whitelists of properties

As mentioned, automatic model binding is potentially dangerous when you have complex types. In such cases, in fact, the default binder attempts to populate all public properties on the complex types for which it finds a match in the posted values. This might end up filling the server type with unexpected data, especially in the case of request tampering. To avoid that, you can use the *Include* property on the *Bind* attribute to create a whitelist of acceptable properties, such as shown here:

```
public ActionResult RepeatOnlyText([Bind(Include = "text")]RepeatText inputModel)
{
    ...
}
```

The binding on the *RepeatText* type will be limited to the listed properties (in the example, only *Text*). Any other property is not bound and takes whatever default value the implementation of *RepeatText* assigned to it. Multiple properties are separated by a comma.

Creating blacklists of properties

The *Exclude* attribute employs the opposite logic: It lists properties that must be excluded from binding. All properties except those explicitly listed will be bound:

```
public ActionResult RepeatOnlyText([Bind(Exclude = "number")]RepeatText inputModel)
{
    ...
}
```

You can use *Include* and *Exclude* in the same attribute if doing so makes it possible for you to better define the set of properties to bind. For instance, if both attributes refer to the same property, *Exclude* will win.

Aliasing parameters by using a prefix

The default model binder forces you to give your request parameters (for example, form and query string fields) given names that match formal parameters on target action methods. Using the *Prefix* attribute, you can change this convention. By setting the *Prefix* attribute, you instruct the model binder to match request parameters against the prefix rather than against the formal parameter name. All in all, alias would have been a much better name for this attribute. Consider the following example:

```
[HttpPost]
[ActionName("Emails")]
public ActionResult EmailForPost([Bind(Prefix = "email")]IList<String> emails)
{
    ...
}
```

For the *emails* parameter to be successfully filled, you need to have posted fields whose name is *email*, not *emails*. The *Prefix* attribute makes particular sense on POST methods and fixes the aforementioned issue with naming conventions and collections of parameters.

Finally, note that if a prefix is specified, it becomes mandatory; subsequently, fields whose names are not prefixed are not bound.

Note Yes, the name chosen for the attribute—*Prefix*—is not really explanatory of the scenarios it addresses. Everybody agrees that *Alias* would have been a much better name. But, now it's too late to change it!

Advanced model binding

So far, we've examined the behavior of the default model binder. The default binder does excellent work, but it is a general-purpose tool designed to work with most possible types in a way that is not specific to any of them. The *Bind* attribute gives you some more control over the binding process, but there are some reasonable limitations to its abilities. If you want to achieve total control over the binding process, all you do is create a custom binder for a specific type.

Custom type binders

There's just one primary reason you should be willing to create a custom binder: The default binder is limited to taking into account only a one-to-one correspondence between posted values and properties on the model.

Sometimes, though, the target model has a different granularity than the one expressed by form fields. The canonical example is when you employ multiple input fields to let users enter content for a single property; for example, distinct input fields for day, month, and year that then map to a single *DateTime* value.

Customizing the default binder

To create a custom binder from scratch, you implement the *IModelBinder* interface. Implementing the interface is recommended if you need total control over the binding process. For example, if all you need to do is to keep the default behavior and simply force the binder to use a non-default constructor for a given type, inheriting from *DefaultModelBinder* is the best approach. Here's the schema to follow:

```
public RepeatTextModelBinder : DefaultModelBinder
{
    protected override object CreateModel(
        ControllerContext controllerContext,
        ModelBindingContext bindingContext,
        Type modelType)
    {
        ...
        return new RepeatText( ... );
    }
}
```

Another common scenario for simply overriding the default binder is when all you want is the ability to validate against a specific type. In this case, you override *OnModelUpdated* and insert your own validation logic, as shown here:

```
protected override void OnModelUpdated(ControllerContext controllerContext,
        ModelBindingContext bindingContext)
{
    var obj = bindingContext.Model as RepeatText;
    if (obj == null)
        return;

    // Apply validation logic here for the whole model
    if (String.IsNullOrEmpty(obj.Text))
    {
        bindingContext.ModelState.AddModelError("Text", ...);
    }
    ...
}
```

You override *OnModelUpdated* if you prefer to keep in a single place all validations for any properties. You resort to *OnPropertyValidating* if you prefer to validate properties individually.

> **Important** When binding occurs on a complex type, the default binder simply copies matching values into properties. You can't do much to refuse some values if they put the instance of the complex type in an invalid state.
>
> A custom binder could integrate some logic to check the values being assigned to properties and signal an error to the controller method or degrade gracefully by replacing the invalid value with a default one.
>
> Although it's possible to use this approach, it's not commonly employed because there are more powerful options in ASP.NET MVC that you can use to deal with data validation across an input form. And that is exactly the topic I address in Chapter 4.

Implementing a model binder from scratch

The *IModelBinder* interface is defined as follows:

```
public interface IModelBinder
{
    Object BindModel(ControllerContext controllerContext,
                ModelBindingContext bindingContext);
}
```

Following is the skeleton of a custom binder that directly implements the *IModelBinder* interface. The model binder is written for a specific type—in this case, *MyComplexType*:

```
public class MyComplexTypeModelBinder : IModelBinder
{
  public Object BindModel(ControllerContext controllerContext,
                          ModelBindingContext bindingContext)
  {
      if (bindingContext == null)
          throw new ArgumentNullException("bindingContext");

      // Create the model instance (using the ctor you like best)
      var obj = new MyComplexType();

      // Set properties reading values from registered value providers
      obj.SomeProperty = FromPostedData<string>(bindingContext, "SomeProperty");
      ...
      return obj;
  }

// Helper routine
private T FromPostedData<T>(ModelBindingContext context, String key)
{
    // Get the value from any of the input collections
    ValueProviderResult result;
    context.ValueProvider.TryGetValue(key, out result);

    // Set the state of the model property resulting from value
    context.ModelState.SetModelValue(key, result);

    // Return the value converted (if possible) to the target type
    return (T) result.ConvertTo(typeof(T));
}
```

The structure of *BindModel* is straightforward. You first create a new instance of the type of interest. In doing so, you can use the constructor (or factory) you like best and perform any sort of custom initialization that is required by the context. Next, you simply populate properties of the freshly created instance with values read or inferred from posted data. In the preceding code snippet, I assume that you simply replicate the behavior of the default provider and read values from registered value providers based on a property name match. Obviously, this is just the place where you might want to add your own logic to interpret and massage what's being posted by the request.

Keep in mind that when writing a model binder, you are in no way restricted to getting information for the model only from the posted data, which represents only the most common scenario. You can grab information from anywhere (for example, from the ASP.NET cache and session state), parse it, and store it in the model.

Note ASP.NET MVC comes with two built-in binders beyond the default one. These additional binders are automatically selected for use when posted data is a Base64 stream (*ByteArrayModelBinder* type) and when the content of a file is being uploaded (*HttpPostedFileBaseModelBinder* type).

Registering a custom binder

You can associate a model binder with its target type globally or locally. In the former case, any occurrence of model binding for the type will be resolved through the registered custom binder. In the latter case, you apply the binding to just one occurrence of one parameter in a controller method.

Global association takes place in the global.asax file as follows:

```
void Application_Start()
{
    ...
    ModelBinders.Binders[typeof(MyComplexTypeModelBinder)] =
                        new MyCustomTypeModelBinder();
}
```

Local association requires the following syntax:

```
public ActionResult RepeatText(
        [ModelBinder(typeof(MyComplexTypeModelBinder))] MyComplexType info)
{
    ...
}
```

Local binders always take precedence over globally defined binders.

As you can glean clearly from the preceding code within *Application_Start*, you can have multiple binders registered. You can also override the default binder, if required:

```
ModelBinders.Binders.DefaultBinder = new MyNewDefaultBinder();
```

However, modifying the default binder can have a considerable impact on the behavior of the application and should therefore be a very thoughtful choice.

A sample *DateTime* model binder

With input forms, it is quite common to have users enter a date. You can sometimes use a jQuery user interface to let users pick dates from a graphical calendar. If you use HTML5 markup on recent browsers, the calendar is automatically provided. The selection is translated to a string and saved to a text box. When the form posts back, the date string is uploaded and the default binder attempts to parse it to a *DateTime* object.

In other situations, you might decide to split the date into three distinct text boxes, one each for day, month, and year. These pieces are uploaded as distinct values in the request. The result is that the default binder can manage them only separately; the burden of creating a valid *DateTime* object out of day, month, and year values is up to the controller. With a custom default binder, you can take this code out of the controller and still enjoy the pleasure of having the following signature for a controller method:

```
public ActionResult MakeReservation(DateTime theDate)
```

Let's see how to arrange a more realistic example of a model binder.

The displayed data

The sample view we consider next shows three text boxes for the items that make up a date as well as a submit button. You enter a date, and the system calculates how many days have elapsed since or how many days you have to wait for the specified day to arrive. Here's the Razor markup:

```
@model DateEditorResponseViewModel
@section title{
    @Model.Title
}

@using (Html.BeginForm())
{
<fieldset>
    <legend>Date Editor</legend>
    <div>
        <table><tr>
        <td>@DateHelpers.InputDate("theDate", Model.DefaultDate)</td>
        <td><input type="submit" value="Find out more" /></td>
        </tr></table>
    </div>
</fieldset>
}
<hr />
@DateHelpers.Distance(Model.TimeToToday)
```

As you can see, I'm using a couple of custom helpers to better encapsulate the rendering of some view code. Here's how you render the date elements:

```
@helper InputDate(String name, DateTime? theDate)
{
    String day="", month="", year="";
    if(theDate.HasValue)
    {
        day = theDate.Value.Day.ToString();
        month = theDate.Value.Month.ToString();
        year = theDate.Value.Year.ToString();
    }
    <table cellpadding="0">
        <thead>
            <th>DD</th>
            <th>MM</th>
            <th>YYYY</th>
        </thead>
        <tr>
            <td><input type="number" name="@(name + ".day")"
                        value="@day" style="width:30px" /></td>
            <td><input type="number" name="@(name + ".month")"
                        value="@month" style="width:30px"></td>
            <td><input type="number" name="@(name + ".year")"
                        value="@year" style="width:40px" /></td>
        </tr>
    </table>
}
```

Figure 3-7 shows the output.

FIGURE 3-7 A sample view that splits date input text into day-month-year elements.

The controller methods

The view in Figure 3-7 is served and processed by the following controller methods:

```
public class DateController : Controller
{
    [HttpGet]
    [ActionName("Editor")]
    public ActionResult EditorForGet()
    {
        var model = new EditorViewModel();
        return View(model);
    }

    [HttpPost]
    [ActionName("Editor")]
    public ActionResult EditorForPost(DateTime theDate)
    {
        var model = new EditorViewModel();
        if (theDate != default(DateTime))
        {
            model.DefaultDate = theDate;
            model.TimeToToday = DateTime.Today.Subtract(theDate);
        }
        return View(model);
    }
}
```

After the date is posted back, the controller action calculates the difference with the current day and stores the results back in the view model by using a *TimeSpan* object. Here's the view model object:

```
public class EditorViewModel : ViewModelBase
{
    public EditorViewModel()
    {
        DefaultDate = null;
        TimeToToday = null;
    }
    public DateTime? DefaultDate { get; set; }
    public TimeSpan? TimeToToday { get; set; }
}
```

What remains to be examined is the code that performs the trick of transforming three distinct values uploaded independently into one *DateTime* object.

Creating the *DateTime* binder

The structure of the *DateTimeModelBinder* object is not much different from the skeleton I described earlier. It is just tailor-made for the *DateTime* type.

```
public class DateModelBinder : IModelBinder
{
    public Object BindModel(ControllerContext controllerContext, ModelBindingContext
bindingContext)
    {
        if (bindingContext == null)
        {
            throw new ArgumentNullException("bindingContext");
        }

        // This will return a DateTime object
        var theDate = default(DateTime);

        // Try to read from posted data. xxx.Day|xxx.Month|xxx.Year is assumed.
        var day = FromPostedData<int>(bindingContext, "Day");
        var month = FromPostedData<int>(bindingContext, "Month");
        var year = FromPostedData<int>(bindingContext, "Year");

        return CreateDateOrDefault(year, month, day, theDate);
    }

    // Helper routines
    private static T FromPostedData<T>(ModelBindingContext context, String id)
    {
        if (String.IsNullOrEmpty(id))
            return default(T);

        // Get the value from any of the input collections
        var key = String.Format("{0}.{1}", context.ModelName, id);
        var result = context.ValueProvider.GetValue(key);
        if (result == null && context.FallbackToEmptyPrefix)
```

```
    {
        // Try without prefix
        result = context.ValueProvider.GetValue(id);
        if (result == null)
            return default(T);
    }

    // Set the state of the model property resulting from value
    context.ModelState.SetModelValue(id, result);

    // Return the value converted (if possible) to the target type
    T valueToReturn = default(T);
    try
    {
        valueToReturn = (T)result.ConvertTo(typeof(T));
    }
    catch
    {
    }

    return valueToReturn;
}

private DateTime CreateDateOrDefault(Int32 year, Int32 month, Int32 day,
                                     DateTime? defaultDate)
{
    var theDate = defaultDate ?? default(DateTime);
    try
    {
        theDate = new DateTime(year, month, day);
    }
    catch (ArgumentOutOfRangeException e)
    {
    }

    return theDate;
}
}
```

The binder makes some assumptions about the naming convention of the three input elements. In particular, it requires that those elements be named day, month, and year, possibly prefixed by the model name. It is the support for the prefix that makes it possible to have multiple date input boxes in the same view without conflicts.

With this custom binder available, all you need to do is register it either globally or locally. Here's how to make it work with just a specific controller method:

```
[HttpPost]
[ActionName("Editor")]
public ActionResult EditorForPost([ModelBinder(typeof(DateModelBinder))] DateTime theDate)
{

}
```

Figure 3-8 shows the final page in action.

FIGURE 3-8 Working with dates using a custom type binder.

Summary

In ASP.NET MVC as well as in ASP.NET Web Forms, posted data arrives within an HTTP packet and is mapped to various collections on the *Request* object. To offer a nice service to developers, ASP.NET then attempts to expose that content in a more usable way.

In ASP.NET Web Forms, the content is parsed and passed on to server controls; in ASP.NET MVC, on the other hand, it is bound to parameters of the selected controller's method. The process of binding posted values to parameters is known as model binding and occurs through a registered model-binder class. Model binders provide you with complete control over the deserialization of form-posted values into simple and complex types.

In functional terms, the use of the default binder is transparent to developers—no action is required on your end—and it keeps the controller code clean. By using model binders, including custom binders, you also keep your controller's code free of dependencies on ASP.NET intrinsic objects and thus make it cleaner and more testable.

The use of model binders is strictly related to posting and input forms. In Chapter 4, I discuss aspects of input forms, input modeling, and data validation.

Input forms

Whatever you can do or dream, begin it.

—Wolfgang Goethe

Classic ASP.NET bases its programming model on the assumption that state is maintained across postbacks. This is not true at all at the HTTP-protocol level, but it is brilliantly simulated by using the page view-state feature and a bit of work in the Web Forms page life cycle. The view state, which is so often kicked around as a bad thing, is a great contribution to establishing a stateful programming model in ASP.NET, and that programming model was one of the keys to ASP.NET's success and rapid adoption. Data entry is a scenario in which server controls really shine and in which their postback and view-state overhead save you from doing a lot of work. Server controls also give you a powerful infrastructure for input validation.

If you've grown up with Web Forms and its server controls, you might be shocked when you're transported into the ASP.NET MVC model. In ASP.NET MVC, you have the same functional capabilities as in Web Forms, but they're delivered through a different set of tools. The ASP.NET MVC framework uses a different pattern, one that is not page based and relies on a much thinner abstraction layer than Web Forms. As a result, you don't have rich native components such as server controls to quickly arrange a nice user interface in which elements can retain their content across postbacks. This fact seems to cause a loss of productivity, at least for certain types of applications, such as those heavily based on data entry.

Is this really true, though?

For sure, in ASP.NET MVC you write code that is conceptually and physically closer to the metal; therefore, it takes more lines, but it gives you a lot more control over the generated HTML and actual behavior of the run-time environment. You don't have to write everything from scratch, however. You have HTML helpers to automatically create (quite) simple but functional viewers and editors for any primitive or complex type. You have data annotations to declaratively set your expectations about the content of a field and its display behavior. You have model binders to serialize posted values into more comfortable objects for server-side processing. And, you have tools for both server and client validation.

This chapter aims to show you how to grab input data through forms in ASP.NET MVC and then validate and process it against a persistence layer.

> **Note** Growing attention is being garnered these days by Ajax-based solutions for input forms. For example, it's becoming common to display a modal dialog box to the user in which to enter input data. Displaying a modal dialog box is as easy as creating a separate <div> and have client frameworks such as Twitter Bootstrap or jQuery UI to manage the presentation. As far as posting data is concerned, however, using a plain FORM post and full or partial page refresh under the control of the ASP.NET MVC API being discussed in this chapter is still a common and widely used option. The other option that would make the content of this chapter less interesting is managing the HTTP POST yourself by using plain JavaScript code.

General patterns of data entry

Input forms revolve around two main patterns: Edit-and-Post and Select-Edit-Post. The former displays an HTML form and expects users to fill the fields and post data when they're done. The latter pattern just extends the former by adding an extra preliminary step. The users select an item of data, place it into edit mode, play with the content, and then save changes back to the storage layer.

I'm not explicitly covering the Edit-and-Post pattern because it is merely a simpler version of the Select-Edit-Post pattern. The sections "Editing data" and "Saving data" later in the chapter, which provide a description of the Select-Edit-Post pattern, also provide one of the Edit-and-Post pattern. Let's proceed with an example.

A classic Select-Edit-Post scenario

I'll illustrate the Select-Edit-Post pattern through an example that starts by letting users pick a customer from a drop-down list. Next, the record that contains information about the selected customer is rendered into an edit form, where you can enter updates and eventually validate and save them.

In this example, the domain model consists of an Entity Framework model inferred from the canonical Northwind database. Figure 4-1 shows the initial user interface of the sample application.

FIGURE 4-1 The initial screen of the sample application, where users begin by making a selection.

Note Examples discussed in this chapter don't actually use any database linked or embedded in some way in the project. All examples end up placing simple query calls to a web service, available at my personal site *http://www.expoware.org*. You can find the details of this in the file northwind.cs in the BookSamples.Components library project.

Presenting data and handling the selection

The listing that follows shows the controller action that is used to populate the drop-down list to offer the initial screen to the user. Observe that I'm designing controllers according to the Coordinator stereotype defined in the Responsibility Driven Design (RDD) methodology. (I talk more about RDD and MVC controllers as coordinators in Chapter 7, "Design considerations for ASP.NET MVC controllers." For now, suffice it to say that a coordinator is a component that reacts to events and delegates any further action to an external component.) A coordinator is limited to passing input and capturing output. Having controllers implemented as coordinators in ASP.NET MVC is beneficial because it decouples the layer that receives requests from the layer (or layers) that processes requests. For the sake of simplicity, at this time the code doesn't make use of dependency injection. The next obvious step would be injecting the instance of the coordinator class—*HomeService*—via Inversion of Control (IoC).

```csharp
public class HomeController : Controller
{
    private readonly HomeService _service = new HomeService();
    public ActionResult Index()
    {
        var model = _service.GetModelForIndex();
        return View(model);
    }
}
```

The method *Index* obtains a view-model object that contains the list of customers to display.

```
public class IndexViewModel : ViewModelBase
{
    public IndexViewModel()
    {
        Customers = new List<SimpleCustomer>();
    }
    public IEnumerable<SimpleCustomer> Customers { get; set; }
}
```

Here's the implementation of the *GetModelForIndex* method in the coordinator component:

```
public class HomeService
{
    public IndexViewModel GetModelForIndex()
    {
        var model = new IndexViewModel {Customers = NorthwindCustomers.GetAll()};
        return model;
    }
}
```

The view that produces the interface in Figure 4-1 is shown here:

```
@model Sep.ViewModels.Home.IndexViewModel

<div class="floating">
    <p class="legend">Customers</p>
    @using(Html.BeginForm("edit", "home"))
    {
        @Html.DropDownList("customerList", new SelectList(Model.Customers, "Id", "Company"))
        <input type="submit" name="btnEdit" value="Edit" />
    }
</div>
```

After the user has selected a customer from the list (by clicking a submit button), he submits a POST request for an *Edit* action on the *HomeController* class.

Editing data

The request for the *Edit* action moves the application into edit mode, and an editor for the selected customer is displayed. As you can see in Figure 4-2, you should also expect the successive view to retain the current drop-down list status. The following code shows a possible implementation for the *Edit* method on the *Home* controller:

```
public ActionResult Edit([Bind(Prefix = "customerList")] String customerId)
{
    var model = _service.GetModelForEdit(customerId);
    return View(model);
}
```

Chapter 3, "The model-binding architecture," points out that the *Bind* attribute instructs the default model binder to assign the value of the posted field named *customerList* to the specified parameter. In this case, the *GetModelForEdit* method retrieves information about the specified customer and passes that to the view engine so that an input form can be arranged and displayed to the user:

```
public EditViewModel GetModelForEdit(String id)
{
    var model = new EditViewModel
                    {
                        Title = "Edit customer",
                        Customer = NorthwindCustomers.Get(id),
                        Customers = NorthwindCustomers.GetAll()
                    };
    return model;
}
```

Why does the *GetModelForEdit* method also need to retrieve the list of customers?

This is a direct consequence of not having the view state around. Every aspect of the view must be recreated and repopulated each time. This is a key part of the HTTP contract and relates to the inherent HTTP stateless-ness. In ASP.NET Web Forms, most of the refilling work is done automatically by the abstraction layer of the framework through information stored in the view state. In ASP.NET MVC, it's just up to you.

In the preceding code snippet, I just place another call to the service layer; a more serious application would probably cache data and reload from there. The caching layer, however, could also be incorporated in the repository itself.

Here's the code for the view:

```
@model Sep.ViewModels.Home.EditViewModel

<div class="container">
    <div class="floating">
        <p class="legend">Customers</p>
        @using(Html.BeginForm("edit", "home"))
        {
            @Html.DropDownList("customerList",
                new SelectList(Model.Customers, "Id", "Company", Model.Customer.Id))
            <input type="submit" name="btnEdit" value="Edit" />
        }
    </div>
    <div class="floating-spacer">
        @Html.Partial("uc_customerEditor", Model.Customer)
    </div>
</div>
```

The structure of the view is nearly the same as in Figure 4-1, the only difference being the table-based editor on the right of the view. The editor (*uc_customerEditor.cshtml*) is created through the *Partial* HTML helper. If you look into the list of native HTML helpers, you find two apparently similar helpers: *Partial* and *RenderPartial*. What's the difference? As is hinted in Chapter 2, "ASP.NET MVC views," *Partial* just returns a string, whereas *RenderPartial* performs the action of rendering a string. If the goal is only that of creating a view, they are nearly identical but still require a slightly different programming syntax. To call *RenderPartial*, you need the following in Razor:

```
@{ Html.RenderPartial(view) }
```

Figure 4-2 shows the editor in action.

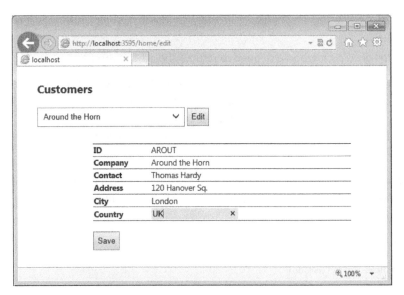

FIGURE 4-2 Users can make changes to the selected customer.

Saving data

After the input form is displayed, the user enters any data she reckons to be valid and then presses the button that posts the content of the form to the server. Here's the markup for a typical form that posts changes. (The markup is the content of the uc_customerEditor.cshtml file.)

```
@model BookSamples.Components.Data.SimpleCustomer

<div class="container">
@using(Html.BeginForm("update", "customer", new { customerId = Model.Id }))
{
    <table id="__tableCustomerEditAscx" rules="rows" frame="hsides">
        <tr>
            <td width="100px"><b>ID</b></td>
            <td width="350px">@Model.Id</td>
        </tr>
```

```
            <tr>
                <td><b>Company</b></td>
                <td><span>@Model.Company</span></td>
            </tr>
            <tr>
                <td><b>Contact</b></td>
                <td>@Html.DisplayTextFor(c => c.Contact)</td>
            </tr>
                ...
            <tr>
                <td><b>Country</b></td>
                <td>@Html.TextBoxFor(c => c.Country,
                        new Dictionary<String, Object>() { { "class", "textBox" } })
                    <br />
                    @Html.ValidationMessage("country")
                </td>
            </tr>
        </table>
        <br/>
        <input id="btnSave" type="submit" value="Save" />
}
</div>
```

Typically, you group any editable field (for example, a text box) with a *ValidationMessage* helper. The validation helper displays any message that originates as a result of invalid values being entered in the field. Furthermore, you ensure that the resulting URL includes a key value that uniquely identifies the record to be updated. Here's an example:

```
Html.BeginForm("update", "home", new { customerId = Model.CustomerID })
```

Internally, *BeginForm* matches the data it has received to the parameters of registered URL routes in an attempt to create the proper URL to post the form. The preceding code generates the following URL:

```
http://yourserver/customer/update?customerId=alfki
```

Thanks to the default model binder, the method *Update* receives the fields of the input form as members of the *SimpleCustomer* class:

```
public ActionResult Update(SimpleCustomer customer)
{
    var modelState = ViewData.ModelState
    var model = _service.TryUpdateCustomer(modelState, customer);
    return View("edit", model);
}
```

The method needs to do a couple of things: update the data layer, and display the edit view so that the user can continue making changes. Except perhaps for some unrealistically simple scenarios, the update operation requires validation. If validation of the data being stored is unsuccessful, detected errors must be reported to the end user through the user interface.

The ASP.NET MVC infrastructure offers built-in support for displaying error messages that result from validation. The ModelState dictionary—a part of the *Controller* class—is where methods add notifications of an error. Errors in the ModelState dictionary are then displayed through the *Validation Message* helper, as illustrated here:

```
public EditCustomerViewModel TryUpdateCustomer(ModelStateDictionary modelState, Customer
customer)
{
    if (Validate(modelState, customer))
        Update(customer);

    return EditCustomer(customer.CustomerID);
}

private static Boolean Validate(ModelStateDictionary modelState, Customer customer)
{
    var result = true;

    // Any sort of specific validation you need ...
    if (!CountryIsValid(customer.Country)))
    {
        // For each detected error, add a message and set a new display value
        modelState.AddModelError("Country", "Invalid country.");
        result = false;
    }

    return result;
}

private static void Update(Customer customer)
{
    NorthwindCustomers.Update(customer);
}
```

As the name suggests, the ModelState dictionary is the key/value repository for any messages that relate to the state of the model behind the view. The value is the error message; the key is the unique name used to identify the entry (such as the string "Country" in the preceding example). The key of a model state entry will match the string parameter of the *Html.ValidationMessage* helper. Figure 4-3 shows the system's reaction when the user attempts to enter an invalid value.

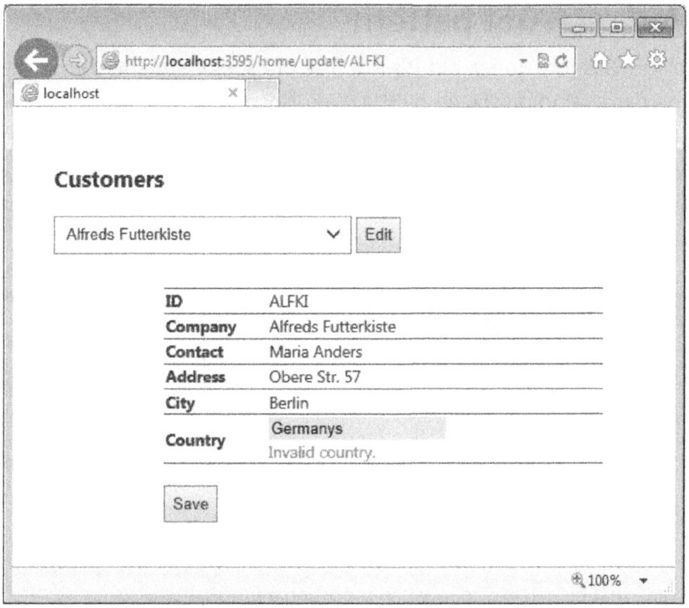

FIGURE 4-3 Handling invalid input.

During the validation process, every time you detect an error in the posted data, you add a new entry to the ModelState dictionary, as demonstrated here:

```
modelState.AddModelError("Country", "Invalid country.");
```

It is your responsibility to provide localized error messages.

Observe that the model binder always sets parameters to null if a corresponding match cannot be found through the various value providers (for example, the form, route parameters, or the query string). In particular, this means that string parameters or string members can be set to null. You should always check against nullness before you attempt to consume a value that came through model binding. The following code shows a possible way to deal with this condition when strings are involved:

```
// In the examples for this chapter, validation is really coding in this way. In the end,
// validation is a plain logical expression suggested by business. While this condition
// is not much realistic, it still makes perfectly sense in a demo. Anyway, note that in light
// of this code any "valid" country name you enter is denied except "USA".
if (String.IsNullOrEmpty(customer.Country) || !customer.Country.Equals("USA"))
{
    ...
}
```

With respect to the earlier code, you would place the test against nullness in the *CountryIsValid* method.

Applying the Post-Redirect-Get pattern

The previous approach to input forms is functional, but it's not free of issues. First, the URL in the address bar might not reflect the data being displayed by the page. Second, repeating the last action (Refresh or an F5 keystroke) might not simply prompt the user with the annoying confirmation message shown in Figure 4-4. As the user goes ahead, she can easily get a run-time exception if the repeated operation is not implemented as idempotent (that is, if it doesn't always produce the same result regardless of how many consecutive times it is called).

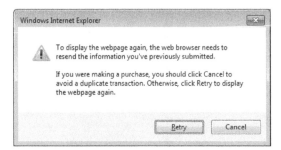

FIGURE 4-4 The confirmation message that browsers display when reposting a form.

However, these aspects of ASP.NET applications are not specific to ASP.NET MVC. They exist in ASP.NET Web Forms, too, but this is not a good reason to avoid using a better implementation.

The lack of synchronization between the URL in the browser's address bar and the content displayed might not be a problem in most cases. Your users might not even notice that. In fact, the confirmation dialog box that prompts the user when she refreshes the current page is an old (and not really pleasant) acquaintance of ASP.NET developers and the users of their applications. Let's see how the Post-Redirect-Get (PRG) pattern can help fix both aspects.

Keeping the URL and content synchronized

In the previous example, the URL shown in the address bar after the user has selected, for instance, user ALFKI is the following:

```
// Action EDIT on CUSTOMER controller
http://yourserver/customer/edit
```

If the user repeats the last action (for example, by pressing F5), he gets the dialog box shown in Figure 4-4 and then the view updates as expected. Wouldn't it be preferable for the URL to reflect the selected customer and have the page be refreshed without side effects?

The side effect represented by the dialog box in Figure 4-4 has a well-known origin. When F5 is pressed, the browser just blindly reiterates the last HTTP request. And, the selection of a customer from a drop-down list (shown in Figure 4-1) is an HTTP POST request for the action *Edit* on the *Customer* controller.

The PRG pattern recommends that each POST request, after having been processed, terminates with a redirect to a resource accessed via GET. If you do so, the URL stays nicely synchronized with the customer displayed, and your users forget the annoying dialog box that you saw in Figure 4-4.

Splitting POST and GET actions

The first step on the way to applying PRG to ASP.NET MVC applications is neatly separating POST actions from GET actions. Here's how to rewrite the *Edit* action:

```
[HttpPost]
[ActionName("edit")]
public ActionResult EditViaPost([Bind(Prefix = "customerList")] String customerId)
{
    // POST, now REDIRECT via GET to Edit
    return RedirectToAction("edit", new {id = customerId});
}

[HttpGet]
[ActionName("edit")]
public ActionResult EditViaGet(String id)
{
    var model = _service.GetModelForEdit(id);
    return View("edit", model);
}
```

Every time the user posts the *Edit* method to select a given customer, all that happens is a redirect (HTTP 302) to the same action via GET. The GET method for the action *Edit* receives the ID of the customer to edit and does its job as usual.

The beautiful effect is that you can change the selection in either of two ways: by typing the URL in the address bar (as a command) or just by clicking the drop-down list. Moreover, when the user interface is updated, the last action tracked by the browser is a GET—and you can repeat the GET as many times as you like without incurring any boring warnings or annoying exceptions.

Updating only via POST

Take a look back at Figure 4-3, which represents the next page after an update. In particular, the figure shows a failed update, but that is not relevant here. What's relevant instead is the URL.

```
http://yourserver/customer/update?customerId=ALFKI
```

This is the URL that will be repeated by pressing F5. I can hardly believe that any regular user will ever attempt to manually edit this URL and try to push updates to another customer. But, as unlikely as that is, it's definitely a possibility.

The URL of an update operation should never be visible to users. The user performs the update, but the operation remains hidden between two displays of the same page. This is exactly what you get with the PRG pattern. Here's how to rewrite the *Update* action:

```
[HttpPost]
public ActionResult Update(SimpleCustomer customer)
{
    var modelState = ViewData.ModelState;
    _service.TryUpdateCustomer(modelState, TempData, customer);
    return RedirectToAction("edit", new { id = customer.Id });
}
```

As you can see, you need only the *HttpPost* leg. A user orders the update from a page created via a GET that displays the customer being edited. The update takes place, and the next view is obtained by redirecting again to the *Edit* action for the same customer. It's simple, clean, and effective.

Saving temporary data across redirects

There's one final issue to take into account. The PRG pattern makes the overall code look cleaner but requires two requests to update the view. This might or might not be a problem with regard to performance—I don't think it is. Anyway, this is primarily a functional problem: if the update fails, how do you pass feedback to the view? In fact, the view is being rendered in the GET action subsequent to the redirect; it's quite another blank request.

Overall, the best option you have is saving feedback messages to the *Session* object. ASP.NET MVC provides a slightly better option that still uses session state, but which does so through a smart wrapper—the *TempData* dictionary. Here's how to modify the code that validates before updating:

```
private static Boolean Validate(ModelStateDictionary modelState,
                                TempDataDictionary tempData,
                                SimpleCustomer customer)
{
    var result = true;

    if (String.IsNullOrEmpty(customer.Country) || !customer.Country.Equals("USA"))
    {
        modelState.AddModelError("Country", "Invalid country.");

        // Save model-state to TempData
        tempData["ModelState"] = modelState;
        result = false;
    }

    return result;
}
```

You first add feedback messages to the ModelState dictionary as usual. Then, you save a reference to the ModelState in the TempData dictionary. The TempData dictionary stores any data you provide in the session state for as long as two requests. After the second request past the storage has been processed, the container clears the entry.

You do the same for any other message or data that you need to pass to the view object. For example, Figure 4-5 depicts the message that is added by the following code if the update operation completes successfully:

```
private Boolean Update(TempDataDictionary tempData, SimpleCustomer customer)
{
    // Perform physical update
    var result = _repository.Update(customer);

    // Add a message for the user
    var msg = result
                    ? "Successfully updated."
                    : "Update failed. Check your input data!";
    tempData["OutputMessage"] = msg;
    return result;
}
```

FIGURE 4-5 A post-update message.

You still might want to give some clear feedback to users about what has happened before redisplaying the same edit form for them to keep on working. If your update operation takes the user to a completely different page, you might not need the previous trick.

Saving data to the TempData dictionary is only half the effort. You also need to add code that re-trieves the dictionary from the session state and merges that with the current model state. This logic belongs to the code that actually renders the view.

```
[HttpGet]
[ActionName("edit")]
public ActionResult EditViaGet(String id)
{
    // Merge current ModelState with any being recovered from TempData
    LoadStateFromTempData();

    ...
}
private void LoadStateFromTempData()
{
    var modelState = TempData["ModelState"] as ModelStateDictionary;
    if (modelState != null)
        ModelState.Merge(modelState);
}
```

With these few changes, you can arrange input forms that are clean to write and read and that work effectively. The only wrinkle in an input form built in accordance with the PRG pattern is that you need a second request the redirect for each operation. Furthermore, you still need to pack the view model with any data required to render the view, including data calculated by the ongoing op-eration and any other data around the page, such as menus, breadcrumbs, and lists.

To go beyond this level, however, you need to embrace the Ajax approach.

> ## Beyond classic browser-led content form submission
>
> Classic form submission for the most part takes place over a full page refresh and in some cases over two HTTP requests, as in the PRG pattern. Is there a way to implement input forms without a full page refresh?
>
> There are a few ways, but all of them have quirks and therefore are subject to personal pref-erences. In general, I use two possible approaches for building my own forms: plain-old form posts over PRG, and modal input forms via Ajax. ASP.NET MVC does have some native support for Ajax-driven posts through the *Ajax.BeginForm* HTML helper. In addition, you can manually build modal input forms by using technologies such as Twitter Bootstrap for the user interface (and modal pop-up infrastructure), jQuery Validate for client-side checks, and XmlHttpRequest (XHR) for posting.
>
> You can find a good startup example of a modal input forms in the context of an ASP.NET MVC application in this post from my blog at *http://software2cents.wordpress.com/2013/06/07/modal-input-forms-with-bootstrap/*. The post illustrates the use of Twitter Bootstrap—the CSS library you find integrated in ASP.NET MVC 5.

Automating the writing of input forms

Input forms play a central part in the organization of views. Often input forms contain images, require the specific placement of fields, and are enriched with client-side goodies. In all of these cases, you probably need to write the template of the input form from scratch.

Generally speaking, however, there are a number of other situations in which you can automate the building of the input form. This is often the case, for example, when you write the back office of a website. A back-office system typically consists of a bunch of forms for editing records; however, as a developer, you don't care much about the graphics. You focus on effectiveness rather than style. In a nutshell, a back-office system is the perfect case for which you don't mind using an automatic generator of form input templates.

Predefined display and editor templates

Chapter 2 presents templated HTML helpers such as *DisplayXxx* and *EditorXxx*. These helpers can take an object (even the entire model passed to the view) and build a read-only or editable form. You use the following expression to specify the object to display or edit:

```
Html.DisplayFor(model => model.Customer)
Html.EditorFor(model => model.Customer)
```

The *model* argument is always the model being passed to the view. You can use your own lambda expression to select a subset of the entire model. To select the entire model (say, for editing), you can choose either of the following functionally equivalent expressions:

```
Html.EditorFor(model => model)
Html.EditorForModel()
```

Attributes placed on public members of the model class provide guidance on how to display individual values. Let's find out how it works in practice.

Annotating data members for display

In ASP.NET MVC, templated helpers use metadata associated with class members to decide how to display or edit your data. Metadata is read through a metadata provider object; the default metadata provider grabs information from data annotations attributes. The most commonly used attributes are listed in Table 4-1.

TABLE 4-1 Some annotations that affect the rendering of data

Attribute	Description
DataType	Indicates the presumed data type you'll be editing through the member. It accepts values from the *DataType* enumeration. Supported data types include *Decimal*, *Date*, *DateTime*, *EmailAddress*, *Password*, *Url*, *PhoneNumber*, and *MultilineText*.
DisplayFormat	Use this to indicate a format through which to display (and/or edit) the value. For example, you might use this annotation to indicate an alternate representation for null or empty values. In this case, you use the *NullDisplayText* property.
DisplayName	Indicates the text to use for the label that presents the value.
HiddenInput	Indicates whether a hidden input field should be displayed instead of a visible one.
UIHint	Indicates the name of the custom HTML template to use when displaying or editing the value.

Annotations are spread across a variety of namespaces, including *System.ComponentModel* and *System.ComponentModel.DataAnnotations*. If you explore these (and other) namespaces, you can find even more attributes, but some of them don't seem to work with ASP.NET MVC, at least not in the way that you would expect.

Data annotations are attributes, and attributes don't typically contain code. They just represent meta-information for other modules to consume. By using data annotations, you decorate your model objects with metadata. This isn't really expected to produce any visible effect: It all depends on how other components consume metadata.

In ASP.NET MVC, default display and editor helpers simply consume only a few of the possible annotations. However, metadata information is there, and if you override default templates, you have available a lot more meta-information to consume at your leisure. The *ReadOnly* attribute is a good example of an annotation that default templates ignore but that ASP.NET MVC regularly understands and exposes to helpers.

Note Data annotations include descriptive attributes that instruct listeners how to display or edit data as well as validation attributes that instruct listeners how to validate the content of a model class. I'll discuss validation attributes later.

The following code shows a view-model class decorated with annotations:

```
public class CustomerViewModel : ViewModelBase
{
    [DisplayName("Company ID")]
    [ReadOnly(true)]  // This will be blissfully ignored by default templates!
    public Int32 Id { get; set; }

    [DisplayName("Is a Company (or individual)?")]
    public Boolean IsCompany { get; set; }

    [DisplayFormat(NullDisplayText = "(empty)")]
    public String Name { get; set; }
```

```
    [DataType(DataType.MultilineText)]
    public String Notes { get; set; }

    [DataType(DataType.Url)]
    public String Website { get; set; }

    [DisplayName("Does this customer pay regularly?")]
    public Boolean? IsReliable { get; set; }
}
```

Note that you don't need data annotations if you are not using *DisplayForModel* or *EditorForModel* to generate input forms automatically. Like any other metadata, annotations are transparent to any code that is not specifically designed to consume them.

Figure 4-6 shows the input form that *EditorForModel* creates for the previous model object.

FIGURE 4-6 An autogenerated input form.

Meta-information instructs the *Editor/Display* helpers how to edit and display values. This results in ad hoc HTML templates being used, such as a *TextArea* element for multiline types and check boxes for Boolean values. For nullable Boolean values, helpers also automatically display a tri-state drop-down list. Not all data types show up in edit mode or display mode. For example, the *EmailAddress* and *Url* data types are reflected only in display mode.

To be precise, the form displayed in the figure also passed through a slight set of graphical changes due to the application of a style sheet. The *Editor/Display* helpers automatically read style information from a few cascading style sheet (CSS) classes with a conventional name, as shown here:

```css
.display-label, .editor-label {
    margin: 1em 0 0;
    font-weight: bold;
}
.display-field, .editor-field {
    margin: 0.5em 0 0;
}
.text-box {
    width: 30em;
    background: yellow;
}
.text-box.multi-line {
    height: 6.5em;
}
.tri-state {
    width: 6em;
}
```

In particular, classes named *display-label* and *editor-label* refer to labels around input values. You can insert these styles either inline in views or inherit them from a globally shared CSS file.

Default templates for data types

Display/Editor helpers work by mapping the data type of each member to render to a predefined display or edit template. Next, for each of the template names, the system asks the view engines to return a proper partial view. Predefined display templates exist for the following data types: *Boolean*, *Decimal*, *EmailAddress*, *HiddenInput*, *Html*, *Object*, *String*, *Text*, and *Url*. Data types are resolved through the *DataType* annotation or the actual type of the value. If no match can be found, the default template is used, which consists of plain text for display and a text box for editing. Let's see what a template looks like. The following listing shows a sample implementation of the Razor template for displaying the *Url* data type:

```
@inherits System.Web.Mvc.WebViewPage<String>
<a href="@Model">
    @ViewData.TemplateInfo.FormattedModelValue
</a>
```

The *Url* data type is rendered through a hyperlink in which the *Model* object references the data being displayed—most likely, a string representing a website. As you can see, the real value is used to set the URL but not the text of the hyperlink. The *FormattedModelValue* property on the *TemplateInfo* object is either the original raw model value or a properly formatted string, if a format string is specified through annotations.

Note The *TemplateInfo* property is defined on the *ViewData* object, but it is always null, except when you're inside of a template.

The *Url* template is a fairly simple one. The template for *Boolean* values is a more interesting example to consider:

```
@model bool?

@if (Model == null)
{
    <text>Not Set</text>
}
else
{
    if (Model.Value)
    {
        <text>True</text>
    }
    else
    {
        <text>False</text>
    }
}
```

The example contains a mix of logic and markup as the template applies to *Boolean* and *Nullable<Boolean>* values.

Editor templates are not that different from display templates, at least in terms of structure; however, the code might be a bit more complex. ASP.NET MVC provides a few predefined editors for *Boolean, Decimal, HiddenInput, Object, String, Password,* and *MultilineText.* Here's a sample editor for a password:

```
@Html.Password("",
        ViewData.TemplateInfo.FormattedModelValue,
        new { @class = "text-box single-line password" })
```

As you can see, conventions regarding styles descend from the implementation of default templates. By changing the default template for a given data type, you can choose to style it according to different rules.

Object.cshtml is the template used to recursively loop through the public members of a type. It builds an entire form by using type-specific editors. The default implementation of Object.cshtml vertically stacks labels and editors. Although it's valuable for quick prototyping, it is not usually something you want to seriously consider for a realistic application. Let's move ahead and see how to customize editor templates.

Custom templates for data types

Display/editor helpers are customizable to a great extent. Any custom template consists of a custom view located in the Views\[controller]\DisplayTemplates folder for display helpers and in the Views\ [controller]\EditorTemplates folder for editor helpers. If you want templates shared by all controllers, you place them in Views\Shared. If the name of the view matches the data type, the view becomes the new default template for that data type. If it doesn't, the view won't be used until it's explicitly called through the *UIHint* annotation, as shown here:

```
public CustomerViewModel
{
    ...
    [UIHint("CustomerViewModel_Url")]
    public String Url {get; set;}
}
```

The *Url* property is now displayed or edited by using the *CustomerViewModel_Url* template. Properties whose data type is *Url* will continue to be served by the default template, instead.

Let's see how to create a custom display and editor template for a type that doesn't even have predefined templates—the *DateTime* type. Here's the content for a Razor display template:

```
@model DateTime
@Model.ToString("ddd, dd MMM yyyy")
```

In this example, you just display the date in a fixed format (but one controlled by you) that includes day of the week, name of the month, and year. Here's a sample editor template for a date:

```
@model DateTime
<div>
<table>
<tr>
    <td>@Html.Label("Day")</td>
    <td>@Html.TextBox("Day", Model.Day)</td>
</tr>
<tr>
    <td>@Html.Label("Month")</td>
    <td>@Html.TextBox("Month", Model.Month)</td>
</tr>
<tr>
    <td>@Html.Label("Year")%></td>
    <td>@Html.TextBox("Year", Model.Year)</td>
</tr>
</table>
</div>
```

You can style elements in the template by using any class names you like; as long as those classes are defined in some style sheets in the application, they will be automatically used. Observe that IDs you set in your templates are always automatically prefixed in the emitted markup by the name of the member. For example, if the preceding date template is applied to a property named *BirthDate*, the actual IDs emitted will be *BirthDate_Day*, *BirthDate_Month*, and *BirthDate_Year*.

Note It's probably not a very realistic scenario, but if you happen to have two editors for the same model in the same page, well, in this case you're going to have ID conflicts that the model binder might not be able to resolve without a bit of effort on your own. If you are in this position, you might want to consider the tricks we discussed in Chapter 3 for binding a collection of custom types to a controller method.

How do you name these templates? If the *UIHint* attribute is specified, its value determines the template name. If it's not specified, the *DataType* attribute takes precedence over the actual type name of the member. Given the following class definition, the expected template name is date. If none of the view engines can provide such a view, the default template is used, instead. Figure 4-7 shows the table-based date editor defined earlier.

FIGURE 4-7 A custom template for editing dates.

Read-only members

If you decorate a member of the view model with the *ReadOnly* attribute, you probably expect it not to be editable in the editor. You probably expect that the display template is used within the editor for the model. You'll be surprised to see that this is not the case. The *ReadOnly* attribute is properly recognized by the metadata provider, and related information is stored in the metadata available for the model. For some reason, though, this is not transformed into a template hint.

As weird as it might sound, you have data annotations to indicate a given member is read-only, but this is not reflected by default templates. There are a few workarounds to this problem. First and foremost, you can use the *UIHint* annotation to specify a read-only template like the one shown here, named *readonly.cshtml*:

```
<span>@Model</span>
```

You need to place the *readonly.cshtml* template in the editor folder.

Although it's effective, this solution bypasses the use of the *ReadOnly* attribute. Not that this is a big problem, but you might wonder if there's a way to solve the issue by forcing the metadata provider to process the *ReadOnly* attribute differently. You need a different metadata provider, such as the one shown here:

```
public class ExtendedAnnotationsMetadataProvider : DataAnnotationsModelMetadataProvider
{
    protected override ModelMetadata CreateMetadata(IEnumerable<Attribute> attributes,
        Type containerType,
        Func<Object> modelAccessor,
        Type modelType,
        String propertyName)
    {
        var metadata = base.CreateMetadata(
            attributes,
            containerType,
            modelAccessor,
            modelType,
            propertyName);

        if (metadata.IsReadOnly)
            metadata.TemplateHint = "readonly";    // Template name is arbitrary
        return metadata;
    }
}
```

You create a new class that inherits the *DataAnnotationsModelMetadataProvider* class and overrides the *CreateMetadata* method. The override is simple—you call the base method and then check what the *IsReadOnly* property returns. If the member is declared read-only, you can programmatically set the *TemplateHint* property to your custom read-only template. (It is then your responsibility to ensure that such a template is available in the Views folder.)

You must register a custom metadata provider with the system. You can do that in either of two ways. You can just store an instance of the new provider in the *Current* property of the *Model MetadataProviders* class, as shown next (this needs be done in *Application_Start* in global.asax):

```
ModelMetadataProviders.Current = new ExtendedAnnotationsMetadataProvider();
```

In ASP.NET MVC, you have another equally effective option: using dependency resolvers. I discuss the topic of dependency resolvers in Chapter 7. For now, it suffices to say that all internal components of ASP.NET MVC that were pluggable in earlier versions, and a bunch of new ones, are in ASP. NET MVC and are discovered by the system by using a centralized service (the dependency resolver) that acts like a service locator. A service locator is a general-purpose component that gets a type (for example, an interface) and returns another (for example, a concrete type that implements that interface).

In ASP.NET MVC, the *ModelMetadataProvider* type is discoverable through the dependency resolver. So, all you have to do is register your custom provider with a made-to-measure dependency resolver. A dependency resolver is a type that knows how to get an object of a requested type. A simple dependency resolver tailor-made for this scenario is shown in the code that follows:

```
public class SampleDependencyResolver : IDependencyResolver
{
    public object GetService(Type serviceType)
    {
        try
        {
            return serviceType == typeof(ModelMetadataProvider)
                ? new ExtendedAnnotationsMetadataProvider()
                : Activator.CreateInstance(serviceType);
        }
        catch
        {
            return null;
        }
    }

    public IEnumerable<object> GetServices(Type serviceType)
    {
        return Enumerable.Empty<Object>();
    }
}
```

You register the resolver in global.asax like so:

```
DependencyResolver.SetResolver(new SampleDependencyResolver());
```

Be aware that ASP.NET MVC attempts to find a valid implementation of *ModelMetadataProvider*, first by looking into registered resolvers and then by looking into the *ModelMetadataProviders*. *Current* property. Double registration for the *ModelMetadataProvider* type is not allowed, and an exception will be thrown if that occurs.

 Note Another approach to support read-only properties in editors consists of modifying the default template used. I'll discuss this in a moment.

Custom templates for model data types

So far, we've exposed a lot of details about display and editor templates that work on primitive types of values. The internal architecture of helpers such as *EditorForModel* and *DisplayForModel*, however, provides for some inherent ability to reflect through the public interface of the model type and build a hierarchical view. This behavior is hardcoded, but it's too simple to be useful in real-world scenarios.

In this section, I'll show you how to rewrite the display and editor template for a generic type to make it look tabular. In other words, instead of getting a vertically stacked panel of label and value <div>s, you get a two-column table with labels on the left and values on the right. The template to overwrite is named object.

Tabular templates

Writing a table-based layout is a relatively simple exercise that consists of looping over the properties of the model object. Here is the Razor code:

```
@inherits System.Web.Mvc.WebViewPage
@if (Model == null)
    <span>@ViewData.ModelMetadata.NullDisplayText</span>
else
{
    <table cellpadding="0" cellspacing="0" class="display-table">
    @foreach (var prop in ViewData
                    .ModelMetadata
                    .Properties
                    .Where(pm => pm.ShowForDisplay && !ViewData.TemplateInfo.Visited(pm)))
    {
        <tr>
            <td>
                <div class="display-label">
                    @prop.GetDisplayName()
                </div>
            </td>
            <td>
                <div class="display-field">
                    <span>@Html.Display(prop.PropertyName)</span>
                </div>
            </td>
        </tr>
    }
    </table>
}
```

If the model is null, you just emit the default null text for the model class. If it's not, you proceed to looping all the properties and creating a table row for each property that has not been previously visited and that is set up for display. For each property, you then recursively call the *Display* HTML helper. You can style every little piece of markup at will. In this example, I'm introducing a new table-level style called *display-table*. Figure 4-8 shows the results.

FIGURE 4-8 A tabular default display template.

The editor template is a bit more sophisticated because it takes care of validation errors and required fields. The template has an extra column to indicate which fields are required (based on the *Required* annotation), and each editor is topped with a label for validation messages. Here is the source code:

```
@inherits System.Web.Mvc.WebViewPage
@if (Model == null)
    <span>@ViewData.ModelMetadata.NullDisplayText</span>
else {
    <table cellpadding="0" cellspacing="0" class="editor-table">
    @foreach (var prop in ViewData
                    .ModelMetadata
                    .Properties
                    .Where(pm => pm.ShowForDisplay && !ViewData.TemplateInfo.Visited(pm)))
    {
        <tr>
            <td>
                <div class="editor-label">
                    @prop.GetDisplayName()
                </div>
            </td>
            <td width="10px"> @(prop.IsRequired ? "*" : "") </td>
            <td>
                <div class="editor-field">
                    @if(prop.IsReadOnly)
                    {
                        <span>@Html.Display(prop.PropertyName)</span>
                    }
```

```
                    else
                    {
                        <span>@Html.Editor(prop.PropertyName)</span>
                        <span>@Html.ValidationMessage(prop.PropertyName, "*")</span>
                    }
                </div>
            </td>
        </tr>
    }
    </table>
}
```

Figure 4-9 shows the editor in action.

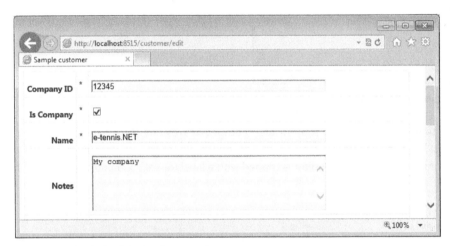

FIGURE 4-9 A tabular default editor template.

Dealing with nested models

One final point to cover is the expected behavior of the templates when the model type has nested models. The code shown so far recursively digs out properties of nested models and renders them as usual. Imagine that you have the following model:

```
public class CustomerViewModel
{
    ...
    public ContactInfo Contact {get; set;}
}

public class ContactInfo
{
    public String FullName {get; set;}
    public String PhoneNumber {get; set;}
    public String Email {get; set;}
}
```

Figure 4-10 shows the results.

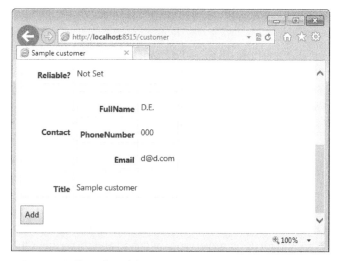

FIGURE 4-10 Nested models.

As a developer, you can control this behavior to some extent. By adding an extra *if* branch to the code of the template, you can limit the nesting level to what you like (1 in this example).

```
@if (Model == null)
    <span>@ViewData.ModelMetadata.NullDisplayText</span>
else
if (ViewData.TemplateInfo.TemplateDepth > 1)
{
    <span>@ViewData.ModelMetadata.SimpleDisplayText</span>
}
else
{ ... }
```

The property *TemplateDepth* measures the allowed nesting level. With this code enabled, if the nesting level is higher than 1, you resort to a simplified representation of the child model. You can control this representation by overriding *ToString* on the child model type.

```
public class ContactInfo
{
    ...
    public override string ToString()
    {
        return "[ContactInfo description here]";
    }
}
```

Alternatively, you can select one column and use that for rendering. You select the column by using the *DisplayColumn* attribute on the child model type.

```
[DisplayColumn("FullName")]
public class ContactInfo
{
    ...
}
```

The attribute *DisplayColumn* takes precedence over the override of *ToString*.

> **Note** As you've seen, the *HiddenInput* attribute gives you a chance to hide a given member from view while uploading its content through a hidden field. If you just want the helpers to ignore a given member, you can use the *ScaffoldColumn* attribute and pass it a value of *false*.

Input validation

Programming books are full of statements such as "Input is evil," and of course, a chapter mostly dedicated to input forms can't leave out a section on input validation. If you want to discuss it in terms of what's really a necessity, you should focus on server-side validation and think about the best technology available that facilitates validation in the most effective way for your application and business domain.

However, having said that, there's really no reason for skipping a client-side validation step that would simply prevent patently invalid data from making it to the server, consuming valuable CPU cycles. So, you're likely interested in both client-side and server-side validation. But, even in moderately complex web applications, validation applies at least at two levels: to validate the input received from the browser, and to validate the data the back end of your system is going to store.

These two levels might sometimes be just one, but this is not what typically happens in the real world and outside of books and tutorials about some cool pieces of technology. Unless your domain model is essentially aligned one-to-one with the storage and the user interface is mostly Create/Read/Update/Delete (CRUD), you have to consider (and make plans for) two levels of validation: presentation and business.

In the rest of this chapter, I'll review a bunch of other data annotations attributes that are well integrated with the ASP.NET MVC plumbing.

Using data annotations

As mentioned, data annotations are a set of attributes which you can use to annotate public properties of any .NET class in a way that any interested client code can read and consume. Attributes fall into two main categories: display and validation. We've just discussed the role that display attributes play with metadata providers in ASP.NET MVC. But, before we dig out validation attributes, let's learn a bit more about data validation in ASP.NET MVC.

Validation provider infrastructure

Chapter 3 explains how controllers receive their input data through the model-binding subsystem. The model binder maps request data to model classes and, in doing so, it validates input values against validation attributes set on the model class.

Validation occurs through a provider. The default validation provider is based on data annotations. The default validation provider is the *DataAnnotationsModelValidatorProvider* class. Let's see which attributes you can use that the default validation provider understands.

Table 4-2 lists the most commonly used data annotation attributes that express a condition to verify on a model class.

TABLE 4-2 Data annotation attributes for validation

Attribute	Description
Compare	Checks whether two specified properties in the model have the same value.
CustomValidation	Checks the value against the specified custom function.
EnumDataType	Checks whether the value can be matched to any of the values in the specified enumerated type.
Range	Checks whether the value falls in the specified range. It defaults to numbers, but you can configure it to consider a range of dates, too.
RegularExpression	Checks whether the value matches the specified expression.
Remote	Makes an Ajax call to the server and checks whether the value is acceptable.
Required	Checks whether a non-null value is assigned to the property. You can configure it to fail if an empty string is assigned.
StringLength	Checks whether the string is longer than the specified value.

All of these attributes derive from the same base class: *ValidationAttribute*. As you'll see in a moment, you can also use this base class to create your own custom validation attributes.

You use these attributes to decorate members of classes being used in input forms. For the entire mechanism to work, you need to have controller methods that receive data in complex data types, as shown here for the *Memo* controller:

```
public ActionResult Edit()
{
    var memo = new Memo();
    return View(memo);
}


[HttpPost]
public ActionResult Edit(Memo memo)
{
    // ModelState dictionary contains error messages
    // for any invalid value detected according to the annotations
    // you might have in the Memo model class.

    return View(memo);
}
```

The model-binder object edits the ModelState dictionary while binding posted values to the *Memo* model class. For any invalid posted value being mapped to an instance of the *Memo* class, the binder automatically creates an entry in the ModelState dictionary. Whether the posted value is valid depends on the outcome returned by the currently registered validation provider. The default validation provider bases its response on the annotations you might have set on the *Memo* model class. Finally, if the next view makes use of *ValidationMessage* helpers, error messages show up automatically. This is exactly the case if you use *EditorForModel* to create the input form.

Decorating a model class

The following listing shows a sample class—the aforementioned *MemoDocument* class—that makes extensive use of data annotations for validation purposes:

```
public class MemoDocument : ViewModelBase
{
    public MemoDocument()
    {
        Created = DateTime.Now;
        Category = Categories.Work;
    }

    [Required]
    [StringLength(100)]
    public String Text { get; set; }

    [Required]
    [Range(1, 5]
    public Int32 Priority { get; set; }

    [Required]
    public DateTime Created { get; set; }

    [EnumDataType(typeof(Categories))]
    [Required]
    public Categories Category { get; set; }

    [StringLength(50, MinimumLength=4)]
    [RegularExpression(@"\b[A-Z0-9._%+-]+@[A-Z0-9.-]+\.[A-Z]{2,4}\b")]
    public String RelatedEmail { get; set; }
}

public enum Categories
{
    Work,
    Personal,
    Social
}
```

Given the class, you should expect to receive error messages if the *Text* property is longer than 100 characters or if it is left empty. Likewise, the *Priority* members must be an integer between 1 and 5 (extremes included) and the *Created* date cannot be omitted. The *RelatedEmail* member can be empty; however, if given any text, the text must be between 4 and 50 characters long and matching the regular expression. Finally, the *Category* member must contain a string that evaluates to one of the constants in the *Categories* enumerated type. Figure 4-11 shows the validation of a sample memo.

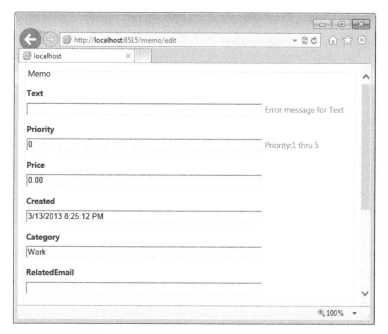

FIGURE 4-11 Validation messages.

Dealing with enumerated types

You might wonder why the *Category* field is being edited as a plain string. It would be smarter if a drop-down list could be provided. That won't just happen for free. The *EnumDataType* is recognized by the validation provider, which ensures that the value belongs to the enumeration; it is ignored by editors. If you want a drop-down list with enumerated values, you need to write a String.cshtml custom template and place it in an EditorTemplates folder. Because enumerated types are paired to strings, you overwrite String.cshtml (or .aspx) to change the way in which an enumeration is edited. In the code, you determine the markup based on the actual type of the *Model* property. Here's the simple code you need:

```
@model Object
@if (Model is Enum)
{
    <div class="editor-field">
        @Html.DropDownList("", new SelectList(Enum.GetValues(Model.GetType())))
        @Html.ValidationMessage("")
    </div>
}
else
{
    @Html.TextBox("", ViewData.TemplateInfo.FormattedModelValue,
        new { @class = "text-box single-line" })
}
```

Figure 4-12 shows the same form when the just-created editor template is used.

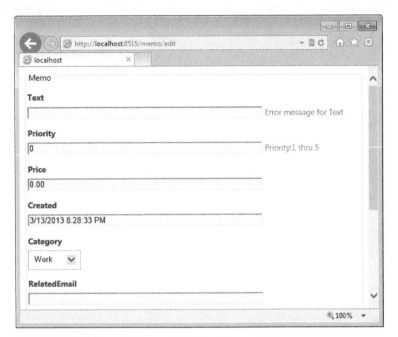

FIGURE 4-12 Mixing validation and display data annotations.

Controlling error messages

In Figure 4-12, you see some messages that attempt to explain what went wrong. You have total control over those messages. Each attribute has an *ErrorMessage* property for you to set the text. Note, though, that attribute properties can accept only constant strings.

```
[Required(ErrorMessage = "A description is required.")]
public String Text { get; set; }
```

You might not like the idea of having plain strings interspersed with class definition. A way to decouple the class definition from error messages is by using resources. Using resources makes it possible for you to make offline changes to the text without touching classes. It also facilitates localization, but it still doesn't give you programmatic control over the text being displayed. For programmatic control, the only option you have is editing the ModelState dictionary in the controller method, as shown here:

```
[HttpPost]
public ActionResult Edit(MemoDocument memo)
{
    if (!ModelState.IsValid)
    {
        var newModelState = new ModelStateDictionary();
```

```
            // Create a new model-state dictionary with values you want to overwrite
            newModelState.AddModelError("Text", "...");
            newModelState.AddModelError("Priority", "...");
            ...

            // Merge your changes with the existing ModelState
            ModelState.Merge(newModelState);
        }
        return View(memo);
}
```

Basically, you create a new model-state dictionary and then merge it with one calculated during the model-binding stage. When you merge the dictionaries, the values in the new dictionary are copied into the ModelState dictionary, overwriting any existing value.

If having constant messages works for you and all you need to do is avoid magic strings in software, you can use a resource file which, incidentally, also sets the stage for easy localization. Each validation attribute accepts an error message expressed as a resource index:

```
[Required(ErrorMessageResourceName="MustSetPriority",
        ErrorMessageResourceType = typeof(Strings))]
[Range(1, 5, ErrorMessageResourceName="InvalidPriority",
        ErrorMessageResourceType=typeof(Strings))]
public Int32 Priority { get; set; }
```

You indicate the resource through a pair of arguments: the resource container data type, and the name of the resource. The former is expressed through the *ErrorMessageResourceType* property; the latter is expressed by *ErrorMessageResourceName.* When you add a resource file to an ASP.NET MVC project, the Microsoft Visual Studio designer creates a container type that exposes strings as public members. This is the type to assign to the *ErrorMessageResourceType* property. By default, the name of this auto-generated type matches the name of the resource (.resx) file.

Advanced data annotations

The beauty of data annotations is that after you have defined attributes for a model type, you're pretty much done. Most of what follows happens automatically, thanks to the deep understanding of data annotations that the ASP.NET MVC infrastructure has. However, in this imperfect world, none of the things you really need are completely free. So it is for data annotations, which cover a lot of relatively simple situations very well, but leave some extra work for you to do on your own in many realistic applications. Let's explore a few more advanced features that you can build on top of data annotations.

Cross-property validation

The data annotations we've considered so far are attributes you use to validate the content of a single field. This is definitely useful, but it doesn't help that much in a real-world scenario in which you likely need to validate the content of a property in light of the value stored in another. Cross-property validation requires a bit of context-specific code. The problem is this: how and where do you write it?

The solution that springs to mind is probably not too far from the following outline:

```
public ActionResult Edit(MemoDocument memo)
{
    if (ModelState.IsValid)
    {
        // If here, then properties have been individually validated.
        // Proceed with cross-property validation, and merge model-state dictionary
        // to reflect feedback to the UI.
        ...
    }
}
```

If the model state you receive from the binder is valid, all of the decorated properties passed the validation stage. So, taken individually, each property is OK. You proceed with context-specific, cross-property validation, add errors to a new state dictionary, and merge it to the existing ModelState.

You might be pleased to know that the *CustomValidation* attribute serves exactly this purpose and, overall, you can consider it a shortcut for the approach I just suggested. Consider the following code:

```
[Required]
[EnumDataType(typeof(Categories))]
[CustomValidation(typeof(MemoDocument), "ValidateCategoryAndPriority")]
public Categories Category { get; set; }
```

The *CustomValidation* attribute takes two parameters: a type and a method name. The type can also be the same model you're decorating. The method must be public and static with any of the following signatures:

```
public static ValidationResult MethodName(Categories category)
public static ValidationResult MethodName(Categories category, ValidationContext context)
```

Using the first overload is the same as defining custom validation logic for an individual value. It is sort of equivalent to creating a custom data annotations attribute—it's quicker to write but more rigid as far as the signature is concerned. Much more interesting is the second overload. In fact, through the *ValidationContext* parameter, you can get a reference to the model object and check as many properties as you like.

```
public static ValidationResult ValidateCategoryAndPriority(
            Categories category, ValidationContext context)
{
    // Grab the model instance
    var memo = context.ObjectInstance as MemoDocument;
    if (memo == null)
        throw new NullReferenceException();

    // Cross-property validation
    if (memo.Category == Categories.Personal && memo.Priority > 3)
        return new ValidationResult("Category and priority are not consistent.");
    return ValidationResult.Success;
}
```

You can attach the *CustomValidation* attribute to an individual property as well as to the class. In the preceding example, the attribute is attached to *Category*, but it ensures that if the value is *Personal*, the property *Priority* must be set to a value not higher than 3. If the validation fails, the entry in the model-state dictionary uses *Category* as the key. If you attach *CustomValidation* to the class, be aware that the validation is performed only if everything went fine for all individual properties. This is exactly the declarative counterpart of the pattern outlined earlier:

```
[CustomValidation(typeof(MemoDocument), "ValidateMemo")]
public class MemoDocument
{
    ...
}
```

Here's the signature of the method if the *CustomValidation* attribute is attached to the class:

```
public static ValidationResult ValidateMemo(MemoDocument memo)
{
    ...
}
```

When you use *CustomValidation* at the class level, you have the problem of capturing error messages, because error messages are usually associated with properties. You can easily solve the issue by using the helper *Html.ValidationSummary*, which brings up all error messages regardless of the originating properties. I'll return to the topic of class-level validation later in the chapter.

Finally, the *Compare* attribute is available to serve far more quickly a specific cross-property scenario; for example, when you need to ensure that the value of a property matches the value of another. The canonical example is retyping a new password:

```
[Required]
[DataType(DataType.Password)]
public String NewPassword {get; set;}

[Required]
[DataType(DataType.Password)]
[Compare("NewPassword")]
public String RetypePassword {get; set;}
```

The comparison is made by using the *Equals* method as implemented on the specific type.

Creating custom validation attributes

The *CustomValidation* attribute forces you to validate the value stored in the property without the possibility of adding any extra parameters. The problem here is not so much gaining access to other properties on the model object—which you can do through *ValidationContext*—but enriching the signature of the attribute that defines additional attribute-level parameters. For example, suppose that you want to validate a number to ensure that it is an even number. Optionally, however, you want to turn on the attribute to check whether the number is also a multiple of 4. You want an attribute such as the one shown here:

```
[EvenNumber(MultipleOf4=true)]
public Int32 MagicNumber {get; set;}
```

There's no way to pass an optional Boolean value in the signature recognized by *CustomValidation*. In the end, the difference between the *CustomValidation* attribute and a custom validation attribute is that the latter is designed to be (easily) reusable. Here's how to write a custom data annotation attribute:

```
[AttributeUsage(AttributeTargets.Property)]
public class EvenNumberAttribute : ValidationAttribute
{
    // Whether the number has to be checked also for being a multiple of 4
    public Boolean MultipleOf4 { get; set; }

    public override Boolean IsValid(Object value)
    {
        if (value == null)
            return false;

        var x = -1;
        try
        {
            x = (Int32) value;
        }
        catch
        {
            return false;
        }

        if (x % 2 > 0)
            return false;
        if (!MultipleOf4)
            return true;

        // Is multiple of 4?
        return (x % 4 == 0);
    }
}
```

You create a class that inherits from *ValidationAttribute* and override the method *IsValid*. If you need extra parameters such as *MultipleOf4*, you just define public properties.

In ASP.NET MVC, you can create custom attributes that perform cross-property validation. All you do is override a slightly different overload of the *IsValid* method:

```
protected override ValidationResult IsValid(Object value, ValidationContext context)
```

Using the properties on the *ValidationContext* object, you can gain access to the entire model object and perform a full validation.

Enabling client-side validation

All of the examples considered work across a postback or through an Ajax form. To use them with Ajax, you need to make just a small change to the view that displays the editor so that it uses *Ajax.BeginForm* instead of *Html.BeginForm*. In addition, the controller method should return a partial view instead of a full view, as shown here:

```
[HttpPost]
public ActionResult Edit(MemoDocument memo)
{
    if (Request.IsAjaxRequest())
        return PartialView("edit_ajax", memo);
    return View(memo);
}
```

Here's how to convert the original view to an *edit_ajax* partial view:

```
@model DataAnnotations.ViewModels.Memo.MemoDocument
@{
    Layout = "";   // Drop the master page
}

@using (Ajax.BeginForm("edit", "memo",
    new AjaxOptions() { UpdateTargetId="memoEditor" }))
{
    <div id="memoEditor">
    <fieldset>
        <legend>Memo</legend>
        @Html.EditorForModel()
        <p>
        <input type="submit" value="Create" />
        </p>
    </fieldset>
    </div>
}
```

In this way, your form is validated on the server but doesn't refresh the full page. However, at least for a few basic annotations, it can be helpful in turning on client-side validation so that if the data is patently invalid (for example, a required field is empty), no HTTP request is ever started.

To turn on client-side validation, you need to perform a couple of easy steps. First, ensure that your *web.config* file contains the following:

```
<appSettings>
    <add key="ClientValidationEnabled" value="true" />
    <add key="UnobtrusiveJavaScriptEnabled" value="true" />
</appSettings>
```

Observe that both settings are set by default. In addition, you need to link a couple of JavaScript files: *jquery.validate.js* (the jQuery validation plugin) and *jquery.validate.unobtrusive.js*, or their minified versions. The simplest way to find and add these files is via NuGet. Needless to say, you need to link the jQuery library on top of everything.

> **Important** When you turn on client-side validation, all built-in data annotation attributes gain a client-side behavior and, to the extent that it is possible, perform their validation in JavaScript within the browser. If the validation fails, no request is made to the web server. However, custom validation attributes such as *EvenNumber* don't automatically work in this way. To add client-side validation for custom attributes also, you need to implement an additional interface, *IClientValidatable*, which I'll cover in a moment.

Culture-based, client-side validation

When it comes to data-type validation, you likely have the additional problem of globalization. For example, consider the following:

```
public Decimal Price {get; set;}
```

The editor correctly handles the type and displays a default format of "0.00". However, if you enter "0,8" where the decimal separator is the comma, your input is rejected and the form won't post. As you can see, it is a problem of setting the correct culture on the client-side validation. The jQuery Validation plugin defaults to the United States culture on the client; on the server-side, instead, it depends on the value of the *Culture* property on the thread. (See Chapter 5, "Aspects of ASP.NET MVC applications," for more details on localization and globalization.)

To support a specific culture on the client, you must first link the official jQuery globalization plugin as well as the script file for the specific culture in which you're interested. Both files must be included after regular validation scripts. In addition, you must instruct the globalization plugin as to which culture you intend to use. Finally, the validator plugin must be informed that it needs to use globalization information when parsing a number.

```
<script type="text/javascript">
    $.validator.methods.number = function (value, element) {
        if (Globalization.parseFloat(value)) {
            return true;
        }
        return false;
    }
    $(document).ready(function () {
        $.culture = jQuery.cultures['it-IT'];
        $.preferCulture($.culture.name);
        Globalization.preferCulture($.culture.name);
    });
</script>
```

With this code in place, you can enter decimals using the culture-specific settings. Taking this approach further, you can customize on a culture basis most of the client-side validation work.

Validating properties remotely

Validation might happen on the client, but you should see it as a way to save a few HTTP-heavy requests for pages. To be on the safe side, you should always validate any data on the server. However, to give users a nicer experience, you might want to perform a server-side validation without leaving the browser. The typical example is when users are registering to some service and enter a nickname. That name must be unique, and uniqueness can be verified only on the server. Wouldn't it be cool if you could inform the user in real time whether the nickname is already taken? In this way, she could change it and avoid annoying surprises when finally posting the registration request.

Data annotations offer an attribute that helps code this feature: the *Remote* attribute. Attached to a property, the attribute invokes a method on some controller and expects a Boolean response. The controller method receives the value to validate plus an additional list of related fields. Here's an example:

```
[Remote("CheckCustomer", "Memo",
        AdditionalFields="Country",
        ErrorMessage="Not an existing customer")]
public String RelatedCustomer { get; set; }
```

When validating *RelatedCustomer* on the client, the code silently places a jQuery call to the method *CheckCustomer* on the *Memo* controller. If the response is negative, the specified error message is displayed.

```
public ActionResult CheckCustomer(String relatedCustomer)
{
    if (CustomerRepository.Exists(relatedCustomer))
        return Json(true, JsonRequestBehavior.AllowGet);
    return Json(false, JsonRequestBehavior.AllowGet);
}
```

The controller must return true/false wrapped up in a JSON payload. If additional fields have been specified, they are added to the query string of the URL and are subject to the classic model-binding rules of ASP.NET MVC. Multiple fields are separated by a comma. Here's a sample URL:

```
http://yourserver/memo/checkcustomer?relatedCustomer=dino&Country=...
```

The Ajax call is placed every time the input field loses the focus after having been modified. The property decorated with the *Remote* attribute honors the client-side validation contract and doesn't allow the form to post back until a valid value is entered.

Important Data annotations can be specified only statically at compile time. Currently, there's no way to read attributes from an external data source and bind them to model properties on the fly. To turn this feature on, you probably need to consider replacing the default validation provider with a custom one that reads metadata for validation from a different source.

I've found this to be a real issue more in business-layer validation than in presentation. In business-layer validation, you likely need to inject business rules as requirements change, and more flexibility is therefore welcome. In business-layer validation, I often use the Enterprise Library Validation Application Block, which can read validation attributes from the configuration file. (I'll return to the Enterprise Library in a moment.)

Self-validation

Data annotations attempt to automate the validation process around data being posted from forms. Most of the time, you use only stock attributes and get error messages for free. In other cases, you create your own attributes at a bit higher development cost, but still what you do is create components that fit nicely in an existing infrastructure. In addition, data annotations are designed to work mostly at the property level. In ASP.NET MVC, you can always access the entire model via the validation context; however, ultimately, when the validation is complex, many developers prefer to opt for a handcrafted validation layer.

In other words, you stop fragmenting validation in myriad combinations of data annotations and move everything into a single place—a method that you call on the server from within the controller:

```
public ActionResult Edit(MemoDocument memo)
{
    if (!Validate(memo))
        ModelState.AddModelError(...);
    ...
}
```

The *MemoDocument* class might or might not have property annotations. As I see things, if you opt for self-validation, for reasons of clarity you should just stop using data annotations. In any case, self-validation doesn't prevent you from using data annotations, as well.

The *IValidatableObject* interface

When it comes to building a layer of self-validation, you can unleash your creativity and choose the application model that best suits you. ASP.NET MVC attempts to suggest an approach. Basically, ASP.NET MVC guarantees that any model class that implements the *IValidatableObject* interface is automatically validated, with no need for the developer to call out validation explicitly. The interface is shown here:

```
public interface IValidatableObject
{
    IEnumerable<ValidationResult> Validate(ValidationContext validationContext);
}
```

If the interface is detected, the *Validate* method is invoked by the validation provider during the model-binding step. The parameter of type *ValidationContext* makes available the entire model for any sort of cross-property validation.

> **Important** If the model is also decorated with data annotations, the *Validate* method is not invoked if some of the properties are not in a valid state. (To avoid pitfalls, I suggest that you drop annotations entirely if you opt for *IValidatableObject*.)

Using *IValidatableObject* is functionally equivalent to using the *CustomValidation* attribute at the class level. The only difference is that with *IValidatableObject* you can implement a validation layer with a single method, using your own architecture and remaining independent of data annotations.

Benefits of centralized validation

When you have really complex validation logic in which cross-property validation is predominant, mixing per-property validation and class-level validation might result in an unpleasant experience for the end user. As mentioned, class-level validation won't fire until properties are individually validated. This means that users initially see a few error messages related to properties and are led to think that they are safe as soon as these errors are fixed. Instead, they might get an entirely new group of errors because of cross-property validation. Users won't have any clue about these other possible errors until they show up. To avoid this, if class-level validation is predominant, just focus on that and drop per-property validation.

To implement class-level validation, choosing between *IValidatableObject* or *CustomValidation* at the class level is entirely your call. For years, I used my own interface, which looked nearly identical to today's *IValidatableObject*.

The *IClientValidatable* interface

Custom validation attributes won't produce any visible effect when client-side validation is active. In other words, a custom attribute is not able per se to run any client-side code to attempt to validate values in the browser. It doesn't mean, however, that you can't add this ability. It just takes more code. Here's how to extend a custom attribute to turn it on for the client:

```
[AttributeUsage(AttributeTargets.Property)]
public class ClientEvenNumberAttribute : ValidationAttribute, IClientValidatable
{
    ...

    // IClientValidatable interface members
    public IEnumerable<ModelClientValidationRule> GetClientValidationRules(
            ModelMetadata metadata, ControllerContext context)
```

```
    {
        var errorMessage = ErrorMessage;
        if (String.IsNullOrEmpty(errorMessage))
            errorMessage = (MultipleOf4 ? MultipleOf4ErrorMessage : EvenErrorMessage);

        var rule = new ModelClientValidationRule
                    {
                        ValidationType = "iseven",
                        ErrorMessage = errorMessage
                    };
        rule.ValidationParameters.Add("multipleof4", MultipleOf4);
        yield return rule;
    }
}
```

You simply make it implement a new interface: the *IClientValidatable* interface. The method returns a collection of validation rules. Each rule is characterized by an error message, a JavaScript function name used for validation, and a collection of parameters for the JavaScript code. Names of parameters and functions should be lowercase.

Next, you need to write some JavaScript code that performs the validation on the client. Preferably, you should do so by using jQuery and the jQuery validation plugin. Here's the JavaScript you need to turn on the previous *EvenNumber* attribute to work on the client, too:

```
$.validator.addMethod('iseven', function (value, element, params) {
    var mustBeMultipleOf4 = params.multipleof4;
    if (mustBeMultipleOf4)
        return (value % 4 === 0);
    return (value % 2 === 0);
});

$.validator.unobtrusive.adapters.add('iseven', ['multipleof4', 'more_parameters'],
    function (options) {
        options.rules['iseven'] = options.params;
        options.messages['iseven'] = options.message;
    });
```

The *addMethod* function registers the validation callback for the *iseven* rule. The validation callback receives the value to validate and all parameters previously added to the rule in the implementation of *IClientValidatable*.

In addition, you need to specify adapters to generate JavaScript-free markup for the validation scenario. To add an adapter, you indicate the name of the function, its parameters, and error message.

You don't need anything else; if it doesn't work, first check that all required scripts are available and then check function and parameter names in JavaScript code and in the C# implementation of *IClientValidatable*. Be aware that you won't be receiving any JavaScript error if something goes wrong.

Dynamic server-side validation

Validation is about conditional code, so in the end, it is a matter of combining together a few *if* statements and returning Booleans. Writing a validation layer with plain code and without any ad hoc framework or technology might work in practice, but it might not be a great idea in design. Your resulting code would be hardly readable and hard to evolve even though some recently released fluent-code libraries are making it easier.

Subject to real business rules, validation is a highly volatile matter, and your implementation must necessarily account for that. In the end, it is not simply about writing code that validates, but code that is open to validating the same data against different rules. Data annotations are a possible choice; another valid choice is the Validation Application Block (VAB) in Microsoft's Enterprise Library.

Data annotations and VAB have a lot in common. Both frameworks are attribute-based and you can extend both frameworks with custom classes representing custom rules. In both cases, you can define cross-property validation. Finally, both frameworks have a validator API that evaluates an instance and returns the list of errors. So, where's the difference?

Data annotations are part of the .NET Framework and don't need any separate download. Enterprise Library is a separate NuGet package. It might not be a big deal in a large project, but it is still an issue because it might require additional approval in some corporate scenarios.

In my opinion, VAB is superior to data annotations in one aspect: It can be fully configured via *XML rulesets*. An XML ruleset is an entry in the configuration file in which you describe the validation you want. Needless to say, you can change things declaratively without even touching your code. Here's a sample ruleset:

```xml
<validation>
  <type assemblyName="..." name="Samples.DomainModel.Customer">
    <ruleset name="IsValidForRegistration">
      <properties>
        <property name="CompanyName">
          <validator type="NotNullValidator" />
          <validator lowerBound="6" lowerBoundType="Ignore"
                     upperBound="40" upperBoundType="Inclusive"
                     messageTemplate="Company name cannot be longer ..."
                     type="StringLengthValidator" />
        </property>
        <property name="Id">
          <validator type="NotNullValidator" />
        </property>
        <property name="PhoneNumber">
          <validator negated="false"
                     type="NotNullValidator" />
          <validator lowerBound="0" lowerBoundType="Ignore"
                     upperBound="24" upperBoundType="Inclusive"
                     negated="false"
                     type="StringLengthValidator" />
        </property>
```

```
          . . .
        </properties>
      </ruleset>
    </type>
</validation>
```

A ruleset lists the attributes that you want to apply to a given property on a given type. In code, you validate a ruleset as follows:

```
public virtual ValidationResults ValidateForRegistration()
{
    var validator = ValidationFactory
            .CreateValidator<Customer>("IsValidForRegistration");
    var results = validator.Validate(this);
    return results;
}
```

The method above applies the validators listed in the *IsValidForRegistration* ruleset to the specified instance of the class. (The *ValidateForRegistration* method is expected to be a method on an entity class of yours.)

> **Note** There are two approaches to validation: sometimes, you want to yell out if invalid data is passed; sometimes, you want to collect errors and report that to other layers of code. In .NET, Code Contracts is another technology that you probably want to take into account for validation. Unlike annotations and VAB, however, Code Contracts just check conditions and then throw at first failure. You need to use a centralized error handler to recover from exceptions and degrade gracefully. In general, I would recommend using Code Contracts in a domain entity only to catch potentially severe errors that can lead to inconsistent states. For example, it makes sense to use Code Contracts in a factory method. In this case, if the method is passed patently invalid data, you want it to throw an exception. Whether you use Code Contracts also in the setter methods of properties is your call. I prefer to take a softer route and validate via attributes.

Summary

Input forms are common in any web application, and ASP.NET MVC applications are no exception. For a while, there was a sentiment in the industry that ASP.NET MVC was not well suited to support data-driven applications because they required a lot of data entry and validation. Ultimately, ASP.NET MVC measures up nicely to the task. It does use a different set of tools than Web Forms, but it is still effective and to the point.

ASP.NET MVC offers templated helpers for autogenerated, repetitive forms and server-side and client-side forms of input validation. Input validation can be largely streamlined if you build your user interface around view-model objects annotated with display and validation attributes. These attributes—known as data annotations—are recognized by the ASP.NET MVC infrastructure (model metadata and validation providers), and they're processed to produce templated helpers and feedback messages for the user.

With this chapter, we've nearly covered all the fundamentals of ASP.NET MVC programming. Chapter 5 covers what remains to be dealt with, including localization, security, and integration with intrinsic objects, primarily *Session* and *Cache*.

ASP.NET MVC
software design

Aspects of ASP.NET MVC applications

A multitude of rulers is not a good thing. Let there be one ruler, one king.

—*Homer*

There's a lot more to a web application than just a request/response sequence. If it were as simple as that, with a well-done set of ASP.NET MVC controllers, you would be all set. Unfortunately, things are a bit more complex. An effective ASP.NET MVC application results from the insightful consideration and implementation of various aspects, including Search Engine Optimization (SEO), state management, error handling, and localization, just to name a few (and fairly important aspects, at that).

This chapter is a collection of distinct and, to some extent, self-contained topics, each touching on an aspect that many ASP.NET MVC applications out there already have or are considering to have.

> **Note** Not every web application needs to manage session or global state. Likewise, not every application is written for an international audience or makes a point of being highly ranked by search engines. Having said that, though, there's no application I can think of that needs none of these aspects.

ASP.NET intrinsic objects

ASP.NET MVC works and thrives on top of the classic ASP.NET infrastructure. To a good extent, you can consider ASP.NET MVC as a specialization of the classic ASP.NET runtime environment that just supports a different application and programming model. ASP.NET MVC applications have full access to any built-in components that populate the ecosystem of ASP.NET, including *Cache*, *Session*, *Response*, and the authentication and error-handling layer.

Nothing is different in ASP.NET MVC in the way in which you can access these components. But what about the way you should use these components from within ASP.NET MVC? Describing that is precisely the purpose of this chapter.

> **Note** In ASP.NET—and in this book—the expression "intrinsic objects," or just "intrinsics," is frequently used to indicate the entire set of fundamental objects wrapped up by *HttpContext*. The list includes *HttpRequest*, *HttpResponse*, *HttpSessionState*, *Cache*, and the objects that identify the logged-on user.

HTTP response and SEO

Let's start our analysis of ASP.NET intrinsic objects with the *HttpResponse* object. This object is used to describe the HTTP response being sent back to the browser at the end of request processing. The public interface of the *HttpResponse* object makes it possible for you to set cookies and content type, append headers, and pass instructions to the browser regarding the caching of the response data. In addition, the *HttpResponse* object facilitates redirecting to other URLs.

To customize any aspects of the response stream, you write a custom action result object and make a controller method return an instance of your type instead of *ViewResult* or any other predefined typed deriving from *ActionResult*. Chapter 8, "Customizing ASP.NET MVC controllers," discusses this in detail.

SEO is an extremely valid reason to pay more attention to the features of the ASP.NET *HttpResponse* object. Permanent redirection is the first practical programming aspect to take into account.

Permanent redirection

In ASP.NET, when you invoke *Response.Redirect*, you return to the browser an HTTP 302 code indicating that the requested content is now available from another specified location. Based on that, the browser makes a second request to the specified address and gets any content. However, a search engine that visits your page takes the HTTP 302 code literally. The actual meaning of the HTTP 302 status code is that the requested page has been temporarily moved to a new address. As a result, search engines don't update their internal tables, and when someone later clicks to see your page, the engine returns the original address. Consequently, the browser receives an HTTP 302 code and needs to make a second request to finally display the desired page.

> **Note** To view a good resource for learning more about HTTP return codes and how they work, go to *http://www.w3.org/Protocols/rfc2616/rfc2616-sec10.html*.

If the redirection is used to convey requests to a given URL, permanent redirection is a better option because it represents a juicier piece of information for a search engine. To set up a permanent redirection, you return the HTTP 301 response code. This code informs search agents that the location has been permanently moved. Search engines know how to process an HTTP 301 code and use that information to update the page URL reference. The next time they display search results that involve the page, the linked URL is the new one. In this way, users can get to the page quickly and a second roundtrip is avoided. The following code shows what's required to arrange a permanent redirection programmatically:

```
void PermanentRedirect(String url, Boolean endRequest)
{
    Response.Clear();
    Response.StatusCode = 301;
    Response.AddHeader("Location", url);
    ...

    // Optionally end the request
    if (endRequest)
        Response.End();
}
```

Starting with ASP.NET 4, the *HttpResponse* class features a new method for such a thing. It is named *RedirectPermanent*. You use the method in the same way you used the classic *Response. Redirect*, except that this time the caller receives an HTTP 301 status code. For the browser, it makes no big difference, but it is a key difference for search engines.

In ASP.NET MVC, things are much easier because a new Boolean member named *Permanent* has been added to the *RedirectResult* type. The entire thing is wrapped by the *RedirectPermanent* method on the *Controller* class that you'll likely use.

```
public ActionResult Index()
{
    ...
    return RedirectPermanent(url);
}
```

As mentioned, you can read more on the topic of advanced customization of action results in Chapter 8.

Devising routes and URLs

A huge difference between ASP.NET Web Forms and ASP.NET MVC is that in the latter, URLs look more like commands you send to the web application than server paths to pages and resources. Because the routing mechanism is under your total control as a developer, you are responsible for devising URLs for your application properly.

If you have SEO in mind, devising URLs properly mostly means guaranteeing URL uniqueness. One of the primary purposes of a search engine is determining how relevant the content to which a given URL points actually is. Of course, a given piece of information is much more relevant if you can find it only in one place and through a unique URL. Sometimes, however, even if the content is unique, it can be reached through multiple, subtly different URLs. In this case, you run the risk of getting a lower ranking from search engines and, worse yet, have references to that portion of your site lost in the last result pages and hardly noticed by potential visitors. The problem here does not have much to do with storage and page content, but with the shape and format of URLs. Even though the World Wide Web Consortium (W3C) suggests that you consider using case-sensitive URLs, from an SEO perspective, using single-case (and lowercase) URLs are a better choice. If you can keep all of your URLs lowercase, that adds consistency to the site while reducing duplicate URLs.

Note Unlike Unix systems, ASP.NET and Internet Information Services (IIS) make no distinction about the case when a URL is requested. Probably because of the W3C standpoint and Unix practices, search engines apply a case-sensitive policy to URLs. Recently, most search engines (and primarily Google) added forms of mitigation, ultimately trying to join ranks for URLs that only differ for the case. At any rate, if the site exposes endpoints spelled differently, the final rank is hardly just the sum of all distinct ranks. So, the bottom line is that by not paying attention to have single-case in URLs your SEO rank is penalized.

What about inbound links?

Well, there's not much you can do to avoid having external sites link to pages in your site using the case they prefer. Most likely, they will just copy your URLs, thus repeating the same case you have chosen. If this is not the case, you can always force a permanent redirect via an HTTP module that intercepts the *BeginRequest* event. Forcing all inbound links to use the same case saves you from splitting traffic across multiple URLs instead of concentrating all of it on a single URL with a higher rank. (We can call this strategy "Unite and Conquer" as opposed to the "Divide and Conquer" strategy that is so popular in other software scenarios.)

To address this problem, the canonical URL format also has been defined. The canonical URL describes your idea of a URL in the form of a preferred URL scheme. All you do is add a <link> tag to the <head> section, as shown here:

```
<link rel="canonical" href="http://myserver.com/" />
```

If your site has a significant amount of content that can be accessed through multiple URLs, the canonical URL gives more information to search engines so that they can treat similar URLs as a single one and come to a more appropriate ranking of the content of the resource. A possible effect of the canonical URL feature (which has zero cost on your side) is that it can clear up the controversy regarding having or not having the trailing slash. With a canonical URL that defaults to either choice, it makes no difference to a search engine which one is actually linked.

The trailing slash

There are some SEO concerns related to the trailing slash. In particular, a search engine incorporates a filter that detects and penalizes duplicate content in search results. Duplicate content is any page (that is, any distinct URL) in the search results that is regarded as serving the same content as others. From the perspective of the search engine, a URL with a trailing slash and the same URL without the trailing slash are just two URLs serving the same content.

To serve the most relevant content possible to the user, a search engine tries to rank lower the pages that seem nearly the same as others. But, this process can accidentally reduce the rank of good pages.

What about ASP.NET MVC and the routing system? Should you force a trailing slash?

Ultimately, an ASP.NET MVC application is entirely responsible for its URLs and subsequently for what a search engine will request. In a new application, it's ultimately up to you because your routes determine how the request is processed. Helpers that are used to generate URLs in the markup tend to avoid trailing slashes, so let's say that not having trailing slashes is a more common solution in ASP.NET MVC. However, keep in mind that the other approach is equally valid. In ASP.NET MVC, it's up to you to resolve (or not resolve) URLs with and without the trailing slash in the same way. You ultimately decide about your page rank. Whether you use or don't use the trailing slash is not as important as being consistent with whatever choice you make.

If you're porting an existing site to ASP.NET MVC, you might have many legacy URLs to maintain. You can install a custom route handler and permanently redirect (HTTP 301) from legacy URLs to new URLs. This approach works, but in practice it might take weeks for the search engine to physically update the internal tables of links to reflect all of your permanent redirects. In the meantime, you might lose quite a bit of income.

The search engine always likes to deal with the existing URLs. In this case, you might want to install a rewrite module in Microsoft IIS to map an ASP.NET MVC URL to a legacy URL.

 Note Speaking of SEO, there's another point to make, even though it is not strictly related to pages or controller actions: subdomains. In general, there are many reasons to consider subdomains in the setup of a website. Common reasons to split a domain into subdomains are to distinguish the site by language, product, or feature while making administration easier. Unfortunately, search engines treat subdomains (including naked domains such as *myserver.com*) as separate sites.

Managing the session state

All real-world applications of any shape and form need to maintain their own state to serve users' requests. Web applications are no exception. However, unlike other types of applications, web applications need special system-level tools to achieve the result. The reason for this peculiarity lies in the stateless nature of the underlying protocol upon which web applications still rely. As long as HTTP remains the transportation protocol for the web, all applications will run into the same trouble: figuring out the most effective way to persist state information.

In ASP.NET, the *HttpSessionState* class provides a dictionary-based model of storing and retrieving session-state values. The class doesn't expose its contents to all users operating on the application at a given time. Only the requests that originate in the context of the same session—that is, generated across multiple page requests made by the same browser instance—can access the session state. The session state can be stored and published in a variety of ways, including in a web farm or web garden scenario. By default, though, the session state is held within the ASP.NET worker process.

Using the *Session* object

As an ASP.NET MVC developer, you have no technical limitations on your way to the intrinsic *Session* object. You have just the same issues and benefits as a developer of an ASP.NET Web Forms application. The ASP.NET MVC infrastructure uses the session state internally, and you can do so also in your code. In particular, the ASP.NET MVC infrastructure uses the session state to persist the content of the *TempData* dictionary, as is illustrated in Chapter 4, "Input forms."

So, if you feel the need to store data across sessions, you store it and then read it back through the familiar *Session* object, as demonstrated here:

```
public ActionResult Config()
{
    Session[StateEntries.PreferredTextColor] = "Green";
    ...
}
```

As you can see, nothing is different from classic ASP.NET programming. Just keep in mind that the session dictionary is a name/value collection, so it requires plain strings to identify entries. Using constants in code is a good technique to prevent nasty errors. When you read from session state, casting and null-checking are unavoidable, as shown in the following:

```
var preferredTextColor = "";
var data = Session[StateEntries.PreferredTextColor];
if (data ! null)
        preferredTextColor = (String) data;
```

Any data stored in the session state is returned as an *Object*.

Never outside the controller

The most important aspect that relates to accessing the session state in ASP.NET MVC is that you should be using it only from within the controller. Generally speaking, data stored in the session state can be consumed in either of two ways. It can be used to drive some back-end calculation on input data, or it can be passed as is to the view.

In the latter case, ensure that you copy individual values to proper members on the view model class or to whatever predefined view data structures you use (*ViewData* or *ViewBag*). Technically speaking, you could access the session state (and other intrinsic objects) also from within a Razor or ASPX view. Although any code like this works, you should avoid doing this so that you can preserve a strong Separation of Concerns (SoC) between controllers and views. The golden rule is that the view receives from the outside world whatever data it needs to incorporate.

 Note The aforementioned golden rule holds also for render actions, which are special controller methods you invoke directly from the view. Render actions add a bit of logic to your views but don't break the separation between controllers and views—the view continues to have its only contact in the controller.

Caching data

Caching indicates the application's ability to save frequently used data to an intermediate storage medium. In a typical web scenario, the canonical intermediate storage medium is the web server's memory. However, you can design caching around the requirements and characteristics of each application, thus using as many layers of caching as needed to reach your performance goals.

In ASP.NET, built-in caching capabilities come through the *Cache* object. The *Cache* object is created on a per-*AppDomain* basis, and it remains valid while that *AppDomain* is up and running. The object is unique in its capability to automatically scavenge the memory and get rid of unused items. You can prioritize and associate cached items with various types of dependencies, such as disk files, other cached items, and database tables. When any of these items change, the cached item is automatically invalidated and removed. Aside from that, the *Cache* object provides the same familiar, dictionary-based programming interface as *Session*. Unlike Session, however, the *Cache* object does not store data on a per-user basis.

The bright side and dark side of the native *Cache* object

Using the *Cache* object in ASP.NET MVC is just the same as in ASP.NET Web Forms. You should be accessing the *Cache* object preferably from a controller class or from infrastructure classes such as global.asax, as shown here:

```
protected void Application_Start()
{
    var data = LoadFromSomeRepository();
    Cache[CacheEntries.CustomerRecords] = data;
    ...
}
```

To read from cache, you use the same pattern you just saw for session state, check for nullness, and cast to a known valid type, as demonstrated in the following:

```
var customerRecords = new CustomerRecords();
var data = Cache[CacheEntries.CustomerRecords];
if (data ! null)
        customerRecords = (CustomerRecords) data;
```

If cached data needs to be displayed in the view, you just add that data to the view-model class for the specific view. Alternatively, you define render actions on the controller class.

So far, so good. What's the dark side of caching in ASP.NET MVC?

As mentioned, the *Cache* object is limited to the current *AppDomain* and subsequently to the current process. This design was fairly good a decade ago, but it shows more and more limitations today. If you're looking for a global repository object that, similar to *Session*, works across a web farm or web garden architecture, the native *Cache* object is not for you. You must resort to Windows Server AppFabric Caching services or to some commercial frameworks (such as ScaleOut or NCache) or open-source frameworks (such as Memcached).

However, the issue is that the implementation of the *Cache* object is not based on the same popular provider model as session state. This means that you can't replace the cache data holder if you need to scale it up, not even for testing your controllers.

Injecting a caching service

The currently recommended approach for caching in ASP.NET MVC consists of injecting caching capabilities into the application. You define a contract for an abstract caching service and make your controllers work against this contract. Injection can happen the way you like, either through your favorite Inversion-of-Control (IoC) framework or via an ad hoc controller constructor. The latter is jokingly called "the poor-man's dependency injection approach."

The following code shows a minimal but functional example of how to abstract the caching layer:

```
public interface ICacheService
{
    Object Get(String key);
    void Set(String key, Object data);
    Object this[String key] { get; set; }
    ...
}
```

You are responsible for making this interface as rich and sophisticated as you need. For example, you might want to add members to support dependencies, expiration, and priorities. Just keep in mind that you are not writing the caching layer for the entire ASP.NET subsystem; you're simply writing a segment of your application. In this respect, the YAGNI principle (You Aren't Gonna Need It) holds true as never before.

Any controller class that needs caching will accept an *ICacheService* object through the constructor, as shown here:

```
private ICacheService _cacheService;
public HomeController(ICacheService cacheService)
{
    _cacheService = cacheService;
}
```

The next step consists of defining a few concrete implementations of the *ICacheService* interface. The concrete type simply uses a particular cache technology to store and retrieve data. Here's the skeleton of a class that implements the interface by using the native ASP.NET *Cache* object:

```
public class AspNetCacheService : ICacheService
{
    private readonly Cache _aspnetCache;
    public AspNetCacheService()
    {
        if (HttpContext.Current != null)
            _aspnetCache = HttpContext.Current.Cache;
    }
```

```
    public Object Get(String key)
    {
        return _aspnetCache[key];
    }

    public void Set(String key, Object data)
    {
        _aspnetCache[key] = data;
    }

    public object this[String name]
    {
        get { return _aspnetCache[name]; }
        set { _aspnetCache[name] = value; }
    }
    ...
}
```

Finally, let's complete the controller's code that uses this caching service so that the service can be properly injected:

```
public class HomeController
{
    private readonly ICacheService _cacheService;
    public HomeController() : this(new AspNetCacheService())
    {
    }
    public HomeController(ICacheService cacheService)
    {
        _cacheService = cacheService;
    }
    ...
}
```

In this way, your controller classes that need caching are not tightly bound to a specific implementation of a cache object and are, at a minimum, easier to test.

A better way of injecting a caching service

Injecting a cache service into a controller instance requires that a new cache service must be created for each request. Because the caching service is a plain wrapper around an existing and external cache data holder (for example, the ASP.NET *Cache* object or Windows Server AppFabric Caching Services), this is not going to have a great impact on the performance of the request. In fact, the cache data holder is initialized only once at application startup.

Can you manage things to save your application a few CPU cycles per request and expose a global cache object that is in turn based on a replaceable provider? You bet. Try adding the following code to global.asax:

```
public class MvcApplication : HttpApplication
{
    ...

    // Internal reference to the cache wrapper object
    private static ICacheService _internalCacheObject;

    // Public method used to inject a new caching service into the application.
    // This method is required to ensure full testability.
    public void RegisterCacheService(ICacheService cacheService)
    {
        _internalCacheObject = cacheService;
    }

    // Use this property to access the underlying cache object from within
    // controller methods. Use this instead of native Cache object.
    public static ICacheService CacheService
    {
        get { return _internalCacheObject; }
    }

    protected void Application_Start()
    {
        ...

        // Inject a global caching service
        RegisterCacheService(new AspNetCacheService());

        // Store some sample app-wide data
        CacheService["StartTime"] = DateTime.Now;
    }
}
```

In this way, you have no need to inject the actual caching service in the selected controller for each request. The caching service is initialized and injected once at application startup. Controllers use a public static method on the application object (as defined in global.asax) to access the cache.

```
var data = MvcApplication.CacheService[...]
```

The public method *RegisterCacheService* preserves testability. In any unit test for which you want to test a cache-aware controller, you place the following call in the preliminary phase of the unit test:

```
MvcApplication.RegisterCacheService(new FakeCacheService());
```

Next, you proceed calling the controller method which will transparently use the fake cache service.

Distributed caching

Easier testing is not the only benefit you gain by using a public contract for your cache-related tasks: By keeping your controllers aware of a cache interface—not a cache implementation—you keep them able to work with any object that provides caching services through the specified interface. In other words, you can replace the aforementioned *AspNetCacheService* class with another similar-looking class that relies on a different caching infrastructure.

For example, you can transparently plug in a cache service based on a distributed framework, such as Windows Server AppFabric Caching Services or another open-source or commercial framework. Nearly all of these frameworks expose a public API that is analogous to the basic ASP.NET *Cache* object, so there's not really much work that you need to do to set it up beyond configuration.

Nicely enough, if you're just not interested in distributed caching, you can still replace the ASP. NET native *Cache* object with the newest *MemoryCache* object introduced in the .NET Framework 4 for the precise purpose of giving caching capabilities to any .NET applications. For this reason, the class is defined outside the ASP.NET realm in a brand new assembly named *System.Runtime.Caching*. The *MemoryCache* object works like the ASP.NET *Cache* except that it throws an exception if you try to store null values. The *MemoryCache* class inherits from a base class, *ObjectCache*. By deriving your own cache object, you can take control of the internal storage and management of cached data. This is not a recommended approach for everybody, but it's definitely possible. Keep in mind, however, that *ObjectCache* and derived types are not designed to provide the behavior of a distributed cache. If you intend to create your own distributed cache, the hard work of maintaining multiple caches in synchronization is entirely up to you.

Caching the method response

The classic mechanism of ASP.NET output caching survived in ASP.NET MVC, too. It takes the form of the *OutputCache* attribute that you can attach to a controller method or to the controller class to affect all action methods.

```
[OutputCache(Duration=10, VaryByParam="None")]
public ActionResult Index()
{
    ...
}
```

The *Duration* parameter indicates how long (in seconds) the method's response should stay cached in memory. On the other hand, the *VaryByParam* attribute, indicates how many distinct versions of the response you should cache, one for each distinct value of the specified property. If you use *None*, you're informing the system that you don't want multiple versions of the same method's response.

Table 5-1 lists the properties supported by the attribute. They are a subset of the attributes of the *@OutputCache* directive of ASP.NET. Missing attributes are those limited to ASP.NET user controls.

TABLE 5-1 Properties of the *OutputCache* attribute

Attribute	Description
CacheProfile	Associates a response with a group of output-caching settings specified in the web.config file.
Duration	The amount of time (in seconds) for which the response is cached.
Location	Specifies the location (browser, proxy, or server) to store the response of the method call. The attribute takes its value from the *OutputCacheLocation* enumeration.
NoStore	Indicates whether to send a Cache-Control:no-store header to prevent browser-side storage of the response.
SqlDependency	Indicates a dependency on the specified table on a given Microsoft SQL Server database. Whenever the contents of the table changes, the response is removed from the cache.
VaryByContentEncoding	Content encoding by which you intend to differentiate cached responses.
VaryByCustom	A semicolon-separated list of strings with which you can maintain distinct cached copies of the response based on the browser type or user-defined strings.
VaryByHeader	A semicolon-separated list of HTTP headers.
VaryByParam	A semicolon-separated list of strings representing query string values sent with GET method attributes, or parameters sent by using the POST method.

These properties communicate the same output-caching infrastructure of the ASP.NET runtime and work exactly the same in ASP.NET Web Forms.

Note It should be pretty obvious, but let's state it clearly. Methods for which you set the *OutputCache* attribute are not executed for requests that hit the server when a valid cached response is available.

Partial output caching

Partial caching is not limited to the entire response of the method. You can also attach the *Output Cache* attribute to child actions. A child action is a method on the controller that the view can call back by using the *Html.RenderAction* helper. The *RenderAction* helper can invoke any method on the controller; however, some methods can be marked as exclusive child actions. You do this using the *ChildActionOnly* attribute, as demonstrated here:

```
[ChildActionOnly]
public ActionResult RenderSiteMap()
{
    ...
}
```

Such a method is clearly designed to render a small section of the view. It is logically equivalent to a user control in ASP.NET Web Forms. By decorating this method with the *OutputCache* attribute, you can cache the response for the specified duration.

Error handling

Because ASP.NET MVC works on top of the classic ASP.NET runtime environment, you can't expect to find a radically different infrastructure to handle run-time errors. This means that you can still opt for the classic ASP.NET strategy of mapping any 400 or 500 HTTP status codes to a specific URL that provides error information. Switching programmatically to a different page in cases of error requires an HTTP redirect. You control the mapping through the <customErrors> section of the web.config file.

As I see things, although functional, this approach is less than ideal in ASP.NET MVC, given that you can easily switch to an error interface by simply changing the name of the view template invoked by the controller.

Let's see what ASP.NET MVC has to offer when it comes to error handling. Overall, error handling in ASP.NET MVC spans two main areas: the handling of program exceptions, and route exceptions. The former is concerned with catching errors in controllers and views; the latter is more about redirection and HTTP errors.

Handling program exceptions

Most of the code you write in ASP.NET MVC applications resides in controller classes. In a controller class, you can deal with possible exceptions in a number of equivalent ways: handling exceptions directly via *try/catch* blocks, overriding the *OnException* method, and using the *HandleError* attribute.

Handling exceptions directly

In the first place, you can use local *try/catch* blocks to protect yourself against a possible exception in a specific section of the code. This is the approach that gives you maximum flexibility, but it does so at the cost of adding some noise to the code. I'm not one to question the importance of exception handling—which, by the way, is the official .NET approach to error handling—however, the presence of *try/catch* blocks makes reading code a bit harder. For this reason, I always welcome any alternative solution that aims to centralize exception-handling code to the extent it is legitimately possible.

To execute a piece of code with the certainty that any (or just some) exceptions it might raise will be caught, you use the following code:

```
try
{
    // Your regular code here
    ...
}
catch
{
    // Your recovery code for all exceptions
    ...
}
```

The preceding snippet catches any exceptions originated by the code in the *try* block. Because of its extreme generality, it doesn't put you in the position of implementing an effective recovery strategy. The sample code snippet can have a number of variations and extensions. For example, you can list multiple *catch* blocks, one per each significant exception. You can also add a *finally* block, which will finalize the operation and run regardless of whether the execution flow went through the *try* block or the *catch* block:

```
try
{
    // Your regular code here
    ...
}
catch(NullReferenceException nullReferenceException)
{
    // Your recovery code for the null reference exception
    ...
}
catch(ArgumentException argumentException)
{
    // Your recovery code for the argument exception
    ...
}
finally
{
    // Finalize here, but DON'T throw exceptions from here
    ...
}
```

Exceptions are listed from the most specific to the least specific. From a *catch* block, you are also allowed to consume the exception so that other top-level modules will never know about it. Alternatively, you can handle the situation gracefully and recover. Finally, you can do some work and then rethrow the same exception or arrange a new one with some extra or modified information in it.

When it comes to writing direct code for handling exceptions, you might want to keep a few guidelines in mind. First, the *catch* block is fairly expensive if your code gets into it. Therefore, you should use it judiciously—use it only when it's really needed and without overcatching.

 Note For a long time, Microsoft said you should derive your exception classes from *System. ApplicationException*. More recently, there's been a complete turnaround on this point: the new directive indicates the opposite. You should ignore *ApplicationException* and derive your exception classes from *Exception* or other, more specific, built-in classes. And, don't forget to make your exception classes serializable. For more background, refer to the following thread (and contained links) on StackOverflow at *http://stackoverflow.com/ questions/5685923/what-is-applicationexception-for-in-net*.

Furthermore, you should never throw an exception as an instance of the root *System.Exception* class. It is strictly recommended that you try to use built-in exception types such as *InvalidOperation Exception*, *NullReferenceException*, and *ArgumentNullException* whenever these types apply. You should resist the temptation of having your own exceptions all the way through, although for program errors you should consider defining your own exceptions. In general, you should be very specific with exceptions. *ArgumentNullException* is more specific than *ArgumentException*. An exception comes with a message, and the message must be targeted to developers and, ideally, localized.

> **Note** Another key guideline from Microsoft about exception handling is to use built-in types for general errors (for example, null reference, invalid argument, I/O or network exceptions) and create application-specific types for exceptions that are specific to the application you're creating.

Overriding the *OnException* method

As discussed in Chapter 1, "ASP.NET MVC controllers," the execution of each controller method is governed by a special system component known as the action invoker. An interesting aspect of the default action invoker is that it always executes controller methods within a *try/catch* block. Here's some pseudocode that illustrates the behavior of the default action invoker:

```
try
{
    // Try to invoke the action method
    ...
}
catch(ThreadAbortException)
{
    throw;
}
catch(Exception exception)
{
    // Prepare the context for the current action
    var filterContext = PrepareActionExecutedContext( ..., exception);

    // Go through the list of registered action filters, and give them a chance to recover
    ...

    // Re-throw if not completely handled
    if (!filterContext.ExceptionHandled)
    {
        throw;
    }
}
```

If an exception is thrown at some point during the method's execution or during the rendering of the view, the control passes to the code in the *catch* block, as long as the exception is not a *Thread AbortException*. Handling the exception entails looping through the list of registered action filters and giving each its own chance to fix things. At the end of the loop, if the exception has not been marked as handled, the caught exception is thrown again.

An action filter is a piece of code that can be registered to handle a few events fired during the execution of an action method. One of these system events is fired when the invoker intercepts an exception. (I cover action filters in detail in Chapter 8.) To have your own code added to the list of filters, the simplest thing you can do is override the *OnException* method on the controller class, as shown in the following:

```
protected override void OnException(ExceptionContext filterContext)
{
    ...
}
```

Defined in any of your controller classes (or in a base class of yours), this method is always invoked when an unhandled exception occurs in the course of the action method.

Note No exception will be caught by *OnException* that originates outside the realm of the controller, such as null references resulting from a failure in the model-binding layer or a not-found exception resulting from an invalid route. I'll tackle this aspect in a more specific way later in the chapter.

Overall, there's just one reason for you to override *OnException* in a controller class: you want to control the behavior of the system and degrade gracefully in the case of an exception. This means that the code in *OnException* is given the power of controlling the entire response for the request that just failed. The method receives a parameter of type *ExceptionContext*. This type comes with a *Result* property of type *ActionResult*. As you can guess, the property refers to the next view or action result. If the code in *OnException* omits setting any result, the user won't see any error screen (neither the system's nor that of the application); the user will see just a blank screen. Here's the typical way to implement *OnException*:

```
protected override void OnException(ExceptionContext filterContext)
{
    // Let other exceptions just go unhandled
    if (filterContext.Exception is InvalidOperationException)
    {
        // Default view is "error"
        filterContext.SwitchToErrorView();
    }
}
```

The *SwitchToErrorView* method is an extension method for the *ExceptionContext* class coded as shown here:

```
public static void SwitchToErrorView(this ExceptionContext context,
                                     String view = "error", String master = "")
{
    var controllerName = context.RouteData.Values["controller"] as String;
    var actionName = context.RouteData.Values["action"] as String;
    var model = new HandleErrorInfo(context.Exception, controllerName, actionName);
    var result = new ViewResult
                     {
                         ViewName = view,
                         MasterName = master,
                         ViewData = new ViewDataDictionary<HandleErrorInfo>(model),
                         TempData = context.Controller.TempData
                     };
    context.Result = result;

    // Configure the response object
    context.ExceptionHandled = true;
    context.HttpContext.Response.Clear();
    context.HttpContext.Response.StatusCode = 500;
    context.HttpContext.Response.TrySkipIisCustomErrors = true;
}
```

Altogether, this code provides an effective framework-level *try/catch* block that is not limited to catching the exception but switches to an error view. In the code just shown, the default error view is *error*, but you can change it at will as well as its layout.

Using the *HandleError* attribute

As an alternative to overriding the *OnException* method, you can decorate the class (or just individual methods) with the *HandleError* attribute or any custom class that derives from it.

```
[HandleError]
public class HomeController
{
    ...
}
```

Note that *HandleError* is a bit more than a simple attribute; it is an action filter. As such, it contains executable code and is not limited to providing meta-information to some other modules. In particular, *HandleError* implements the *IExceptionFilter* interface, as illustrated here:

```
public interface IExceptionFilter
{
    void OnException(ExceptionContext filterContext);
}
```

The interface is the same one that all controllers implement. However, on the base *Controller* class, *OnException* has just an empty body.

Internally, *HandleError* implements the *OnException* method by using a piece of code very similar to *SwitchToErrorView*. The only difference is in the conditions under which the change of view is operated. The *HandleError* attribute traps the specified exceptions only if they haven't been previously fully handled and are not resulting from child actions. To control the exceptions you want to handle, you do as follows:

```
[HandleError(ExceptionType=typeof(NullReferenceException), View="SyntaxError")]
```

Each method can have multiple occurrences of the attribute, one for each exception in which you're interested. The *View* and *Master* properties indicate the view to display after the exception. By default, *HandleError* switches to a view named error. (Such a view is purposely created by the Microsoft Visual Studio ASP.NET MVC standard template.)

Important For *HandleError* to produce any visible results in debug mode, you need to turn on custom errors at the application level, as shown here:

```
<customErrors mode="On">
</customErrors>
```

If you leave on the default settings for the <customErrors> section of the configuration file, only remote users will get the selected error page. Local users (for example, developers doing some debugging) will receive the classic error page with detailed information about the stack trace as produced by the normal ASP.NET exception handler.

Tip Even when everything is fully configured to display a custom error page, it can happen that Internet Explorer shows a built-in error page. This is due to a little known feature of Internet Explorer that has existed since 2006. In practice, if Internet Explorer detects that your error page has a body less than 512 bytes, it simply prefers to display a built-in page because—or so it believes—that this is likely nicer to see for the user! This isn't a big deal for realistic sites and pages, but during initial phases of development, it can easily be a source of headaches.

Just like any other action filter in ASP.NET MVC, you can automatically apply the *HandleError* attribute to any method of any controller class by registering it as a global filter. Incidentally, this is exactly what happens within the code generated by the Visual Studio tooling for ASP.NET MVC. Here's an excerpt from *Application_Start* in global.asax:

```
public class MvcApplication : System.Web.HttpApplication
{
    protected void Application_Start()
    {
        RegisterGlobalFilters(GlobalFilters.Filters);
        ...
    }
```

```
public static void RegisterGlobalFilters(GlobalFilterCollection filters)
{
    filters.Add(new HandleErrorAttribute());
}
}
```

A global filter is an action filter that the default action invoker automatically adds to the list of filters before it invokes any action method. I have more to say on global action filters in Chapter 8.

Global error handling

For the most part, *OnException* and the *HandleError* attribute provide controller-level control over error handling. This means that each controller which requires error handling must host some exception-handling code. More important than this, however, is that dealing with errors at the controller level doesn't ensure that you intercept all possible exceptions that might be raised around your application.

You can create a global error handler at the application level that catches all unhandled exceptions and routes them to the specified error view.

Global error handling from global.asax

Since the very first version of the ASP.NET runtime, the *HttpApplication* object—the object behind global.asax—has featured an *Error* event. The event is raised whenever an unhandled exception reaches the outermost shell of code in the application. Here's how to write such a handler:

```
void Application_Error(Object sender, EventArgs e)
{
    ...
}
```

You could do something useful in this event handler, such as sending an email to the site administrator or writing to the Microsoft Windows event log to report that the page failed to execute properly. Here's an example:

```
void Application_Error(Object sender, EventArgs e)
{
    var exception = Server.GetLastError();
    if (exception == null)
        return;

    var mail = new MailMessage { From = new MailAddress("automated@contoso.com") };
    mail.To.Add(new MailAddress("administrator@contoso.com"));
    mail.Subject = "Site Error at " + DateTime.Now;
    mail.Body = "Error Description: " + exception.Message;
    var server = new SmtpClient { Host = "your.smtp.server" };
    server.Send(mail);
```

```
    // Clear the error
    Server.ClearError();

    // Redirect to a landing page
    Response.Redirect("home/landing");
}
```

With the preceding code, the administrator will receive an email message (as shown in Figure 5-1), but the user will still receive a system error page. If you want to avoid that, after you manage the error you can redirect the user to a landing page. Finally, be aware that if the SMTP server requires authentication, you need to provide your credentials through the *Credentials* property of the *SmtpClient* class.

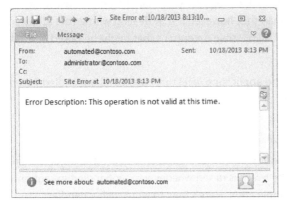

FIGURE 5-1 An email message to the site administrator.

Global error handling using an HTTP module

In ASP.NET, there's just one way to capture any fatal exceptions: writing a handler for the *Http Application* object *Error* event. However, you can do this in two ways. You can write code directly in the application's global.asax file, or you can plug a made-to-measure HTTP module to the web.config file. The HTTP module registers its own handler for the *Error* application event. The two solutions are functionally equivalent, but the one based on the HTTP module can be turned on and off and modified without recompiling the application. It is, in a way, less obtrusive.

When you consider a global error handler, you have a couple of ideas in mind: alerting the administrator about an exception, and logging the exception. Especially for the second task, an HTTP module seems like an easier-to-manage solution than having code in global.asax.

A tool that is very popular among ASP.NET developers is Error Logging Modules And Handlers (ELMAH). ELMAH is essentially made of an HTTP module that, once configured, intercepts the *Error* event at the application level and logs it according to the configuration of a number of back-end repositories. ELMAH comes out of an open-source project (*http://code.google.com/p/elmah*) and has a number of extensions, mostly in the area of repositories. ELMAH offers some nice facilities such as a webpage on which you can view all recorded exceptions and look more closely into each of them. Architecturally speaking, any error-reporting system specifically designed for ASP.NET can't be much different from ELMAH.

Intercepting model-binding exceptions

A centralized error handler is also good at catching exceptions that originate outside the controller, such as exceptions caused by incorrect parameters. If you declare a controller method with one, for instance, integer argument and the current binder can't match any posted value to it, you get an exception. Technically, the exception is not raised by the model binder itself; it is raised by an internal component of the action invoker while preparing the method call. If this component doesn't find a value for a non-optional method parameter, it just throws an exception.

This exception is not fired from within the controller code, but it still falls under the control of the overall *try/catch* block in the action invoker. Why doesn't a global (or local) *HandleError* do the trick of trapping the exception? It does, but only if you turn on the custom error flag in the web.config file. With the custom error flag turned off, your only chance to intercept a model-binding error is through the centralized error handler in global.asax. Figure 5-2 shows the page served gracefully to the user and the email message sent to the administrator.

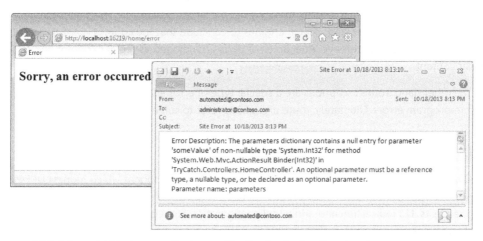

FIGURE 5-2 A model-binder exception trapped by the *Application_Error* handler.

Handling route exceptions

In addition to any detected program errors, your application might be throwing exceptions because the URL of the incoming request doesn't match any of the mapped routes—either because of an invalid URL pattern (an invalid action or controller name) or a violated constraint. In this case, your users receive an HTTP 404 error. Letting users receive the default 404 ASP.NET page is something you might want to avoid for a number of reasons, primarily to be friendlier to end users.

The typical solution enforced by the ASP.NET framework consists of defining custom pages (or routes in ASP.NET MVC) for common HTTP codes such as 404 and 403. Whenever the user types or follows an invalid URL, she is redirected to another page where some useful information (hopefully) is provided. Here's how to register ad hoc routes in ASP.NET MVC:

```
<customErrors mode="On">
    <error statusCode="404" redirect="/error/show" />
    ...
</customErrors>
```

This trick works just fine, and there's no reason to question it from a purely functional perspective. So, where's the problem, then?

The first problem is with security. By mapping HTTP errors to individualized views, hackers can distinguish between the different types of errors that can occur within an application and use this information for planning further attacks. Thus, you explicitly set the *defaultRedirect* attribute of the <customErrors> section to a given and fixed URL and ensure that no per-status codes are set.

A second issue with per-status code views has to do with SEO. Imagine a search engine requesting a URL that doesn't exist in an application that implements custom error routing. The application first issues an HTTP 302 code and informs the caller that the resource has been temporarily moved to another location. At this point, the caller makes another attempt and finally lands on the error page. This approach is great for humans, who ultimately get a pretty message; it is less than optimal from an SEO perspective because it leads search engines to conclude that the content is not missing at all, it's just harder than usual to retrieve. And, an error page is cataloged as regular content and related to similar content.

On the other hand, route exceptions are a special type of error and deserve a special strategy distinct from program errors. Ultimately, route exceptions refer to some missing content.

Dealing with missing content

The routing subsystem is the front end of your application and the door at which request URLs knock to get some content. In ASP.NET MVC, it is easy to treat requests for missing content in the same way as valid requests. No redirection and additional configuration are required if you create a dedicated controller that catches all requests that would go unhandled.

Catch-all route

A common practice to handle this situation consists of completing the route collection in global.asax with a catch-all route that traps any URLs sent to your application that haven't been captured by any of the existing routes.

```
public static void RegisterRoutes(RouteCollection routes)
{
    // Main routes
    ...
```

```
    // Catch-all route
    routes.MapRoute(
      "Catchall",
      "{*anything}",
      new { controller = "Error", action = "Missing" }
    );
}
```

Obviously, the catch-all rule needs to go at the very bottom of the routes list. This is necessary because routes are evaluated from top to bottom, and parsing stops at the first match found. The catch-all route maps the request to your application-specific *Error* controller. (You don't have an *Error* controller out of the box in ASP.NET MVC, but it is highly recommended that you create one on your own.) The *Error* controller, in turn, looks at content and headers and then decides which HTTP code to return. Here's an example of such an *Error* controller:

```
public class ErrorController : Controller
{
    public ActionResult Missing()
    {
        HttpContext.Response.StatusCode = 404;
        HttpContext.Response.TrySkipIisCustomErrors = true;

        // Log the error (if necessary)
        ...

        // Pass some optional information to the view
        var model = ErrorViewModel();
        model.Message = ...;
        ...

        // Render the view
        return View(model);
    }
}
```

The *ErrorViewModel* class in the example is any view-model class that you intend to use to pass data to the underlying view in a strongly typed manner. Using the ViewData dictionary is fine, as well, and overall it's an acceptable compromise in this specific and relatively simple context.

By using an error controller, you can improve the friendliness of the application and optimize it for search engines. In fact, you actually serve a pretty user interface to users while returning a direct (that is, not redirected) error code to any callers.

 Note A catch-all route is simply a route selected for a URL that didn't match any other routes. Many routes, however, are matched by the standard route, which overall is quite a generic catch-almost-all route. In other words, a URL such as /foo matches the default route and never reaches the catch-all route. Then, if it's missing a *Foo* controller, it results in a 404 error. To intercept 404 errors that occur because of an invalid controller name, you should override the controller factory. (Chapter 7 discusses this in more detail.)

Skipping IIS error-handling policies

In the preceding code snippet, the *Missing* method on the *ErrorController* class at some point sets to true the *TrySkipIisCustomErrors* property on the *Response* object. It is a property introduced with ASP.NET 3.5 that specifically addresses a feature of the IIS 7 integrated pipeline.

When an ASP.NET application (either Web Forms or ASP.NET MVC) runs under IIS 7 within an integrated pipeline, some of the ASP.NET configuration settings will be merged with the settings defined at the IIS level, as demonstrated in Figure 5-3.

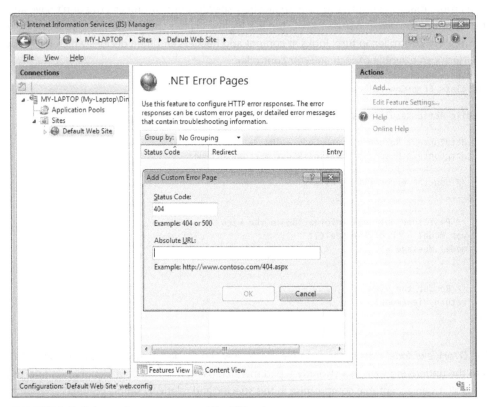

FIGURE 5-3 Defining custom error pages at the IIS level.

In particular, if error pages are defined in IIS for common HTTP status codes, in the default case these pages will take precedence over the ASP.NET-generated content. As a result, your application might trap an HTTP 404 error and serve a nice-looking ad hoc page to the user. Like it or not, your page never makes it to the end user because it is replaced by another page that might be set at the IIS level.

To ensure that the IIS error handling is always bypassed, you set the *TrySkipIisCustomErrors* property to *true*. The property is useful only for applications that run under IIS 7 in integrated pipeline mode. In integrated pipeline mode, the default value of the property is *false*. The implementation of the *HandleError* exception filter, for example, takes this aspect into careful consideration and sets the property to *true*.

Localization

The entire theme of localization is nothing new in the .NET Framework, and ASP.NET is no exception. You have had tools to write culture-specific pages since the very first version of ASP.NET. The beauty is that nothing has changed, so adding localization capabilities to ASP.NET MVC applications is neither more difficult nor different than in classic ASP.NET.

Considering localization from the perspective of an entire application with a not-so-short expectation of life, there are three aspects of it that need to be addressed: how to make (all) resources localizable, how to add support for a new culture, and how to use (or whether to use) databases as a storage place for localized information.

Using localizable resources

Resources are just user interface items that you might want to adapt to a specific culture. Resources span the entire application and are not limited to text to translate. I recommend forgetting about old-fashioned ASP.NET Web Forms practices and outlining your own resource management strategy specific to modern web applications. Such a strategy is based on two pillars: the organization of RESX resource files, and the granularity of the content.

What's the role of the RESX file?

A RESX file is ultimately an XML file that is compiled on the fly by the Visual Studio designer. As a developer, you have some control over the namespace and the access modifier of the class members. In other words, when you add a resource to the project, you can choose whether to make all of the properties public or internal (the default) and decide which namespace will group them. A public modifier is necessary if you're compiling resources in their own assembly.

Localizable text

Localizable text is the only type of resource that can still comfortably sit in a classic RESX file. From what I have learned on the battlefield, having a single global file to hold all localizable resources turns into a not-so-pleasant experience even for a moderately complex application.

One issue is the size of the file, which grows significantly; another issue, which is even more painful, is the possible concurrent editing that multiple developers might be doing on the same file with the subsequent need for a continuous merge. However, I encourage you not to overlook the naming issue. When you have hundreds of strings that cover the entire application scope, how do you name them? Many strings look the same or differ only in subtle points. Many strings are not entire strings with some sensible meaning; they often are bits and pieces of some text to be completed with dynamically generated content. Trust me: naming a few of them in the restricted context of only some pages is doable; handling hundreds of them for the entire application is really painful.

Overall, the best approach seems to be having multiple resource files. Ideally, you might want to consider one RESX per view. This is not necessarily leading to a proliferation of files: for a minimally complex view, an individual RESX files makes the process of localization far easier and manageable.

As for grouping of files, I'd recommend having a subfolder named after the controller that invokes the view. In more concrete terms, this means creating a Resources folder in your project that contains multiple RESX files distributed in a bunch of subfolders organized according to some criteria. It could be per logical functional area or, probably better, on a per-controller basis. A Shared subfolder might be good to gather resource files with content referenced from multiple views. Figure 5-4 shows a Resources folder that groups multiple files.

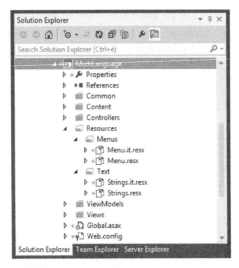

FIGURE 5-4 A custom Resources folder.

Any string you place in such RESX files is global and can be referenced from any view and controller class. Here's what you need in Razor:

```
@using MultiLanguage.Resources.Text;
...
<p>@Strings.OurServices</p
```

The preceding expression guarantees that either the language-neutral value or the localized value is retrieved and displayed. The resource manager will pick up the right assembly resource for the current culture.

All RESX files that use the default language are compiled to the same assembly as the application. This is the case for files whose name doesn't include a culture reference, such as errors.resx, strings. resx, menus.resx, and so forth. Culture-specific resources are compiled in separate assemblies, one per culture. You localize text to a culture by adding a new RESX file, named according to the pattern shown here:

```
filename.XX.resx
```

Here, the XX stands for the two-letter name of the culture; for example, it, fr, en, es, de, and so on. Those localized files are copies of the original (culture-neutral) file and just translate text into the language.

Tip I also suggest that you consider keeping even default resources in their own assembly. All you need to do is create a new class library project, drop the Resources folder in it (including localized versions), and reference the library from the main application.

In ASP.NET MVC, another effective way of organizing files within a project is to group all resources in the default Content folder. In my current project, I have Scripts, Styles, Images, and Text subfolders within Content. The Text subfolder contains RESX files, and RESX files are limited to strings.

Localizable files

In ASP.NET MVC, it is common to use the *Url.Content* method to reference content files such as images or style sheets. The major benefit of this method is that it transparently converts a relative path to an absolute path. More specific, the method understands the tilde (~) operator. When used in a URL, the tilde operator indicates the root path regardless of what it is and regardless of whether your application is deployed as a root application or a subapplication. For this reason, I always recommend you reference external files through *Url.Content*.

Wouldn't it be great if this method could handle localization, too? You request the path for, say, welcome.jpg and you get back welcome.it.jpg if the current culture is IT (the country, not the department...). The method itself can't be altered; but, as is illustrated here, writing an extension method that extends the *Url.Content* syntax is easy:

```
public static class UrlExtensions
{
    public static String Content(this UrlHelper helper,
                            String contentPath, Boolean localizable=false)
    {
        var url = contentPath;
        if (localizable)
            url = GetLocalizedUrl(helper, url);
        return helper.Content(url);
    }

    public static String GetLocalizedUrl(UrlHelper helper, String resourceUrl)
    {
        var cultureExt = String.Format("{0}{1}",
            Thread.CurrentThread.CurrentUICulture.TwoLetterISOLanguageName,
            Path.GetExtension(resourceUrl));
        var url = Path.ChangeExtension(resourceUrl, cultureExt);

        // Check if localized URL exists, and return file.XX.jpg (or whatever)
        return VirtualFileExists(helper, url) ? url : resourceUrl;
    }

    public static Boolean VirtualFileExists(UrlHelper helper, String url)
    {
        var fullVirtualPath = helper.Content(url);
        var physicalPath = helper.RequestContext.HttpContext.Server.MapPath(fullVirtualPath);
        return File.Exists(physicalPath);
    }
}
```

Basically, the new *Content* method is a thin wrapper around *Url.Content*. The method checks whether a localized resource exists. If one does exist, the method returns the localized URL; otherwise, it returns the original URL. Here's an example of how to use the method:

```
@using BookSamples.Components.Localization;
...
<link href="@Url.Content("~/content/site.css", localizable:true)" rel="stylesheet" type="text/css" />
```

Keep in mind that the type of the resource you reference (image, style sheet, or script) is not relevant; the *Content* method just processes URLs and changes the extension if conditions apply.

Referencing embedded files

When you embed a file (a script, CSS, or image) in the resource section of an assembly, you need to do some extra work to retrieve it. On the up side, however, you don't need to deploy the files separately; deploying the assembly is all you need to do.

There are two ways of embedding a resource in an assembly. You can add the resource file to a RESX file. You open up the RESX file, and use the interface of the designer to pick up an existing image or create a new one. The image is stored as a bitmap object in the resources of the assembly. You can retrieve this information by using the *ResourceManager* class or the *GetGlobalResourceObject* method on the *HttpContext* class. (The latter only works if the RESX files is placed in the old-fashioned App_GlobalResources folder.) In both cases, you can't transform the content in the assembly into a URL that you can attach to an HTML tag. One possibility is to create an ad hoc controller method like the one shown here:

```
public Object Image(String name)
{
    var bits = (Bitmap) HttpContext.GetGlobalResourceObject("AllResources", name);
    Response.ContentType = "image/jpeg";
    bits.Save(Response.OutputStream, ImageFormat.Jpeg);
    return bits;
}
```

The <img> tag looks like this:

```
<img alt="" src="/home/image?name=trees" />
```

A better approach consists of adding the resource to the assembly as an individual embedded resource. Figure 5-5 shows how to do it with a JPEG image. You add the image to your project and then change the build action to *Embedded Resource*.

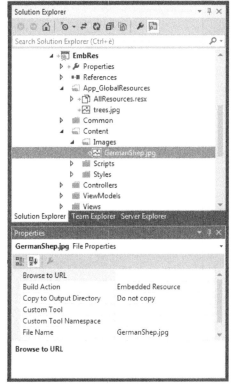

FIGURE 5-5 Adding an image as an embedded resource.

Next, and more important, you decorate your assembly as one that contains embedded resources. In the Properties project folder, in the AssemblyInfo file, add the following:

```
[assembly: WebResource("EmbRes.Content.Images.GermanShep.jpg", "image/jpg")]
```

The path is just the fully qualified name of the resource. To retrieve the resource, here's all you need to do in Razor:

```
@{
    var p = new Page();
    var url = p.ClientScript.GetWebResourceUrl(typeof(MvcApplication),
                                    "EmbRes.Content.GermanShep.jpg");
}
...
<img alt="" src="@url" />
```

Another tricky point to consider is the first argument of *GetWebResourceUrl*. Setting it to the application's type works just fine. Figure 5-6 shows the image displayed.

FIGURE 5-6 Displaying an image from embedded resources.

Localizable views

Views are another part of the application that might need to be adapted to the current locale. In ASP. NET MVC, you call out the view from within an action method. In addition, each view invoked from the controller can include partial views that might need to be localized, as well. This means that you need to add localization capabilities at two levels, using the action method and the extension methods commonly used to link partial views.

The best way to add localization logic to action methods is through an action filter. In the end, all you need to do is determine the name of the view algorithmically and call it. An action filter keeps the code clean and moves localization logic elsewhere, where it can be managed separately. You can read more about this particular action filter in Chapter 8. For now, let's focus on HTML extensions to invoke localized partial views.

In ASP.NET MVC, you use *Html.RenderPartial* when you just want to render a view; you use *Html.Partial* when you want to get back the HTML markup and write it yourself to the stream. Adding localization logic here is nearly the same process as we used earlier for resource files. Here's a new HTML extension method that extends *Partial*:

```
public static class PartialExtensions
{
    public static MvcHtmlString Partial(this HtmlHelper htmlHelper,
            String partialViewName, Object model, ViewDataDictionary viewData,
            Boolean localizable = false)
    {
        // Attempt to get a localized view name
        var viewName = partialViewName;
        if (localizable)
            viewName = GetLocalizedViewName(htmlHelper, viewName);

        // Call the system Partial method
        return System.Web.Mvc.Html.PartialExtensions.Partial(htmlHelper, viewName, model,
                                                    viewData);
    }

    public static MvcHtmlString Partial(this HtmlHelper htmlHelper, String partialViewName,
                                Boolean localizable=false)
    {
        // Attempt to get a localized view name
        var viewName = partialViewName;
        if (localizable)
            viewName = GetLocalizedViewName(htmlHelper, viewName);

        // Call the system Partial method
        return htmlHelper.Partial(viewName, null, htmlHelper.ViewData);
    }

    public static String GetLocalizedViewName(HtmlHelper htmlHelper, String partialViewName)
    {
        var urlHelper = new UrlHelper(htmlHelper.ViewContext.RequestContext);
        return UrlExtensions.GetLocalizedUrl(urlHelper, partialViewName);
    }
}
```

The structure of the code is quite intuitive. The new method checks whether a localized view exists according to the established convention. If one does exist, the method proceeds and calls the original *Partial* method with the localized name; otherwise, everything proceeds as usual. The extra step can be controlled through the localizable Boolean parameter:

```
@using BookSamples.Components.Localization;
...
@Html.Partial("_aboutdetails", localizable:true)
```

The code for *RenderPartial* is nearly identical, and you can find it in the source code download.

Dealing with localizable applications

So far, you've seen what you can do to deal with individual resources that must be localized. However, localizing an application requires more than just localizing a collection of single resources. In particular, you should have a clear idea of what you intend to accomplish by localizing an application. Do you want your application to support multiple languages but to configure each language at setup time? Or, do you want the user to be able to switch between a few predefined languages? Or, finally, is an auto-adapting application what you want to have? Let's examine the three scenarios.

Auto-adapting applications

An auto-adapting application is an application that in some way decides the culture to use based on user-provided information. Such an application supports a number of predefined cultures, and it falls back to the neutral culture when the detected locale doesn't match any of the supported cultures. The neutral culture is just the native default language of the application. Neutral resources are those that don't have any culture ID in the name.

The most characteristic aspect of an auto-adapting application is how the application determines the culture to use. This is commonly done in a couple of ways. The most common approach entails having the application read the list of accepted languages that the browser sends with each request. Another approach is based on geolocalization, where the server-side part of the application in some way gets the current location of the user (the IP address or just the client-side geolocalization) and chooses the culture accordingly. The first approach is gently offered by the ASP.NET runtime; the second approach requires some extra work on your part and likely uses some extra framework. Let's examine the first approach.

In ASP.NET, you use the *Culture* and *UICulture* properties to get and set the current culture. You do that on a per-request basis—for example, from within the constructor of each controller class or in the constructor of some base controller class. The property *Culture* governs all application-wide settings, such as dates, currency, and numbers. The property *UICulture* governs the language being used to load resources. These string properties are publicly available from the view classes in both the ASPX and Razor view engines.

Be aware that the two properties default to the empty string, which means that the default culture is the culture set on the web server. If culture properties are set to auto, the first preferred language sent by the browser through the Accept-Languages request header is picked up. To make your views automatically localized (if resources for that culture are available), you must add the following line to the web.config file:

```
<system.web>
   ...
   <globalization culture="auto" uiCulture="auto" />
</system.web>
```

That's all you need to do (in addition to using localized resources) to get an auto-adapting localized application up and running.

Multilingual applications

Another possible scenario is when you have a multilingual application that is deployed with multiple localized assemblies but is configured to use only one set of resources. Also, in this case you don't need to write ad hoc code anywhere; all you need to do is write the correct information in the globalization section of the web.config file:

```
<system.web>
   ...
  <globalization culture="it" uiCulture="it" />
</system.web>
```

In addition, of course, you need to have culture-specific resources available so that they can be invoked automatically by the ASP.NET framework.

Changing culture programmatically

Most of the time, though, what you really want is the ability to set the culture programmatically and the ability to change it on the fly as the user switches to a different culture by clicking an icon or using a culture-specific URL.

To change the culture programmatically as you go, you need to satisfy two key requirements. First, define the policies you'll be using to retrieve the culture to set. The policy can be a value you read from some database table or perhaps from the ASP.NET cache. It can also be a value you retrieve from the URL. Finally, it can even be a parameter you get via geolocation—that is, by looking at the IP address by which the user is connecting. In any case, at some point you know the magic string that identifies the culture to set. How do you apply that?

The following code shows what you need to instruct the ASP.NET runtime about the culture to use:

```
var culture = "...";    // i.e., it-IT
var cultureInfo = CultureInfo.CreateSpecificCulture(culture);
Thread.CurrentThread.CurrentCulture = cultureInfo;
Thread.CurrentThread.CurrentUICulture = cultureInfo;
```

You pick up the ASP.NET current thread and set the *CurrentCulture* and *CurrentUICulture* properties. Note that the two culture properties might or might not have the same value. For example, you can switch the language of text and messages according to the browser's configuration while leaving globalization settings (such as dates and currency) constant.

The culture must be set for each request because each request runs on its own thread. In ASP.NET MVC, you can achieve this in a number of ways. For example, you can embed the preceding code in a base controller class. This forces you to derive any controllers from a given base class. If you find this unacceptable, or you just prefer to take another route, you can go for a custom action invoker or a global action filter. (Chapter 8 looks at invokers and action filters in more detail.) In both cases, you write the code once and attach it to all controllers in a single step. The following is what it takes to use a global filter for localization:

```
[AttributeUsage(AttributeTargets.Class|AttributeTargets.Method, AllowMultiple=false,
Inherited=true)]
public class CultureAttribute : ActionFilterAttribute
{
    private const String CookieLangEntry = "lang";

    public String Name { get; set; }
    public static String CookieName
    {
        get { return "_LangPref"; }
    }

    public override void OnActionExecuting(ActionExecutingContext filterContext)
    {
        var culture = Name;
        if (String.IsNullOrEmpty(culture))
            culture = GetSavedCultureOrDefault(filterContext.RequestContext.HttpContext.
                                               Request);

        // Set culture on current thread
        SetCultureOnThread(culture);

        // Proceed as usual
        base.OnActionExecuting(filterContext);
    }

    public static void SavePreferredCulture(HttpResponseBase response, String language,
                                            Int32 expireDays=1)
    {
        var cookie = new HttpCookie(CookieName) { Expires = DateTime.Now.AddDays(expireDays) };
        cookie.Values[CookieLangEntry] = language;
        response.Cookies.Add(cookie);
    }

    public static String GetSavedCultureOrDefault(HttpRequestBase httpRequestBase)
    {
        var culture = "";
        var cookie = httpRequestBase.Cookies[CookieName];
        if (cookie != null)
            culture = cookie.Values[CookieLangEntry];
        return culture;
    }

    private static void SetCultureOnThread(String language)
    {
        var cultureInfo = CultureInfo.CreateSpecificCulture(language);
        Thread.CurrentThread.CurrentCulture = cultureInfo;
        Thread.CurrentThread.CurrentUICulture = cultureInfo;
    }
}
```

The *CultureAttribute* class offers public static methods to read and write a specific culture string to a custom cookie. The filter overwrites the *OnActionExecuting* method, meaning that it might kick in before any controller method runs. For this to happen, though, the filter must be registered as a global filter. In the implementation of *OnActionExecuting*, the filter reads the user's preferred culture that was previously stored to a cookie and sets it to the current request thread.

The following code shows how to register the filter as a global filter that applies to all controller methods within the application:

```
public class MvcApplication : HttpApplication
{
    public static void RegisterGlobalFilters(GlobalFilterCollection filters)
    {
        filters.Add(new HandleErrorAttribute());
        filters.Add(new CultureAttribute());
    }
    ...
}
```

With this infrastructure in place, you can add links to your pages (typically, the master page) to switch languages on the fly:

```
@Html.ActionLink(Menu.Lang_IT, "Set", "Language", new { lang = "it" }, null)
@Html.ActionLink(Menu.Lang_EN, "Set", "Language", new { lang = "en" }, null)
```

To follow the actions just shown, you need an action method. I prefer to isolate this code to a specific controller, such as the *LanguageController* class shown here:

```
public class LanguageController : Controller
{
    public void Set(String lang)
    {
        // Set culture to use next
        CultureAttribute.SavePreferredCulture(HttpContext.Response, lang);

        // Return to the calling URL (or go to the site's home page)
        HttpContext.Response.Redirect(HttpContext.Request.UrlReferrer.AbsolutePath);
    }
}
```

The action method simply stores the newly selected language in the store you selected—a custom cookie in the example—and redirects. Figure 5-9 shows a sample page whose content can be displayed in multiple languages.

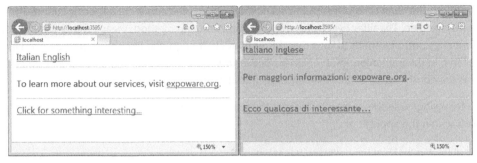

FIGURE 5-7 An application in which users can switch languages on the fly.

You can apply this approach regardless of the technique you use to determine the desired language, whether by choice, IP address, or geolocation.

Note More and more websites check the location from which a user is connected and suggest a language and a culture. This feature requires an API that looks up the IP address and maps that to a country and then a culture.

Storing localized resources in a database

While discussing localization, it seems inevitable that you have to talk about databases as a possible store for localized data. Is this an option? You bet. However, there are some pros and cons to consider.

In the first place, using a database adds latency even though you don't make a database call for each segment of a view to be localized. Instead, most likely you'll read a bunch of records and probably cache them for a long time. The performance hit represented by using the database in this way is therefore less devastating than one might think at first.

Storing localization data within a database requires a custom localization layer, whereas going through the classic XML-based approach of resource files doesn't lead you to writing much extra code and offers you excellent support from the Visual Studio designers.

When the number of views becomes significant (for example, in the hundreds), the number of resource items will be at least in the thousands. At this point, managing them can be problematic. You can have too many assemblies loaded in the *AppDomain* consuming run-time memory, and that will have an impact on the overall performance of the site. Hence, a database is probably the best way to go for a large share of localizable content.

Data stored within a relational database is easier to manage, query, and cache, and the size is not an issue. In addition, with a database and a custom localization layer, you gain more flexibility in the overall retrieval process of local resources. In fact, you can ask the layer for a group of strings—or, better yet, for raw data—to then be formatted for the needs of the UI. In other words, a custom localization layer decouples you from maintaining a direct binding between a resource item and specific pieces of the user interface.

Getting localized data from a service

Yet another option made popular by mobile applications is getting data from a localization service. The service can be owned by the same team that arranged the site or it can even be some third-party service. More important, this approach makes it possible for you to add new languages with a minimal effort but also improve the quality of translated text over time and without redeploying anything new.

 Note The external service–based approach and the approach that uses a local database can be encapsulated in an ASP.NET resource provider—a class using the *IResourceProvider* interface.

Summary

An application built with ASP.NET MVC is primarily a web application. Modern web applications have more numerous requirements than only a few years ago. For example, a web application today must be SEO-friendly and very likely must support full localization to be able to drive the user's actions by employing the user's specific language and culture. Finally, serving a notorious yellow-screen-of-death (namely, one of those default error pages of ASP.NET) is hardly acceptable; it still happens, but it is really a bad statement about the site. (An unhandled error has always been a bad thing, but the level of forgiveness that users were willing to give only a few years ago is definitely a thing of the past.)

For all these reasons, the infrastructure of any web application (and, in this context, the infrastructure of ASP.NET MVC applications) needs to be stronger and richer. In particular, you need to pay more attention to the URLs you recognize and design both for SEO and error handling. You need to design views and controllers to check the current locale and adjust graphics and messages automatically. You also need to detect the culture and let users switch among the languages that you support.

This chapter offered a detailed overview of how to proceed. In Chapter 6, "Securing your application," we discuss safeguarding an ASP.NET MVC application.

Securing your application

It does not matter how slowly you go, so long as you do not stop.

—Confucius

Security means a variety of things to users and developers. In a web context, security is related to preventing injection of malicious code in the running application. Likewise, security relates to actions aimed at preventing disclosure of private data. Finally, security relates to building applications (and sections of an application) that only authenticated and authorized users can access.

The aspect of security that application developers deal with more frequently is certainly the authentication and authorization of users. Recently, more and more websites started implementing authentication also via popular social providers. Although not ideal for just any applications, and even though it is sometimes ineffective if used as the sole form of membership, social authentication is going to be more and more popular. As you'll see later in the chapter, ASP.NET MVC provides facilities for integrating authentication and authorization via social-oriented apps in websites.

Security in ASP.NET MVC

ASP.NET provides a range of authentication and authorization mechanisms implemented in conjunction with Internet Information Services (IIS), the Microsoft .NET Framework, and the underlying security services of the operating system. If IIS and the ASP.NET application are working in integrated mode—the most common scenario these days with IIS 7 and newer versions—the request goes through a single pipeline that includes an authentication step and an optional authorization step. If IIS and ASP.NET are running their own process, some requests might be authenticated or authorized at the gate by IIS, whereas others (for example, requests for ASPX pages) are handed over to ASP.NET along with the IIS security token of the authenticated, or anonymous, user.

Originally, ASP.NET supported three types of authentication methods: Windows, Passport, and Forms. A fourth possibility is *None*, meaning that ASP.NET does not even attempt to perform its own authentication and completely relies on the authentication already carried out by IIS. In this case, anonymous users can connect, and resources are accessed by using the default ASP.NET account. Although Passport authentication is now obsolete and no longer used, some of its inspiring principles and purposes are revived and better served by emerging security standards such as OAuth and OpenID—protocols behind social network authentication.

Authentication and authorization

Windows authentication is seldom practical for real-world Internet applications. Windows authentication is based on Microsoft Windows accounts and NTFS ACL tokens and, as such, assumes that clients are connecting from devices running Windows. Although this is useful and effective in intranet scenarios and possibly in some extranet scenarios, Windows authentication is simply unrealistic in more common situations because web-application users are required to have Windows accounts in the application's domain.

Forms authentication is the most commonly used way to collect and validate user credentials; for example, against a database of user accounts.

Configuring authentication in ASP.NET MVC

In ASP.NET MVC as well as in Web Forms, you choose the authentication mechanism by using the <authentication> section in the root web.config file. Child subdirectories inherit the authentication mode chosen for the application. By default, ASP.NET MVC applications are configured to use Forms authentication. The following code snippet shows an excerpt from the auto-generated web.config file in ASP.NET MVC (I just edited the logon URL):

```
<authentication mode="Forms">
    <forms loginUrl="~/Auth/LogOn" timeout="2880" />
</authentication>
```

Configured in this way, the application redirects the user to the specified logon URL every time the user attempts to access a URL reserved to authenticated users. But, how would you mark an ASP.NET MVC URL (for example, a controller method) to require authentication?

Restricting access to action methods

You use the *Authorize* attribute when you want to restrict access to an action method and ensure that only authenticated users can execute it. Here's an example:

```
[Authorize]
public ActionResult Index()
{
    ...
}
```

If you add the *Authorize* attribute to the controller class, any action methods on the controller will be subject to authentication.

```
[Authorize]
public class HomeController
{
    public ActionResult Index()
    {
        ...
    }

    ...
}
```

The *Authorize* attribute is inheritable. This means that you can add it to a base controller class of yours and ensure that any methods of any derived controllers are subject to authentication. You should never use the *Authorize* attribute as a global filter. In fact, the following code would restrict access to any resource, including the logon page:

```
public class MvcApplication : System.Web.HttpApplication
{
    public static void RegisterGlobalFilters(GlobalFilterCollection filters)
    {
        // Don't do this!
        filters.Add(new AuthorizeAttribute());
        ...
    }
}
```

Allowing anonymous callers

ASP.NET MVC supplies another security-related attribute: the *AllowAnonymous* attribute. When applied to a method, it instructs the ASP.MVC runtime to let it pass if the caller is not authenticated. The scenario when the *AllowAnonymous* method comes in handy is when you apply *Authorize* at the class level and then need to enable free access to some methods, logon methods in particular.

Handling authorization for action methods

The *Authorize* attribute is not limited to authentication; it also supports a basic form of authorization. Any methods marked with the attribute can be executed only by an authenticated user. In addition, you can restrict access to a specific set of authenticated users with a given role. You achieve this by adding a couple of named parameters to the attribute, as shown here:

```
[Authorize(Roles="admin", Users="DinoE, FrancescoE")]
public ActionResult Index()
{
    ...
}
```

If a user is not authenticated or doesn't have the required user name and role, the attribute prevents access to the method and the user is redirected to the logon URL. In the example just shown, only users DinoE or FrancescoE can have access to the method (if they are in the role of Admin). Note that *Roles* and *Users*, if specified, are combined in a logical AND operation.

Authorization and output caching

What if a method that requires authentication and/or authorization is also configured to support output caching? Output caching—specifically, the *OutputCache* attribute—instructs ASP.NET MVC to not really process the request every time but return any cached response that was previously calculated and that is still valid (that is, not expired). With output caching turned on, it can happen that a user requests a protected URL already in the cache. What should be the behavior?

ASP.NET MVC ensures that the *Authorize* attribute takes precedence over output caching. In particular, the output caching layer returns any cached response for a method subject to *Authorize* only if the user is authenticated and authorized.

Hiding critical user interface elements

You might also want to prevent users from accessing restricted resources by simply disabling or hiding action links and buttons that might trigger restricted action methods. By checking the authentication state of the current user and any assigned role, you can just turn off the visibility flag of critical input elements if users don't have appropriate privileges.

I like this approach, but I would never implement it as the only solution to handle roles and permissions. In the end, hiding user interface (UI) elements (which is more effective and simpler than disabling them) is fine as long as you still restrict access to action methods also by using programmatic checks.

Separating authentication from authorization

Until the advent of ASP.NET MVC 5, the *Authorize* attribute was the only security-related action filter supported by ASP.NET MVC. It can handle authentication and authorization, but it sometimes misses some details.

To make execution of the method possible, the *Authorize* attribute requires first and foremost that the user be authenticated. Next, if *Users*, *Roles*, or both are specified, it checks whether the user is also authorized (by name and role) to access the method. The effect of this is that the attribute doesn't ultimately distinguish between users who are not logged on and and those who are but who do not have the rights to invoke a given action method. In both cases, in fact, the attempt to call the action method redirects the user to the logon page.

In ASP.NET MVC 5, authentication filters have been added to give you a chance to intervene and take control of the workflow when authentication fails. However, before digging out authentication filters, let's first have a look at how you can improve the *Authorize* attribute to distinguish between anonymous users and unauthorized users.

Anonymous or not authorized?

Let's create an enhanced attribute class that extends the built-in *Authorize* attribute, as shown here:

```
public class AuthorizedOnlyAttribute : AuthorizeAttribute
{
    public AuthorizedOnlyAttribute()
    {
        View = "error";
        Master = String.Empty;
    }

    public String View { get; set; }
    public String Master { get; set; }

    public override void OnAuthorization(AuthorizationContext filterContext)
    {
        base.OnAuthorization(filterContext);
        CheckIfUserIsAuthenticated(filterContext);
    }

    private void CheckIfUserIsAuthenticated(AuthorizationContext filterContext)
    {
        // If Result is null, we're OK: the user is authenticated and authorized.
        if (filterContext.Result == null)
            return;

        // If here, you're getting an HTTP 401 status code
        if (filterContext.HttpContext.User.Identity.IsAuthenticated)
        {
            if (String.IsNullOrEmpty(View))
                return;
            var result = new ViewResult {ViewName = View, MasterName = Master};
            filterContext.Result = result;
        }
    }
}
```

In the new class, you override the *OnAuthorization* method and run some extra code to check whether you're getting an HTTP 401 message. If this is the case, you then check whether the current user is authenticated and redirect to your own error page (if any). You have *View* and *Master* properties to configure the target error view with instructions for the user.

The net effect is that if you're getting an HTTP 401 error because the user is not logged on, you'll go to the logon page. Otherwise, if the request failed because of authorization permissions, the user receives a friendly error page. Using the new attribute couldn't be easier, as is demonstrated here:

```
[AuthorizedOnly(Roles="admin", Users="DinoE")]
public ActionResult Index()
{
    ...
}
```

In terms of effectiveness, the presented solution just works, but from a design perspective, it's probably less than ideal.

Authentication filters

In ASP.NET MVC 5, an authentication filter is any class that implements the *IAuthenticationFilter* interface, such as shown here:

```
public interface IAuthenticationFilter
{
    void OnAuthentication(AuthenticationContext filterContext);
    void OnAuthenticationChallenge(AuthenticationChallengeContext filterContext);
}
```

The only class in the framework that natively implements the interface is the *Controller* class. Internally, authentication filters are the very first set of filters that are invoked on an incoming request. The method *OnAuthentication* takes care of the actual authentication logic and decides whether authentication should really take place. You perform here any action that is preliminary to the challenge through which the user enters credentials or additional information. The *OnAuthenticationChallenge* method is where you redirect the user to a logon page or any additional page after authentication has occurred. A common scenario is redirecting the user to a page where she can enter an email address following, for example, an OAuth authentication via Facebook, LinkedIn, or Twitter.

It is important to notice that you don't need to write authentication filters in order to direct users to a logon page; authentication filters don't change the way you write security in your applications. Authentication filters might only come in handy if you need to customize the default processing of authentication and authorization. For example, you can create an authentication filter to decide on the fly whether the request needs be authenticated based on run-time conditions such as parameters in the URL.

```
[AttributeUsage(AttributeTargets.Class | AttributeTargets.Method, Inherited = true)]
public class OptionalAuthenticationAttribute : FilterAttribute, IAuthenticationFilter
{
    public void OnAuthentication(AuthenticationContext filterContext)
    {
        var page = filterContext.ActionDescriptor.ActionName;
        if (CheckYourRuntimeCondition())
        {
            filterContext.Result = new HttpUnauthorizedResult();
            return;
        }
        else
        {
        }
    }

    public void OnAuthenticationChallenge(AuthenticationChallengeContext filterContext)
    {
    }
}
```

Instead, you can use the *OnAuthenticationChallenge* to redirect the user to another page where she can provide additional data or pass another level of security check.

A quick look at Windows authentication

Although Forms authentication is by far the most common authentication mechanism for ASP. NET applications, there are some scenarios in which you want to opt for Windows authentication. Typically, you use the Windows authentication method in intranet scenarios when the users of your application also have Windows accounts that can be authenticated by the web server.

When using Windows authentication, ASP.NET works in conjunction with IIS. The real authentication is performed by IIS, which uses one of its two authentication methods: Basic or Integrated Windows. After IIS has authenticated the user, it passes the security token on to ASP.NET. When configured to operate in Windows authentication mode, ASP.NET does not perform any further authentication steps and just uses the IIS token to authorize access to the resources.

For example, let's assume that you configured the web server to work with the Integrated Windows authentication mode and that you turned off anonymous access. What happens when a user connects to the ASP.NET application? If the account of the local user doesn't match any accounts on the web server or in the trusted domain, IIS displays a dialog box asking the user to enter valid credentials. Next, if credentials are determined to be valid, IIS generates a security token and hands it over to ASP.NET.

Implementing a membership system

To authenticate a user, you need some sort of a membership system that supplies methods to manage the account of any users. Building a membership system means writing the software and the UI to create a new user and update or delete existing users. It also means writing the software for editing any information associated with a user, such as the user's email address, password, and roles.

How do you create a user? Typically, you add a new record to some data store. Each data store can have its own set of properties, but core tasks are common and to a large extent abstracted by the ASP.NET native membership API. In ASP.NET MVC, you build a membership system integrating the ASP.NET membership API with one or two specific account controllers. A bunch of views and view model classes complete the infrastructure.

 Note The Microsoft Visual Studio tooling for ASP.NET MVC generates a sample application with full support for authentication and authorization. Although it's fully functional, the sample code you get is not exactly a paragon of software virtue. In any of my own significant applications, I just wipe out all the autogenerated files and start from scratch, taking the approach described next.

Defining a membership controller

At a minimum, you need to have a controller that knows how to log users on and off. The following sample *AuthController* class shows a possible way of getting one. The following code reworks the sample *AccountController* class created by the Visual Studio tooling for ASP.NET MVC:

```
public class AuthController : Controller
{
    [HttpGet]
    public ActionResult Logon()
    {
        // Just displays the login view
        return View();
    }

    [HttpPost]
    public ActionResult Logon(LogonViewModel model, String returnUrl)
    {
        // Gets posted credentials and proceeds with
        // actual validation
        ...
    }

    public ActionResult Logoff(String defaultAction="Index", String defaultController="Home")
    {
        // Logs out and redirects to the home page
        FormsAuthentication.SignOut();
        return RedirectToAction(defaultAction, defaultController);
    }
}
```

The *Logon* method must be split in two: one overload to simply display the logon view, and one to handle posted credentials and proceed with the actual validation. The *Logoff* method signs out of the application and redirects to the specified page—typically, the application's home page. To sign out, you use the native forms authentication services of ASP.NET. To top it off, you can also consider adding the following overload for *Logoff*:

```
public ActionResult Logoff (String defaultRoute)
{
    FormsAuthentication.SignOut();
    return RedirectToRoute(defaultRoute);
}
```

The method accepts a route name instead of a controller/action pair to identify the return URL.

Validating user credentials

Figure 6-1 shows a canonical UI for a logon view. It contains two text boxes: one for the user name and password, and a check box in case the user wants to be remembered on the site.

FIGURE 6-1 A canonical logon view.

Here's a possible implementation for the controller method that handles data posted from this form:

```
[HttpPost]
public ActionResult LogOn(LogonViewModel model, String returnUrl,
                    String defaultAction="Index", String defaultController="Home")
{
    var isValidReturnUrl = IsValidReturnUrl(returnUrl);
    if (!ModelState.IsValid)
    {
        ModelState.AddModelError("", "The user name or password provided is incorrect.");
        return View(model);
    }

    // Validate and proceed
    if (Membership.ValidateUser(model.UserName, model.Password))
    {
        FormsAuthentication.SetAuthCookie(model.UserName, model.RememberMe);
        if (isValidReturnUrl)
        {
            return Redirect(returnUrl);
        }
```

```
        else
        {
            return RedirectToAction(defaultAction, defaultController);
        }
    }

    // If we got this far, something failed; redisplay form.
    return View(model);
}
```

Chapter 4, "Input forms," demonstrates that input data can be collected in a handy data structure and processed on the server. That's just what you do with the *LogonViewModel* class. The *returnUrl* parameter is only set if an original request was redirected to a logon view because the user needed to be authenticated first. In this case, the redirect response contains the new URL in the location header and the URL includes a *returnUrl* query string parameter.

Validation occurs through the ASP.NET membership API. If validation is successful, a valid authentication cookie is created via the *FormsAuthentication* class. Next, the user is redirected to the originally requested page or to the home page.

Integrating with the membership API

Centered on the *Membership* static class, the ASP.NET membership API shields you from the details of how the credentials and other user information are retrieved and compared. The *Membership* class doesn't directly contain any logic for any of the methods it exposes. The actual logic is supplied by a provider component.

You select the membership in the configuration file. ASP.NET comes with a couple of predefined providers that target MDF files in Microsoft SQL Server Express and Active Directory. However, it is not unusual that you end up creating your own membership provider so that you can reuse any existing store of users' data and are in total control over the structure of the data store.

Defining a custom membership provider is not difficult at all. All you do is derive a new class from *MembershipProvider* and override all abstract methods. At a minimum, you override a few methods such as *ValidateUser*, *GetUser*, *CreateUser*, and *ChangePassword*.

```
public class PoorManMembershipProvider : MembershipProvider
{
    public override bool ValidateUser(String username, String password)
    {
        ...
    }

    public override MembershipUser GetUser(String username, Boolean userIsOnline)
    {
        ...
    }
```

```
    public override MembershipUser CreateUser(String username, String password,
            String email, String passwordQuestion, String passwordAnswer,
            Boolean isApproved, Object providerUserKey,
            out MembershipCreateStatus status)
    {
      ...
    }

    public override Boolean ChangePassword(String username, String oldPassword, String
                                           newPassword)
    {
      ...
    }

    // Remainder of the MembershipProvider interface
    ...
}
```

In particular, in the implementation of *ValidateUser*, you pick up the user name and password and check them against your database. As a security measure, it is recommended that you store your passwords in a hashed format. Here's a quick demo of how to check a typed password against a stored hashed password:

```
public override bool ValidateUser(String username, String password)
{
    // Validate user name
    ...

    // Runs a query against the data store to retrieve the
    // password for the specified user. We're assuming that the
    // retrieved password is hashed.
    var storedPassword = GetStoredPasswordForUser(username);

    // No user found
    if (storedPassword == null)
      return false;

    // Hash the provided password and see if that matches the stored password
    var hashedPassword = Utils.HashPassword(password);
    return hashedPassword == storedPassword;
}
```

The default membership API has been criticized for being cumbersome and in clear violation of the Interface Segregation Principle—the "I" principle in the popular SOLID acronym (which stands for *S*ingle responsibility, *O*pen-closed, *L*iskov substitution, *I*nterface segregation and *D*ependency inversion principle). The membership API attempts to cover a reasonable number of situations and is probably too complex and unnecessarily rich for the most common scenarios these days. Creating a custom membership provider helps, but it doesn't solve the issue entirely because it only builds a simpler façade.

Using the *SimpleMembership* API

If you don't want to create your own membership layer completely from scratch, another middle-way option that you can try is represented by the *SimpleMembership* API, as originally available in ASP.NET Web Pages.

The *SimpleMembership* API is just a wrapper on top of the ASP.NET membership API and data stores. With it, you can work with any data store you have, and it requires only that you indicate which columns operate as the user name and user ID. The *WebSecurity* class offers a simplified API with which to do your membership chores, where the major difference with the classic membership API is a radically shorter list of parameters for any methods and greater freedom with regard to the schema of the storage. Here's how you create a new user:

```
WebSecurity.CreateUserAndAccount(username, password,
    new{ FirstName = fname, LastName = lname, Email = email });
```

As a result, until ASP.NET MVC 4, you had two parallel routes for membership implementation: classic membership API centered on the *MembershipProvider* class, and simple membership API centered on the *ExtendedMembershipProvider* class. The two APIs are incompatible. In ASP.NET MVC 5, there's an effort to unify the membership experience. This comes at the cost of adding yet another API—ASP.NET Identity. I'll get to ASP.NET Identity in a moment.

Integrating with the role API

Roles in ASP.NET simplify the implementation of applications that require authorization. A role is just a logical attribute assigned to a user. An ASP.NET role is a plain string that refers to the logical role the user plays in the context of the application. In terms of configuration, each user can be assigned one or more roles. ASP.NET looks up the roles for the current user and binds that information to the *User* object. ASP.NET uses a role provider component to manage role information for a given user.

The role provider is a class that inherits the *RoleProvider* class. The schema of a role provider is not much different from that of a membership provider and shares the same complexity issues, as well. To keep things simpler or to wrap existing data storage, you might want to create a custom role provider or switch to the simple role API that is the role counterpart of the simple membership API.

The code snippet that follows shows how to programmatically correlate roles and users. You use the *Roles* class, which works on top of the concrete role provider.

```
// Create Admin role
Roles.CreateRole("Admin");
Roles.AddUsersToRole("DinoE", "Admin");

// Create Guest role
Roles.CreateRole("Guest");
var guests = new String[2];
guests[0] = "Joe";
guests[1] = "Godzilla";
Roles.AddUsersToRole(guests, "Guest")
```

At run time, information about the logged-on user is available through the HTTP context *User* object. The following code demonstrates how to determine whether the current user is in a certain role and subsequently enable specific functions:

```
if (User.IsInRole("Admin"))
{
    // Enable functions specific to the role
    ...
}
```

ASP.NET identity

The purpose of authentication is getting the identity associated with the current user. The identity is retrieved matching provided credentials to records stored in a database. Subsequently, an identity system is based on two primary blocks: the user authentication manager and the store manager.

The new ASP.NET Identity system is the offspring of the "One ASP.NET" approach to web development that Visual Studio 2013 heralds, and is slated to become the preferred way to handle user authentication in all ASP.NET applications, whether based on Web Forms or MVC. The main purpose of ASP.NET Identity—the standard way of authenticating users in Visual Studio 2013 and ASP.NET MVC 5—is to unify the approach to authentication by factoring out the entire system in two key components and using dependency injection to keep the entire system easily testable.

In the ASP.NET Identity framework, the authentication manager takes the form of the *UserManager<TUser>* class. This class basically provides a façade for signing users in and out. The *UserManager* class is declared as follows:

```
public class UserManager<TUser> : IDisposable where TUser : IUser
{
    :
}
```

The type *TUser* refers to the current description of the user to be managed. The *IUser* interface contains a very minimal definition of the user, limited to ID and name. The ASP.NET Identity API defines the *IdentityUser* type that implements the *IUser* interface and adds a few extra properties.

```
public class IdentityUser : IUser
{
    public string Id { get; }
    public string UserName { get; set; }
    public string PasswordHash { get; set; }
    public string SecurityStamp { get; set; }
    public ICollection<IdentityUserRole> Roles { get; private set; }
    public ICollection<IdentityUserClaim> Claims { get; private set; }
    public ICollection<IdentityUserLogin> Logins { get; private set; }
}
```

The sample ASP.NET MVC 5 application you get out of the Visual Studio 2013 wizard also features the *ApplicationUser* class that just inherits from *IdentityUser* but makes things ready for further extension. You can easily add extra profile data for the user your application is going to handle by adding more properties to the following class:

```
public class ApplicationUser : IdentityUser
{
}
```

The central class for user storage is *UserStore<TUser>*. The *TUser* type must be *IdentityUser* or a further inherited class such as *ApplicationUser*. The user store class implements the *IUserStore* interface which summarizes the actions allowed on the user store.

```
public interface IUserStore<TUser> : IDisposable where TUser : IUser
{
    Task CreateAsync(TUser user);
    Task DeleteAsync(TUser user);
    Task<TUser> FindByIdAsync(string userId);
    Task<TUser> FindByNameAsync(string userName);
    Task UpdateAsync(TUser user);
}
```

As you can see, the user store interface looks a lot like a canonical repository interface like those you might build around a data access layer. The *UserManager<TUser>* and *UserStore<TUser>* classes live in different namespaces and assemblies. In particular, *UserManager* lives in *Microsoft.AspNet. Identity.Core*, whereas *UserStore* is defined in *Microsoft.AspNet.Identity.EntityFramework* and has some dependency on the actual storage technology.

The entire infrastructure is glued together in the account controller class. Here's the skeleton of an ASP.NET MVC account controller class that is fully based on the ASP.NET Identity API:

```
public class AccountController : Controller
{
    public UserManager<ApplicationUser> UserManager { get; set; }
    public AccountController(UserManager<ApplicationUser> manager)
    {
        UserManager = manager;
    }
    public AccountController() : this(
        new UserManager<ApplicationUser>(new UserStore<ApplicationUser>(new
ApplicationDbContext())))
    {
    }
    ...
}
```

The controller holds a reference to the authentication identity manager. An instance of the authentication identity manager is injected in the controller.

The identity store is injected in the identity manager where it is used to verify credentials. The identity store needs to know about the actual data source though. User data is managed through

Entity Framework Code First. This means that you don't strictly need to create a physical database to store your users' credentials; instead, you can define an *ApplicationUser* class and have the underlying framework create the most appropriate database to store such records. The link between user store and data store is established in the *ApplicationDbContext* class that the wizard creates for you.

```
public class ApplicationDbContext : IdentityDbContext<ApplicationUser>
{
    public ApplicationDbContext() : base("DefaultConnection")
    {
    }
}
```

The base *IdentityDbContext* class inherits from *DbContext* and is dependent on Entity Framework. Right from the constructor, you see that the class refers to an entry in the web.config file where the actual connection string is read.

The use of Entity Framework Code First is a great move here because it makes the structure of the database a secondary point. You still need one, but you can have the code to create one based on classes. In addition, you can use Entity Framework Code First Migration tools to modify a previously created database as you make changes to the class behind it. (See *http://msdn.microsoft.com/data/ jj591621.aspx*)

Authenticating users by using ASP.NET Identity

ASP.NET Identity is also based on the newest Open Web Interface for .NET (OWIN) authentication middleware. This means that the typical steps of authentication (cookies check and creation) can be carried out through the abstract OWIN interfaces and not directly in ASP.NET/IIS interfaces. Support for OWIN requires that the account controller has another handy property, such as the following:

```
private IAuthenticationManager AuthenticationManager
{
    get {
        return HttpContext.GetOwinContext().Authentication;
    }
}
```

The *IAuthenticationManager* interface is defined in the *Microsoft.Owin.Security* namespace. This property is crucial because it needs to be injected in any operation that involves authentication-related steps. Let's have a look at a typical logon method.

```
private async Task SignInAsync(ApplicationUser user, bool isPersistent)
{
    AuthenticationManager.SignOut(DefaultAuthenticationTypes.ExternalCookie);
    var identity = await UserManager.CreateIdentityAsync(user,
                              DefaultAuthenticationTypes.ApplicationCookie);
    AuthenticationManager.SignIn(
            new AuthenticationProperties() { IsPersistent = isPersistent }, identity);
}
```

For registering a new user, you need the following code:

```
var user = new ApplicationUser() { UserName = model.UserName };
var result = await UserManager.CreateAsync(user, model.Password);
if (result.Succeeded)
{
    await SignInAsync(user, isPersistent: false);
    return RedirectToAction("Index", "Home");
}
```

All in all, ASP.NET Identity provides a unified API for most of the tasks related to authentication. Personally, I like the expressiveness of the API and the attempt to fuse together different forms of authentication—built-in and OAuth-based, for example. Another great plus is the integration with OWIN which makes it kind of independent from a specific runtime such IIS/ASP.NET. Whether you use it in the current project or not, you should definitely look at ASP.NET Identity.

The Remember-Me feature and Ajax

Today, nearly any logon view features a check box labeled "Remember me" or "Keep me logged on," as Facebook does. Selecting the box usually results in an authentication cookie that lasts longer; how much longer depends on the code behind the page. The flag just indicates the user's preference of getting a more persistent cookie that keeps him connected to the site for a longer time without having to retype credentials.

If the cookie expires, on the next access the user will be automatically redirected to the logon page and politely asked to re-enter his user name and password. This pattern is not new, and every developer is used to it. However, it might give you a few problems in an Ajax scenario.

Reproducing the problem

Imagine that a user clicks somewhere and places an Ajax call to the server. Imagine also that the authentication cookie has expired. Subsequently, the server returns an HTTP 302 status code, which redirects the user to the logon page. This is just what one would expect, isn't it? What's the issue, then?

In an Ajax scenario, it's the *XMLHttpRequest* object, not the browser, that handles the request. *XMLHttpRequest* correctly handles the redirect and goes to the logon page. Unfortunately, the original issuer of the Ajax call will get back the markup of the logon page instead of the data it was expecting. As a result, the logon page will likely be inserted in any DOM location where the original response was expected, as illustrated in Figure 6-2.

FIGURE 6-2 An Ajax request to a restricted URL injects the logon view.

Solving the problem

To work around the issue, you must intercept the request during the authorization stage and verify that it is an Ajax request. If it is and if the request is being rejected, you hook up the status code and change it to 401. The client-side script you have then takes that into account and displays the proper HTML, as demonstrated here:

```
<script type="text/javascript">
    function failed(xhr, textStatus, errorThrown) {
        if (textStatus == "error") {
            if (xhr.status === 401) {
                $("#divOutput").html("You must be logged in.");
            }
        }
    }
</script>
```

The failed JavaScript function is the callback used by the Ajax infrastructure (as discussed in Chapter 4) when a form post or a link request fails. Here's the code for the form in Figure 6-2:

```
@using (Ajax.BeginForm("Now", "Home",
            new AjaxOptions { UpdateTargetId = "divOutput", OnFailure="failed" }))
{
    <input type="submit" value="What time is it?" />
}
<hr />
<div id="divOutput">
</div>
```

The real work is done by a slightly revised version of the *Authorize* attribute. All in all, you can just extend the *AuthorizedOnly* attribute, as shown next, and use it in any case in which restricted access to a method is necessary. Replace the previous implementation of the internal method *CheckIfUserIs Authenticated* with this one:

```
private void CheckIfUserIsAuthenticated(AuthorizationContext filterContext)
{
    // If Result is null, we're OK
    if (filterContext.Result == null)
        return;

    // Is this an Ajax request?
    if (filterContext.HttpContext.Request.IsAjaxRequest())
    {
        // For an Ajax request, just end the request
        filterContext.HttpContext.Response.StatusCode = 401;
        filterContext.HttpContext.Response.End();
    }

    // If here, you're getting an HTTP 401 status code
    if (filterContext.HttpContext.User.Identity.IsAuthenticated)
    {
        var result = new ViewResult {ViewName = View, MasterName = Master};
        filterContext.Result = result;
    }
}
```

With this final update, the *AuthorizedOnly* attribute has now become the definitive replacement for the system's *Authorize* attribute. Here's a sample restricted controller method that can be invoked both via Ajax and regular posts. Figure 6-3 shows the desired effect.

```
[AuthorizedOnly]
public ActionResult Now()
{
    ViewBag.Now = DateTime.Now.ToString("hh:mm:ss");
    if (Request.IsAjaxRequest())
        return PartialView("aNow");
    return View();
}
```

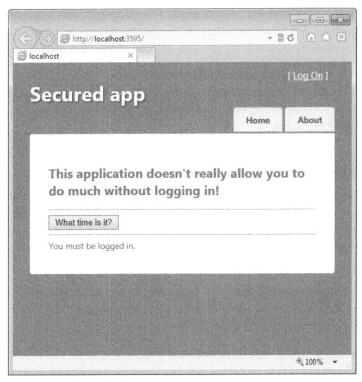

FIGURE 6-3 No logon view shows up in case of Ajax requests.

Note The Remember-Me problem manifests only if you are using *Ajax.BeginForm* (or partial rendering). If you are making direct calls to an HTTP endpoint and are updating the user interface according to the response you get, everything is under your control. Moreover, if you're calling an endpoint that returns JavaScript Object Notation (JSON) instead of HTML, you have more chances to understand the response and process it accordingly.

External authentication services

Implementing your own authentication layer in a site is definitely an option. These days, however, it is becoming just one option, and it's probably not even the most compelling one for users. By implementing your own authentication layer, you make yourself responsible for storing passwords safely and charge your team with the extra work required to fully manage an account. From the perspective of users, any new sites they're interested in might add a new user name/password pair to the list. For a user, a forgotten password is really frustrating.

Years ago, the Microsoft Passport initiative was an early attempt to make users' lives easier when they moved across a few related sites. With Passport, users just needed to do a single logon and, if they were successfully authenticated, they could freely navigate through all the associated sites.

The Passport initiative, and its related API, is now officially considered obsolete because it was superseded by OpenID (*http://openid.net*). For websites that depend on lots of traffic and a large audience, the OpenID authentication is an interesting feature to have on board that can really help attract and retain more and more visitors to the site.

The OpenID protocol

The main purpose of OpenID is to make access to a website easier, quicker, and especially, not annoying for end users. The visitors of any sites that support OpenID can sign in using an existing identity token that has been issued by another site. An OpenID-enabled website authenticates its users against an existing (external) identity provider and doesn't need to store passwords and implement a membership layer.

Although offering the standard, site-specific membership solution remains an option, many sites today also make it possible for visitors to use an OpenID they received from some provider for authenticating. One form or authentication doesn't exclude the other.

Figure 6-4 provides an overall view of the authentication logic employed by a site that supports OpenID. When the user clicks to sign in with one of the supported OpenIDs, the site connects to the specified provider and gets an access token about the user. The user might be requested to type in credentials for the OpenID provider site. A user who is already logged on with the provider is automatically logged on also with the site of interest. In this case, the few redirects taking place under the hood never show intermediate pages and the transition is as smooth as within two distinct pages of the same application.

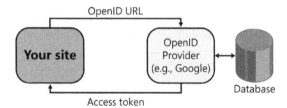

FIGURE 6-4 Authenticating via OpenID.

Your site doesn't have to be an OpenID identity provider, but it can easily become a consumer of identity tokens supplied by a few of the OpenID providers available today. Yahoo!, Flickr, and Google are popular OpenID providers. Overall, OpenID is not different from the original Windows Live ID, except that it relies on a number of service providers and doesn't force people to get yet another account from a specific provider. By supporting OpenID, you make it possible for your users to log on to your site by using whatever credentials they already have. Users can essentially choose from where they log on.

Identifying users through an OpenID provider

There are quite a few libraries that help integrate OpenID into websites. A very popular one for .NET developers is DotNetOpenAuth (DNOA), available from *http://www.dotnetopenauth.net*. Figure 6-5 shows a sample application using the DNOA library to perform authentication against any valid OpenID URL that the user can provide.

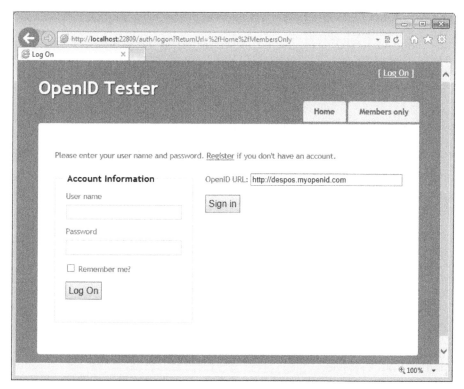

FIGURE 6-5 A sample application for connecting to any OpenID provider you might know of.

As a developer, the first piece of information you should grab is the OpenID URL of the service (or services) that you intend to support. This information might be the same for each user or it can differ for each user. For example, Google and Yahoo! always use the same URL regardless of the user. Here are the URLs for Google and Yahoo!, respectively:

- *https://www.google.com/accounts/o8/id*

- *http://yahoo.com*

The provider in this case will figure out from the details of the request (for example, a cookie) the account name of the user to authenticate. If no details can be gleaned, or the user is not currently logged on to the service, the service displays a logon page to collect credentials and redirects back if all is fine (possibly with a cookie for further access). Other providers such as *myOpenID* (*http://www.myopenid.com*) require a different URL for each user. User-specific URLs are of the form *http://name.myopenid.com*. The service recognizes the account name from the URL and then proceeds as shown earlier.

As a developer, if you intend to support an OpenID provider that uses a fixed URL, you can avoid the text box shown in Figure 6-5 and replace it with a link or a button. In general, you might want to reduce typing on the user's part to a minimum. For example, for myOpenID, all you really need is the first part of the URL. Here's the HTML for the small form shown in Figure 6-5:

```
@using (Html.BeginForm("authenticate", "auth", new { returnUrl = Request.
QueryString["ReturnUrl"] }))
{
    <label for="openid_identifier">OpenID URL: </label>
    <input id="openid_identifier" name="openid_identifier" size="40" /><br />
    @Html.ValidationMessage("openid_identifier")
    <br />
    <input type="submit" value="Sign in" />
}
```

The sign-in button posts to a method such as the one shown here:

```
public ActionResult Authenticate(String returnUrl, [Bind(Prefix="openid_identifier")]String url)
{
    // First step: issuing the request and returning here
    var response = RelyingParty.GetResponse();
    if (response == null)
    {
        if (!RelyingParty.IsValid(url))
            return View("Logon");

        try
        {
            return RelyingParty.CreateRequest(url).RedirectingResponse.AsActionResult();
        }
        catch (ProtocolException ex)
        {
            ModelState.AddModelError("openid_identifier", ex.Message);
            return View("LogOn");
        }
    }

    // Second step: redirected here by the provider
    switch (response.Status)
    {
        case AuthenticationStatus.Authenticated:
            FormsAuthentication.SetAuthCookie(response.ClaimedIdentifier, true);
            return Redirect(returnUrl);

        case AuthenticationStatus.Canceled:
            return View("Logon");

        case AuthenticationStatus.Failed:
            return View("Logon");
    }
    return new EmptyResult();
}
```

In the preceding code, the method belongs to a controller class that has a *RelyingParty* property defined as follows:

```
protected static OpenIdRelyingParty RelyingParty = new OpenIdRelyingParty();
```

The controller of the example is derived from a base class that just provides the *RelyingParty* property.

The type *OpenIdRelyingParty* is defined in the DNOA library. The authentication develops in two phases within the same controller method. The method *CreateRequest* prepares the proper HTTP request and associates it with the specified OpenID URL. The provider receives instructions to redirect back to the same URL and the same controller method. The second time, though, the response is not null, and you can create a regular ASP.NET authentication cookie for which the user name is the name of account as returned by the OpenID provider.

Note that you have no control over this aspect—the provider decides what to return as the friendly name of the authenticated user. For example, for security reasons, Google doesn't return any significant friendly name; the *FriendlyIdentifierForDisplay* property is set to the generic OpenID URL. When you use myOpenID, it sets the *FriendlyIdentifierForDisplay* of the response to the URL, simply removing the scheme information and any trailing slash. To finalize the integration with the ASP.NET authentication infrastructure, you need to create a regular authentication cookie so that the user name can be displayed in the logon area. Figure 6-6 shows the authentication step through the myOpenID provider.

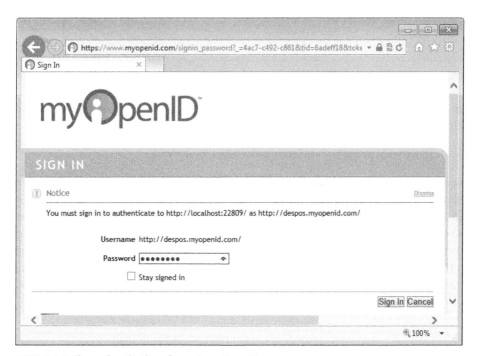

FIGURE 6-6 The authentication phase via myOpenID.

Figure 6-7 shows the page that is displayed after the user has been successfully authenticated by myOpenID and returns to the originally requesting site.

FIGURE 6-7 User authenticated via myOpenID.

The user name depends on the first parameter you pass when you create the cookie. (The second argument is whether you want a persistent cookie to keep the user logged on.)

```
FormsAuthentication.SetAuthCookie(response.ClaimedIdentifier, true);
```

The name you use here is up to you. If you still maintain a list of application-specific nicknames, you can map the claimed identifier to the nickname and display the nickname. Or, you can simply update the UI to notify the user of the successful sign-in without displaying any user name. Yet another option is to create a slightly customized authentication cookie where you use the *UserData* property of the authentication ticket (the actual content of the cookie) to persistently store the friendly name to display. The benefit of this approach is that you save both the claimed identifier and your own adapted friendly name. Here's an extension method that creates a custom authentication cookie:

```
public delegate String UserNameAdapterDelegate(String userName);
public static HttpCookie CreateAuthCookie(this IAuthenticationResponse response,
                                          Boolean persistent = true,
                                          UserNameAdapterDelegate fnAdapter = null)
{
    var userName = response.ClaimedIdentifier;
    var userDisplayName = response.FriendlyIdentifierForDisplay;
    if (fnAdapter != null)
        userDisplayName = fnAdapter(userDisplayName);

    return CreateAuthCookie(userName, userDisplayName, persistent);
}

private static HttpCookie CreateAuthCookie(String username,
                                           String userDisplayName,
                                           Boolean persistent)
{
    // Let ASP.NET create a regular authentication cookie
    var cookie = FormsAuthentication.GetAuthCookie(username, persistent);

    // Modify the cookie to add friendly name
    var ticket = FormsAuthentication.Decrypt(cookie.Value);
    var newTicket = new FormsAuthenticationTicket(ticket.Version,
            ticket.Name, ticket.IssueDate, ticket.Expiration, ticket.IsPersistent,
userDisplayName);
    cookie.Value = FormsAuthentication.Encrypt(newTicket);

    // This modified cookie MUST be re-added to the Response.Cookies collection
    return cookie;
}
```

Here's a slightly modified version of the *Authenticated* method in the controller that takes this extension method into account:

```
switch (response.Status)
{
    case AuthenticationStatus.Authenticated:
        var cookie = response.CreateAuthCookie(true, StopAtFirstToken);
        Response.Cookies.Add(cookie);
        if (isValidReturnUrl)
            return Redirect(returnUrl);
        return RedirectToAction("Index", "Home");
    ...
}
```

The delegate *UserNameAdapterDelegate* indicates the template of a function that you can inject to determine the friendly name to be displayed.

```
public String StopAtFirstToken(String name)
{
    var tokens = name.Split('.');
    return tokens[0];
}
```

Finally, you need to edit the logon view to display the content of the *UserData* field in the cookie instead of the canonical user name.

```
@if(Request.IsAuthenticated) {
    <text>Welcome <strong>@(((FormsIdentity)User.Identity).Ticket.UserData)</strong>!
    [ @Html.ActionLink("Log Off", "LogOff", "Auth") ]</text>
}
```

Figure 6-8 shows the result.

FIGURE 6-8 The user is logged on, and a custom nickname is shown.

> **Note** When you need to add more data to the authentication cookie, the *UserData* property of the internal ticket structure is the first option to consider. The *UserData* property exists exactly for this purpose. However, you can always create an additional and entirely custom cookie or just add values to the authentication cookie. The name of the authentication cookie results from the value of the property *FormsAuthentication.FormsCookieName*.

OpenID vs. OAuth

OpenID is a single–sign-on scheme and, as such, it just aims to uniquely identify users in the simplest possible way. OpenID is not related to granting users access to resources managed by the service provider. Or, put another way, the only resources that an OpenID provider manages are the identities of registered users.

The advent of social networks such as Facebook, Twitter, and LinkedIn put the classic single–sign-on problem under a different light. Not only do users want to use a single (popular) identity to log on to multiple sites without registering every time, but they also want to be granted some permissions to a site to access information and resources they have on the site, such as posts, tweets, followers, friends, contacts, and so forth.

OAuth (*http://oauth.net*) is another single–sign-on scheme with additional capabilities as compared to OpenID. A website that acts as an OAuth provider operates as an identity provider, and when the user logs on, the OAuth provider specifies permissions on resources. A website that offers OAuth authentication just acts as the client of a provider using the specific OAuth protocol. Such a website authenticates users and gains an access token it can further use to access resources (for example, merge tweets or contacts with its own user interface). Finally, from the user's perspective, OAuth grants a website (or desktop application) user's controlled access to one account without giving away logon details.

Popular OAuth providers are Twitter and Facebook.

> **Note** Overall, I don't think that as a website developer you need to make a choice between using OpenID or OAuth for authentication. You decide which external provider you want to authenticate against (for example, Twitter) and then go with the API it requires, whether it's OpenID, OAuth, or a proprietary API. If you're developing a website and want to allow your users to share their account (and related information) with other sites, you make a decision between OpenID, OAuth, or a proprietary protocol. In this case, I recommend you consider OAuth as the first option.

> **Important** Authentication via social networks is a required feature today by all those websites that are expected to have a consumer target. Authentication via social networks is appreciated by users because it saves them the burden of creating yet another account and remembering yet another pair of credentials. At the same time, though, social networks might hide pieces of information about the user that are essential for developers of websites. If you request users to log on, it's likely that you want to capture their email address. This might not be easy to achieve via social networks. For this reason, it is becoming common that consumer-oriented websites first give you the option to authenticate via Twitter or Facebook and then ask you to finalize the logon or registration step by entering an email address as well as some other personal information.

Authenticating via social networks

Let's see what it takes to authenticate users via Twitter and Facebook. In the next example, we'll use the same DNOA library to encapsulate the details of the protocols. I'll limit the code to authentication (OpenID and OAuth overlap somewhat in the examples of this chapter) but will call out the points where OAuth extends the OpenID scheme.

Registering your application with Twitter

Dealing with an OAuth provider requires some preliminary steps. First and foremost, you must register your application with the social network and get two strings: the *consumer key* and *consumer secret*. You'll be embedding these strings in any further programmatic request to the provider.

The process is nearly identical for Facebook and Twitter. I'll discuss Twitter here. The entire process begins at *http://dev.twitter.com*. Figure 6-9 shows the configuration page for an existing application.

FIGURE 6-9 Registering an application with Twitter.

In particular, you set the application type and the default permission you require on the user's resources. The Callback URL field deserves some attention. The URL is where Twitter returns after successfully authenticating a user. You don't likely want this URL to be constant. However, Twitter requires that you don't leave the field blank if your application is a web application. If you leave the field blank because you intend to specify the callback URL on a per-call basis, Twitter overwrites the application type settings, forcing it to a desktop application. The net effect is that any attempts to authenticate any users return unauthorized. Assigning any URL, including one that results in a 404 message (as shown in the example), will work.

Enabling social authentication in ASP.NET MVC

Until ASP.NET MVC 4, you had to code your way to Twitter and Facebook for authentication. The DNOA library does help a lot, but all it offers it a low-level programming interface that is very close to the very metal of the OAuth protocol. In ASP.NET MVC, you find available a new class—the *OAuthWebSecurity* class—that offers full support for OAuth authentication. In particular, the class offers a few handy methods ready to plug in most popular social networks that support OAuth.

Authentication methods take the form of *RegisterXxxClient*. Available methods exist for Twitter, Facebook, Google, LinkedIn, Yahoo, and Microsoft.

If you start your ASP.NET MVC project from the standard template, you find the following code invoked from global.asax:

```
OAuthWebSecurity.RegisterTwitterClient(
    consumerKey: "...",
    consumerSecret: "...");

OAuthWebSecurity.RegisterFacebookClient(
    appId: "...",
    appSecret: "...");
```

To be precise, this code is commented out and must be completed with actual keys and secrets for the social application in the background. Even if you don't use any of the standard project templates, however, a look at the source code for social authentication in the default template is recommended.

By simply having the preceding two lines of code, you get the the results shown in Figure 6-10 out of the predefined ASP.NET MVC template.

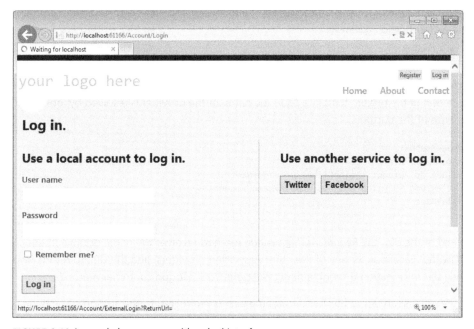

FIGURE 6-10 A sample logon page with a dual interface.

If the user types a user name and password and clicks Log In, everything takes place as usual and the burden of validation and credentials storage is on you. Otherwise, the user will be redirected to either Twitter or Facebook to be authenticated. If authentication is successful she will be redirected back.

The entire process is coded using the DNOA library; ASP.NET MVC, though, offers some wrapper classes that streamline coding and, more important, provide scaffolding for grabbing user information via social networks and then saving data to the local membership system.

> **Important** I don't know how many developers actually start building their ASP.NET MVC applications from the Visual Studio standard templates. However, as far as social authentication is concerned, the patterns implemented in the standard template are definitely worth a look.

Starting the authentication process

When the user clicks the Twitter (or Facebook) button, the site ends up invoking the *ExternalLogin* method on the *Account* controller. Here's the code involved:

```
public ActionResult ExternalLogin(String provider, String returnUrl)
{
    return new ExternalLoginResult(provider,
        Url.Action("ExternalLoginCallback",
                    new { ReturnUrl = returnUrl }));
}
```

The *ExternalLoginResult* class is a wrapper for the following code that really does the job of contacting the authentication gateway:

```
OAuthWebSecurity.RequestAuthentication(Provider, ReturnUrl);
```

The *ExternalLoginResult* class is a helper class that is also found in the AccountController.cs file. You should note that in the project template code the name of the provider is resolved by looking at the name attribute of the button.

```
<button type="submit"
        name="provider"
        value="@p.AuthenticationClient.ProviderName"
        title="Log in using your @p.DisplayName account">
    @p.DisplayName
</button>
```

At the end of the day, the *RequestAuthentication* method receives the name of the authentication provider (Twitter, Facebook, or any of the other supported providers) and the URL to return. You can also provide this information through a direct call right from a logon controller method.

When the request arrives at the Twitter site, the user is redirected to the authorization page shown in Figure 6-11.

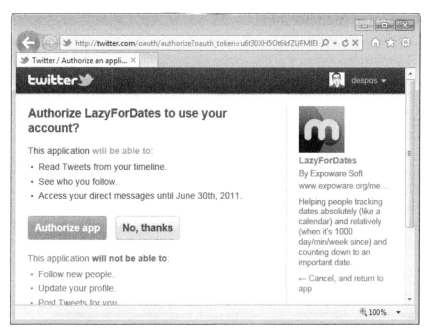

FIGURE 6-11 The user authenticates on Twitter and authorizes the requesting application to access account information.

If the user (me, in this case) is already logged on to Twitter, he's simply asked to authorize the requesting application. Otherwise, he first needs to sign in with Twitter and then authorize. Next, Twitter redirects back to the specified URL.

Dealing with the Twitter response

If the user enters credentials that Twitter (or the social network of choice) recognizes as valid, the Twitter site redirects back to the provided return URL. The next method with which you regain control past the authentication is *ExternalLoginCallback*.

What you know at this point is only that the user who's trying to access your application has been successfully recognized as a Twitter user. You don't know anything about her; not even the user name. I can hardly think of an application that needs authenticated users and can blissfully ignore user name or email address. Back from the authentication step, the application only receives a code but has not been authorized yet to access the Twitter API programmatically. For this to happen, the code received at this stage must be exchanged for an access token (usually time-limited to prevent misuse). This is the purpose of the call to the *VerifyAuthentication* method you find in the body of *ExternalLoginCallback*.

The *AuthenticationResult* object you get back from *VerifyAuthentication* brings back some information about the user. The actual information you get might be slightly different depending on the provider; however, it usually contains at least the user name.

From authentication to membership

Authenticating a user is only the first step; next, you need to track the user by name within the site. In a classic ASP.NET membership system, you first display a logon form, validate credentials, and then create an authentication cookie stuffed with user name and optionally other key information. Twitter and Facebook save you the burden of arranging a logon form and validating the credentials plus the nontrivial burden of storing and managing accounts with sensitive information such as passwords.

The bottom line, though, is that nearly any application that needs authenticated users also needs a membership system within which each regular user is tracked by name. Building such a system is still a task you must accomplish on your own. As mentioned, the ASP.NET MVC basic template comes to the rescue by offering an extra step during which the user is automatically given a chance to enter her display name which is then saved to a local membership table. This is required only the first time a user logs on to a given site. In other words, the form shown in Figure 6-12 serves the purpose of joining registration and first logon.

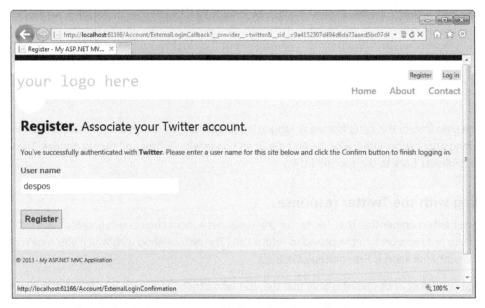

FIGURE 6-12 Completing the logon process with the registration to the site

The name entered at this stage is used to create the ASP.NET authentication cookie which definitely closes the circle: you used Twitter to check credentials, asked the user to enter her display name, and created a regular authentication cookie. From now on, everything works as usual in ASP.NET for sites subject to authentication.

Important Whether you decide to merge logon and registration, it is necessary that you nonetheless manage to create a classic ASP.NET authentication cookie using the user name returned by the OAuth provider (if any).

The sample application, which is heavily based on the default ASP.NET MVC project template, saves user data to an MDF local database created under the *App_Data* folder. The table is managed by using the simple membership API inherited from the Web Pages framework.

The following code shows how the sample project template retrieves the user display name presented in Figure 6-12.

```
var loginData = OAuthWebSecurity.SerializeProviderUserId(
    result.Provider, result.ProviderUserId);
var name = OAuthWebSecurity
                .GetOAuthClientData(result.Provider)
                .DisplayName;
return View("ExternalLoginConfirmation",
        new RegisterExternalLoginModel {
            UserName = result.UserName,
            ExternalLoginData = loginData
        });
```

The call to *GetOAuthClientData* is where you access any information that the Twitter provider shares about the logged user. Next, the view *ExternalLogicConfirmation* provides the actual markup of Figure 6-12. When the user clicks to register, another call back to the account controller is made, precisely to the method *ExternalLoginConfirmation*. In the body of this method, two key things happen, which are summarized by the following code:

```
OAuthWebSecurity.CreateOrUpdateAccount(
    provider, providerUserId, model.UserName);
OAuthWebSecurity.Login(
    provider, providerUserId, createPersistentCookie: false);
```

The first line sets up the new record in the membership local database for the application. The second line actually creates the authentication cookie. The default template provides for a bunch a database tables such as *UserProfiles* and *webPages_OAuthMembership*. The latter table stores the record with the name of the provider (for example, Twitter), the provider unique ID for the user, and a pointer to an internal ID that uniquely identifies the user in the *UserProfiles* table with the display name the user himself has chosen on the page in Figure 6-12.

> **Important** To test the Twitter authentication, you need a real consumer key/consumer secret pair, but you don't strictly need to test it from a public web server. You can do everything comfortably from your Visual Studio environment and use *localhost:port* as the root of the callback URL.

Beyond authentication

Although most websites just use social networks to authenticate users, as described in the preceding sections, there's a lot more that they can do. After the user's credentials are verified, nearly any external providers (and surely Twitter and Facebook) return an alphanumeric string known as the *access token*.

The access token is an important piece of information because it authorizes the website to operate on the social network on behalf of the user and within the range of permissions required and granted by the user, as depicted in Figure 6-9. In a nutshell, grabbing and storing the access token is not important if you only want to authenticate a user, but it becomes essential when you want to provide more functionality, such as post on behalf of the user or just retrieve more personal information.

> **Note** An access token might not last forever. For example, Facebook tokens tend to expire quickly; Twitter tokens last a lot longer. You decide how to deal with access tokens case by case, but in general a good strategy is saving the access token every time the user logs on. You can save it to the session state or, better yet, to a database.

How would you retrieve the access token?

The access token is available within the *ExternalLoginCallback* method; that is, the first entry point in your code after successful authentication. Specifically, you find it stored in the *ExtraData* property of the *AuthenticationResult* object.

```
if (result.ExtraData.Keys.Contains("accesstoken"))
{
    // Save the access token for later use: result.ExtraData["accesstoken"]
    ...
}
```

For example, you can use the access token to retrieve more information about a user. Keep in mind that functions that go beyond the simple authentication require an ad hoc software development kit (SDK) for a particular social network. To interact with Twitter, you might want to use TweetSharp. For Facebook, instead, the best option is the Facebook Client SDK for C#. Both libraries are easily accessible via NuGet. Here's a code snippet to grab extra information for a Facebook user:

```
var client = new FacebookClient(accesstoken);
dynamic user = client.Get("/me", new { fields = "first_name,last_name,email" });
```

With a similar syntax, you can access the timeline of the current user. For more information, you might want to refer to the developer pages on the site of the social network of choice.

Summary

Security is always perceived as a hot topic for web applications. Therefore, nearly any class or book on a web technology is expected to host a section on how to write secure applications. Assuming that one knows the basics of security and Forms authentication for classic ASP.NET (for example, Web Forms), there's not much else left to cover that is specific to ASP.NET MVC.

The run-time pipeline is the same as in Web Forms, and trust levels and process identities are established in exactly the same manner. Also, Forms authentication works in the same way through an HTTP module and a highly configurable cookie. You can find an in-depth discussion of these topics in Chapter 19 of my latest ASP.NET book *Programming ASP.NET 4* (Microsoft Press, 2011).

Specific to ASP.NET MVC is the way in which one restricts access to action methods and controls authorization. I covered this in the first half of the chapter. The second half touched on features that more and more applications are incorporating these days—authenticating users through external services. You can do this via a couple of single–sign-on schemes and underlying protocols: OpenID and OAuth. Whereas OpenID is essentially for uniquely identifying users, OAuth can do that and more. OAuth can get permissions from the user about resources held by the service provider that the application can use. This chapter presented an OAuth sample application that authenticates users by using the popular Twitter social network, thus gaining for itself the permission to read the tweets and connect to followers of logged-on users.

CHAPTER 7

Design considerations for ASP.NET MVC controllers

Part of the inhumanity of the computer is that, once it is competently programmed and working smoothly, it is completely honest.

—Isaac Asimov

The controller is the central element of any operation you perform in ASP.NET MVC. The controller is responsible for getting posted data, executing the related action, and then preparing and requesting the view. More often than not, these apparently simple steps generate a lot of code. Worse yet, similar code ends up being used in similar methods, and similar helper classes sprout up from nowhere.

ASP.NET MVC comes with the promise that it makes it easier for you to write cleaner and more testable code. For sure, ASP.NET MVC is based on some infrastructure that makes this possible and easier than in Web Forms. However, a lot is left to you, the developer, and to your programming discipline and design vision.

Architecturally speaking, the controller is just the same as the code-behind class in Web Forms. It is part of the presentation layer, and in some way it exists to forward requests to the back end of the application. Without development discipline, the controller can easily grow as messy and inextricable as an old-fashioned code-behind class. So, it isn't just choosing ASP.NET MVC that determines whether you're safe with regard to code cleanness and quality.

In this chapter, we explore an approach to ASP.NET MVC design that simplifies the steps you need to mechanize the implementation of the controller classes. The idea is to make the controller an extremely lean and mean class that delegates responsibility rather than orchestrating tasks. This design has an impact on other layers of the application and also on some portions of the ASP.NET MVC infrastructure.

Shaping up your controller

Microsoft Visual Studio makes it easy to create your own controller class. To do so, you simply right-click the project folder in the current ASP.NET MVC project and add a new controller class. In a controller class, you'll have one method per each user action that falls under the responsibility of the controller. How do you code an action method?

> **Note** Visual Studio tooling for ASP.NET MVC is no longer limited to letting you add a controller class exclusively in the Controllers folder. You can place a controller class anywhere, and right-clicking any folder displays the command to create a new empty controller class.

An action method should collect input data and use it to prepare one or multiple calls to some endpoint exposed by the middle tier of the application. Next, it receives output and ensures that output is in the format that the view needs to receive. Finally, the action method calls out the view engine to render a specific template.

Well, all this work might add up to several lines of code, making even a controller class with just a few methods quite a messy class. The first point—getting input data—is mostly solved for you by the model-binder class. Invoking the view is just one call to a method that triggers the processing of the action result. The core of the action method is in the code that performs the task and prepares data for the view.

Choosing the right stereotype

Generally speaking, an action method has two possible roles: it can be that of a controller, or it can be a coordinator. Where do words like "controller" and "coordinator" come from? Obviously, in this context the word "controller" has nothing to do with an ASP.NET MVC controller class.

These words refer to object stereotypes, a concept that comes from a methodology known as Responsibility-Driven Design (RDD). Normally, RDD applies to the design of an object model in the context of a system, but some of its concepts also apply neatly to the relatively simpler problem of modeling the behavior of an action method.

> **Note** For more information about RDD, check out *Object Design: Roles, Responsibilities, and Collaborations* by Rebecca Wirfs-Brock and Alan McKean (Addison-Wesley, 2002).

RDD at a glance

The essence of RDD consists of breaking down a system feature into a number of actions that the system must perform. Next, each of these actions is mapped to an object in the system being designed. Executing the action becomes a specific responsibility of the object. The role of the object depends on the responsibilities it assumes. Table 7-1 describes the key concepts of RDD and defines some of the terms associated with its use.

TABLE 7-1 Standard RDD concepts and terms

Concept	Description
Application	Refers to a collection of interconnected and interacting objects.
Collaboration	Refers to an established relation between two objects that work together to provide some meaningful behavior. The terms of collaboration are defined through an explicit contract.
Object	Refers to a software component that implements one or multiple roles.
Role	Refers to the nature of a software component that takes on a collection of (related) responsibilities.
Responsibility	Refers to the expected behavior of an object. Stereotypes are used to classify responsibilities.

Table 7-2 summarizes the main classes of responsibility for an object. These are referred to as object role stereotypes.

TABLE 7-2 Standard RDD stereotypes

Stereotype	Description
Controller	Orchestrates the behavior of other objects, and decides what other objects should do.
Coordinator	Solicited by events, it delegates work to other objects.
Information holder	Holds (or knows how to get) information and provides information.
Interfacer	Represents a façade to implement communication between objects.
Service provider	Performs a particular action upon request.
Structurer	Manages relations between objects.

In RDD, every software component has a role to play in a specific scenario. When using RDD, you employ stereotypes to assign each object its own role. Let's see how you can apply RDD stereotypes to an action method.

Breaking down the execution of a request

I've described some common steps that all action methods should implement. We can break down the responsibility of an action method as follows:

- Getting input data sent with the request

- Performing the task associated with the request

- Preparing the view model for the response

- Invoking the next view

You can use both the Controller and Coordinator RDD stereotypes to implement an action method—but they won't produce the same effects.

Acting as a "Controller"

Let's consider an action method in the apparently simple *place-an-order* use-case. In the real-world, placing an order is never a simple matter of adding a record to some Orders table, as you too often see happen in entry-level tutorials.

Place-an-order is an action that usually involves several steps and objects. For example, it might require querying the database to find out about the availability of the ordered goods. It might also require a separate order to be placed to a provider to refill the inventory, and typically requires checking the credit status of the customer and synchronizing with the bank of the customer and the shipping company. Finally, it also involves doing some updates on some database tables. After the order has been successfully placed, the system should display back to the user the ID, maybe an invoice to print, and possibly an estimated date of delivery.

The following pseudo-code gives you an idea of the concrete steps you need to take:

```
[HttpPost]
public ActionResult PlaceOrder(OrderInfo order)
{
    // Input data already mapped thanks to the model binder

    // Step 1-Check goods availability
    ...
    // Step 2-Check credit status of the customer
    ...
    // Step 3-Sync up with the shipping company
    ...
    // Step 4-Update databases
    ...
    // Step 5-Notify the customer
    ...

    // Prepare the view model
    var model = PlaceOrderViewModel { ... };
    ...

    // Invoke next view
    return View(model);
}
```

At a minimum, having all these steps coded in the controller means that you end up with calls made to the data access layer from the presentation. For simple Create, Read, Update, Delete (CRUD) applications, this is acceptable, but it's not acceptable for more complex applications.

Even when each of the steps outlined resolves in one or two lines of code, you have quite a long and soon unmanageable method. The RDD Controller stereotype applied to ASP.NET MVC controller classes suggests that you should use the previous layout of the code. This is not ideal even for moderately complex applications.

Important The business workflow behind the implementation of a use-case touches on multiple components possibly belonging to various layers or tiers in the system architecture. Some of the steps might be accomplished by a domain service (for example, prepare an invoice); other steps might be implemented by external services (for example, getting delivery information from the interconnected system of a partner shipping company); some more steps might simply be a database call (getting the order ID). All these calls should be seen as steps of a single workflow triggered by the presentation layer.

Acting as a "Coordinator"

The RDD Coordinator stereotype suggests that you group all of the steps that form the implementation of the action within a single worker object. From within the action method, you place a single call to the worker and use its output to feed the view-model object. Here's the layout:

```
[HttpPost]
public ActionResult PlaceOrder(OrderInfo order)
{
    // Input data already mapped thanks to the model binder

    // Perform the task invoking a worker service
    var service = new OrderService();
    var response = service.PerformSomeTask();

    // Prepare the view model
    var model = PlaceOrderViewModel(response);
    ...

    // Invoke next view
    return View(model);
}
```

The overall structure of the ASP.NET MVC controller method is much simpler now. Solicited by an incoming HTTP request, the action method relays most of the job to another component that coordinates all further steps. I call these components *worker services*, or just *application services*.

Important Worker services or application services belong to the application layer of the system. The application layer is where you have the application logic implemented that results from use-cases. This layer is not reusable, because it is specific to the application (and front end). Reusability should be pushed one layer down in the domain layer. The idea is that core functions are reusable (the domain), but presentation workflows are specific to the application. Here's a simple example to illustrate the point: In a desktop front end, you might have a single form to capture all data, whereas in a mobile front end you might need to go through multiple forms, each of which might require some interaction with the back end. Core functions (for example, placing an order or just synchronizing with the shipping company) remain reusable; workflows need to be adjusted.

Fat-free controllers

ASP.NET MVC is a framework that is designed to be testable and promotes important principles such as Separation of Concerns (SoC) and Dependency Injection (DI). ASP.NET MVC informs you that an application is separated in a part known as the controller and a part referred to as the view (not to mention the model discussed here). Being forced to create a controller class doesn't mean that you'll automatically achieve the right level of SoC, and it certainly doesn't mean that you're writing testable code. As mentioned in Chapter 1, "ASP.NET MVC controllers," ASP.NET MVC gets you off to a good start, but any further (required) layering is up to you.

What I haven't probably stated clearly enough is that if you don't pay close attention, you end up with a fat and messy controller class, which certainly isn't any better than a messy (and justifiably despised) code-behind class. So, you should aim to create controller classes as lean and mean collections of endpoints and remove any fat from them.

Note According to my standards, I wasn't precise earlier when I called DI a principle. More specifically, DI is just the most popular pattern used to implement the *Dependency Inversion Principle*, according to which the surface of contact between dependent classes should always be an interface instead of an implementation. Much less known (and understood) than DI in the wild, the Dependency Inversion Principle is the "D" in the popular SOLID acronym (*Single responsibility, Open-closed, Liskov substitution, Interface segregation and Dependency inversion principle*) that summarizes the five key design principles for writing clean, high-quality code.

Short is always better

If you have a method that is about 100 logical lines long, that code probably includes 10 to 15 lines of comments. Generally, 10 percent is considered to be a fair ratio of code to comments; I'd even go as high as a comment for every three logical lines if you want to ensure that you explain clearly the whys and wherefores of what you're doing and really want to help whomever deals with that piece of code after you.

However, regardless of what you decide the ideal ratio is, my point is that a method that's 100 lines long makes little sense, anyway. You can probably break it into three or four smaller methods and get rid of some comments, too.

I don't call myself an expert in software metrics, but I usually try to keep my methods below 30 lines—which more or less matches the real estate available in the Visual Studio editor on a typical laptop. How can you manage to keep the code of action methods as short as possible? Surprisingly enough, applying the RDD Coordinator stereotype is what you must do, but even that's not always sufficient.

Note A quick rule-of-thumb pattern I follow to break down code and improve readability is simply getting suspicious about every method that requires scrolling in a Visual Studio window that uses a font of regular size.

Action methods coded as view-model builders

A method designed to be a coordinator invokes a method on a worker object, has some work done, and gets some data back. This data should simply be packed into a dictionary or a strongly typed class and then passed down to the view engine.

The worker class, though, is attempting to bridge the gap between the data model you have on the middle tier—the domain model—and the data model you have in the presentation layer—the view model, or the data being worked on in the view. (By the way, "the data being worked on in the view" is the wording originally used in the MVC paper to define the role of the model.)

If the business objects you invoke on your middle tier return collections or aggregates of domain objects, you probably need to massage this data into view-model objects that faithfully represent the contracted user interface. If you move this work into the controller class, you're back to square one. The lines of code you cut off by using worker services and the RDD Coordinator stereotype are replaced by just as many lines for building a view model.

To support your efforts in getting fat-free controllers, I recommend a strategy based on the following points:

- Relay any action to a controller-specific worker service class (part of the application layer and not expected to be reusable).

- Make methods of the worker service class accept data as it comes from the model binder.

- Make methods of the worker service class return data expressed as view-model objects that are ready to be passed down to the view engine.

- Grab exceptions via attributes.

- Use .NET Code Contracts for checking preconditions and, where applicable, ensure postconditions.

- For anything else that requires additional logic, consider using custom action filters.

Let's see how I envision a worker service class.

Worker services

A worker service is a helper class that goes hand in hand with the controller. You might reasonably expect to have a distinct worker service class for each controller. On the other hand, the worker service is just an extension of a controller and results from the logical split of the controller behavior pushed by the RDD Coordinator role.

I'm using the word *service* here to indicate that this class provides a service to callers; it has nothing to do with any technology you might know for implementing services such as Windows Communication Foundation (WCF). At the same time, if you decide to scale out the application layer over multiple computers, WCF is an excellent technology to turn logical worker services into actual WCF services.

Figure 7-1 shows an architectural perspective of worker services in ASP.NET MVC.

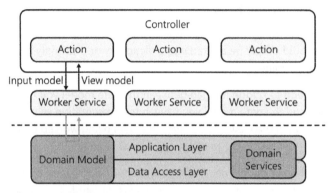

FIGURE 7-1 Worker services and controllers.

A worker service is just a matter of design, and design is design, regardless of its complexity. So, you don't have to wait for a giant project to experiment with these features. Let's go through a simple example that shows the power of the worker service approach. Admittedly, it might sound like a lot of work to do for a simple demonstration, but in the end, it costs you just an extra interface—and it scales exceptionally well with the complexity of the domain.

Implementing a worker service

You can start by creating a Services folder in your ASP.NET MVC project. Which folders you create within it is entirely your responsibility. I usually go with one folder for each controller plus an extra folder for interfaces. Figure 7-2 shows a glimpse of a project that uses this approach.

FIGURE 7-2 Worker services in an ASP.NET MVC project.

If you prefer, you can move the Services section to a separate assembly—it's your call. As mentioned, you create one worker service for each controller. For the *Home* controller, you can create the *IHomeService* interface and the *HomeService* class, as illustrated in the following:

```
public interface IHomeService
{
    IndexViewModel GetIndexViewModel();
}
public class HomeService : IHomeService
{
    private IHomeService _homeService;
    public IndexViewModel GetHomeViewModel()
    {
        ...
    }
    ...
}
```

In the sample application we're considering, the home page picks up a list of featured dates and renders the time span in days between those days and the current day. On the middle tier, you have a repository that returns information about featured dates such as the date, whether it is absolute or relative (for example, February 8, regardless of the year), and a description for the date. Here's an example for a featured date object for a domain model:

```
namespace FatFree.Backend.Model
{
    public class MementoDate
    {
        public DateTime Date { get; set; }
        public String Description { get; set; }
        public Boolean IsRelative { get; set; }
    }
}
```

The repository will likely fill up a collection of these objects when querying some database. At any rate, the worker service gets a collection of *MementoDate* objects and processes them up to the point of obtaining a collection of *FeaturedDate* objects—a type that belongs to another object model, the view model.

```
namespace FatFree.ViewModels.Shared
{
    public class FeaturedDate
    {
        public DateTime Date { get; set; }
        public Int32 DaysToGo { get; set; }
        public String Description { get; set; }
    }
}
```

There are two operations that need be done: First, any relative date must be transformed into an absolute date, and second, the time span between the given date and the current day must be calculated. For example, suppose that you want to calculate the distance to the next occurrence of February 8. The target date is different if you're computing January 2 or March 5. Here's a portion of the code in the worker service:

```
private IDateRepository _repository;
...
public HomeViewModel GetHomeViewModel()
{
    // Get featured dates from the middle tier
    var dates = _repository.GetFeaturedDates();

    // Adjust featured dates for the view
    //     For example, calculate distance from now to specified dates
    var featuredDates = new List<FeaturedDate>();
    foreach(var mementoDate in dates)
    {
        var fd = new FeaturedDate
                    {
                        Description = mementoDate.Description,
                        Date = mementoDate.IsRelative
                                    ? DateTime.Now.Next(mementoDate.Date.Month,
                                                        mementoDate.Date.Day)
                                    : mementoDate.Date
                    };
```

```
        fd.DaysToGo = (Int32)(DateTime.Now - fd.Date).TotalDays;
        featuredDates.Add(fd);
    }

    // Package data into the view model as the view engine expects
    var model = new HomeViewModel
                {
                    Title = "Memento (BETA)",
                    MessageFormat = "Today is <span class='dateEmphasis'>{0}</span>",
                    Today = DateTime.Now.ToString("dddd, dd MMMM yyyy"),
                    FeaturedDates = featuredDates
                };
    return model;
}
```

What about the controller? Here is the code you need:

```
public ActionResult Index()
{
    var model = _homeService.GetHomeViewModel();
    return View(model);
}
```

Figure 7-3 shows the sample page in action.

FIGURE 7-3 Worker services processing dates.

As you can see, there's no magic behind worker services. As the name suggests, they are worker classes that just break up the code that would logically belong to the processor of the request—the ASP.NET MVC controller.

Do we really need controllers?

The code of each controller method will hardly be as simple as what I've shown here, which was just one logical line. In real-world scenarios, you might need to pass some input data to the worker service; perhaps you might use an *if* statement to quickly rule out some cases, or even further edit the view-model object. This latter scenario might occur when you attempt to gain some reusability and get one worker service method to serve the needs of two or more controllers' action methods.

To flesh out the code in action methods, use exception handling, null checks, and preconditions. In the end, to keep action methods lean and mean, you need to push the RDD Coordinator role to the limit and move any processing logic out of the controller.

Does this mean that you don't need controllers anymore? Each HTTP request maps to an action method, but you need some plumbing to make the connection. In ASP.NET MVC, the controller is just part of the infrastructure, it shouldn't contain much of your code and, big surprise, there should be no need to test it. If you consider controllers to be part of the infrastructure, you take their basic behavior for granted; you need to test your worker services, instead. (This point is also touched upon in Chapter 9, "Testing and testability in ASP.NET MVC," which is entirely dedicated to testing ASP.NET MVC applications.)

The ideal action method code

Let's top off this discussion by analyzing an ideal fragment of code you should find in your action methods. It uses attributes to handle exceptions and Code Contracts to determine preconditions.

```
[HandleError(...)]
public class DateController : Controller
{
    private readonly IDateService _workerService;
    public DateController() : this(new DateService())
    {
    }
    public DateController(IDateService service)
    {
        _workerService = service;
    }


    [MementoInvalidDateException]
    [MementoDateExistsException]
    [HttpPost]
    public ActionResult Add(DateTime date, String description)
    {
        Contract.Requires<ArgumentException>(date > DateTime.MinValue);
        Contract.Requires<ArgumentException>(!String.IsNullOrEmpty(description));

        var model = _workerService.AddNewDate(date, description);
        return View(model);
    }
}
```

In this example, custom exception attributes are used to catch specific exceptions that might be raised by the worker service. In this case, you don't need to spoil your code with *if* statements and *null* checks. (I have nothing against using *if* statements, but if I can save myself and my peers a few lines of code and still keep code highly readable, well, by all means I do that.)

> **Important** As an attentive reader, you might have noticed that I completely ignored an important point: how to get a hold of an instance of the worker service. And, how does the worker service, in turn, get a hold of an instance of the repository? Techniques and tools to inject dependencies in your code is exactly the next topic. (Chapter 8, "Customizing ASP. NET MVC controllers," covers more about injection points and related techniques in the entire ASP.NET MVC framework.)

Connecting the presentation and back end

Assuming that we've agreed that you don't want to orchestrate the entire flow of logic for a given request within the context of a controller's action method, the next problem to address is where and how you cross the invisible border between the presentation layer and the back end of the application. In Figure 7-1, a subtly dashed line separates worker service blocks from the application layer—the topmost layer in an application back end.

Implementing action methods as RDD coordinators forces you to relay requests to other layers, but at some point you need to cross the border and invoke enterprise services, databases, business components, calculators, and whatever else you might have. So, choosing the coordinator route does have an impact on how you organize the downward layers and tiers of your application.

> **Note** Terms such as *layer* and *tier* are often used interchangeably, and sometimes with reason. Generally, though, a layer and a tier are neatly distinct entities. A layer refers to a logical separation, such as introducing a different assembly in the same process space. A tier refers to something physical, such as a software module that, although reachable, resides in a different process space and perhaps is hosted on a different hardware/software platform. To call a tier, you need data serialization, contracts, and, likely, a service technology such as WCF in the .NET space.

The Layered Architecture pattern

Everybody agrees that a multilayer system has a number of benefits in terms of maintainability, ease of implementation, extensibility, scalability, and testability. Most of the time, you arrange a three-level architecture with some flavors of service orientation just to make each layer ready for a possible move to a different physical tier. There are various reasons to move a layer onto its own tier: a quest for increased scalability, the need for stricter security measures, and also increased reliability in case the layers become decoupled because of computer failure.

In a three-level scenario, you typically have a presentation segment where you first take care of processing any user input and then arrange responses; a business logic segment that includes all the functional algorithms and calculations that make the system work and interact with other components; and the data access segment where you find all the logic required to read and write from storage.

Although this layout is still rock-solid in general terms, it probably needs to be refreshed in light of technologies available and findings and progress made in the industry with patterns and solutions.

Beyond classic layers

Terms like *presentation*, *business*, and *data access* mean everything and nothing today and are becoming quite blurred indeed. How do you really design and implement them? Too many variables apply, and too many choices, patterns, and practices can be adopted. The Layered Architecture pattern described next attempts to expand each of these segments into something more specific and provides guidance on how to do things.

In modern software architecture you find layers like presentation, application, domain and infrastructure. Figure 7-4 provides an overall view of a layered architecture. Mapping to classic Presentation+Business+Data layers is relatively simple. The classic Business layer usually expands to take a bit of everything: a bit of presentation, a bit of infrastructure, and the entire domain. The data layer is in the infrastructure. This is just to restate that layered architecture is nothing really new; it's just a more modern and pragmatic way of applying some old but still rock-solid theory.

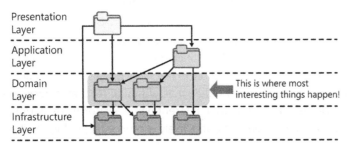

FIGURE 7-4 An example of layered architecture.

We can summarize a layered architecture as follows:

The presentation layer intercepts a request and relays it to the application layer. The application layer (also referenced as the *service layer*) is the segment of the application that implements use-cases. In this regard, it is specific to each application and not reusable. The application layer exposes endpoints to the presentation layer and decouples it from the rest of the system. The application layer orchestrates domain services as well as external services and business-specific enterprise components that you might have. Finally, the infrastructure layer encapsulates data access.

Observe that storage is not necessarily a relational database. These days, it can be a document database (NoSQL), a cloud data store, or perhaps an enterprise Customer Relationship Management (CRM) system. It varies to the point that "data access" is probably no longer the best term to describe it.

The (idiomatic) presentation layer

The key lesson that software architects have learned in the past decade is that no application can be built successfully without deeply involving the customer. Already mentioned as one of the key points in the Agile manifesto back in 2001, the collaboration between customers and development team, in reality, is often left to the good will of the involved parties. More often than not, collaboration remains just a good intention that's never entirely pursued.

Today, software is used to guide users to do their everyday job in the best and simplest possible way. The software must morph into what users expect, not the other way around—as was the case for too many years. I have quite a few memories of discussions I had with customers some 25 years ago in which I felt no shame in saying, "No, this feature is impossible to program the way you suggest; the language we're using doesn't support this." Such an answer is hard to imagine today.

Regardless of the technology you employ to build the client side of an application, the presentation layer is the part of the code that collects input from the user and triggers the expected behavior. If the application is distributed, the presentation layer is the segment of code responsible for preparing and executing the remote call and for arranging the new user interface after results are back. The important aspect is that the presentation logic invokes methods designed according to the user interface (UI) needs. These methods receive and return data formatted for the UI. The rule these days is that the UI receives exactly what it needs, in the form and shape that it likes it. This approach makes you a winner regardless of the various flavors of UI technologies that you might encounter—Microsoft Windows, browser, HTML5, mobile, Microsoft Silverlight, and so forth.

When it comes to implementation, the presentation layer is necessarily *idiomatic* in the sense that its actual code depends on the framework you're using. Although the overall idea remains the same, the presentation layer is based on code-behind pages in Web Forms, controllers (plus, optionally, worker services) in ASP.NET MVC, model-view-viewmodel (MVVM) classes in Silverlight and WPF, and so forth. For example, if you're having an entirely client-side single-page application (SPA), you might want to use some JavaScript frameworks that let you code by using either MVC or MVVM patterns, as well.

As far as ASP.NET MVC is concerned, applying the Layered Architecture pattern means delegating the production of a response for a request to a worker service which, in turn, will contact the back end to get a response. The response comes filled with data in the format required by the presentation layer.

The application layer

The application layer contains the implementation of use-cases, and you can view it as the aggregation of components that work as orchestrators. The term *orchestration* here refers to the implementation of any algorithm that serves a given use-case. For the *place-an-order* use-case, the orchestrator is the method that arranges the expected flow of data and coordinates domain services (for example, checking the credit status and refilling the inventory), external services (for example, sychronizing with the shipping company), business components (calculating prices), and storage (updating internal databases).

In relatively simple cases, or where you just don't have specific scalability requirements, the controller's worker service might coincide with the application layer. When it comes to this, keep in mind a popular Service-Oriented Architecture (SOA) warning: be chunky, not chatty. (See Figure 7-5.)

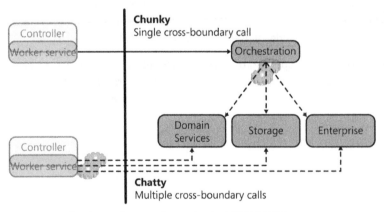

FIGURE 7-5 Chunky vs. chatty orchestration in ASP.NET MVC.

If services you orchestrate reside (for the most part) in the same process space as the worker service, you probably don't need to introduce yet another layer. In this case, orchestration coincides with worker services. You might want to compile worker services as a distinct assembly and upgrade their logical rank from a plain helper class to a constituent architectural block.

If services to orchestrate are remote or capable of being remote, you might want to introduce an extra orchestration layer in the same space as the services to orchestrate. In this case, you go from the worker service directly to this additional layer with a single call that wires all the data required for the various steps to take. Orchestrating from another tier—the presentation layer—would cost you a lot in terms of distributed computing, serialization, and network latency. This is the chatty antipattern of SOA design.

The domain layer

Although it hasn't been officially declared obsolete, the *DataSet* is a thing of the past for most developers. Not that there's something wrong with the *DataSet* design, it's just that a decade in software is really a long time. The pace of technology is such that a compelling solution devised 10 years ago can hardly have the same effectiveness in the next decade. Today, Entity Framework—not to mention NHibernate and other commercial solutions—makes it really quick to create a basic domain model around which to design your application. You can use Entity Framework and its Visual Studio tools to create entities and relationships and make these appear to be the actual database to the application's eyes. You don't need be a Domain-Driven Design (DDD) master to keep database details distinct from the objects you use to implement business operations.

A lot of developers today find it easy and effective to create an entity model and persist it with an Object/Relational Mapper (O/RM) tool such as Entity Framework or NHibernate.

This leads you to having an assembly with plain-old CLR (POCO) classes padded with data and behavior. This object model represents the model of data you have in the back end of the application. You have classes such as *Customer* with descriptive properties logically equivalent to some database columns: *Name*, *Address*, *Website*, *Email*, *Contact*, *Orders*. In addition, the *Customer* class will likely have a bunch of methods that validate the state of the object and implement object-specific operations on the property values associated with the instance. For example, you might have a method that calculates the total of *Orders* associated with the customer. Or, perhaps, for an *Invoice* class with properties like *Date* and *PaymentMode*, you can have a method that returns the estimated date of payment. In this object model, classes know nothing about persistence and things like connection strings.

Note *Object model*, *domain model*, and *entity model* are all similar terms often used interchangeably. However, each term has its own specific meaning. Sometimes, you don't need to go into the level of detail that requires using the precise meaning, so using them interchangeably is just fine. This casual usage, however, doesn't cancel the real meaning that each term holds. An object model is a plain, generic collection of objects. A domain model is special type of object model for which each class is POCO, aggregate roots are identified, factories are used over constructors, and value types tend to replace primitive types most of the time. Finally, an entity model is mostly an Entity Framework term that indicates a collection of (mostly anemic) classes, which might or might not be POCO. An anemic class has data but nearly no behavior.

What about more business-oriented behaviors, such as checking the credit status of a customer or perhaps verifying that a customer has placed enough orders to qualify for an elevated level of service or rewards? And, more generally, what about functionalities that produce or manipulate aggregated data that span multiple entities and require database access? These are special forms of orchestration limited to domain entities and their persistence. You implement them through another collection of classes called domain services. You likely have a domain service component for each significant entity or, to use DDD terminology, for each aggregate root. The domain model and domain services form the domain layer.

Exposing entities of the domain

What's the visibility of the classes in the domain layer? Should they emerge in the presentation layer, or are they destined to live and thrive in the folds of the back-end system? The world would be a better place if one could use domain objects everywhere. If your particular scenario makes it possible to move data around by using just one object model—the domain model—by all means call yourself lucky and go ahead. The fact is, however, that this is almost never an option except for conference demos and tutorials.

The presentation is built around use-cases, and each use-case might have a different definition of an entity. The order might have a different representation in use-cases, such as "The user places an order" and "The user reviews pending orders." Sometimes, it is affordable to use the same domain-based representation of the *Order* entity because the various use-cases need only a subset of the original *Order*. More often than not, though, each use-case needs objects that select some information from the original *Order* and some from other entities such as *Products*. In the domain model, you just don't have such aggregates. Hence, a view-focused object model must be created, and data must be transferred to and from it.

The view-focused object model is based on data-transfer objects (DTOs). A DTO is a plain container class (only data, no behavior) that is used to pass data around layers, tiers, and even within the same layer. With DTOs, you can definitely work any place with the data you need. But, the devil is in the details. A DTO-based solution is expensive and painful to code, period.

To deal with the extra complexity of DTOs, you can take advantage of tools such as AutoMapper (*http://automapper.codeplex.com*), which saves you from writing repetitive (and boring) code, or you can use T4 templates for saving some common code and just write the custom parts yourself.

The infrastructure layer

How would you get a reference to a domain object? In general, a domain object can be *transient* or *persistent*. It is said to be transient if a new instance is created in memory and populated with run-time data. It is said to be persistent if the instance contains data read from storage. You typically deal with transient entities when you're about to insert a new order; you deal with persistent entities when you fetch an order from storage for display or processing reasons.

The infrastructure layer is mostly the database layer, renamed to lower focus and emphasis on data and models. In modern systems, you still need persistence but that doesn't necessarily come out of relational models and is anyway limited to mere storage of raw data with everything else (for example, constraints, validation, actions) taking place at a higher layer of the system.

So, the infrastructure layer deals with persistence and consists of repository classes—one per significant entity (or, if you prefer, aggregate root). The repository class uses a given storage API to implement persistence. Repositories are classes whose implementation logically belongs to the data access layer. The repository class collects multiple methods that serve the data access needs of that entity. In a repository, you typically find methods to fetch, add, delete, and update data.

The repository exposes an interface to the application layer and uses a storage API internally. Thus, you can have a repository that uses Entity Framework and a POCO model or one that uses NHibernate. You can have a repository that persists the domain through a plain ADO.NET layer. You can also make the repository point to some cloud storage, Dynamics CRM, or a NoSQL service. Created on a per-entity basis (precisely, major entities only), the repository is the gateway to the actual persistence layer.

Using repositories is important also for another reason—making your business services testable by mocking the persistence layer.

What's the typical structure of a repository class? There are two main schools of thought. Some prefer to have a generic repository that provides basic CRUD methods for each entity, such as that shown here:

```
public abstract class Repository<T> where T : IAggregateRoot
{
    internal YourContext ActiveContext { get; set; }
    public Repository()
    {
        ActiveContext = new YourContext();
    }
    public void Add(T item)
    {
        this.AddObject(item);
        this.ActiveContext.SaveChanges();
    }
}
```

```
    public bool Remove(T item)
    {
        try {
            this.DeleteObject(item);
            this.ActiveContext.SaveChanges();
            return true;
        } catch {
            return false;
        }
    }
    public void Update(T item)
    {
        this.ActiveContext.SaveChanges();
    }
    :
}
```

As far as queries are concerned, here's a list of methods you might have in a generic repository class:

```
T[] GetAll<T>();
T[] GetAll<T>(Expression<Func<T, bool>> filter);
T GetSingle<T>(Expression<Func<T, bool>> filter);
```

You pass the details of the query to be executed as a function via either *GetAll* or *GetSingle*.

Others prefer to just have a regular class with as many methods as required by the logic to be implemented. In this case, you end up with a class that is tailor-made to the entity. You can easily treat special cases for deletions and insertions appropriately and have a specific *get* method to call for each necessary query. In the end, the choice is up to you because none of these approaches is clearly better than the other. Personally, I like to have specific (nongeneric) repositories.

> **Note** Speaking of repositories, there is another point I should mention. It is related to the lifetime of the context object if you use an O/RM to persist data. In the previous listing, you see an *ActiveContext* property instantiated by the constructor. In this way, the context lives as long as the instance is live. Multiple calls you make to the same instance will have access to the same identity map and can track changes. An alternative is to use locally scoped instances that are dismissed at the end of each repository operation.

Injecting data and services in layers

The primary reason for using layers (and tiers) is SoC. As an architect, you determine which layer talks to which layer, and you have testing, code inspection, and perhaps check-in policies enforce these rules. However, even when two layers are expected to collaborate, you don't want them to be tightly coupled. In this regard, the Dependency Inversion Principle (recall from earlier in the chapter that this is the "D" in the SOLID acronym) helps a lot. I'd even say that the Dependency Inversion Principle is much more important than the Dependency Injection pattern, which seems to be on everybody's mind these days.

The Dependency Inversion Principle

Defined, the Dependency Inversion Principle (DIP) states that high-level classes should not depend on lower-level classes. Instead, high-level classes should always depend on abstractions of their required lower-level classes. In a way, this principle is a specialization of one of the pillars of object-oriented design; program to an interface, not to an implementation.

DIP is the formalization of a top-down approach to defining the behavior of any significant class method. In using this top-down approach, you focus on the work flow that happens at the method level rather than focusing on the implementation of its particular dependencies. At some point, though, lower-level classes should be linked to the mainstream code. DIP suggests that this should happen via injection.

In a way, DIP indicates an inversion of the control flow whenever a dependency is encountered—the main flow doesn't care about details of the dependency as long as it has access to an abstraction of it. The dependency is then injected in some way when necessary. Figure 7-6 shows a personalized version of the classic diagram for the canonical example of DIP as originally presented by Robert Martin in the paper that you can find at *http://www.objectmentor.com/resources/articles/dip.pdf*.

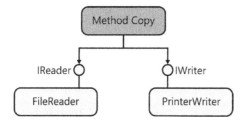

FIGURE 7-6 The DIP diagram.

The paper describes a sample *Copy* function that reads from a source and writes to a target stream. The *Copy* function ideally doesn't care about the details of the reader and writer components. It should care only about the interface of the reader and writer. The reader and writer are then injected or resolved in some way around the implementation of the *Copy* function. How this point is approached depends on the actual pattern you intend to use.

To address DIP, you commonly use either of two patterns: the *Service Locator* pattern or the *Dependency Injection* pattern.

The Service Locator pattern

The Service Locator pattern defines a component that knows how to retrieve the services that an application might need. The caller has no need to specify the concrete type; the caller normally indicates an interface, a base type, or even a nickname of the service in the form of a string or a numeric code.

The *Service Locator* pattern hides the complexity of component lookup, handles the caching or pooling of instances and, in general, offers a common façade for component lookup and creation. Here's the typical implementation of a service locator:

```
public class ServiceLocator
{
    private static const String SERVICE_QUOTEPROVIDER = "quoteprovider";

    // You might also want to have a generic method GetService<T>()...
    public static Object GetService(Type t)
    {
      if (t == typeof(IQuoteProvider))
      {
         return new SomeQuoteProvider();
      }
      ...
    }

    public static Object GetService(String serviceName)
    {
       switch(serviceName)
       {
           case SERVICE_QUOTEPROVIDER:
               return new SomeQuoteProvider();
           ...
       }
    }
}
```

As you can see, the locator is merely a wrapper around a *Factory* object that knows how to get an instance of a given (or indirectly referenced) type. Let's have a look now at the code that calls the locator. The following code illustrates a class that first gets quotes for the specified list of symbols and then renders values out to an HTML string:

```
public class FinanceInfoService
{
  public String GetQuotesAsHtml(String symbols)
  {
    // Get dependencies
    var renderer = ServiceLocator.GetService("quoterenderer");
    var provider = ServiceLocator.GetService("quoteprovider");

    // Use dependencies
    var stocks = provider.FindQuoteInfo(symbols);
    var html = renderer.RenderQuoteInfo(stocks);

    return html;
  }
}
```

The locator code lives within the method that manages the abstraction, and the factory is part of the deal. By simply looking at the signature of the *FinanceInfoService* class, you can't say whether it has dependencies on external components. You must inspect the code of the *GetQuotesAsHtml* method to find it out.

The main *Service Locator* focus is to achieve the lowest possible amount of coupling between components. The locator represents a centralized console that an application uses to obtain all the external dependencies it needs. In doing so, the *Service Locator* pattern also produces the pleasant side effect of making your code more flexible and extensible.

Using the *Service Locator* pattern is not a bad thing from a purely functional perspective. However, in more practical terms, a better option exists: the *Dependency Injection* pattern.

The *Dependency Injection* pattern

The biggest difference between *Service Locator* and *Dependency Injection* is that with dependency injection, the factory code lives outside of the class being worked on. The pattern suggests that you design the class in such a way that it receives all of its dependencies from the outside. Here's how to rewrite the *FinanceInfoService* class for making use of *Dependency Injection* pattern:

```
public class FinanceInfoService
{
  private IQuoteProvider _provider;
  private IRenderer _renderer;

  public FinanceInfoService(IQuoteProvider provider, IRenderer renderer)
  {
      _provider = provider;
      _renderer = renderer;
  }

  public string GetQuotesAsHtml(string symbols)
  {
    var stocks = _provider.FindQuoteInfo(symbols);
    string html = _renderer.RenderQuoteInfo(stocks);
    return html;
  }
}
```

When it comes to using *Dependency Injection* in classes, a critical decision that the developer must make is about how and where to allow for code injection. There are three ways to inject dependencies into a class: using the constructor, a settable property, or the parameters of a method. All three techniques are valid, and the choice is ultimately up to you. In general terms, the consensus is to use constructors for necessary dependencies, and setters for optional dependencies. However, some considerations apply.

What if you have many dependencies? In this case, your constructor would look dangerously messy. Even though a long list of parameters in the constructor is often the sign of some design issues, this isn't a hard-and-fast rule. You might encounter situations in which you have complex constructors with many parameters. In this case, grouping dependencies in a compound object is a solution. In a nutshell, your goal should be to reveal dependencies and intentions right at construction time. You can do this in two ways: via a set of classic constructors you manage to keep as simple as possible, or via factories.

Factories are the preferred approach in the DDD methodology. Using a factory, you can express more clearly the context in which you need an instance of the type. You can also deal with dependencies inside the factory code and ensure that you return valid objects from the beginning. In addition, your classes end up having only the default constructor (probably implemented as a protected member).

Using constructors also hinders inheritance because derived classes might have the need to receive dependencies, as well. When you add a new dependency, this design scheme might require more refactoring work.

When the dependency is optional, however, there's no strict need to make it show up at the constructor level. In this case, using a setter property is fine and probably the recommended approach because it helps keep the constructor (or factory code) leaner and cleaner.

In summary, there are good reasons for using the constructor and good reasons for going with setter properties. As with many other architectural questions, the right answer is, "It depends." It also depends on your personal taste.

Using tools for Inversion of Control

DI takes any code that relates to the setup of dependencies out of the class. When dependencies are nested, this code might be quite a few lines long; furthermore, for the most part it is boilerplate code. For this reason, developers have created ad hoc frameworks known as Inversion of Control (IoC) frameworks. An IoC container is a framework specifically created to support DI. You can consider it a productivity tool for implementing DI quickly and effectively. From the perspective of an application, a container is a rich factory that provides access to external objects to be retrieved and consumed later.

All IoC frameworks are built around a container object that, when bound to some configuration information, resolves dependencies. The caller code instantiates the container and passes the desired interface as an argument. In response, the IoC framework returns a concrete object that implements that interface. An IoC container holds a dictionary of type mappings where typically an abstract type (for example, an interface) is mapped to a concrete type or an instance of a given concrete type. Table 7-3 lists some of the most popular IoC frameworks available today.

TABLE 7-3 Popular IoC frameworks

Framework	URL
Autofac	*http://code.google.com/p/autofac*
Castle Windsor	*http://www.castleproject.org/container/index.html*
Ninject	*http://www.ninject.org*
Spring.NET	*http://www.springframework.net*
StructureMap	*http://structuremap.net/structuremap/index.html*
Unity	*http://unity.codeplex.com*

After it is configured, an IoC container gives you the ability to resolve the entire chain of dependencies between your types with a single call. In addition, you save yourself all the intricacies of inner dependencies. For example, if you have some *ISomeService* parameter in a class constructor or property, you can be sure you'll get it at run time as long as you instruct the IoC container to resolve it. The beauty of this approach is that if the constructor of the concrete type mapped to *ISomeService* has its own dependencies, these are resolved, as well, and automatically.

Take this further and you see the point: with an IoC container, you stop caring about the cloud of dependencies. Furthermore, all you do is design the graph of dependencies using the syntax supported by the IoC of choice. Everything else happens free of charge.

IoC containers differ in terms of the syntax they support (for example, lambda expressions), the configuration policies used (for example, the external XML scheme), plus additional features that are available. Two features are gaining a lot of importance today: aspect-orientation capabilities (specifically, interception) and specialized modules that facilitate integration with WCF services.

Note With regard to Unity (Microsoft's IoC library) you can find coverage of advanced features, including interception, in my Cutting Edge column in *MSDN Magazine*; specifically, in the January/February 2011 issues. You can find an excellent article that can help you to understand how to use Unity to inject dependencies during the initialization of a WCF service at *http://blogs.microsoft.co.il/blogs/gadib/archive/2010/11/30/wcf-and-unity-2-0.aspx*.

The poor-man's DI

Today, many tend to confuse the *Dependency Injection* pattern with using an IoC framework. Using an IoC framework is a matter of productivity; as such, it often requires a minimum critical mass of complexity to become really effective. In simpler cases, you can opt for what many like to call the poor-man's DI. You can find an example of this technique in the source code of the FatFree example you saw back in Figure 7-3.

How would you inject a worker service in a controller class and a repository in a worker service? The most obvious way is by letting controllers and services create a fresh new instance of the dependent object. This route, however, creates a tight dependency between objects that hinders extensibility and testability. Here's a better approach:

```
public class HomeController : Controller
{
    private readonly IHomeService _workerService;
    public HomeController() : this(new HomeService())
    {
    }
    public HomeController(IHomeService service)
    {
        _workerService = service;
    }
    ...
}
```

When the default constructor is used to instantiate a controller, the worker service member points to a freshly created instance of a default worker service class. A second constructor is available to manually inject any instance you like, at least for testability reasons. Likewise, you do the same for injecting the repository dependency into the worker service.

However, ASP.NET MVC always uses the default constructor for each controller class, unless you gain control of the controller factory.

 Note ASP.NET MVC is designed with several extensibility points, but generally it lacks a comprehensive support for DI. A service locator is probably the most effective way of making an existing framework more loosely coupled by the addition of new extensibility points because it is the least intrusive solution. A service locator acts as a black box that you install in a specific point and let it figure out what contract is required and how to get it. ASP.NET MVC has its own model of service locator, called *dependency resolvers*, and I cover them in Chapter 8.

Gaining control of the controller factory

In ASP.NET MVC, the instantiation of the controller class is a topical moment. The ASP.NET MVC infrastructure includes a factory that uses the default constructor of the selected controller class. What if you have parameterized constructors on your controller class and need to pass in some data? This scenario is not supported out of the box, but the extremely extensible design of ASP.NET MVC offers a hook for you to replace the default controller factory with your own.

A common way to replace the default controller factory is to integrate an IoC container in it so that any parameter can be resolved brilliantly by looking at the table of registered types. The following sections explain how to do it.

Registering a custom controller factory

It all starts in *Application_Start*, where you register your own controller factory. A controller factory is a class that implements the *IControllerFactory* interface. To register the factory, you create a proper configuration class in accordance with the new pattern pushed by ASP.NET MVC. (Other approaches are fine, as well, though.)

```
protected void Application_Start()
{
    // Register a custom controller factory
    ControllerConfig.RegisterFactory(ControllerBuilder.Current);
    ...
}
```

The *ControllerConfig* class is a simple class with a static method, as shown in the following:

```
public static void RegisterFactory(ControllerBuilder builder)
{
    var factory = new UnityControllerFactory();
    builder.SetControllerFactory(factory);
}
```

Let's see a controller factory from the inside.

Building a custom controller factory

A typical controller factory class inherits from *DefaultControllerFactory* and overrides a few methods, as detailed in Table 7-4.

TABLE 7-4 Popular IoC frameworks

Overridable methods	Description
CreateController	Governs the creation of a controller instance. It takes the name of the controller (for example, home) and returns a controller instance. The default implementation first invokes *GetControllerType* to map the controller name to a type and then calls *GetControllerInstance* to actually create an instance.
GetControllerInstance	Gets a controller type and the request context, and returns a newly created instance of the controller.
GetControllerSessionBehavior	Gets the session state behavior for the controller type. Note: You override this method if you want to control programmatically how the session state behavior is determined. By default, it is controlled by the *SessionState* attribute.
GetControllerType	Gets the controller name and the request context and returns the expected type of the controller. Note: You override this method if you don't like the convention that the controller type is always given by a name followed by "Controller".
ReleaseController	Performs any cleanup task for when the controller instance is dismissed.

Note that the *CreateController* and *ReleaseController* methods are public; all of the other methods are protected. Creating your own factory also makes it possible for you to perform any sort of custom work on freshly created instances of controllers. For example, you might want to centralize the initialization of some custom properties (if you're deriving your controllers from a base class). More likely, you might want to use this hook to give a controller instance a handmade action invoker. (I discuss action invokers in Chapter 8.)

A Unity-based controller factory

When you introduce a custom factory based on Unity, at a minimum you want to override *GetController Instance* to use the Unity infrastructure to resolve the controller type, as demonstrated here:

```
public class UnityControllerFactory : DefaultControllerFactory
{
    public static IUnityContainer Container { get; private set; }

    public UnityControllerFactory()
    {
        Container = new UnityContainer();
        Container.LoadConfiguration();
    }

    protected override IController GetControllerInstance(
                    RequestContext requestContext, Type controllerType)
    {
        if (controllerType == null)
            return null;
        return Container.Resolve(controllerType) as IController;
    }
}
```

Using the Unity engine guarantees that further dependencies rooted in the controller type are identified and resolved. With reference to the FatFree example, this is just what happens with worker service and date repository dependencies.

The code just shown looks pretty generic—which is the reason why IoC tools ultimately became so successful. IoC tools enhance productivity because they save you a lot of boilerplate code. Where are the details?

Just like any other IoC framework, Unity needs some configuration data. You can place this data in the *web.config* file or use the Unity API to add it programmatically. In the end, this configuration data consists of specifying which interface type maps to which concrete type and where these types can be found. Here's a modified *web.config* file that contains a Unity section:

```
<configuration>
  <configSections>
    <section name="unity" type="Microsoft.Practices.Unity.Configuration.
    UnityConfigurationSection,
                            Microsoft.Practices.Unity.Configuration, ..." />
  </configSections>

  ...
  <unity xmlns="http://schemas.microsoft.com/practices/2010/unity">
    <assembly name="FatFreeIoC" />
    <namespace name="FatFreeIoC.Backend.DAL" />
    <namespace name="FatFreeIoC.Services.Abstractions" />
    <namespace name="FatFreeIoC.Services.Home" />
    <container>
      <register type="IHomeService" mapTo="HomeService">
      </register>
      <register type="IDateRepository" mapTo="DateRepository">
      </register>
    </container>
  </unity>
</configuration>
```

The namespace entry registers a namespace that Unity uses to qualify types. The assembly entry lists assemblies to be considered to resolve types. Under the container group, you register types. The register node can contain a bunch of child nodes to provide additional information for injection and interception. (These aspects are not relevant in this book. For more information, refer to the official Unity documentation online at *http://msdn.microsoft.com/en-us/library/ff663144.aspx.*)

Summary

In this chapter, I tried to call each entity involved in a typical ASP.NET MVC application with its own name and role. I wouldn't be surprised if, at first glance, you're tempted to dismiss the material and be a bit annoyed by what seems to be unnecessary complexity. Why on earth should you create a worker service that is apparently just a cool way to waste CPU cycles?

If the complexity of your application compares to that of many tutorials available out there (for example, Music Store), I say good for you. You should go ahead and call the Entity Framework data context right from action methods and forget about layers and layered architecture. You can blissfully and happily design quite a few applications in this way. The idea of ignoring entry-level tutorials couldn't be more foreign to me. They do a great job of getting you started and demonstrating things concretely.

However, it should be clear that it is only the first step. Many common practices just don't scale well with increased complexity of the model and domain. In this chapter, I summarized a few practices that take your ASP.NET MVC application up to the next level of complexity. A key good practice is keeping the controller class lean and mean by moving most of the logic out to worker services. Another good practice is keeping the view as humble and passive as possible by moving code to HTML helpers and controllers, preferably through strongly typed view models, but render actions also are acceptable. Yet another practice is layering the back end of the application to distinguish between domain model, domain services, and repositories. Repositories should be the only way to access data, and services should invoke them whenever possible, thus shielding controllers from them.

So, are simpler tutorials the wrong way to demonstrate these things? No, as long as you consider the code in them as a special case of more general patterns discussed in this chapter (and in the rest of the book, to a good extent).

For simple applications, ASP.NET MVC is an easy framework to use; for complex applications, it might get tricky. But, if you manage it well, your resulting code will definitely be high-quality code—much more so than in Web Forms, assuming a similar level of effort and skills.

CHAPTER 8

Customizing ASP.NET MVC controllers

We need men who can dream of things that never were.

—*John F. Kennedy*

The entire ASP.NET MVC stack is full of extensibility points. An extensibility point is a place in the code at which the actual behavior that takes place can be read from an external and replaceable provider. In the previous chapters, you saw a few examples of extensibility points. You saw, for example, how to replace the controller factory—that is, the component that returns fresh instances of controller classes for each incoming request. (See Chapter 7, "Design considerations for ASP.NET MVC controllers.") Chapter 4, "Input forms," discusses how to replace a model metadata provider—that is, the component that reads meta-information about classes to be used in HTML forms.

In a programming framework such as ASP.NET MVC, the benefits of an extensible design will ripple across any applications built on top of it. In this chapter, my goal is to help you discover the points of extensibility you find in ASP.NET MVC and to illustrate them with a few examples. I'll start with a brief discussion of the extensibility model in ASP.NET MVC and then proceed with a thorough examination of aspects of controllers that you can customize at your leisure and that will result in lean and mean controllers as well as improved maintainability and readability.

The extensibility model of ASP.NET MVC

An extensibility point is tightly coupled with an *extensibility* model. This is the programming model according to which a developer can unplug the existing implementation of a component and create his own. In ASP.NET MVC, you have two functionally equivalent extensibility models that differ in the API they require you to use. One is based on providers you register explicitly using a fluent syntax. The other is based on the classic Service Locator pattern and is introduced to let developers benefit more and more from Inversion-of-Control (IoC) frameworks.

These two models cover the replacement of internal components, such as view engines, action invokers, metadata providers, and factories. Another segment of the ASP.NET MVC extensibility model is based on special attributes—named action filters—that you use to inject custom (and even optional) code in the execution flow of controller methods. Let's tackle the replacement of internal components first.

The provider-based model

Replaceable internal components of the ASP.NET MVC stack exist for very specific situations. You don't want to take advantage of them in just any application you write. Suppose that these extensibility points are there only in case they're needed. If at some point you decide to replace them, be aware that you're interacting with the internal machinery of ASP.NET MVC. Your components, therefore, are the first suspect in the case of performance or functional issues.

Gallery of extensibility points

Table 8-1 provides a quick list of extensibility points.

TABLE 8-1 Replaceable components

Provider	Interface or base class	Description
Action invoker	*DefaultActionInvoker*	Governs the execution of action methods and the generation of the browser response. It interacts with filters and view engines. (I'll say more about this later.)
Controller factory	*DefaultControllerFactory*	Serves as the factory for controller instances. It can be used to set a custom action invoker for the freshly created controller instance.
Dictionary values	*IValueProvider*	Reads values to be added to the dictionary of input values for a request. Built-in value providers read from query strings, forms, input files, and routes. Custom providers might read from cookies or HTTP headers.
Model binder	*IModelBinder*	Defines a binder type that transforms raw values in some value provider dictionaries into a specific complex type.
Model binder provider	*IModelBinderProvider*	Defines a model binder factory that dynamically selects the right model binder to use for a given type.
Model metadata	*ModelMetadataProvider*	Retrieves meta-information about members of a class, and associates that information with any instance of that type. The default provider reads meta-information from *DataAnnotations* attributes.
Model validator	*ModelValidatorProvider*	The description is the same as for the preceding model metadata item, except that it focuses on validation aspects. The default provider reads meta-information from validation *DataAnnotations* attributes.
TempData	*ITempDataProvider*	Serves as the storage of any data being placed in the *TempData* collection. The default provider uses session state.
View engine	*IViewEngine*	Serves as a component capable of interpreting a view template and producing HTML markup for the browser. Default view engines can translate ASPX and Razor markup to HTML.

As you can see, these are not the components you use every day. However, I've customized most of them at least once in my years of programming, but usually I haven't customized more than one or two components at a time.

A realistic scenario: alternate TempData storage

The TempData dictionary is used to store data that logically belongs to the current request but must survive across a redirect. Chapter 4 demonstrates using TempData in the context of the Post-Redirect-Get (PRG) pattern for input forms. According to the PRG pattern, you should terminate a POST request with a GET redirect to the view that displays results. The entire state of the request (for example, validation messages) might be lost across the redirect. The TempData dictionary provides a temporary store for any data (mostly *ModelState*) you need.

By default, the TempData dictionary saves its content to the session state. The key difference between using *Session* directly or through TempData is that any data stored in TempData is automatically cleared up after the successive request terminates. In other words, data stays in memory for just two requests: the current request and the next redirect. TempData, in the end, puts much less pressure on memory.

What if your application is not allowed to use session state?

Either you work out an entirely different solution based on the query string or you just provide different storage for TempData content. What would be different storage? It can be a cookie (if the overall size of your data matches the limitations on cookie size), or it can be a (distributed) cache. If you choose the latter, storing the data on a per-user basis is entirely your responsibility. Here's what a custom TempData provider looks like:

```
public class CookieTempDataProvider : ITempDataProvider
{
    protected override IDictionary<String, Object> LoadTempData(ControllerContext
controllerContext)
    { ... }
    protected override void SaveTempData(ControllerContext controllerContext,
                             IDictionary<String, Object> values)
    { ... }
}
```

You can find a working example of this class (as well as many other replacements for the components listed in Table 8-1) by simply checking StackOverflow questions, which you can access at *http://www.stackoverflow.com*. Here's one in particular that I like: *http://brockallen.com/2012/06/11/cookie-based-tempdata-provider.*

Using custom components in your applications

For a long time, there was no standard way to register custom components. Each component listed in Table 8-1 required its own API to be integrated into a user application. As you'll see in a moment, you have now an additional model based on dependency resolvers that is for the most part parallel to the custom model supported in earlier version of ASP.NET MVC.

Table 8-2 describes how to register the special replaceable components listed in Table 8-1.

TABLE 8-2 Registering replaceable components

Provider	Description
Action invoker	`// In the constructor of a controller class` `this.ActionInvoker = new YourActionInvoker();`

Controller factory	`// In global.asax, Application_Start`
	`var factory = new YourControllerFactory();`
	`ControllerBuilder.Current.SetControllerFactory(factory);`

Dictionary values	`// In global.asax, Application_Start`
	`var providerFactory = new YourValueProviderFactory();`
	`ValueProviderFactories.Factories.Add(providerFactory);`

Model binder	`// In global.asax, Application_Start` `ModelBinders.Binders.Add(typeof(YourType), new YourTypeBinder());`

Model binder provider	`// In global.asax, Application_Start`
	`var provider = new YourModelBinderProvider();`
	`ModelBinderProviders.BinderProviders.Add(provider);`

Model metadata	`// In global.asax, Application_Start ModelMetadataProviders.Current = new` `YourModelMetadataProvider();`

Model validator	`// In global.asax, Application_Start`
	`var validator = new YourModelValidatorProvider();`
	`ModelValidatorProviders.Providers.Add(validator);`

TempData	`// In the constructor of a controller class this.TempDataProvider = new` `YourTempDataProvider();`

View engine	`// In global.asax, Application_Start`
	`ViewEngines.Engines.Clear();`
	`ViewEngines.Engines.Add(new YourViewEngine());`

I want to take a few more moments to discuss value providers. As the code snippets in Table 8-2 show, you don't manage a collection of value providers, you manage a collection of value provider factories. This means that for each custom value provider you intend to add, you should write two distinct classes: the value provider and its factory. However, only the factory class should be registered with the system at startup. The value provider factory is a thin wrapper, as shown here:

```
public class HttpCookieValueProviderFactory : ValueProviderFactory
{
    public override IValueProvider GetValueProvider(ControllerContext controllerContext)
    {
        return new HttpCookieValueProvider(controllerContext);
    }
}
```

The class represents a factory for a custom value provider; also in this case, there are quite a few implementations that have been contributed by the community of developers. You can find some on StackOverflow.

The Service Locator pattern

Service Locator is a popular pattern used in the design of loosely coupled systems. The core of the pattern is a globally accessible factory class responsible for serving instances of classes that implement a given contract. The basic interaction taking place between a service locator and its clients can be summarized as a conversation that starts like this: I need an object that behaves like this type; do you know about some concrete type that you can instantiate for me? The service locator then replies by returning such an instance or null.

The term "Service Locator" (and variations such as "Service Location") is often used to indicate a scenario in which a class gets external dependencies, thus remaining open for extension but closed for modifications. What's the difference, really, between the Service Locator (or Location) pattern and Dependency Injection?

Service Locator vs. Dependency Injection

Functionally speaking, the Service Locator (SL) pattern is nearly identical to Dependency Injection (DI), and both are concrete implementations of the Dependency Inversion Principle—the "D" in the popular SOLID acronym (which in its entirety stands for *S*ingle responsibility, *O*pen-closed, *L*iskov substitution, *I*nterface segregation and *D*ependency inversion principle). SL is historically the first pattern that was widely employed in the building of loosely coupled, testable systems. Later on, DI was introduced as a slightly better way of doing the same things. The difference between SL and DI is more or less blurred, depending on the level of abstraction from which you're looking at them. For sure, there's a difference at the source-code level. With SL, a class queries an external component for getting its dependencies. With DI, a class is given its dependencies through the constructor (or public properties).

Here's what a class that uses SL looks like:

```
public class FinanceInfoService
{
  private IFinder _finder;
  private IRenderer _renderer;

  public FinanceInfoService()
  {
    _finder = ServiceLocator.GetService<IFinder>();
    _renderer = ServiceLocator.GetService<IRenderer>();
  }

  public String GetQuotesAsHtml(String symbols)
  {
    var stocks = _finder.FindQuoteInfo(symbols);
    return _renderer.RenderQuoteInfo(stocks);
  }
}
```

The same class refactored to use DI looks like this:

```
public class FinanceInfoService
{
  private IFinder _finder;
  private IRenderer _renderer;

  public FinanceInfoService(IFinder f, IRenderer r)
  {
      _finder = f;
      _renderer = r;
  }

  public string GetQuotesAsHtml(string symbols)
  {
    var stocks = _finder.FindQuoteInfo(symbols);
    return _renderer.RenderQuoteInfo(stocks);
  }
}
```

The difference is all in the constructor and in how dependencies are retrieved. Which approach should you use?

For new systems built from scratch, DI is preferable; it keeps your code cleaner and makes it easier to read and test. With DI, dependencies are explicit in the class signature. The surrounding framework, however, is entirely responsible for preparing dependencies and injecting them. For existing systems, SL is far easier to plug in because it only requires you to encapsulate calls in a sort of black box that expose an interface.

SL in ASP.NET MVC

ASP.NET MVC is designed with several extensibility points but lacks comprehensive support for DI. The various APIs listed in Table 8-2 prove this statement beyond any reasonable doubt. To make an existing framework more loosely coupled through the addition of new extensibility points, a service locator is probably the most effective because it's the least intrusive solution. A service locator acts as a black box that you install in a specific point and then let it figure out what contract is required and how to get it.

Parallel to the APIs listed in Table 8-2, ASP.NET MVC offers you the ability to register your own service locator that the framework will use any time it needs to resolve a dependency. The service locator is optional, and using it or sticking with the APIs listed in Table 8-2 is equivalent in terms of functionality.

When resolving a dependency, ASP.NET MVC always uses the internal service locator first. The actual behavior changes slightly if the dependency can be registered singly or multiple times. From a developer's perspective, however, all that matters is that if a custom component is registered in two ways (using the service locator or any of the APIs in Table 8-2), the service locator is given precedence.

Note A singly registered component is a component that must be unique to the application. An example is the controller factory—you can't have two factories in the same application. Examples of components registered multiple times are the view engine and the model validator providers. In both cases, you can have multiple instances registered and exposed to the rest of the system.

Defining your dependency resolver

The implementation of the ASP.NET MVC service locator consists of a thin wrapper around a user-defined object known as the dependency resolver. A dependency resolver—which is unique to each application—is an object that implements the following interface:

```
public interface IDependencyResolver
{
    Object GetService(Type serviceType);
    IEnumerable<Object> GetServices(Type serviceType);
}
```

The logic you put in the resolver is entirely up to you. It can be as simple as a switch statement that checks the type and returns a newly created instance of a fixed type. It can be made more sophisticated by reading information from a configuration file and using reflection to create instances. Finally, it can be based on Unity or any other IoC framework. Here's a simple yet functional resolver:

```
public class SampleDependencyResolver : IDependencyResolver
{
    public object GetService(Type serviceType)
    {
        if (serviceType == typeof(ISomeClass))
            return new SomeClass();
        ...
    }

    public IEnumerable<object> GetServices(Type serviceType)
    {
        return Enumerable.Empty<Object>();
    }
}
```

The code shown next is an example of a resolver that uses Unity (and its configuration section) to resolve dependencies:

```
public class UnityDependencyResolver : IDependencyResolver
{
  private readonly IUnityContainer _container;
```

```
public UnityDependencyResolver() : this(new UnityContainer().LoadConfiguration())
{
}
public UnityDependencyResolver(IUnityContainer container)
{
  _container = container;
}

public Object GetService(Type serviceType)
{
  return _container.Resolve(serviceType);
}

public IEnumerable<Object> GetServices(Type serviceType)
{
  return _container.ResolveAll(serviceType);
}
}
```

You register your own resolver with the ASP.NET MVC framework through the *SetResolver* method of the *DependencyResolver* class, as shown here:

```
protected void Application_Start()
{
    // Prepare and configure the IoC container
    var container = new UnityContainer();
    ...

    // Create and register the resolver
    var resolver = new UnityDependencyResolver(container);
    DependencyResolver.SetResolver(resolver);
}
```

If you use an IoC framework from within the resolver, you need to figure out the best way to provide it with the list of registered types. If you prefer to pass this information via fluent code, you need to fully configure the IoC container object before you create the resolver. If you intend to configure the IoC by using the web.config file, you can use the default constructor of the resolver—as far as Unity is concerned—which includes a call to load configuration data. However, be aware that you might need to change this code if you target a different IoC framework.

> **Important** The dependency resolver is an internal tool that developers can optionally use to create their own customized components in lieu of system components. The power of dependency resolvers is limited by the use that ASP.NET MVC makes of them. In other words, if ASP.NET MVC doesn't invoke the resolver before creating, for instance, the controller cache, there's not much you can do to replace the built-in cache with your own.

Adding aspects to controllers

An entirely different form of customization you find in ASP.NET MVC is based on attributes that you can attach to controller classes and methods. These attributes are generally known as *action filters*. An action filter is a piece of code that runs around the execution of an action method and can be used to modify and extend the behavior hardcoded in the method itself.

Action filters

An action filter is fully represented by the following interface:

```
public interface IActionFilter
{
    void OnActionExecuting(ActionExecutingContext filterContext);
    void OnActionExecuted(ActionExecutedContext filterContext);
}
```

As you can see, it offers a hook for you to run code before and after the execution of the action. From within the filter, you have access to the request and controller context and can read and modify parameters.

Embedded and external filters

Each user-defined controller inherits from the class *Controller*. This class implements *IActionFilter* and exposes *OnActionExecuting* and *OnActionExecuted* methods as protected members that can be overridden. This means that each controller class gives you the chance to decide what to do before, after, or both before and after a given method is invoked. Let's see some code that adds an ad hoc response header any time the method *Index* is invoked.

```
protected DateTime StartTime;
protected override void OnActionExecuting(ActionExecutingContext filterContext)
{
    var action = filterContext.ActionDescriptor.ActionName;
    if (String.Equals(action, "index", StringComparison.CurrentCultureIgnoreCase))
    {
        StartTime = DateTime.Now;
    }

    base.OnActionExecuting(filterContext);
}
```

```
protected override void OnActionExecuted(ActionExecutedContext filterContext)
{
    var action = filterContext.ActionDescriptor.ActionName;
    if (String.Equals(action, "index", StringComparison.CurrentCultureIgnoreCase))
    {
        var timeSpan = DateTime.Now - StartTime;
        filterContext.RequestContext.HttpContext.Response.AddHeader(
            "despos-mvc4", timeSpan.Milliseconds.ToString());
    }

    base.OnActionExecuted(filterContext);
}
```

Figure 8-1 demonstrates that the method counts how many milliseconds it takes to execute and writes that number to a new response header.

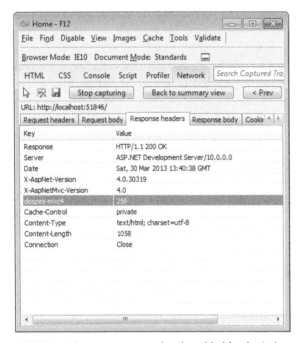

FIGURE 8-1 A custom response header added for the *Index* method.

If you override these methods in a controller class, you end up having a single repository of before/after code for all controller methods. This approach works as long as you want to perform the same operations for each method. If you need to distinguish operations on a per-method basis, using action filters as attributes is probably a better trick to try.

Implemented as an attribute, an action filter provides a declarative means to attach some behavior to a controller's action method. By writing an action filter, you can hook up the execution pipeline of an action method and adapt it to your needs. In this way, you also take out of the controller class any logic that doesn't strictly belong to the controller. In doing so, you make this particular behavior reusable and, more important, optional. Action filters are ideal for implementing solutions to cross-cutting concerns that affect the life of your controllers.

Classification of action filters

Action filters are classified in different types according to the tasks they actually accomplish. An action filter is characterized by an interface; you have a different interface for each type of filter. Special action filters are exception filters, authorization filters, and result filters. Table 8-3 lists the types of action filters in ASP.NET MVC.

TABLE 8-3 Types of action filters in ASP.NET MVC

Filter interfaces	Description
IActionFilter	Defines two methods, one that executes before and one that executes after the controller action
IAuthenticationFilter	Defines a method that executes early in the action pipeline, giving you a chance to customize the process of authentication and also to use different authentication strategies on different action methods and controllers
IAuthorizationFilter	Defines a method that executes after authentication, giving you a chance to verify whether the user is authorized to perform the action
IExceptionFilter	Defines a method that runs whenever an exception is thrown during the execution of the controller action
IResultFilter	Defines two methods, one that executes before and one that executes after the processing of the action result

The implementation of all the interfaces in Table 8-3 results in a few additional methods on the *Controller* class. Table 8-4 lists them and comments on them all.

TABLE 8-4 Filter methods in the *Controller* class

Method	Description
OnActionExecuting	Invoked just before an action method is executed
OnActionExecuted	Invoked right after the execution of an action method is completed
OnAuthentication	Invoked when authentication of an action method occurs
OnAuthorization	Invoked when authorizing the execution of an action method
OnException	Invoked when an exception occurs in an action method
OnResultExecuting	Invoked just before an action result is executed
OnResultExecuted	Invoked right after the execution of an action result is completed

All these methods are protected and virtual, and they can therefore be overridden in your controller classes to achieve more specialized behavior.

Let's take a closer look at some predefined action filters.

Built-in action filters

ASP.NET MVC comes with a few predefined filters, some of which are discussed in earlier chapters: *HandleError*, *Authorize*, and *OutputCache* are just a few of them. Table 8-5 lists the built-in filters available in ASP.NET MVC.

TABLE 8-5 Predefined filters in ASP.NET MVC

Filter	Description
AsyncTimeout	Marks an action method as one that will execute asynchronously and terminate in the specified number of milliseconds. A companion attribute also exists for asynchronous methods that do not set a timeout. This companion attribute is *NoAsyncTimeout*.
Authorize	Marks an action method as one that can be accessed only by specified users, roles, or both.
ChildActionOnly	Marks an action method as one that can be executed only as a child action during a render-action operation.
HandleError	Marks an action method as one that requires automatic handling of any exceptions thrown during its execution.
OutputCache	Marks an action method as one whose output needs to be cached.
RequireHttps	Marks an action method as one that requires a secure request. If the method is invoked over HTTP, the attribute forces a redirect to the same URL but over an HTTPS connection, if that's ever possible.
ValidateAntiForgeryToken	Marks an action method as one that requires validation against the antiforgery token in the page for each POST request.
ValidateInput	Marks an action method as one whose posted input data might (or might not) need validation.

Each controller method can be decorated with multiple filters. The order in which filters are processed is therefore important. All the attributes listed in Table 8-5 derive from the base class *Filter Attribute*, which defines a base property, *Order*. The *Order* property indicates the order in which multiple attributes will be applied. By default, the *Order* property is assigned a value of –1, which means that the order is unspecified. However, any filter with an unspecified order is always executed before a filter with a fixed order. Finally, note that if you explicitly set the same order on two or more action filters on a method, an exception will be thrown.

Global filters

You can apply filters to individual methods or to the entire controller class. If you apply filters to the controller class, they will have an effect on all action methods exposed by the controller. By contrast, global filters are those that, when registered at application startup, are automatically applied to any action of any controller class.

By default, the *HandleError* filter is globally registered in global.asax, meaning that it provides some exception-handling capabilities to any action methods. Global filters are plain action filters that are just registered in a different way, as demonstrated here:

```
GlobalFilters.Filters.Add(new HandleError());
```

The *GlobalFilters* collection is checked by the current action invoker before each action is invoked, and all found filters are added to the list of filters enabled to preprocess and post-process the action. I'll return to action invokers and the list of filters for each action later in the chapter.

Gallery of action filters

Overall, action filters form an embedded aspect-oriented framework within ASP.NET MVC. ASP.NET MVC provides many predefined filters but also makes it possible to write your own. When it comes to writing an action filter, you typically inherit from *FilterAttribute* and then implement one or more of the interfaces defined in Table 8-3. Most of the time, however, you take a shorter route—deriving from *ActionFilterAttribute*. The *ActionFilterAttribute* class is another, richer, base class for creating your custom action filters. It inherits from *FilterAttribute* and provides a default implementation for all the interfaces listed in Table 8-3. Let's find out what it takes to write a few sample action filters.

 Note Action filters are custom components that encapsulate a specific behavior. You write an action filter whenever you want to isolate this behavior and replicate it with ease. Reusability of the behavior is one of the factors for deciding whether to write action filters, but it's not the only one. Action filters also serve the purpose of keeping the controller's code lean and mean. As a general rule, whenever your controller's method code is padded with branches and conditional statements, stop and consider whether some of those branches (or repetitive code) can be moved to an action filter. The readability of the code will be largely improved.

Adding a response header

The classic scenario for having a custom action filter is to encapsulate any repetitive behavior you want to apply to many (but not necessarily all) action methods. A canonical example is adding a custom header to a method response. Earlier in the chapter, you saw how to achieve this by using the native implementation of *IActionFilter* in the controller class. The following code shows how to move that code out of the controller to a distinct class:

```
public class AddHeaderAttribute : ActionFilterAttribute
{
    public String Name { get; set; }
    public String Value { get; set; }

    public override void OnActionExecuted(ActionExecutedContext filterContext)
    {
        if (!String.IsNullOrEmpty(Name) && !String.IsNullOrEmpty(Value))
            filterContext.RequestContext.HttpContext.Response.AddHeader(Name, Value);
        return;
    }
}
```

You now have an easily managed piece of code. You can attach it to any number of controller actions, to all actions of a controller, and even globally to all controllers. All you need to do is to add an attribute, as shown here:

```
[AddHeader(Name="Action", Value="About")]
public ActionResult About()
{ ... }
```

You might argue that this example is not completely equivalent to the previous one, in which we calculated the time elapsed between the start and the completion of the action. Indeed, the AddHeader filter just adds a fixed header. You can derive a new class—for example, *ReportDuration*— and apply all the logic you need there:

```
public class ReportDurationAttribute : AddHeaderAttribute
{
    protected DateTime StartTime;

    public override void OnActionExecuting(ActionExecutingContext filterContext)
    {
        StartTime = DateTime.Now;
        base.OnActionExecuting(filterContext);
    }

    public override void OnActionExecuted(ActionExecutedContext filterContext)
    {
        var timeSpan = DateTime.Now - StartTime;
        Value = timeSpan.Milliseconds.ToString();
        base.OnActionExecuted(filterContext)
    }
}
```

Let's see a slightly more sophisticated example. In this one, we will compress the method response, which is a useful feature, especially when large HTML or binary chunks are returned.

Compressing the response

These days, HTTP compression is a feature that nearly every website can afford because the number of browsers that have trouble with that is approaching zero. (Any browser released in the past 10 years recognizes the most popular compression schemes.)

In ASP.NET Web Forms, compression is commonly achieved through HTTP modules that intercept any request and compress the response. You can also turn on compression at the Internet Information Services (IIS) level. Both options work well in ASP.NET MVC, so the decision is up to you. You typically make your decision based on the parameters you need to control, including the MIME type of the resource to compress, level of compression, files to compress, and so forth.

ASP.NET MVC makes it particularly easy to implement a third option: an action-specific filter that sets things up for compression. In this way, you can control a specific URL without the need to write an HTTP module. Let's go through another example of an action filter that adds compression to the response stream for a particular method.

In general, HTTP compression is controlled by two parameters: the Accept-Encoding header sent by the browser with each request, and the Content-Encoding header sent by the web server with each response. The Accept-Encoding header indicates that the browser is able to handle only the specified encodings—typically, *gzip* and *deflate*. The Content-Encoding header indicates the compression format of the response. Note that the Accept-Encoding header is just a request header sent by the browser; in no way should the server feel obliged to return compressed content.

When it comes to writing a compression filter, the hardest part is gaining a full understanding of what the browser is requesting. Here's some code that works:

```
public class CompressAttribute : ActionFilterAttribute
{
    public override void OnActionExecuting(ActionExecutingContext filterContext)
    {
        // Analyze the list of acceptable encodings
        var preferredEncoding = GetPreferredEncoding(filterContext.HttpContext.Request);

        // Compress the response accordingly
        var response = filterContext.HttpContext.Response;
        response.AppendHeader("Content-encoding", preferredEncoding.ToString());

        if (preferredEncoding == CompressionScheme.Gzip)
            response.Filter = new GZipStream(response.Filter, CompressionMode.Compress);
        if (preferredEncoding == CompressionScheme.Deflate)
            response.Filter = new DeflateStream(response.Filter, CompressionMode.Compress);

        return;
    }


    private CompressionScheme GetPreferredEncoding(HttpRequestBase request)
    {
        var acceptableEncoding = request.Headers["Accept-Encoding"].ToLower();

        if (acceptableEncoding.Contains("gzip"))
            return CompressionScheme.Gzip;
        if (acceptableEncoding.Contains("deflate"))
            return CompressionScheme.Deflate;

        return CompressionScheme.Identity;
    }

    enum CompressionScheme
    {
        Gzip = 0,
        Deflate = 1,
        Identity = 2
    }
}
```

You apply the *Compress* attribute to the method as follows:

```
[Compress]
public ActionResult Index()
{ ... }
```

Figure 8-2 demonstrates that the Content-Encoding response header is set correctly and the response is understood and decompressed within the browser.

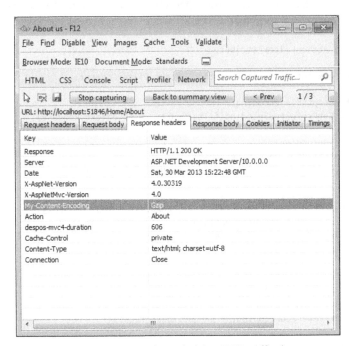

FIGURE 8-2 An inspection to the underlying HTTP traffic shows a custom header with the description of the encoding that was used.

Almost any browser sets the Accept-Encoding header to the string "gzip, deflate", which is not the only possibility. As you can read in RFC 2616 (available at *http://www.w3.org/Protocols/rfc2616/ rfc2616-sec14.html*), an Accept header field supports the *q* parameter as a way to assign a priority to an acceptable value. The following strings are acceptable values for an encoding:

```
gzip, deflate
gzip;q=.7,deflate
gzip;q=.5,deflate;q=.5,identity
```

Even though gzip appears in all strings, only in the first one is it the preferred choice. If a value is not specified, the *q* parameter is set to 1; this assigns to deflate in the second string and to identity in the third string a higher rank than gzip. So, simply checking whether gzip appears in the encoding string still sends back something the browser can accept, but it doesn't take the browser's preference into full account. To write a *Compress* attribute that takes into account the priority (if any) expressed through the *q* parameter, you need to refine the *GetPreferredEncoding* method, as shown here:

```
private CompressionScheme GetPreferredEncoding(HttpRequestBase request)
{
   var acceptableEncoding = request.Headers["Accept-Encoding"].ToLower();
   acceptableEncoding = SortEncodings(acceptableEncoding);

   if (acceptableEncoding.Contains("gzip"))
       return CompressionScheme.Gzip;
   if (acceptableEncoding.Contains("deflate"))
       return CompressionScheme.Deflate;

   return CompressionScheme.Identity;
}
```

The *SortEncodings* method will parse the header string and extract the segment of it that corresponds to the choice with the highest priority.

View Selector

Chapter 5, "Aspects of ASP.NET MVC applications," discusses the *CultureAttribute* filter, which you use to force a specific culture for a given action method, thus obtaining the effect of enabling localization for that request. The *CultureAttribute* filter works great if it's installed as a global filter. I won't be discussing the use of an action filter to implement localization any further. My next filter, however, still belongs to the class of filters that can select a different view for a given action. Suppose that you want to switch to a different view template following the capabilities of the requesting browser.

> **Note** Although the following example is still useful from the perspective of understanding the scope of action filters in ASP.NET MVC, the specific feature demonstrated can be implemented in a more effective and compact way in the newest ASP.NET MVC by using a new feature called *display modes*. I'll cover display modes in detail in Chapter 13, "Building sites for multiple devices."

Creating a multiserving application is not easy and, more important, is always a project-specific solution. What I'm going to do is illustrate the role that filters can play in helping you arrange a multiserving solution. To clarify, a multiserving application is one that can serve the same request in different ways depending on the requesting browser.

Until a few years ago, a classic example of multiserving was having pages for rich browsers and having pages for less-rich desktop browsers. Today, Ajax and JavaScript libraries have significantly mitigated the impact of this problem because JavaScript libraries (for example, jQuery) can now hide most of the differences to the developer. However, an emerging dichotomy is between desktop and mobile browsers. The boundaries of the two categories are not as clear as it might seem. In the end, defining boundaries is up to you. Defining boundaries means deciding how to treat smartphones and tablets as well as deciding what to do with less powerful browsers embedded in mobile devices and cell phones. For the purpose of this chapter, however, I'll assume that you know exactly where your boundaries are. So, I'll proceed with an action filter that knows how to switch views based on the user agent string and your rules.

The idea is to write a filter that kicks in just after the action executed and before the action invoker begins processing the results. According to the classification introduced with Table 8-3, this technically is a result filter. Let's have a look at the source code in the following example:

```
public class BrowserSpecificAttribute : ActionFilterAttribute
{
    public override void OnResultExecuting(ResultExecutingContext filterContext)
    {
        ...
    }
}
```

The filter inherits from *ActionFilterAttribute* and overrides the method *OnResultExecuting*. The method is invoked after the execution of the action method but before the result of the action is processed to generate the response for the browser.

```
public override void OnResultExecuting(ResultExecutingContext filterContext)
{
    var viewResult = filterContext.Result as ViewResult;
    if (viewResult == null)
        return;

    // Figure out the view name
    var context = filterContext.Controller.ControllerContext;
    var viewName = viewResult.ViewName;
    if (String.IsNullOrEmpty(viewName))
        viewName = context.RouteData.GetRequiredString("action");
    if (String.IsNullOrEmpty(viewName))
        return;

    // Resolve the view selector
    var viewSelector = DependencyResolver.Current.GetService(typeof (IViewSelector))
                    as IViewSelector;
    if (viewSelector == null)
        viewSelector = new DefaultViewSelector();

    // Figure out the browser name
    var isMobileDevice = context.HttpContext.Request.Browser.IsMobileDevice;
    var browserName = (isMobileDevice ?"mobile" :context.HttpContext.Request.Browser.Browser);

    // Get the name of the browser-specific view to use
    var newViewName = viewSelector.GetViewName(viewName, browserName);
    if (String.IsNullOrEmpty(newViewName))
        return;

    // Is there such a view?
    var result = System.Web.Mvc.ViewEngines.Engines.FindView(context, newViewName,
                                        viewResult.MasterName);
    if (result.View != null)
        viewResult.ViewName = newViewName;
}
```

The algorithm employed is simple. Using the *ControllerContext* object, the filter retrieves the *Request* object from the request context; from there, it ascertains the capabilities of the current browser. The browser name is used as a discriminator to decide about the next view to select.

An object of type *IViewSelector* resolves the name of the view given the browser name. A default implementation of the view selector is shown here:

```
public class DefaultViewSelector : IViewSelector
{
    public String GetViewName(String viewName, String browserName)
    {
        return String.Format("{0}_{1}", viewName, browserName);
    }

    public String GetMasterName(String masterName, String browserName)
    {
        return String.Format("{0}_{1}", masterName, browserName);
    }
}
```

The code assumes that given a view named Index, an Internet Explorer–specific version of the view is named Index_IE, a version for Firefox is named Index_Firefox, and so forth. After the filter has determined the name of the candidate view to show, it also checks with the current view engine to see whether such a view is supported. If so, the *ViewName* property of the *ViewResult* to render is set to the browser-specific view. If no browser-specific view is found, you need to do nothing else because the generic view invoked by the action method remains in place, as depicted in Figure 8-3.

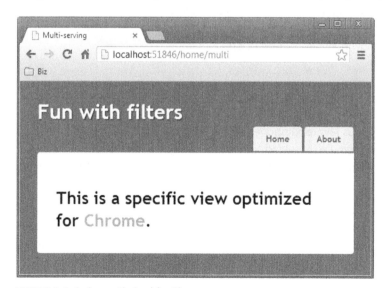

FIGURE 8-3 A view optimized for Chrome.

If the requesting browser turns out to be a mobile device, a view named xxx_mobile is selected.

Using the attribute couldn't be easier. All you need to do is decorate the controller method with it, as shown here:

```
[BrowserSpecific]
public virtual ActionResult Index()
{ ... }
```

An action filter like this saves you from having to add a bunch of *if* statements to each controller method to return a different *ViewResult* object for each supported browser:

```
public virtual ActionResult Index()
{
    if(GetCurrentBrowser() == "IE")
        return View("Index_IE");
    ...
}
```

You might still regard this code as necessary in some corner cases that you encounter, but an action filter gives you a great chance to take it from the controller class, thus simplifying the entire design.

> **Note** From this example, you can see quite clearly why and how ASP.NET MVC is different from Web Forms. Switching views is definitely possible in Web Forms also, but it requires a bit of hacking—switching the master page, loading user controls programmatically, and changing templates programmatically. This is an aspect of programming that was not given a high priority when Web Forms was designed because it addresses an issue to which people were not really sensitive. Today is different, and ASP.NET MVC makes it simpler to address issues that are now relevant to developers.

Special filters

The action filters considered thus far are components aimed at intercepting a few stages of the execution of action methods. What if you want to add some code to help decide whether a given method is fit to serve a given action? For this type of customization, another category of filters is required: *action selectors*.

Action selectors come in two distinct flavors: *action name selectors* and *action method selectors*. Name selectors decide whether the method they decorate can be used to serve a given action name. Method selectors decide whether a method with a matching name can be used to serve a given action. Method selectors typically give their response based on other run-time conditions.

Action name selectors

The base class for action name selectors is *ActionNameSelectorAttribute*. The class has a simple structure, as the code here demonstrates:

```
public abstract class ActionNameSelectorAttribute : Attribute
{
    public abstract Boolean IsValidName(ControllerContext controllerContext,
                                        String actionName, MethodInfo methodInfo);
}
```

The purpose of the selector is simple: checking whether the specified action name is a valid action name for the method.

In ASP.NET MVC, there's just one action name selector: the *ActionName* attribute that you can use to alias a controller method. Here's an example:

```
[ActionName("Edit")]
public ActionResult EditViaPost(String customerId)
{
    ...
}
```

The implementation of the *ActionName* attribute is trivial, as the following code demonstrates:

```
public sealed class ActionNameAttribute : ActionNameSelectorAttribute
{
    public ActionNameAttribute(String name)
    {
        if (String.IsNullOrEmpty(name))
            throw new ArgumentException();
        Name = name;
    }

    public override Boolean IsValidName(ControllerContext controllerContext,
                                        String actionName, MethodInfo methodInfo)
    {
        // Check that the action name matches the specified name
        return String.Equals(actionName, Name, StringComparison.OrdinalIgnoreCase);
    }

    public String Name { get; set; }
}
```

The overall effect of the attribute is that it logically renames the controller method to which it's applied. For example, in the previous example the method is named *EditViaPost*, but it won't be invoked unless the action name that results from the routing process is *Edit*.

Action method selectors

Action method selectors are a more powerful and interesting tool for developers. During the preliminary stage in which the system is looking for a controller method that can serve the request, a method selector just indicates whether a given method is valid. Obviously, such a selector determines its response based on certain run-time conditions. Here's the definition of the base class:

```
public abstract class ActionMethodSelectorAttribute : Attribute
{
    public abstract Boolean IsValidForRequest(
        ControllerContext controllerContext, MethodInfo methodInfo);
}
```

In ASP.NET MVC, quite a few predefined method selectors exist. They are *AcceptVerbs*, *NonAction*, plus several HTTP-specific selectors introduced to simplify coding (*HttpDelete*, *HttpGet*, *HttpPost*, and *HttpPut*). Let's have a look at some of them.

The *NonAction* attribute just prevents the decorated method from processing the current action. Here's how it's implemented:

```
public override Boolean IsValidForRequest(
    ControllerContext controllerContext, MethodInfo methodInfo)
{
    return false;
}
```

The *AcceptVerbs* attribute receives the list of supported HTTP verbs as an argument and checks the current verb against the list. Here are some details:

```
public override Boolean IsValidForRequest(
    ControllerContext controllerContext, MethodInfo methodInfo)
{
    if (controllerContext == null)
        throw new ArgumentNullException("controllerContext");

    // Get the (overridden) HTTP method
    var method = controllerContext.HttpContext.Request.GetHttpMethodOverride();

    // Verbs is an internal member of the AcceptVerbsAttribute class
    return Verbs.Contains<String>(method, StringComparer.OrdinalIgnoreCase);
}
```

Note the use of the *GetHttpMethodOverride* method to retrieve the actual verb intended by the client. The method reads the value in a header field or parameter named *X-HTTP-Method-Override*. (Go to *http://code.google.com/apis/gdata/docs/2.0/basics.html#UpdatingEntry* for more information about *X-HTTP-Method-Override*.) This is a common protocol for letting browsers place any HTTP verbs even if the physical request is either GET or POST. The method is not defined natively on the *HttpRequest* object, but it was added in ASP.NET MVC as an extension method on *HttpRequestBase*.

The other selectors are simply implemented in terms of *AcceptVerbs*, as shown here for *HttpPost*:

```
public sealed class HttpPostAttribute : ActionMethodSelectorAttribute
{
    private static readonly AcceptVerbsAttribute _innerAttribute;

    public override bool IsValidForRequest(
        ControllerContext controllerContext, MethodInfo methodInfo)
    {
        return _innerAttribute.IsValidForRequest(controllerContext, methodInfo);
    }
}
```

Let's see how to write a custom method selector.

Restricting a method to Ajax calls only

All you need is a class that inherits from *ActionMethodSelectorAttribute* and overrides the *IsValid ForRequest* method:

```
public class AjaxOnlyAttribute : ActionMethodSelectorAttribute
{
    public override Boolean IsValidForRequest(
            ControllerContext controllerContext, MethodInfo methodInfo)
    {
        return controllerContext.HttpContext.Request.IsAjaxRequest();
    }
}
```

Any method marked with this attribute is only enabled to serve calls placed via the browser's *XMLHttpRequest* object.

```
[AjaxOnly]
public ActionResult Details(Int32 customerId)
{
    var model = ...;
    return PartialView(model);
}
```

If you try to invoke a URL that, according to routes, should be mapped to an Ajax-only method, you'll get a not-found exception.

Restricting a method to a given submit button

In Web Forms, every page has a single HTML form, and nearly every form contains multiple submit buttons. However, each button has its own click handler that determines the action to take in case of a click. In ASP.NET MVC, instead, you can have as many HTML forms as you want, with each posting to a different and fixed URL. How can you determine which button was clicked in an HTML form with two or more submit buttons?

At the HTML level, the posting form uploads the content of input fields plus a name/value pair inherent to the clicked button. The name token refers to the name attribute of the button; the value token refers to the value attribute of the button. Unfortunately, the value attribute of the button is the caption. You can't reliably figure out which button was clicked by examining the caption. At a minimum, it's subject to localization, or it can be missing altogether if an image button is used.

The simplest way to solve the problem in ASP.NET MVC is to add a bit of JavaScript to the form so that when each button is clicked, it changes the action attribute of the form to reflect its name. Here's a brief example of an HTML form with a couple of input fields and two submit buttons, which update or delete some content:

```
<form name="myForm" id="myForm" method="post">
    <input type="text" />
    <input type="text" />
    <hr />
    <input type="submit" value="Update" name="updateAction"
            onclick="setAction('update')" />
    <input type="submit" value="Delete" name="deleteAction"
            onclick="setAction('delete')" />
</form>
```

The JavaScript function named *setAction* does the following:

```
<script type="text/javascript">
    function setAction(action) {
        document.getElementById("myForm").action = action;
    }
</script>
```

This trick works, but annoyingly, you must repeat this code for each form you write in each ASP.NET MVC application. An ad hoc method selector (and the built-in *ActionName* attribute) can do the job better:

```
public class OnlyIfPostedFromButtonAttribute : ActionMethodSelectorAttribute
{
    public String SubmitButton { get; set; }
    public override Boolean IsValidForRequest(ControllerContext controllerContext,
                                              MethodInfo methodInfo)
    {
        // Check if this request is coming through the specified submit button
        var o = controllerContext.HttpContext.Request[SubmitButton];
        return o != null;
    }
}
```

The selector exposes a public property through which you indicate the name of the button with which the method is associated. When evaluated, the selector simply looks for the name of its companion button in the form data collection being posted. By the design of HTML, a match can be found only if the form was posted by clicking that button. Let's see how you use this selector in the following controller code:

```
[HttpPost]
[ActionName("Demo")]
[OnlyIfPostedFromButton(SubmitButton = "updateAction")]
public ActionResult Demo_Update()
{
    ViewData["ActionName"] = "Update";
    return View("demo");
}
```

The code reads like this: the invoker can select this method (*Demo_Update*) only if the request is a POST, the action name is demo, and the form was posted by using the submit button with the name of *updateAction*.

Building a dynamic loader filter

Action filters are definitely a powerful mechanism for developers to use to decide exactly how a given action method executes. From what you've seen so far, however, action filters are also a static mechanism that requires a new compile and deploy step to be modified. Let's explore an approach to loading filters dynamically from an external source.

Interception points for filters

Filters are resolved for each action method within the action invoker. There are two main points of interception: the *GetFilters* and *InvokeActionMethodWithFilters* methods. Both methods are marked as protected and virtual. The signatures of both methods are shown here:

```
protected virtual ActionExecutedContext InvokeActionMethodWithFilters(
    ControllerContext controllerContext,
    IList<IActionFilter> filters,
    ActionDescriptor actionDescriptor,
    IDictionary<string, object> parameters);

protected virtual FilterInfo GetFilters(
    ControllerContext controllerContext,
    ActionDescriptor actionDescriptor)
```

The *GetFilters* method is invoked earlier and is expected to return the list of all filters for a given action. After invoking the base method of *GetFilters* in your custom invoker, you have available the full list of filters for each category (a list including exception, result, authorization, and action filters). Note that the *FilterInfo* class—a public class in *System.Web.Mvc*—offers specific collections of filters for each category:

```
public class FilterInfo
{
    // Private members
    ...

    public IList<IActionFilter> ActionFilters { get; }
    public IList<IAuthorizationFilter> AuthorizationFilters { get; }
    public IList<IExceptionFilter> ExceptionFilters { get; }
    public IList<IResultFilter> ResultFilters { get; }
}
```

The *InvokeActionMethodWithFilters* method is invoked during the process related to the performance of the action method. In this case, the method receives only the list of action filters (those filters that are to execute before or after the code for the method).

To build a mechanism that makes it possible for developers to change filters that apply to a method on the fly, our interest focuses on the *InvokeActionMethodWithFilters* method.

Adding an action filter by using fluent code

By overriding the *InvokeActionMethodWithFilters* method in a custom action invoker class, you can use fluent code to configure controllers and controller methods with action filters. The following code shows how to add the *Compress* attribute on the fly to the *Index* method of the *Home* controller:

```
protected override ActionExecutedContext InvokeActionMethodWithFilters(
    ControllerContext controllerContext,
    IList<IActionFilter> filters,
    ActionDescriptor actionDescriptor,
    IDictionary<string, object> parameters)
{
    // Add the Compress action filter to the Index method of the Home controller
    if (actionDescriptor.ControllerDescriptor.ControllerName == "Home" &&
        actionDescriptor.ActionName == "Index")
    {
        // Configure the filter and add to the list
        var compressFilter = new CompressAttribute();
        filters.Add(compressFilter);
    }

    // Go with the usual behavior and execute the action
    return base.InvokeActionMethodWithFilters(
        controllerContext, filters, actionDescriptor, parameters);
}
```

You can refine this code in a number of aspects. For example, you can support areas and check the controller type rather than the name. In addition, you can read the filters to add from a configuration file and also use an IoC container to resolve them all. More in general, this approach gives you a chance to dynamically configure the filters, and it also lets you keep attributes out of the controller code.

Customizing the action invoker

Let's generalize the idea a tiny bit. Suppose that you create a custom action invoker and override its *InvokeActionMethodWithFilters* method as shown here:

```
protected override ActionExecutedContext InvokeActionMethodWithFilters(
    ControllerContext controllerContext,
    IList<IActionFilter> filters,
    ActionDescriptor actionDescriptor,
    IDictionary<String, Object> parameters)
```

```
{
    // Load (dynamic-loading) filters for this action
    var methodFilters = LoadFiltersForAction(actionDescriptor);
    if (methodFilters.Count == 0)
        return base.InvokeActionMethodWithFilters(controllerContext,
                                        filters, actionDescriptor, parameters);

    // Apply filter(s)
    foreach (var filter in methodFilters)
    {
        var filterInstance = GetFilterInstance(filter);
        if (filterInstance == null)
            continue;

        // Initialize filter (if params are specified)
        InitializeFilter(filter, filterInstance);

        // Add the filter
        filters.Add(filterInstance);
    }

    // Exit
    return base.InvokeActionMethodWithFilters(controllerContext,
                                        filters, actionDescriptor, parameters);
}
```

The code contains a number of placeholder methods that essentially read about dynamically defined filters as they might be found in the web.config file. The provided action descriptor is used to figure out information about the current action. Action details are used to read about defined filters. Finally, filters are instantiated and initialized via reflection and added to the filters collection for the overridden method. You're responsible for the structure of the *web.config* section. A nice-looking section might be the following:

```
<dynamicFilters>
  <action name="Home.Test">
    <filter type="MvcGallery3.Extensions.Filters.CompressAttribute, MvcGallery3.Extensions" />
    <filter type="MvcGallery3.Extensions.Filters.AddHeaderAttribute, MvcGallery3.Extensions">
      <param Name="Name" Value="X-MvcAspectFX" />
      <param Name="Value" Value="3222" />
    </filter>
  </action>
</dynamicFilters>
```

You can find an implementation of this dynamic-loading filter framework in the companion source code of the book.

Registering the custom invoker

Each controller has its own action invoker exposed through a public property. You can replace the action invoker in the constructor of each controller. If you intend to apply the custom invoker to just any controller instance, you can consider moving the code to the controller factory. I usually employ a custom controller base class, defined as shown in the following example, and derive from there any controller that requires dynamic loading of filters:

```
public class AxpectController : Controller
{
    public AxpectController()
    {
        ActionInvoker = new AxpectActionInvoker();
    }
}

public class HomeController : AxpectController
{
    // Attributes for this method come from global filters defined in global.asax
    // and dynamic-loading filters defined in web.config.
    public ActionResult Index()
    {
        return View();
    }
}
```

Using a custom base class for controllers is not a programming technique that all developers like. There might be several reasons for this, including personal preferences, but in general it's because single-inheritance languages (for example, Microsoft C# and Microsoft Visual Basic .NET) offer just one spot for inheritance, and it's always smart to reserve it for later use.

If you don't like using a base controller class to enable the dynamic loading of filters, you can build an alternative on top of filter providers.

Enabling dynamic loading via a filter provider

The *OnActionExecuting* method is the right place to execute some custom code defined in a previously registered action filter before the action method runs. On the other hand, it's too late at this point to add a new filter to execute some custom code. In addition to using a custom action invoker, filter providers are a system-defined hook for you to dynamically register filters based on run-time conditions.

A filter provider is a class that implements the following interface:

```
public interface IFilterProvider
{
    IEnumerable<Filter> GetFilters(
        ControllerContext controllerContext, ActionDescriptor actionDescriptor);
}
```

The *GetFilters* method is invoked by the action invoker to load filters dynamically for a given action. A custom filter provider is therefore exactly the tool that removes the need to explicitly tweak the action invoker and controller class. You register your own filter provider in global.asax, as shown here:

```
protected void Application_Start()
{
    ...
    RegisterFilterProviders(FilterProviders.Providers);
}
public static void RegisterFilterProviders(FilterProviderCollection providers)
{
    providers.Add(new DynamicLoadingFilterProvider());
}
```

That's all the code you need to have in place as far as configuration is concerned. Next, you add information to the configuration file (as was done in the preceding code sample) and run the application. Here's the code for the filter provider:

```
public class DynamicLoadingFilterProvider : IFilterProvider
{
    public IEnumerable<Filter> GetFilters(
            ControllerContext controllerContext, ActionDescriptor actionDescriptor)
    {
        // The method reads from web.config and returns a collection of Filter objects
        return LoadFiltersFromConfiguration(actionDescriptor);
    }
}

public static IList<Filter> LoadFiltersFromConfiguration(ActionDescriptor actionDescriptor)
{
    var methodFilters = LoadFiltersForAction(actionDescriptor);

    var filters = new List<Filter>();
    foreach (var filterName in methodFilters)
    {
        // Instantiate and initialize the filter (if params are specified)
        var filterInstance = GetFilterInstance(filterName);
        if (filterInstance == null)
            continue;
        InitializeFilter(filterName, filterInstance);

        // Add to the list to return
        var filter = new Filter(filterInstance, FilterScope.Action, -1);
        filters.Add(filter);
    }

    return filters;
}
```

A filter provider manages filters through a wrapper class—the *Filter* class. The class wraps up the actual action filter instance plus a value for the order (–1 in the example) and the filter scope. The scope is defined in the *FilterScope* enumeration type. The type is a system type, defined as follows:

```
public enum FilterScope
{
    First = 0,          // First to run
    Global = 10,        // Applies to all controllers/actions
    Controller = 20,    // Applies at controller level
    Action = 30,        // Applies at action level
    Last = 100          // Last to run
}
```

With the filter provider in place, the following code, plus the web.config content shown earlier, produces the output shown in Figure 8-4 when the method *Test* is invoked:

```
// Dynamically bound to action filters via web.config
// (Adding a custom header.)
public ActionResult Test()
{
    return View();
}
```

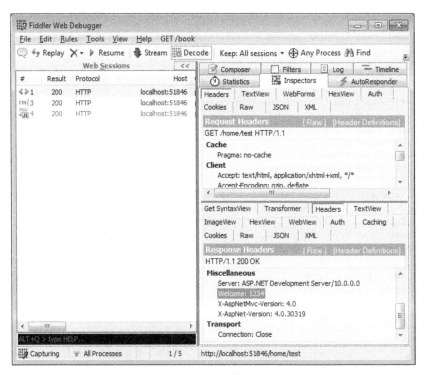

FIGURE 8-4 The response for the request as modified by dynamically added filters.

In this example, we registered the filter provider by using code in global.asax. Alternatively, you can register a filter provider by using your own dependency resolver.

Action result types

In most of the examples you've seen thus far in the book, a controller method always returns an *ActionResult* object. This is just the base class that ASP.NET MVC provides to represent the result of an action. Depending on the method used to return the action result (for example, methods *View*, *PartialView*, and so on) the actual type takes a different form. For example, when a method returns HTML markup, the actual action result type is *ViewResult*.

Action result types are also an aspect of ASP.NET MVC that you can customize to a large extent. So, let's move to the next stage and consider the tools you have at your disposal to customize the action result.

Built-in action result types

The response for the browser is generated and written to the output stream when the *ActionResult* object, as returned by the controller action method, is further processed by the action invoker. In other words, the *ActionResult* type, as well as any type directly derived from it, does not represent the real response being sent to the browser. It's merely a wrapper class that contains response-specific data (for example, headers, cookies, status code, and content type, plus any data that can be used to generate the response), and it knows how to process this data to generate the actual response for the browser.

The *ActionResult* object is defined as follows:

```
public abstract class ActionResult
{
    protected ActionResult()
    {
    }

    public abstract void ExecuteResult(ControllerContext context);
}
```

ExecuteResult is the method that provides the logic to render results to the browser. To understand the mechanics of an action result object, it's useful to look at a couple of action result classes that are built in to ASP.NET MVC.

Returning a custom status code

One of the simplest action result classes is the *HttpStatusCodeResult* class. The class represents an action response that sets a specific HTTP status code and description:

```
public class HttpStatusCodeResult : ActionResult
{
    public HttpStatusCodeResult(Int32 statusCode) : this(statusCode, null)
    {
    }
```

```
    public HttpStatusCodeResult(Int32 statusCode, String statusDescription)
    {
        StatusCode = statusCode;
        StatusDescription = statusDescription;
    }
    public override void ExecuteResult(ControllerContext context)
    {
        if (context == null)
            throw new ArgumentNullException("context");

        // Prepare the response for the browser
        context.HttpContext.Response.StatusCode = StatusCode;
        if (StatusDescription != null)
            context.HttpContext.Response.StatusDescription = StatusDescription;
    }
}
```

As you can see, all it does is set the status code and description of the response. Here is how you use this class to return an HTTP 403 code (Forbidden), as illustrated in Figure 8-5, meaning that the server understood the request but has good reasons to refuse to fulfill it:

```
public ActionResult Forbidden()
{
    return new HttpStatusCodeResult(403);
}
```

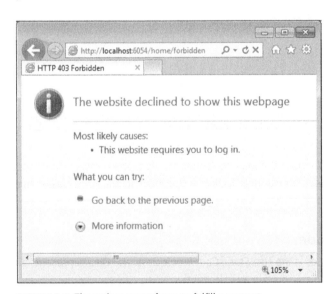

FIGURE 8-5 The web server refuses to fulfill a request.

When you need to return the same status code from several places in your application, it might be a better idea to encapsulate the status code in a custom action result class. It won't really change things that much, but it definitely increases readability. ASP.NET MVC follows this pattern for the 401 code (unauthorized) and offers you the *HttpUnauthorizedResult* class, which is used, among other things, by the *Authorize* action filter. Here's another example for the similarly popular 404 code:

```
public class HttpNotFoundResult : HttpStatusCodeResult
{
    public HttpNotFoundResult() : this(null)
    {}
    public HttpNotFoundResult(String statusDescription) : base(404, statusDescription)
    {}
}
```

Even in their overall simplicity, these classes don't fail to show the core scaffolding of action result classes.

Returning JavaScript code

A slightly more sophisticated example is the *JavaScriptResult* class. This class supplies a public property—the *Script* property—that contains the script code (as a string) to write to the output stream, as shown in the following:

```
public class JavaScriptResult : ActionResult
{
    public String Script { get; set; }

    public override void ExecuteResult(ControllerContext context)
    {
        if (context == null)
            throw new ArgumentNullException("context");

        // Prepare the response
        var response = context.HttpContext.Response;
        response.ContentType = "application/x-javascript";
        if (Script != null)
            response.Write(Script);
    }
}
```

You use the *JavaScriptResult* class from the action method as shown here:

```
public ActionResult Javascript()
{
    var script = "function helloWorld() {alert('hello, world!');}";
    var result = new JavaScriptResult {Script = script};
    return result;
}
```

For some predefined action results, ASP.NET MVC provides helper methods that hide the creation of the action result object. You can rewrite the previous code in a more compact way, as shown here:

```
public ActionResult Javascript()
{
    var script = "function helloWorld() {alert('hello, world!');}";
    return JavaScript(script);
}
```

When the user invokes an action that returns JavaScript, the classic download panel is displayed, as illustrated in Figure 8-6.

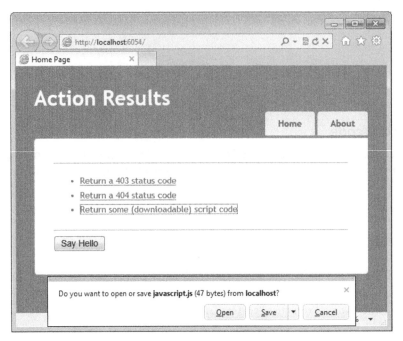

FIGURE 8-6 Script code returned by a JavaScript action result.

It turns out that the right place for action methods returning JavaScript is the <script> tag.

```
<script type="text/javascript" src="/home/javascript"></script>
```

After you place a line like the one just shown in the HTML, you can then programmatically invoke any script function being downloaded.

Returning JavaScript Object Notation data

To return JavaScript Object Notation (JSON) data from within an ASP.NET MVC controller class, all you need is an action method that returns a *JsonResult* object. The *JsonResult* class gets any .NET object and attempts to serialize it to JSON by using the *JavaScriptSerializer* system class. Here's a possible definition for an action method that serves JSON data:

```
public JsonResult GetCountries(String area)
{
    // Grab some data to serialize and return
    var countries = CountryRepository.GetAll(area);
    return Json(countries);
}
```

Defined on the *Controller* class, the *Json* method internally creates a *JsonResult* object. The purpose of the *JsonResult* object is to serialize the specified .NET object—in this example, a list of countries—to the JSON format. The *Json* method has a few overloads through which you can specify the desired content type string (with the default being *application/json*) and request behavior. The request behavior consists of allowing or denying JSON content over an HTTP GET request.

By default, ASP.NET MVC doesn't deliver JSON content through an HTTP GET request. This means that the previous code will fail if it's invoked in the context of a GET, which is the most obvious way to make a JSON call. If you consider your method to be secure and not at risk of potentially revealing sensitive data, you modify the code, as shown in the following:

```
public JsonResult GetCountries()
{
    // Grab some data to serialize and return
    var countries = CountryRepository.GetAll();
    return Json(countries, JsonRequestBehavior.AllowGet);
}
```

Just like script, JSON data returned from an action method will be downloaded if the method is invoked interactively via the browser. If embedded in a <script> tag or invoked via Ajax, content is made available as raw data. The script that follows shows an Ajax call that downloads JSON data through an ASP.NET MVC controller. The downloaded data is then used to populate a drop-down list named *listOfCountries*.

```
function downloadCountries(area) {
    $("#listOfCountries").empty();

    $.getJSON("/home/getcountries", { area: "EMEA" },
            function (data) { _displayCountries(data); });
}

function _displayCountries(data) {
    // Get the reference to the drop-down list
    var listbox = $("#listOfCountries")[0];

    // Fill the list
    for (var i = 0; i < data.length; i++) {
        var country = data[i];
        var option = new Option(country.Name, country.Code);
        listbox.add(option);
    };
}
```

The HTML in the view looks like Figure 8-7.

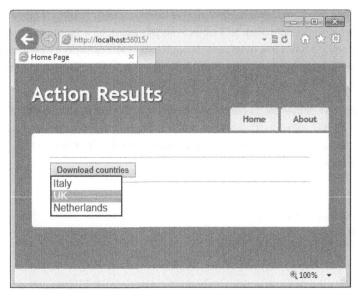

FIGURE 8-7 A drop-down list populated with Ajax-retrieved JSON data.

Returning primitive types

Strictly speaking, a controller action method is not forced to return an *ActionResult* object. You can, for example, make it return a string or an integer and use *String* and *Int32* as declared return types in the method's signature. However, be aware that whatever type you return will be wrapped up in a *ContentResult* object by the ASP.NET MVC framework.

Conversely, if the method is void, the action result will be an *EmptyResult* object. By using action filters, you can modify the result object, and its parameters, at will. So in the end, you can still have a controller method declared to return nothing but tailor that to return a value with an action filter attached that programmatically returns a given result object.

Custom result types

Ultimately, the action result object is a way to encapsulate all the tasks you need to accomplish in particular situations, such as when a requested resource is missing or redirected or when some special response must be served to the browser. Let's examine a couple of interesting scenarios for having custom action result objects.

Returning JSONP Strings

As you might know, browsers don't usually allow pages to place Ajax calls to sites from a different domain. This rule is relatively recent and has been added to reduce to nearly zero the surface attack area for malicious users. The net effect of such restrictions is that you're prevented from making Ajax calls to a website (hosted on a different domain than the requesting page) to download JSON data. More interesting, this restriction is unilaterally applied by browsers and ignores whether the remote site can serve data.

That's much ado for Ajax calls and JSON data, but we still have no control over images and script files, which can be blissfully downloaded from any site that's reachable. It's precisely this feature of browsers that can be exploited to safely download JSON data via Ajax from sites that explicitly allow for it. This is what the JSONP (JSON with Padding) protocol is all about.

JSONP is a convention that some sites use to expose their JSON content in a way that makes it easier for callers to consume data via script even from an external domain. The trick consists of returning the JSON content wrapped up in a script function call. In other words, the site would return the following string instead of a string that contains plain JSON data:

```
yourFunction("{...}");   // instead of plain {...} JSON data
```

After the site URL is invoked from within a <script> tag, the browser receives what looks like a plain function call with a fixed input string. At this point, whether the input is text or JSON text is irrelevant to the browser.

A website that supports JSONP exposes a public way for callers to indicate the name of the wrapper JavaScript function to be used when returning JSON data. Needless to say, the JavaScript function must be local to the requesting site and is expected to contain the logic that processes JSON data. Let's see how to add JSONP capabilities to an ASP.NET MVC controller. Consider the following example:

```
public ActionResult GetCountriesJsonp(String area)
{
    var result = new JsonpResult
                    {
                        JsonRequestBehavior = JsonRequestBehavior.AllowGet,
                        Data = GetCountries(area)
                    };
    return result;
}
```

The *JsonpResult* class extends the native *JsonResult* and wraps up the JSON string being returned into a call to the specified JavaScript function.

```
public class JsonpResult : JsonResult
{
    // The callback name here is the parameter name to be added to the URL to specify the
    // name of the JavaScript function padding the JSON response. This name is arbitrary and
    // is part of your site's SDK.
    private const String JsonpCallbackName = "callback";

    public override void ExecuteResult(ControllerContext context)
    {
        if (context == null)
            throw new ArgumentNullException("context");
```

```
if ((JsonRequestBehavior == JsonRequestBehavior.DenyGet) &&
    String.Equals(context.HttpContext.Request.HttpMethod, "GET"))
    throw new InvalidOperationException();

var response = context.HttpContext.Response;
if (!String.IsNullOrEmpty(ContentType))
    response.ContentType = ContentType;
else
    response.ContentType = "application/json";
if (ContentEncoding != null)
    response.ContentEncoding = this.ContentEncoding;

if (Data != null)
{
    String buffer;
    var request = context.HttpContext.Request;
    var serializer = new JavaScriptSerializer();
    if (request[JsonpCallbackName] != null)
        buffer = String.Format("{0}({1})", request[JsonpCallbackName],
                                           serializer.Serialize(Data));
    else
        buffer = serializer.Serialize(Data);

    response.Write(buffer);
}
}
}
```

The class is nearly the same as *JsonResult* except for a small change in the *ExecuteResult* method. Before serializing to JavaScript, the code checks whether the conventional JSONP parameter has been passed with the request and fixes the JSON string accordingly. Figure 8-8 shows the response body for the following URL:

/home/getcountriesjsonp?callback=_cacheForLater&area=asia

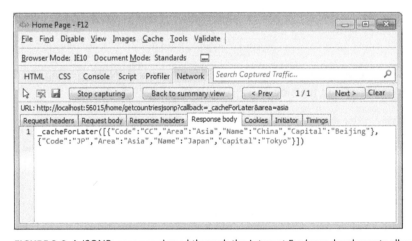

FIGURE 8-8 A JSONP response viewed through the Internet Explorer developer toolbar.

To place JSONP calls, you can follow a couple of routes. You can, for example, just manually arrange a <script> tag to make JSON data globally available to the page:

```
<script type="text/javascript"
        src="/home/getcountriesjsonp?callback=_cacheForLater&area=asia"></script>
```

Alternatively, you can place an Ajax call via jQuery or plain JavaScript. In particular, the jQuery library offers specific support through the *getJSON* function. When the URL you pass to *getJSON* contains an *xxx=?* segment, jQuery interprets it as a JSONP call and processes it in a special way. More precisely, jQuery creates a <script> tag on the fly and downloads the response through it. The name of the padding function is generated dynamically by jQuery and made to point to the *getJSON* callback code you provide. Here's an example:

```
$.getJSON("/home/getcountriesjsonp?callback=?", { area: "NA" },
          function (data) { _displayCountries(data); });
```

The name callback in the URL must match the public JSONP name as defined by the site you're calling. I'm using callback in the example because that's the name recognized by the previously presented implementation of *JsonpResult*.

Returning syndication feed

If you search the web for a nontrivial example of an action result, you'll likely find a syndication action result object at the top of the list. Let's briefly go through this popular example.

The class *SyndicationResult* supports both RSS 2.0 and ATOM 1.0, and it offers a handy property for you to choose one or the other programmatically. By default, the class produces an RSS 2.0 feed. To compile this example, you need to reference the *System.ServiceModel* assembly and import the *System.ServiceModel.Syndication* namespace:

```
public class SyndicationResult : ActionResult
{
    public SyndicationFeed Feed { get; set; }
    public FeedType Type { get; set; }

    public SyndicationResult()
    {
        Type = FeedType.Rss;
    }
    public SyndicationResult(
        string title, string description, Uri uri, IEnumerable<SyndicationItem> items)
    {
        Type = FeedType.Rss;
        Feed = new SyndicationFeed(title, description, uri, items);
    }
    public SyndicationResult(SyndicationFeed feed)
    {
        Type = FeedType.Rss;
        Feed = feed;
    }
```

```
public override void ExecuteResult(ControllerContext context)
{
    // Set the content type
    context.HttpContext.Response.ContentType = GetContentType();

    // Create the feed, and write it to the output stream
    var feedFormatter = GetFeedFormatter();
    var writer = XmlWriter.Create(context.HttpContext.Response.Output);
    if (writer == null)
        return;
    feedFormatter.WriteTo(writer);
    writer.Close();
}

private String GetContentType()
{
    if(Type == FeedType.Atom)
        return "application/atom+xml";
    return "application/rss+xml";
}

private SyndicationFeedFormatter GetFeedFormatter()
{
    if (Type == FeedType.Atom)
        return new Atom10FeedFormatter(Feed);
    return new Rss20FeedFormatter(Feed);
}
}

public enum FeedType
{
    Rss = 0,
    Atom = 1
}
```

The class gets a syndication feed and serializes it to the client by using either the RSS 2.0 or ATOM 1.0 format. Creating a consumable feed is another story, but it's also a concern that relates to the controller rather than to the infrastructure. Here's how to write a controller method that returns a feed:

```
public SyndicationResult Feed()
{
    var items = new List<SyndicationItem>();
    items.Add(new SyndicationItem(
        "Controller descriptors",
        "This post shows how to customize controller descriptors",
        null));
    items.Add(new SyndicationItem(
        "Action filters",
        "Using a fluent API to define action filters",
        null));
    items.Add(new SyndicationItem(
        "Custom action results",
        "Create a custom action result for syndication data",
        null));
```

```
        var result = new SyndicationResult(
            "Programming ASP.NET MVC",
            "Dino's latest book",
             Request.Url,
             items);

    result.Type = FeedType.Atom;
    return result;
}
```

You create a list of *SyndicationItem* objects and provide a title, some content, and an alternate link (null in the code snippet) for each. You typically retrieve these items from some repository you might have in your application. Finally, you pass items to the *SyndicationResult* object along with a title and description for the feed to be created and serialized. Figure 8-9 shows an ATOM feed in Internet Explorer.

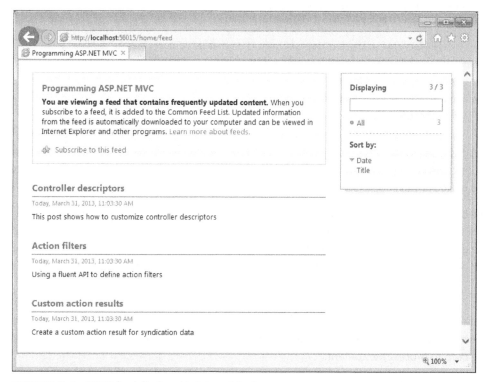

FIGURE 8-9 An ATOM feed displayed in Internet Explorer.

Dealing with binary content

A common developer need is returning binary data from a request. Many different types of data fall under the umbrella of binary data, such as the pixels of an image, the content of a PDF file, or even a Microsoft Silverlight package.

You don't really need an ad hoc action result object to deal with binary data. Among the built-in action result objects, you can certainly find one that helps you when working with binary data. If the content you want to transfer is stored within a disk file, you can use the *FilePathResult* object. If the content is available through a stream, you use *FileStreamResult* and opt for *FileContentResult* if you have it available as a byte array.

All of these objects derive from *FileResult* and differ from one another only in how they write out data to the response stream. Let's review how *ExecuteResult* works within *FileResult*.

```
public override void ExecuteResult(ControllerContext context)
{
    if (context == null)
        throw new ArgumentNullException("context");

    var response = context.HttpContext.Response;
    response.ContentType = this.ContentType;
    if (!String.IsNullOrEmpty(this.FileDownloadName))
    {
        var headerValue = ContentDispositionUtil.GetHeaderValue(FileDownloadName);
        context.HttpContext.Response.AddHeader("Content-Disposition", headerValue);
    }

    // Write content to the output stream
    WriteFile(response);
}
```

The class has a public property named *ContentType* through which you communicate the MIME type of the response and which does all of its work via an abstract method, *WriteFile*, that derived classes must override.

The base class *FileResult* also supports the Save As dialog box within the client browser through the Content-Disposition header. The property *FileDownloadName* specifies the default name the file will be given in the browser's *Save As* dialog box. The Content-Disposition header has the following format, where XXX stands for the value of the *FileDownloadName* property:

```
Content-Disposition: attachment; filename=XXX
```

Note that the file name should be in the US-ASCII character set and no directory path information is allowed. Finally, the MIME type must be unknown to the browser; otherwise, the registered handler will be used to process the content.

The delta between the base class *FileResult* and derived classes is mostly related to the implementation of the *WriteFile* method. In particular, *FileContentResult* writes an array of bytes straight to the output stream, as shown here:

```
// FileContents is a property on FileContentResult that points to the bytes
protected override void WriteFile(HttpResponseBase response)
{
    response.OutputStream.Write(FileContents, 0, FileContents.Length);
}
```

FileStreamResult offers a different implementation. It has a *FileStream* property that provides the data to read, and the code in *WriteFile* reads and writes in a buffered way.

```
protected override void WriteFile(HttpResponseBase response)
{
    Stream outputStream = response.OutputStream;
    using (FileStream)
    {
        byte[] buffer = new byte[0x1000];
        while (true)
        {
            var count = FileStream.Read(buffer, 0, 0x1000);
            if (count == 0)
                return;
            outputStream.Write(buffer, 0, count);
        }
    }
}
```

Finally, *FilePathResult* copies an existing file to the output stream. The implementation of *WriteFile* is quite minimal in this case.

```
// FileName is the name of the file to read and transmit
protected override void WriteFile(HttpResponseBase response)
{
    response.TransmitFile(FileName);
}
```

With these classes available, you can deal with any sort of binary data you need to serve programmatically from a URL. The following code shows how to serve an image:

```
public ActionResult Img()
{
    const String file = "stones.jpg";
    return File(Server.MapPath(String.Format("~/content/images/{0}", file)), "image/jpeg");
}
```

Returning PDF files

As a final example, let's see what it takes to return some PDF data. To be honest, when it comes to this, the biggest problem to solve is how you get the PDF content. If your PDF content is a static resource such as a server file, all you need to do is use *FilePathResult*. Better yet, you can use the ad hoc *File* method, as shown here:

```
public ActionResult About()
{
    ...
    return File(fileName, "application/pdf");
}
```

To create PDF content on the fly, you can use a bunch of libraries, such as iTextSharp (*http://sourceforge.net/projects/itextsharp*). Some commercial products and various open-source projects also can create PDF content from HTML content. This option is particularly interesting for an ASP.NET MVC application because you can grab a partial view and turn it into downloadable PDF content.

More commonly, you need to create and return PDF documents arranged from a template. There are two main routes that you can consider: using Office automation and creating PDFs from Microsoft Word or Microsoft Excel documents, or using Reporting Services. Of the two, using Microsoft Office is perhaps easier to arrange; the other is more reliable and free of hidden costs and subtle issues. By the way, Microsoft itself discourages using Office automation in server applications. (See *http://support. microsoft.com/?id=257757.*) I've used it in a couple of applications without encountering any significant trouble. But, my experience could be the exception rather than the rule.

The companion code for this book provides a sample ASP.NET MVC project that serves a PDF file when you invoke a given action method. The code uses Office automation to create new Word documents from a DOTX template. The template includes a few bookmarks that are replaced programmatically with user-defined values. Figure 8-10 shows the sample PDF document created by previous code.

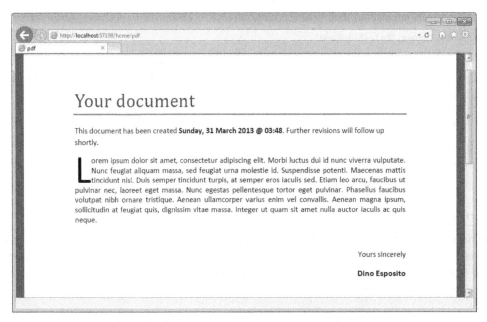

FIGURE 8-10 The sample application creating a PDF document on the fly.

Note The sample PDF application works by creating a local file on the web server disk. As long as you test the application by using the Microsoft Visual Studio environment (and the embedded Visual Studio web server), all goes well. When you start testing it under a real IIS web server, saving the file locally might raise a few problems because of default security permissions. The ASP.NET default account doesn't have write permission on the folder where the file is created. You have to fix this by raising the writing permissions for the ASP.NET account in the folder where you intend to create temporary or persistent PDF files.

Summary

You might or might not like ASP.NET MVC, but you can't honestly deny that it's a highly customizable and extensible framework. In ASP.NET MVC, you can take full control over the execution of each action and intervene before the request has been processed, after it has been processed, or both. Likewise, you can gain control over nearly all aspects of the process that emits the response for the client browser.

Even though you can customize nearly every aspect of ASP.NET MVC, you don't want to rewrite all of them all the time. The aspects of customization that were discussed in this chapter are those that I see as being more frequently customized and, more important, those that deliver the greatest benefits if they're properly customized.

CHAPTER 9

Testing and testability in ASP.NET MVC

In preparing for battle I have always found that plans are useless, but planning is indispensable.

—*Dwight D. Eisenhower*

In the early days of .NET, the average complexity of applications wasn't quite high and the Microsoft Visual Studio debugging tools were powerful enough for the purpose. Rapid Application Development (RAD) was the paradigm of choice for most; subsequently, few developers really cared about writing test programs.

The success of .NET as a platform resulted in many companies across the full spectrum of the industry needing to acquire new line-of-business applications. In doing so, they dumped an incredible amount of complexity and business rules on the various development teams. Being productive became harder and harder with the sole support of the RAD paradigm. It was ultimately a complete change of priorities. In addition to having to be concerned with time to market, developers had to pay much more attention to maintainability and extensibility. Of course, maintainability brought with it the need to write readable code that could deal with a growing requirement churn.

The ability to test software, and in particular to test software automatically, is an aspect of extraordinary importance because automated tests give you a mechanical way to figure out quickly and reliably whether certain features that worked at some point still work after you make some required changes. In addition, tests make it possible for you to calculate metrics and take the pulse of a project, as well. In the end, the big change that has come about is that we can no longer spend money on software projects that do not complete successfully. Testing is an important part of the change.

Productivity is still important, but focusing on productivity alone costs too much because it can lead to low-quality code that is difficult and expensive to maintain. And, if it's hard to maintain, where's the benefit?

The necessity of testing software in an automated way—we could call it the necessity of applying the RAD paradigm to tests—raised another key point: the need to have software that is easy to test. In this chapter, I first try to nail down the technical characteristics that a piece of software needs to have to be testable. Next, I briefly introduce the basics of unit testing—fixtures, assertions, test doubles, and code coverage—and finish up with some ASP.NET MVC–specific examples of unit tests.

> **Note** For quite a long time, many .NET developers considered terms like "testing" and "debugging" to be nearly synonyms. The action of debugging is related to catching and fixing bugs and anomalies in an application. Debugging is carried out by a developer and is mostly an interactive, multistep process. The action of testing is related to ensuring that certain parts of your code behave as expected. Testing is carried out by ad hoc programs and is essentially an unattended task that you can automate and integrate in the build process. The two processes are orthogonal, and one doesn't certainly exclude the other. A test can be an effective way to try to reproduce a bug; on the other hand, tests are a great way to try to prevent bugs.

Testability and design

In the context of software architecture, a broadly accepted definition for testability is "the ease of performing testing." Testing, of course, is the process of checking software to ensure that it behaves as expected, contains no errors, and satisfies its requirements.

Testing software is conceptually simple: just force the program to work on correct, incorrect, missing, or incomplete data, and verify whether the results are in line with any set expectations. How would you force the program to work on your input data? How would you measure the correctness of results? In cases of failure, how would you track the specific module that failed?

These questions are the foundation of a paradigm known as Design for Testability (DfT). Any software built in full respect of DfT principles is inherently testable and, as a very pleasant side effect, it is also easy to read, understand, and subsequently maintain.

> **Important** As I see things, testability is much more important than testing. Testability is an attribute of software that represents a (great) statement about its quality. Testing is a process aimed at verifying whether the code meets expectations. Applying testability (for example, making your code easily testable) is like learning to fish; writing unit tests is like eating a fish.

DfT

DfT was developed as a general concept a few decades ago in a non-software-related field. In fact, the goal of DfT was to improve the process of building low-level circuits within boards and chips.

DfT pioneers employed a number of design techniques and practices with the purpose of enabling effective testing in an automated manner. What pioneers called "automated testing equipment" was nothing more than a collection of ad hoc software programs written to test some well-known functions of a board and report results for diagnostic purposes.

DfT was adapted to software engineering and applied to test units of code through tailor-made programs. Ultimately, writing unit tests is like writing software. When you write regular code, you call classes and functions, but you focus more on the overall behavior of the program and the actual implementation of use-cases. Conversely, when you write unit tests, you need to focus on the input and output of individual methods and classes, which is a different level of granularity.

DfT defines three attributes that any unit of software must have to be easily testable: control, visibility, and simplicity. You'll be surprised to see that these attributes address exactly the questions I outlined earlier when discussing the foundation of DfT.

The attribute of control

The attribute of control refers to the degree to which the code makes it possible for testers to apply fixed input data to the software under test. Any piece of software should be written in a way that makes it clear what parameters are required and what return values are generated. In addition, any piece of software should abstract its dependencies—both parameters and low-level modules—and provide a way for external callers to inject them at will.

The canonical example of the control attribute applied to software is a method that requires a parameter instead of using its knowledge of the system to figure out the parameter's value from another publicly accessible component. In DfT, control is all about defining a virtual contract for a software component that includes preconditions. The easier you can configure preconditions, the easier you can write effective tests.

The attribute of visibility

The attribute of visibility is defined as the ability to observe the current state of the software under test and any output it can produce. After you've implemented the ability to impose ad hoc input values on a method, the next step is being able to verify whether the method behaved as expected. Visibility is all about this aspect—postconditions to be verified past the execution of a method.

The main assumption related to visibility is that if testers have a way to programmatically observe a given behavior, they can easily test it against expected or incorrect values. Postconditions are a way to formalize the expected behavior of a software module.

The attribute of simplicity

Simplicity is always a positive attribute for any system and in every context. Testing is clearly no exception. Simple and extremely cohesive components are preferable for testing because the less you have to test, the more reliably and quickly you can do that.

In the end, DfT is a driving factor when writing the source code, preferably right from the beginning of the project, so that attributes such as visibility, control, and simplicity are maximized. When design for testability is successfully applied, writing unit tests is highly effective and easier overall. In addition, your code maximizes maintainability and is easier to read overall.

Loosen up your design

Testable software is inherently better software from a design perspective. When you apply control, visibility, and simplicity to the software development process, you end up with relatively small building blocks that interact only via contracted interfaces. Testable software is software written for someone else to use it programmatically. The typical programmatic user of testable software is the test harness—the program used to run unit tests. In any case, we are talking about software that uses other software. Therefore, low coupling is the universal principle to apply systematically, and *interface-based programming* is the best practice to follow for creating software that's easier to test.

Interface-based programming

Tight coupling makes software development much simpler and faster. Tight coupling results from an obvious point: if you need to use a component, just get an instance of it. This leads to code such as that in the following listing:

```
public class MyComponent
{
    private DefaultLogger _logger;
    public MyComponent()
    {
        _logger = new DefaultLogger();
    }
    public bool PerformTask()
    {
        // Some work here
        bool success = true;
        <...>

        // Log activity
        _logger.Log(...);

        // Return success or failure
        return success;
    }
}
```

The *MyComponent* class is strictly dependent on *DefaultLogger*. You can't reuse the *MyComponent* class in an environment in which *DefaultLogger* isn't available. Moreover, you can't reuse *MyComponent* in a run-time environment that prevents *DefaultLogger* from working properly. This is an example of where tight coupling between classes can take you. From a testing perspective, you can't test the *MyComponent* class without reproducing a run-time environment that is perfectly compatible with the production environment. For example, if *DefaultLogger* logs to Microsoft Internet Information Services (IIS), your test environment must have IIS properly configured and working.

The beauty of unit testing, on the other hand, is that you run your tests quickly and punctually, focusing on the behavior of a small piece of software and ignoring or controlling dependencies. This is clearly impossible when you program your classes to use a concrete implementation of a dependency. Here's how to rewrite the *MyComponent* class so that it depends on an interface, thus resulting in more maintainable and testable code:

```
public class MyComponent
{
    private ILogger _logger;
    public MyComponent()
    {
        _logger = new DefaultLogger();
    }
    public MyComponent(ILogger logger)
    {
        _logger = logger;
    }
    public bool PerformTask()
    {
        // Some work here
        bool success = true;
        ...

        // Log activity
        _logger.Log(...);

        // Return success or failure
        return success;
    }
}
```

The class *MyComponent* is now dependent on the *ILogger* interface that abstracts the dependency on the logging module. The *MyComponent* class now knows how to deal with any objects that implement the *ILogger* interface, including any objects you might inject programmatically.

The solution just shown is acceptable from a testing perspective, even though it is far from perfect. In the preceding implementation, the class is still dependent on *DefaultLogger*, and you can't really reuse it without having available the assembly where *DefaultLogger* is defined. However, at a minimum you can use it to test the behavior of the class in isolation, bypassing the default logger, as shown here:

```
// Arrange the call
var fakeLogger = new FakeLogger();
var component = new MyComponent(fakeLogger);

// Perform the call and check against expectations
Assert(component.PerformTask());
```

Instructing your classes to work against interfaces rather than implementations is one of five pillars of modern software development. The five principles of development are often summarized by using the acronym SOLID, which is formed from the initials of the five principles:

- Single Responsibility Principle

- Open/Closed Principle

- Liskov's Substitution Principle

- Interface Segregation Principle

- Dependency Inversion Principle

For more information on these principles, check out *Microsoft .NET: Architecting Applications for the Enterprise*, coauthored by myself and Andrea Saltarello (Microsoft Press, 2008).

In modern software, the idea of writing code against interfaces rather than implementations is widely accepted and applied, but it is also often shadowed by another, more specific, concept: *dependency injection*.

We could say that the entire concept of interface-based programming is hardcoded in the Dependency Inversion Principle (DIP) and that dependency injection is a popular design pattern used to apply the principle. Chapter 7, "Design considerations for ASP.NET MVC controllers," discusses DIP and related patterns such as Dependency Injection and Service Locator.

Relativity of software testability

Is design for testability important because it leads to software that is easy to test? Or rather, is it so important because it leads to inherently better-designed software? I definitely favor the second option (even though a strong argument can be made for the first option, too).

You probably won't go to a customer and use the argument of testability to sell a product of yours. You would likely focus on other characteristics, such as the features, overall quality, user-friendliness, and ease of use. Testability is important mostly to developers, because it is an excellent barometer of the quality of design and coding. From the customer's perspective, there might be no difference between *"testable code that works"* and *"untestable code that works."*

On the other hand, a piece of software that is easy to test is necessarily loosely coupled, provides a great Separation of Concerns (SoC) between core parts, and is easy to maintain because it can have a battery of tests to promptly catch any regression. In addition, it is inherently simpler in its structure and typically lends itself well to future extensions.

In the end, pursuing testability is a great excuse to have well-designed software. Additionally, after you get it, you can also easily test it!

> **Note** I just said that from the customer's perspective there might be no difference between *"testable code that works"* and *"untestable code that works."* Well, whether there is a difference really depends on the customer. If the customer engaged you on a long-term project, she might be very interested in the maintainability of the code. In situations like this, whether the code is testable or untestable might make a huge difference. But again, it's more a design point than a testability point.

Testability and coupling

There's a strict relationship between coupling and testability. A class that can't be easily instantiated in a test has some serious coupling problems. This doesn't mean that you can't test it automatically, but you'll probably have to configure some database or external connection also in a test environment, which will definitely produce slower tests and higher maintenance costs.

To be effective, a test must be quick and execute in memory. A project that has good test coverage will likely have a few simple tests per class, which likely amount to a few thousand test calls. It is a manageable problem if each test is quick enough and has no latency caused by synchronization and connections. It is a serious issue otherwise.

If the problem of coupling between components is not properly addressed in the design, you end up testing components that interact with others, producing something that looks more like an integration test than a unit test. Integration tests are still necessary, but they ideally should run on individual units of code (for example, classes) that already have been thoroughly tested in isolation. Integration tests are not run as often as unit tests because of their slow speed and higher setup costs.

In addition, if you end up using integration tests to test a class and a failure occurs, how easily can you identify the problem? Was it in the class you intended to test or was it the result of a problem in some of the dependencies? Finding the right problem becomes significantly more expensive and time consuming. Even when you've found it, fixing it can have an impact on components in the upper layers.

By keeping coupling under control at the design level (for example, by systematically applying dependency injection), you enforce testability. Conversely, by pursuing testability, you keep coupling under control and end up with a better design for your software.

Testability and object orientation

A largely debated point is whether it is acceptable to sacrifice (and if it is, to what degree) some design principles (specifically, object-oriented principles) to testability. As mentioned, testability is a driver for better design, but you can have a great design without unit tests and also have great software that is almost impossible to test automatically.

The point here is slightly different. If you pursue good object-oriented design, you probably have a policy that limits the use of virtual members and inheritable classes to situations in which it is only strictly necessary. However, nonvirtual methods and sealed classes can be hard to test because most test environments need to mock up classes and override members. Furthermore, why should you have an additional constructor that you won't use other than for testing? What should you do?

It is clearly mostly a matter of considering the tradeoffs.

However, consider that commercial tools exist that let you mock and test classes regardless of their design, including sealed classes and nonvirtual methods. An excellent example is Typemock (*http://www.typemock.com*). For quite some time, Microsoft had a framework called Moles included in the Visual Studio 2010 Power Tools (*http://tinyurl.com/b4zuqj*). Moles is no longer supported in Visual Studio 2013 and has been replaced by a new framework called Fakes (*http://bit.ly/zenveW*).

Before we come to the grips with testing in ASP.NET MVC, let's briefly review the basics of unit testing. If you're already familiar with concepts such as fakes, mocks, and testing in isolation, feel free to jump directly to the section "Testing your ASP.NET MVC code."

The basics of unit testing

Unit testing verifies that individual units of code are working properly according to their expected behavior. A unit is the smallest part of an application that you can test—typically, a method on a class.

Unit testing consists of writing and running a small program (referred to as the aforementioned *test harness*) that instantiates test classes and invokes test methods in an automatic way. A test class is a container of test methods, whereas a test method is simply a helper method that invokes the method to test by using a specific set of input values. In the end, running a battery of tests is much like compiling (see Figure 9-1). You click a button in the programming environment of choice (for example, Visual Studio), you run the test harness, and then, at the end of it, you know what went wrong, if anything.

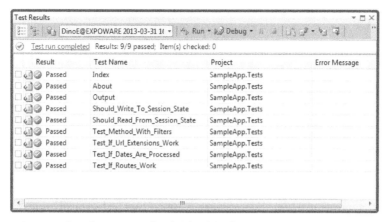

FIGURE 9-1 Running a test project in Visual Studio.

Working with a test harness

In its simplest form, a test harness is a manually written program that reads test-case input values and the corresponding expected results from some external files. Then, the test harness calls methods by using input values and compares the results with the expected values. Obviously, writing such a test harness entirely from scratch is, at a minimum, time consuming and error prone. More important, it is restrictive in terms of the testing capabilities of which you can take advantage.

The most effective and common way to conduct unit testing entails using an automated test framework. An automated test framework is a developer tool that normally includes a run-time engine and a framework of classes for simplifying the creation of test programs.

Choosing a test environment

Popular testing tools are MSTest, NUnit, and its successor, xUnit.net. MSTest is the testing tool incorporated into all versions of Visual Studio. Figure 9-1 shows the user interface of MSTest within Visual Studio.

NUnit (which you can find at *http://www.nunit.org*) is an open-source product that has been around for quite a few years. NUnit is designed to be a stand-alone tool and doesn't natively integrate with Visual Studio, which can be either good or bad news depending on your perspective of things and your needs and expectations. However, an integration package exists in the Visual Studio Gallery to use NUnit within Visual Studio.

xUnit.net (which you can read more about at *http://xunit.codeplex.com*) is the latest framework for unit testing .NET projects. As Figure 9-2 illustrates, it comes with an installer with which you can add it as a new test framework in the default wizard that creates a new ASP.NET MVC application.

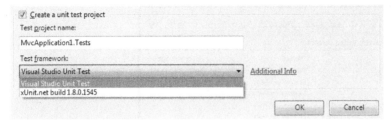

FIGURE 9-2 Picking your favorite test framework.

At the end of the day, picking a testing framework is really a matter of preference. Regardless of which one you choose, you are hardly objectively losing anything really important. The testing matters much more than the framework you use. In my opinion, no significant technical differences exist between MSTest and NUnit. What about xUnit.net, then? As mentioned, xUnit.net is the latest one, and it has been created by the author of NUnit, James Newkirk. For these reasons, xUnit.net is likely to incorporate in its features years of experience and feedback, and you might find it closer to being your ideal tool.

Overall, just because test frameworks are nearly the same functionally speaking doesn't mean you can't make an argument for preferring one over another. However, whatever the argument is, it would likely be more of a personal preference than an argument regarding the capabilities of the tools themselves. I'll use MSTest in this book, but I'll briefly point out differences, especially with regard to xUnit.net.

Test fixtures

You start by grouping related tests in a test fixture. Test fixtures are just test-specific classes where methods typically represent tests to run. In a test fixture, you might also have code that executes at the start and end of the test run. Here's the skeleton of a test fixture with MSTest:

```
using Microsoft.VisualStudio.TestTools.UnitTesting;
...

[TestClass]
public class CustomerTestCase
{
  private Customer customer;

  [TestInitialize]
  public void SetUp()
  {
    customer = new Customer();
  }

  [TestCleanup]
  public void TearDown()
  {
    customer = null;
  }
```

```
    // Your tests go here
    [TestMethod]
    public void ShouldComplainInCaseOfInvalidId()
    {
      ...
    }
    ...
}
```

Test fixtures are grouped in an ad hoc Visual Studio project. When you create a new ASP.NET MVC project, Visual Studio offers to create a test project for you.

You transform a plain .NET class into a test fixture by simply adding the *TestClass* attribute. You turn a method of this class into a test method by using the *TestMethod* attribute, instead. Attributes such as *TestInitialize* and *TestCleanup* have a special meaning and indicate code that runs before and after, respectively, each test in that class. By using attributes such as *ClassInitialize* and *ClassCleanup*, you can define, instead, code that runs only once before and after all tests you have in a class.

> **Note** Some differences exist between xUnit.net and the others regarding test classes (or fixtures). In xUnit.net, you don't need to decorate a test class with a special attribute. The framework will look for all test methods in all public classes available. As far as initialization and cleanup is concerned, xUnit.net requires you to use the class constructor and *Dispose* method for any per-test operations. You implement *IUseFixture* in your test class for one-off, class-level initialization and teardown.

Arrange, act, assert

The typical layout of a test method is summarized by the triple "A" acronym that stands for *arrange, act, assert*. You start arranging the execution context in which you'll test the class by initializing the state of the class and providing any necessary dependencies.

Next, you put in the code that acts on the class under test and performs any required work. Finally, you deal with results and verify that the received output is correct. You do this by verifying assertions based on your expectations.

You write your assertions by using the ad hoc assertion API provided by the test harness. At a minimum, with the test framework, you can check whether the result equals an expected value.

```
[TestMethod]
public void AssignPropertyId()
{
    // Define the input data for the test
    var customer = new Customer();
    string id = "IDS";
    string expected = id;
```

```
    // Execute the action to test.
    customer.ID = id;

    // Test the results
    Assert.AreEqual(expected, customer.ID);
}
```

A test doesn't necessarily have to check whether results are correct. A valid test is also the test aimed at verifying whether under certain conditions a method throws an exception. Here's an example where the setter of the *ID* property in the *Customer* class is expected to raise an *Argument Exception* if the empty string is assigned:

```
[TestMethod]
[ExpectedException(typeof(ArgumentException))]
public void AssignPropertyId()
{
    // Define the input data for the test
    var customer = new Customer();
    var id = String.Empty;

    // Execute the action to test.
    customer.ID = id;

}
```

When writing tests, you can decide to temporarily ignore one because you know it doesn't work, but you have no time to fix it at present. You use the *Ignore* attribute for this, as shown here:

```
[Ignore]
[TestMethod]
public void AssignPropertyId()
{

}
```

Likewise, you can decide to mark the test as temporarily inconclusive because you are currently unable to determine under which conditions the test will succeed or fail.

```
[TestMethod]
public void AssignPropertyId()
{
    ...
    Assert.Inconclusive("Unable to determine success or failure");
}
```

You might think that ignoring a test or marking it as inconclusive is an unnecessary task because you can more simply comment out tests that for some reason just don't work. This is certainly true, but experience teaches us that testing is a delicate task that is always on the borderline between normal priority and low priority. In addition, it is so easy to forget about a test after it has been commented out. It's not by chance that all test frameworks offer a programmatic way to ignore tests while keeping the code active in the project. Test-harness authors know project schedules and budgets are always tight, but they also know that maintaining tests in an executable state is important. Whenever you run the tests, you'll be reminded that some tests were ignored or inconclusive. Overall, this is preferable to just commenting out (and forgetting) tests.

> **Note** xUnit.net replaces the *ExpectedException* attribute with a new method on *Assert*, the *Assert.Throws* method. Ignore is replaced by the *Skip* parameter on the *Fact* attribute—the equivalent for the *TestMethod* attribute. Finally, *Assert.Inconclusive* is not supported in xUnit.net. For more details about differences between xUnit.net and other frameworks, have a look at *http://xunit.codeplex.com/wikipage?title=Comparisons&referringTitle=Home*.

Data-driven tests

When you arrange a test for a class method, you might sometimes need to try it with a range of possible values, including correct and incorrect values and values that represent edge conditions. In this case, a data-driven test is a great help.

MSTest supports two possible data sources: a Microsoft Office Excel .csv file, or any valid ADO. NET data source. The test must be bound to the data source by using the *DataSource* attribute, and an instance of the test will be run for each value in the data source. The data source will contain input values and expected values.

```
var id = TestContext.DataRow["ID"].ToString();
var expected = TestContext.DataRow["Result"].ToString();
...
Assert.AreEqual(id, expected);
```

You use the *TestContext* variable to read input values. In MSTest, the *TestContext* variable is automatically defined when you add a new unit test:

```
private TestContext testContextInstance;
public TestContext TestContext
{
    get { return testContextInstance; }
    set { testContextInstance = value; }
}
```

Among other things, the *DataSource* attribute also lets you specify whether test input values are to be processed randomly or sequentially.

Aspects of testing

Writing unit tests is still a form of programming and has the same need for good practices and techniques as software programming aimed at production code. Writing unit tests, however, has its own set of patterns and characteristics of which you might want to be aware.

Very limited scope

When introducing DfT at the beginning of the chapter, I was careful to make the following point: simplicity is a fundamental aspect of software that is key in enabling testability. When applied to unit testing, simplicity is related to giving a very limited scope to the code under test.

A limited scope makes the test self-explanatory and reveals its purpose clearly. This is beneficial for at least two reasons. First, any developers looking into it, including the same author a few weeks later, can quickly and unambiguously understand the expected behavior of the method under test.

Second, a test that fails poses the additional problem of you needing to figure out why it failed in order to fix the class under test. The simpler the test method is, the simpler it will be to isolate problems within the class being tested. Furthermore, the more layered the class under test is, the easier it will be to apply changes without the risk of breaking the code somewhere else. Finally, writing tests with a very limited scope is significantly easier for classes that control their dependencies on other components.

Unit testing is like a circle: Making it virtuous or vicious is up to you, and it mostly depends on the quality of your design.

Testing in isolation

An aspect of unit tests that is tightly related to having a limited scope is testing in isolation. When you test a method, you want to focus only on the code within that method. All that you want to know is whether that code provides the expected results in the tested scenarios. To get this, you need to get rid of all dependencies the method might have.

For example, if the method invokes another class, you assume that the invoked class will always return correct results. In this way, you eliminate at the root the risk that the method fails under test because a failure occurred down the call stack. If you test method A and it fails, the reason has to be found exclusively in the source code of method A and not in any of its dependencies.

It is highly recommended that you isolate the class being tested from its dependencies. Be aware, though, that this can happen only if the class is designed in a loosely coupled manner. In an object-oriented scenario, class A depends on class B when any of the following conditions are verified:

- Class A derives from class B.

- Class A includes a member of class B.

- One of the methods of class A invokes a method of class B.

- One of the methods of class A receives or returns a parameter of class B.

- Class A depends on a class that in turn depends on class B.

How can you neutralize dependencies when testing a method? You use test *doubles*.

Fakes and mocks

A test double is an object that you use in lieu of another. A test double is an object that pretends to be the real one expected in a given scenario. A class written to consume an object that implements the *ILogger* interface can accept a real logger object that logs to IIS or some database table. At the same time, it also can accept an object that pretends to be a logger but just does nothing. There are two main types of test doubles: fakes and mocks.

The simplest option is to use fake objects. A fake object is a relatively simple clone of an object that offers the same interface as the original object but returns hardcoded or programmatically de-termined values. Here's a sample fake object for the *ILogger* type:

```
public class FakeLogger : ILogger
{
    public void Log(String message)
    {
        return;
    }
}
```

As you can see, the behavior of a fake object is hardcoded; the fake object has no state and no significant behavior. From the fake object's perspective, it makes no difference how many times you invoke a fake method and when in the flow the call occurs. You use fakes when you just want to ignore a dependency.

A more sophisticated option is using mock objects. A mock object does all that a fake does, plus something more. In a way, a mock is an object with its own personality that mimics the behavior and interface of another object.

What more does a mock provide to testers? Essentially, a mock accommodates verification of the context of the method call. With a mock, you can verify that a method call happens with the right preconditions and in the correct order with respect to other methods in the class.

Writing a fake manually is not usually a big issue; for the most part, all the logic you need is simple and doesn't need to change frequently. When you use fakes, you're mostly interested in the state that a fake object might represent; you are not interested in interacting with it. Conversely, you use a mock when you need to interact with dependent objects during tests. For example, you might want to know whether the mock has been invoked, and you might decide within the test what the mock object must return for a given method.

Writing mocks manually is certainly a possibility, but it is rarely an option you want to consider. For the level of flexibility you expect from a mock, you need an ad hoc mocking framework. Table 9-1 lists a few popular mocking frameworks.

TABLE 9-1 Some popular mocking frameworks

Product	URL
Moq	*http://code.google.com/p/moq*
NMock2	*http://sourceforge.net/projects/nmock2*
Typemock	*http://www.typemock.com*
Rhino Mocks	*http://hibernatingrhinos.com/open-source/rhino-mocks*

Note that no mocking framework is currently incorporated in Visual Studio and earlier versions.

With the notable exception of Typemock, all frameworks in the table are open-source software. Typemock is a commercial product with unique capabilities that basically don't require you to (re) design your code for testability. With Typemock, you can test code that was previously considered untestable, such as static methods, non-virtual methods, and sealed classes.

Here's a quick example of how to use a mocking framework such as Moq:

```
[TestMethod]
public void Test_If_Method_Works()
{
    // Arrange
    var logger = new Mock<ILogger>();
    logger.Setup(l => l.Log(It.IsAny<String>()))
    var controller = new HomeController(logger);

    // Act
    ...

    // Assert
    ...
}
```

The class under test (the *HomeController* class) has a dependency on an object that implements the *ILogger* interface:

```
public interface ILogger
{
    void Log(String msg);
}
```

The mock repository supplies a dynamically created object that mocks up the interface for what the test is going to use. The mock object implements the method *Log* in such a way that it does nothing for whatever string argument it receives. You are not really testing the logger here; you are focusing on the controller class and providing a quick and functional mock for the logger component that the controller uses internally.

There's no need for you to create an entire fake class; you just specify the code you need a given method to run when invoked. That's the power of mocks compared to fakes.

Number of assertions per test

How many assertions should you have per test? Should you force yourself to have just one assertion per test in full homage to the principle of narrowly scoped tests? This is a controversial point.

Many people in the industry seem to think so. Arguments used in support of this opinion are good ones, indeed. One assertion per test leads you to write more focused tests and keep your scope limited. One assertion per test makes it obvious what each test is testing.

The need for multiple assertions often hides the fact that you are testing many features within a single test. This is clearly a thing to avoid. If you can choose only one rule to follow, one assertion per test is probably the best. If you're testing the state of an object after a given operation, you probably need to check multiple values and need multiple assertions. You can certainly find a way to express this through a bunch of tests, each with a single assertion. In my opinion, though, that would be a lot of refactoring for little gain.

I don't mind having multiple assertions per test as long as the code in the test is testing just one very specific behavior. Most frameworks stop at the first failed assertion, so you theoretically risk that other assertions in the same test will fail on the next run. If you hold to the principle that you test just one behavior and use multiple assertions to verify multiple aspects of the class related to that behavior, all assertions are related, and if the first one fails, the chances are great that by fixing it you won't get more failures in that test.

Testing inner members

In some situations, a protected method or property needs to be accessed within a test. In general, a class member doesn't have to be public to deserve some tests. However, testing a nonpublic member poses additional issues.

A common approach to testing a nonpublic member consists of creating a new class that extends the class under test. The derived class then adds a public method that calls the protected method. This class is added only to the test project, without spoiling the class design.

As mentioned earlier, in the .NET Framework an even better approach consists of adding a partial class to the class under test. For this to happen, though, the original class needs to be marked as partial itself. However, in terms of design, this is not a big deal.

In .NET, you can also easily make internal members of a class visible to another assembly (for example, the test assembly) by using the *InternalsVisibleTo* attribute, as demonstrated here:

```
[assembly: InternalsVisibleTo("MyTests")]
```

You can add the preceding line to the assemblyinfo.cs file of the project that contains the class with internal members to make available. Note that you can use the attribute multiple times so that you make visible internal members of classes to multiple external executables.

As I see things, using this attribute is a little more obtrusive than using partial classes. In fact, to take advantage of the attribute, you must mark as internal any members you want to recall from tests. Internal members are still not publicly available, but the level of visibility they have is higher than private or protected. In other words, you should use internal and *InternalsToVisible* sparingly and only where a specific need justifies its use.

Finally, MSTest also has a nice programming feature—the *PrivateObject* class—that offers to call nonpublic members via reflection.

```
var resourceId = "WelcomeMessage";
var resourceFile = "MyRes.it.resx";
var expected = "...";
var po = new PrivateObject(controller);
var text = po.Invoke("GetLocalizedText", new object[] { resourceId, resourceFile });
Assert.AreEqual(text, expected);
```

You wrap the object that contains the hidden member in a new instance of the *PrivateObject* class. Next, you call the *Invoke* method to indirectly invoke the method with an array of objects as its parameter list. The *Invoke* method returns an object that represents the return value of the private member.

Code coverage

The primary purpose of unit and integration tests is to make the development team confident about the quality of the software they're producing. Basically, unit testing informs the team whether they are doing well and are on the right track. But, how reliable are the results of unit tests?

Any measure of reliability you want to consider also depends to some extent on the number of unit tests and the percentage of code covered by tests. On the other hand, no realistic correlation has ever been proved to exist between code coverage and the quality of the software.

Typically, unit tests cover only a subset of the code base, but no common agreement has ever been reached on what a "good" percentage of code coverage is. Some say 80 percent is good; some do not even bother quoting a figure. For sure, forms of full code coverage are actually impractical to achieve, if ever possible.

All versions of Visual Studio have code-coverage tools.

In addition, code coverage is a rather generic term that can refer to quite a few different calculation criteria, such as *function*, *statement*, *decision*, and *path* coverage. Function coverage measures whether each function in the program has been executed in some tests. Statement coverage looks more granularly at individual lines of the source code. Decision coverage measures the branches (such as an *if* statement) evaluated, whereas path coverage checks whether every possible route through a given part of the code has been executed.

Each criterion provides a viewpoint into the code, but what you get back are only numbers to be interpreted. So, it might seem that testing all the lines of code (that is, getting 100 percent statement coverage) is a great thing; however, a higher value for path coverage is probably more desirable. Code coverage is certainly useful because it helps you to identify which code hasn't been touched by tests. However, code coverage doesn't indicate to you much about how well tests have exercised the code. Would you like a nice example?

Imagine a method that processes an integer. You can have 100 percent statement coverage for it, but if you lack a test in which the method receives an out-of-range, invalid value, you might get an exception at run time in spite of all the successful tests you have run.

In the end, code coverage is a number subject to specific measurement. Relevance of tests is what really matters. Blindly increasing the code coverage or, worse yet, requiring that developers reach a given threshold of coverage is no guarantee of anything. It is probably still much better than having no tests, but it says nothing about the relevance and effectiveness of tests. Focusing on expected behavior and expected input is the most reasonable way to approach testing. A well-tested application is an application that has a high coverage of relevant scenarios.

 Note The Microsoft Pex add-in for Visual Studio aims to understand the logic of your code and suggests relevant tests that you need to have. Internally, Pex employs static analysis techniques to build knowledge about the behavior of your application. You can download Pex from *http://tinyurl.com/b4zuqj*.

Testing your ASP.NET MVC code

Testability is often presented as an inalienable feature that makes ASP.NET MVC the first option to consider when it comes to web development for the Microsoft platform. For sure, ASP.NET MVC helps developers write more solid and well-designed software with due SoC between view and behavior. The ASP.NET MVC runtime also offers an API that abstracts away any dependencies your code can have on ASP.NET intrinsic objects. This change marks a huge difference from Web Forms as far as testing is concerned. The bottom line is that ASP.NET MVC is definitely a framework that facilitates unit testing.

Which part of your code should you test?

As mentioned, ASP.NET MVC provides neat separation between the pillars of an application—controllers, views, and models. In addition, it loosens the dependencies of your code on intrinsic components of the ASP.NET runtime such as *Request*, *Response*, and *Session*. The template project also serves a global.asax file where all the initialization work is written in a test-oriented way; these are the little details that help.

ASP.NET MVC does its best to enable and support testing. ASP.NET MVC, however, doesn't write your tests and knows nothing about the real structure of your application and the layers of which it is made. You should aim to write tests that are relevant; you should not simply aim for getting a high score in code coverage.

How do I find relevant code to test?

The location of the relevant code to test mostly depends on the layers you have in the code. In light of what is discussed in Chapter 7, I say, "Do not put it in the controller." Too many examples emphasizing the support for unit testing that ASP.NET MVC offers are limited to testing the controller. Consider the following code:

```
[TestClass]
public class HomeControllerTest
{
    [TestMethod]
    public void Index()
    {
        var controller = new HomeController();
        var result = controller.Index() as ViewResult;
        Assert.AreEqual("Welcome to ASP.NET MVC!", result.ViewBag.Message);
    }
}
```

The test creates a new instance of the controller class and invokes the *Index* method. The method returns a *ViewResult* object. The assertion then checks whether the *Message* property in the *View Result* instance equals a given string. Let's review the controller's code here:

```
public ActionResult Index()
{
    ViewBag.Message = "Welcome to ASP.NET MVC!";
    return View();
}
```

The relevant part of this code is the assignment. To keep the controller lean and mean, you should consider moving this code to a worker service as discussed in Chapter 7. Here's how to rewrite the method to isolate the core logic:

```
public ActionResult Index()
{
    _service.GetIndexViewModel(ViewBag);
    return View();
}
```

At this point, you no longer need to test the controller. You might want to test the service class. There might be situations in which the body of the controller method is a bit fleshier; however, it will be mostly glue code made of conditional statements and trivial assignments—nothing you really need to test.

You can apply the same reasoning to the worker service, leading you to write tests for just highly specialized components with extremely clear and limited assertions.

> **Note** When writing a unit test, you should know a lot of details about the internals of the unit you're testing. Unit testing is, in fact, a form of white-box testing, as opposed to black-box testing in which the tester needs no knowledge of the internals and limits testing to entering given input values and expecting given output values.

The domain layer

Chapter 7 defines the context of the domain layer, which refers to the invariant objects of your application's business context—the data and behavior. If you're designing an e-commerce application, your domain is made of entities like invoice, customer, order, shipper, and offer. Each of these entities has properties and methods. For example, an invoice will have properties such as *Number*, *Date*, *Payment*, and *Items* and methods such as *GetEstimatedDayOfPayment*, *GetTotal*, and *CalculateTaxes*. For some of these entities (for example, aggregate roots), you might also need special services that perform ad hoc operations in a cross-entity manner. For example, you might want to have a method that gets a customer and figures out if she has placed enough orders to qualify as a gold-level customer.

This is a portion of the code you absolutely want to test thoroughly; namely, you want to be sure it's extensively covered by relevant unit tests. Because this is the core of your application, you want to ensure that you encounter all corner cases properly and that inconsistent values/states are properly detected. Finally, you want to be sure that a proper battery of tests can alert you to any regression being introduced in later stages of development. If you can cover with tests just one segment of the application, I recommend that segment be the domain layer, if you have one.

The orchestration layer

Depending on how many layers and tiers you really implement, the orchestration layer (which is discussed in Chapter 7) either can be fully identified with the worker services of an ASP.NET MVC controller or can form a layer of its own.

The need to test this layer thoroughly depends on the amount of logic you have in it. In a Create, Read, Update, and Delete (CRUD) system, this layer is mostly thin enough to just test samples of it. However, if the presentation layer offers a significantly different representation of the data than the storage maintains, the orchestration layer is responsible for arranging data in a particular format for the view. In this case, the layer becomes a more critical part of your application and deserves more attention.

If you reduce the controller to be a mere pass-through layer—one that gets view models from the orchestration layer and passes it to the ASP.NET MVC infrastructure—you have no need to test it. Or, better yet, you have other portions of the application that you might focus on first.

The data access layer

What service is providing your data access layer? Is it simply running SQL statements for you? If that is the case, after you determine that the code works at development time (for example, your SQL statements are correct), you're all set.

If the data access layer sums up additional capabilities and incorporates some logic that adapts data into different data structures than storage, you might want to consider some tests. But, in this case, why not separate the CRUD wheat from the adapter chaff and test the adapters only?

> **Important** Unit testing is not really a matter of numbers; it is a matter of quality of numbers. Not only do you need tests, but you need tests that cover relevant aspects of your code. You won't sell an application because of unit tests; you sell an application if the application passes the acceptance tests. And, acceptance tests indicate what behavior is relevant for the end user. Finding what behavior is relevant for the units of code your application is made of is exactly the effort one expects from a great developer.

Unit testing ASP.NET MVC code

Beyond the theory of unit testing—some would even call it the art of unit testing—there are some concrete and pragmatic aspects that you need to handle. Specifically, there a few practices and techniques you want to understand in order to write unit tests for ASP.NET MVC applications.

Writing a unit test is equivalent to calling a method simulating the particular context in which you're interested. A unit test is just software—a method in a class—and with it, like software, you can use most of the tricks and techniques you normally use in a regular code class. In this chapter, I'm just discussing what's relevant to know and not every aspect of writing a unit test for ASP.NET MVC.

> **Note** If you're interested in the art of unit testing, be sure you get a copy of *The Art of Unit Testing* by Roy Osherove (Manning Publications, 2009), which you can find at *http://www.manning.com/osherove*.

Testing whether the returned view is correct

There might be situations in which the controller decides on the fly about the view to render. This happens when the view to render is based on some conditions known only at run time. An example is a controller method that must switch view templates based on the locale, user account, day of the week, or anything else your users might ask you.

In a test, you can catch the view being rendered by using the *ViewName* property of the *Action Result* object, as presented here:

```
[TestMethod]
public void Should_Render_Italian_View()
{
    // Simulate ad hoc runtime conditions here
    ...

    // Parameters
    var productId = 42;
    var expectedViewName = "index_it";

    // Go
    var controller = new ProductController();
    var result = controller.Find(productId) as ViewResult;
    if (result == null)
        Assert.Fail("Invalid result");
    Assert.AreEqual(result.ViewName, expectedViewName);
}
```

The assumption is that the *ProductController* class returns localized views for the selected product. In this case, a good example of the run-time conditions to simulate for the sake of the test is setting the current locale to it.

By checking the public properties of the specific *ActionResult* object returned by the controller method, you can also perform ad hoc checks when a particular response is generated, such as JavaScript Object Notation (JSON), JavaScript, binaries, files, and so forth.

Testing localization

Sometimes, you'll find it useful to have some tests that quickly check whether certain parts of the user interface are going to receive proper localized resources when a given language is selected. Here's how to proceed with a unit test:

```
[TestMethod]
public void Test_If_Localized_Strings_Are_Used()
{
    // Simulate ad hoc runtime conditions here
    const String culture = "it-IT";
    var cultureInfo = CultureInfo.CreateSpecificCulture(culture);
    Thread.CurrentThread.CurrentCulture = cultureInfo;
    Thread.CurrentThread.CurrentUICulture = cultureInfo;

    // Ensure resources are being returned in the correct language
    var showMeMoreDetails = MyText.Product.ShowMeDetails;

    // Assert
    Assert.AreEqual(showMeMoreDetails, "Maggiori informazioni");
}
```

In the unit test, you first set the culture on the current thread and then you attempt to retrieve the value for the resource and assert against expected values.

You can use this technique to test nearly everything that's related to localization, including localized views and resources. Here's a unit test written for the *UrlHelper* extension method, which is discussed in Chapter 5, "Aspects of ASP.NET MVC applications":

```
[TestMethod]
public void Test_If_Url_Extensions_Work()
{
    // Data
    var url = "sample.css";
    var expectedUrl = "sample.it.css";

    // Set culture to IT
    const String culture = "it-IT";
    var cultureInfo = CultureInfo.CreateSpecificCulture(culture);
    Thread.CurrentThread.CurrentCulture = cultureInfo;
    Thread.CurrentThread.CurrentUICulture = cultureInfo;

    // Act & Assert
    var localizedUrl = UrlExtensions.GetLocalizedUrl(url);
    Assert.AreEqual(localizedUrl, expectedUrl);
}
```

This quick demo hides a very interesting story. Chapter 5 shows code that defines the *GetLocalizedUrl* extension method, as shown here:

```
public static String GetLocalizedUrl(UrlHelper helper, String resourceUrl)
```

To test this method, you need to provide an instance of the *UrlHelper* class. Unfortunately, the constructor of the *UrlHelper* class is coupled with the ASP.NET MVC infrastructure.

```
public UrlHelper(RequestContext context)
```

How can you get a valid *RequestContext* in a testing environment? You need to mock up the HTTP context. It's definitely a doable thing, as you'll see in a moment, but it requires too much work in this scenario. A simple refactoring will help you focus on what's really relevant to test.

What you want ultimately is to check the ability of the code to return sample.it.css instead of sample.css when the culture is Italian. You don't need to test whether the resource really exists on the web server. So, you don't strictly need the request context. Let's rewrite the *GetLocalizedUrl* method, as shown here:

```
public static String GetLocalizedUrl(UrlHelper helper, String resourceUrl)
{
    var url = GetLocalizedUrl(resourceUrl);
    return VirtualFileExists(helper, url) ? url : resourceUrl;
}
```

```
public static String GetLocalizedUrl(String resourceUrl)
{
    var cultureExt = String.Format("{0}{1}",
        Thread.CurrentThread.CurrentUICulture.TwoLetterISOLanguageName,
        Path.GetExtension(resourceUrl));
    return Path.ChangeExtension(resourceUrl, cultureExt);
}
```

The effect is the same, but the test is quicker and more focused.

Testing redirections

A controller action might also redirect to another URL or route. Testing a redirection, however, is no harder than testing a context-specific view. A controller method that redirects will return a *Redirect Result* object if it redirects to a specific URL; however, it will return a *RedirectToRouteResult* object if it redirects to a named route.

The *RedirectResult* class has a familiar *Url* property that you can check to verify whether the action completed successfully. The *RedirectToRouteResult* class has properties such as *RouteName* and *Route Values* that you can check to ensure that the redirection worked correctly.

Testing routes

Especially if you make extensive use of custom routes, you might want to test them carefully. In particular, you're interested in checking whether a given URL is matched to the right route and if route data is extracted properly.

To test routes, you must reproduce the global.asax environment and begin by invoking the *RegisterRoutes* method. The *RegisterRoutes* method populates the collection with available routes, as shown in the following:

```
[TestMethod]
public void Test_If_Product_Routes_Work()
{
    // Arrange
    var routes = new RouteCollection();
    MvcApplication.RegisterRoutes(routes);
    RouteData routeData = null;
    // Act & Assert whether the right route was found
    var expectedRoute = "{controller}/{action}/{id}";
    routeData = GetRouteDataForUrl("~/product/id/123", routes);
    Assert.AreEqual(((Route) routeData.Route).Url, expectedRoute);
}
```

The *GetRouteDataForUrl* method in the test is a local helper, defined as follows:

```
private static RouteData GetRouteDataForUrl(String url, RouteCollection routes)
{
    var httpContextMock = new Mock<HttpContextBase>();
    httpContextMock.Setup(c => c.Request.AppRelativeCurrentExecutionFilePath).Returns(url);
    var routeData = routes.GetRouteData(httpContextMock);
    Assert.IsNotNull(routeData, "Should have found the route");
    return routeData;
}
```

The method is expected to invoke *GetRouteData* to retrieve information about the requested route. Unfortunately, *GetRouteData* needs a reference to *HttpContextBase*, where it places all inquiries about the request. In particular, *GetRouteData* needs to invoke *AppRelativeCurrentExecutionFilePath* to know about the virtual path to process. By mocking *HttpContextBase* to provide an ad hoc URL, you completely decouple the route from the run-time environment and can proceed with assertions.

The sample code shown earlier uses the Moq framework to create test doubles. Let's find out more about mocking and how to use mocks to neutralize or replace dependencies.

Dealing with dependencies

As far as testing is concerned, you could say that there are two main types of dependencies: those you want to ignore, and those with which you want to interact but in a controlled manner. In both cases, you need to provide a test-double object—namely, an object that behaves like the expected one while providing an expected behavior. If the classes under test support dependency injection (DI), providing a test double is a piece of cake.

Regardless of the names being used to indicate test doubles (fakes, mocks, stubs), the raw truth is that you need an object that implements a given contract. So, how do you write this test-double object?

About mock and fake objects

A test double is a class you write and add to the test project. This class implements a given interface or inherits from a given base class. After you have the instance, you inject it inside the object under test by using the public interface of the object being tested. (Clearly, I'm assuming the object under test was designed with testability in mind.)

You might need a different test-double class for each test you write. These classes look nearly the same and differ perhaps in terms of the value they return. Should you really write and maintain hundreds of similar looking classes? You shouldn't, and that's why mocking frameworks exist. A mocking framework provides infrastructure for you to quickly create classes that implement a contract. Additionally, a mocking framework provides some facilities with which you can configure the interaction with the methods of this dynamically created class. In particular, you can instruct the mock to get you an instance of a class that exposes the *ISomething* contract and returns 1 when the *ExecuteTask* method is invoked with a given argument.

You probably need to write your own class when in the implementation of one or more methods you need to maintain some state or just execute some custom logic. In the context of this book, I call fakes the classes you specifically write in the test project to neutralize dependencies. I call mocks the classes that you create—for the same purpose—using a mocking framework.

Do you still think that a relevant difference exists between fakes and mocks? If any exists, it's purely about the label you want to attach to each.

Testing code that performs data access

The canonical example of DI in testing is when you have a worker service class (in simple scenarios, it can even be the controller class) that needs to perform data access operations. Chapter 7 defines a worker service class name *HomeService* that gets a list of dates from a repository. The service class is required to do some extra work on the list of dates before packing them into a view model for display. In particular, the worker service calculates the time span between the current day and the specified date. The repository will likely run a query against some database to return dates. Here's how to inject a fake dependency in the service class so that you can test the service class without dealing with queries and connection strings:

```
[TestClass]
public class DateRepositoryTests
{
    [TestMethod]
    public void Test_If_Dates_Are_Processed()
    {
        var inputDate = new DateTime(2013, 2, 8);
        var fakeRepository = new FakeDateRepository();
        var service = new HomeServices(fakeRepository);
        var model = service.GetHomeViewModel();

        var expectedResult = (Int32) (DateTime.Now - inputDate).TotalDays;
        Assert.AreEqual(model.FeaturedDates[0].DaysToGo, expectedResult);
    }
}
```

The *FakeDateRepository* class will look like this:

```
public class FakeDateRepository : IDateRepository
{
   public override IList<MementoDate> GetFeaturedDates()
   {
      return List<MementoDate>
                {
                    new MementoDate {Date = new DateTime(...)}
                });
   }
}
```

You need a new *FakeDateRepository* class for each test you plan to write. For example, suppose that you want to test the behavior of the service both when the date falls before and after the current date. You need two tests and two slightly different versions of *FakeDateRepository*, the only difference being in the returned date. The following demonstrates how a mocking framework can help:

```
[TestClass]
public class DateRepositoryTests
{
    [TestMethod]
    public void Test_If_Dates_Are_Processed()
    {
        var inputDate = new DateTime(2012, 2, 8);
        var fakeRepository = new Mock<IDateRepository>();
        fakeRepository.Setup(d => d.GetFeaturedDates()).Returns(new List<MementoDate>
                                                      {
                                                          new MementoDate {Date = inputDate}
                                                      });

        var service = new HomeServices(fakeRepository.Object);
        var model = service.GetHomeViewModel();

        var expectedResult = (Int32) (DateTime.Now - inputDate).TotalDays;
        Assert.AreEqual(model.FeaturedDates[0].DaysToGo, expectedResult);
    }
}
```

The fake repository is created by using Moq and is injected in the *HomeService* class via the constructor. The *Mock<IDateRepository>* object is a dynamically created class (Moq uses Castle Dynamic Proxy internally to dynamically generate code) that implements the *IDateRepository* interface and returns the input date whenever the *GetFeaturedDates* method is invoked. To write a test against another input, you simply duplicate the test method without explicitly dealing with source classes.

Mocking the HTTP context

I'm not really happy when I have to mock the HTTP context to write some ASP.NET MVC unit tests. Sometimes, you really need it; however, more often than you might think, a bit of refactoring on your code makes mocking the HTTP context unnecessary.

When it comes to unit testing, there's a mistake (or at least I call it this) that I see too often. Some developers seem unable to look beyond the controller level. These developers put large chunks of logic in the controller. They make little use of specific, highly specialized classes. These developers seem to think that beyond the controller, you can have only a Microsoft SQL Server database or an Entity Framework model. Just having a layer of repositories around LINQ-to-Entities queries is already a cutting-edge solution. Chapter 7 attempts to illustrate a different pattern for plain code.

If the granularity of controller methods is fairly coarse, you inevitably need to mock a long list of objects to run your tests. A controller method that deals directly with query strings and session state needs to have a valid HTTP context arranged for a test to run. This is extra work for you. Also, refactoring the controller method to add encapsulation and wrappers is extra work for you, but it's work of a different type.

You see immediately the benefits of a cleaner design: For one, testing is much easier. Efforts expended to make tests work result in more wasted time, instead. When the test finally runs, you feel more relieved than satisfied. Mocking the HTTP context is a constant requirement if you end up with coarse-grained controller methods. It's not just the ASP.NET MVC framework, it's also you.

Having said that, however, sometimes you really need to mock the HTTP context. Let's see how to do it.

Mocking the *HttpContext* object

The *HttpContext* object inherits from *HttpContextBase*, so all you need to do is create a mock for it. The *HttpContext* object is a plain aggregator of object references; it hardly needs to contain extra code. So, a mock is just fine most of the time. Here's how to build a fake HTTP context by using Moq:

```
public void BuildHttpContextForController(Controller controller)
{
    var contextBase = new Mock<HttpContextBase>();
    var request = new Mock<HttpRequestBase>();
    var response = new Mock<HttpResponseBase>();
    var server = new Mock<HttpServerUtilityBase>();
    ...

    contextBase.Setup(c => c.Request).Returns(request);
    contextBase.Setup(c => c.Response).Returns(response);
    contextBase.Setup(c => c.Server).Returns(server);

    // Pass the fake context down to the controller instance
    var context = new ControllerContext(
            new RequestContext(contextBase.Object, new RouteData()), controller);
    controller.ControllerContext = context;
    return;
}
```

This is only the first level of mocking for ASP.NET intrinsic objects. For example, whenever the application queries for *Request* in a unit test, it gets the mocked object. The mocked object, however, is a dummy object and needs its own setup. Let's see a couple of examples.

Mocking the *Request* object

You probably want to extend the mocked *Request* object with expectations regarding some specific members. For example, here's how to simulate a GET or POST request in a test:

```
var method = "get";
contextBase.Setup(c => Request.HttpMethod).Return(method);
```

Earlier in the chapter, while discussing the testing of routes, we also ran into similar code:

```
var url = ...;
contextBase.Expect(c => Request.AppRelativeCurrentExecutionFilePath).Return(url);
```

You probably don't want to use the *Request.Form* object to read about posted data from within a controller, because you might find model binders to be more effective. However, if you have a legacy call to *Request.Form["MyParam"]* in one of your controller's methods, how would you test it?

```
// Prepare the fake Form collection
var formCollection = new NameValueCollection();
formCollection["MyParam"] = ...;

// Fake the HTTP context and bind Request.Form to the fake collection
var contextBase = new Mock<HttpContextBase>();
contextBase.Setup(c => c.Request.Form).Returns(formCollection);

// Assert
...
```

In this way, every time your code reads anything through *Request.Form*, it actually ends up reading from the name/value collection provided for testing purposes.

Mocking the *Response* object

Let's see a few examples that touch on the *Response* object. For example, you might want to mock up *Response.Write* calls by forcing a fake *HttpResponse* object to write to a text writer object, as illustrated here:

```
var writer = new StringWriter();
var contextBase = new Mock<HttpContextBase>();
contextBase.Setup(c => c.Response).Return(new FakeResponse(writer));
```

In this case, the *FakeResponse* class is used as shown here:

```
public class FakeResponse : HttpResponseBase
{
    private readonly TextWriter _writer;
    public FakeResponse(TextWriter writer)
    {
        _writer = writer;
    }

    public override void Write(string msg)
    {
        _writer.Write(msg);
    }
}
```

With this code, you can test a controller method that has calls to *Response.Write*, such as the one shown here:

```
public ActionResult Output()
{
    HttpContext.Response.Write("Hello");
    return View();
}
```

Here's the test:

```
[TestMethod]
public void Should_Response_Write()
{
    // Arrange
    var writer = new StringWriter();
    var contextBase = new Mock<HttpContextBase>();
    contextBase.Setup(c => c.Response).Returns(new FakeResponse(writer));
    var controller = new HomeController();
    controller.ControllerContext = new ControllerContext(
                    contextBase.Object, new RouteData(), controller);

    // Act
    var result = controller.Output() as ViewResult;
    if (result == null)
        Assert.Fail("Result is null");

    // Assert
    Assert.AreEqual("Hello", writer.ToString());
}
```

Similarly, you can configure a dynamically generated mock if you need to make certain properties or methods just return a specific value. Here are a couple of examples:

```
var contextBase = new Mock<HttpContextBase>();

// Mock up the Output property
contextBase.Setup(c => Response.Output).Returns(new StringWriter());

// Mock up the Content type of the response
contextBase.Setup(c => Response.ContentType).Returns("application/json");
```

For cookies, on the other hand, you might want to mock the *Cookies* collection on both *Request* and *Response* to return a new instance of the *HttpCookieCollection* class, which will act as your cookie container for the scope of the unit test. I'll show more details related to mocking the *Response* object later in the chapter while discussing how to test controller methods with action filters.

Mocking the *Session* object

A mock is easier to use, but sometimes you need to assign a behavior to the various methods of the mocked object. This is easy to do when the behavior is as simple as returning a given value. To effectively test whether the method correctly updates the session state, though, you need to provide an in-memory object that simulates the behavior of the original object and has the ability to store information, which is not exactly an easy task to mock. However, using a fake session class makes it straightforward. Here's a minimal yet effective fake for the session state:

```
public class FakeSession : HttpSessionStateBase
{
    private readonly Dictionary<String, Object> _sessionItems =
                                    new Dictionary<String, Object>();
```

```
    public override void Add(String name, Object value)
    {
        _sessionItems.Add(name, value);
    }

    public override Object this[String name]
    {
        get { return _sessionItems.ContainsKey(name) ? _sessionItems[name] : null; }
        set { _sessionItems[name] = value; }
    }
}
```

And here's how to arrange a test:

```
[TestMethod]
public void Should_Write_To_Session_State()
{
    // Arrange
    var contextBase = new Mock<HttpContextBase>();
    contextBase.Setup(c => c.Session).Returns(new FakeSession());
    var controller = new HomeController();
    controller.ControllerContext = new ControllerContext(
                    contextBase.Object, new RouteData(), controller);

    // Act
    var expectedResult = "green";
    controller.SetColor();    // Runs Session["PreferredColor"] = "green";

    // Assert
    var result = controller.HttpContext.Session["PreferredColor"];
    Assert.AreEqual(result, expectedResult);
}
```

If your controller method only reads from *Session*, your test can be even simpler and you can avoid faking the *Session* entirely. Here's a sample controller action:

```
public ActionResult GetColor()
{
    var o = Session["PreferredColor"];
    if (o == null)
        ViewData["Color"] = "No preferred color";
    else
        ViewData["Color"] = o as String;

    return View("Color");
}
```

The following code snippet shows a possible way to test the method just shown:

```
// Arrange
var contextBase = MockRepository.GenerateMock<HttpContextBase>();
contextBase.Expect(s => s.Session["PreferredColor"]).Return("Blue");
var controller = new HomeController();
controller.ControllerContext = new ControllerContext(
                    contextBase.Object, new RouteData(), controller);
```

```
// Act
var result = controller.GetColor() as ViewResult;
if (result == null)
    Assert.Fail("Result is null");

// Assert
Assert.AreEqual(result.ViewData["Color"].ToString(), "Blue");
```

In this case, you instruct the HTTP context mock to return the string "Blue" when its *Session* property is requested to provide a value for the entry "PreferredColor".

In what is likely the much more common scenario, that in which a controller method needs to read and write the session state, you need to use the test solution based on some *FakeSession* class.

Mocking the *Cache* object

Mocking the ASP.NET *Cache* object is a task that deserves a bit more attention, even though mocking a caching layer doesn't require a new approach. The *HttpContextBase* class has a *Cache* property, but you can't mock it up because the property doesn't represent an abstraction of the ASP.NET caching systems; it's a concrete implementation of a particular class, instead. Here's how the *Cache* property is declared on the *HttpContextBase* class:

```
public abstract class HttpContextBase : IServiceProvider
{
    public virtual Cache Cache { get; }
    ...
}
```

The type of the *Cache* property is actually *System.Web.Caching.Cache*—the real cache object, not an abstraction. Even more unfortunate, the *Cache* type is sealed and therefore is not mockable and is unusable in unit tests.

What can you do? There are two options. One entails using testing tools that can deal with sealed classes. An example of one of these tools is Typemock Isolator (a commercial product); another is Microsoft Moles. The other possibility is to use a wrapper class to perform any access to the *Cache* from within any code you intend to test. Chapter 5 examines this approach.

Based on what you've seen, you create a cache service object that implements a given interface; for example, *ICacheService*. Next, you register this class with the application in global.asax and add a public static property to read/write the cache:

```
protected void Application_Start()
{
    ...

    // Inject a global caching service(for example, one based on ASP.NET Cache)
    RegisterCacheService(new AspNetCacheService());
}
```

```
private static ICacheService _internalCacheObject;
public void RegisterCacheService(ICacheService cacheService)
{
    _internalCacheObject = cacheService;
}

public static ICacheService CacheService
{
    get { return _internalCacheObject;  }
}
```

In controller methods, you stop using the *HttpContext.Cache* entirely. Your controller will have the following layout, instead:

```
public partial class HomeController : Controller
{
    public ActionResult SetCache()
    {
        // MvcApplication is the name of the global.asax class; change it at will
        MvcApplication.CacheService["PreferredColor"] = "Blue";
        return View();
    }
    ...
 }
```

How would you test this? Here's an example:

```
[TestMethod]
public void Should_Write_To_Cache()
{
    // Arrange
    var fakeCache = new FakeCache();
    MvcApplication.RegisterCacheService(fakeCache);

    // Act
    controller.SetCache();

    // Assert
    Assert.AreEqual("Blue", fakeCache["PreferredColor"].ToString());
}
```

The *FakeCache* class can be something like this:

```
public class FakeCache : ICacheService
{
    private readonly Dictionary<String, Object> _cacheItems =
                new Dictionary<String, Object>();
```

```
public object this[String name]
{
    get
    {
        if (_cacheItems.ContainsKey(name))
            return _cacheItems[name];
        else
            return null;
    }
    set { _cacheItems[name] = value; }
}
}
```

In this way, you can test controller methods and services, making use of cached data even when the cache is a distributed cache. The cache service hides all details and makes the application more extensible and testable.

Summary

Testability is a fundamental aspect of software, as the paper ISO/IEC 9126 recognized back in 1991. With ASP.NET MVC, designing your code for testability is easier and encouraged. But, you also can write testable code in ASP.NET Web Forms and test it to a good extent. Testability is an excellent excuse to pursue good design. Design makes a difference under the hood.

We all agree that writing tests is helpful, recommended, and even sexy. However, unless you associate it with some test-driven design methodology, writing tests risks being an end in and of itself. On one hand, you have the classes to test; on the other hand, you have classes that promise to test other classes. And, you have nothing in the middle that guarantees that tests are appropriate and meaningful.

An approach that creates the environment for a much more effective refactoring while not excluding unit testing is based on software contracts. A software contract defines the terms and conditions for each method in each class. That gives you an optional run-time checking mechanism as well as concrete guidance on how to refactor when you have to. Software contracts are not a new concept in software, but they have found widespread implementation only in .NET 4. Check out the documentation for code contracts and the articles I wrote on the subject in the Cutting Edge column in MSDN Magazine, which is available at *http://msdn.microsoft.com/en-us/magazine/default.aspx*.

CHAPTER 10

An executive guide to Web API

The visionary lies to himself, the liar only to others.

—*Friedrich Nietzsche*

ASP.NET Web API is a new framework expressly designed to support and simplify the building of HTTP services that can be consumed by a variety of clients; in particular, HTML pages and mobile applications. The core idea behind Web API is nothing new, and developers and architects have been facing the same challenge for at least a decade now. Along the way, several frameworks and technologies have been worked out and each was regularly presented as the definitive solution to the issue. How many times did you hear that Windows Communication Foundation (WCF) was the ideal technology to build a service layer for whatever kind of client, including TCP and HTTP?

In this regard, Web API is at least the latest attempt—and hopefully the last and truly definitive one—to provide an ideal framework for web services over HTTP.

The scope of Web API is broad enough to make it compelling and useful to just about any developer, not just web developers. For some reasons, though, Web API is sometimes presented, or just perceived, as an ASP.NET MVC–related tool. This is misleading; in addition, if you look at core functionality, ASP.NET MVC developers are the only ones in Microsoft's space who can happily live without Web API.

Web API is a well-designed framework for building both RESTful (Representational State Transfer) and remote procedure calls (RPC)–style HTTP services for .NET applications. Web API intersects various aspects of ASP.NET MVC such as routing, security, controllers, and extensibility and has specific areas not directly supported by plain ASP.NET MVC. In short, Web API deserve its own book to be covered appropriately. This chapter represents an executive summary of the key facts of Web API—how to build and use HTTP services—from the perspective of an ASP.NET MVC developer. For more examples and an even deeper look at the internal architecture, I suggest you look at the excellent documentation that you can find at *http://www.asp.net/web-api*.

The whys and wherefores of Web API

Web API is not a framework that was devised overnight, and I'd say it's not even a framework created following some divine inspiration. More simply, it is hopefully the final stage of an evolutionary process that began about a decade ago with the goal of making available standardized web services.

The need for a unified HTTP API

Before being bound to specific technologies and frameworks, the term *web service* was merely intended to describe a software service that is available over the web. The need for shared HTTP endpoints returning data instead of markup was already strong and clear in the late 1990s, when the ASP.NET framework was being crafted.

As it often happens in software development, architects managed to place a specific need into a broader and broader context and ended up creating technologies and patterns that not only addressed the initial need but offered much more. After a few years of experience, the software community is back to the initial need—"All we want is the simplest infrastructure that could possibly allow us to call endpoints via HTTP." Amazingly, there was no such infrastructure within and around ASP.NET and the Microsoft stack. Instead, there was a number of technologies that developers could bend to operate as HTTP services, each of these technologies having its own pros and cons.

Web API addresses the problem of giving developers an effective and unique platform to expose application services via HTTP. Defining the shape and form of "application services" is up to the architect. It could be that the software development kit (SDK) of the application is published to the web. It could be, instead, that the application's SDK is over the web but accessed in a controlled way and then is not publicly available. Finally, it could be that you use Web API just to publish a service in the Service-Oriented Architecture (SOA) sense—an autonomous, stand-alone application with no user interface, just serving data in a variety of formats.

Beyond WCF

When the world realized about the power of web services, a standard protocol was worked out quickly to become the currency that web services could exchange with callers: Simple Object Access Protocol (SOAP). On top of that, a number of more in-depth specifications became a work-in-progress collectively known as *WS-* protocols*.

WCF was initially conceived to support SOAP and WS-* over a wide variety of transportation layers including TCP, Message Queuing (MSMQ), named pipes, and last but not least, HTTP.

It didn't take much to see that although WCF had its own solid motivation and rationale, developers were mostly using it as a shortcut to HTTP endpoints. This raised the need for the WCF infrastructure to support more effectively non-SOAP services becoming able to serve plain XML, text, and JavaScript Object Notation (JSON) over HTTP. Over the years, we had first the *webHttpBinding* binding mechanism from the WCF team and then came bolted-on frameworks such as the REST starter kit.

In the end, it was a matter of providing some "syntactic sugar" to make the pill of using HTTP as a mere transportation layer easier to swallow. HTTP facilities on top of WCF didn't eliminate the true roadblocks that developers were facing such as notorious WCF over-configuration and overuse of attributes, and its structure not being specifically designed for testability.

The key change was separating multitransport services from plain HTTP services and removing all the heavy machinery of WCF to create a thin and HTTP-focused framework for HTTP services. This is Web API.

Note As the focus for services shifts away from WCF, does it mean that WCF is a dead technology with no realistic application left? Indeed, it does not. WCF is the only significant option when you really need to expose a service that can be invoked over protocols other than HTTP. WCF also remains a key solution when you really need advanced features such as security and support for transactions.

What Web API means for client applications

Web API fits nicely in what today appears to be a fairly common application scenario: a client application needing to invoke a remote back end to download data or request processing. The client application can take many forms: a JavaScript-intensive webpage, a rich client, or a mobile application.

In all of these cases, the HTTP protocol seems to be as effective as SOAP but far simpler and subsequently faster. You can use HTTP verbs and headers to identify operations to perform on remote resources; you can use URL templates to express semantics if you prefer an approach that focuses more on actions. Either way, you use the body of messages to serialize any input value and receive content. The JSON format is ideal to serialize objects between clients and HTTP services.

What Web API means for ASP.NET Web Forms applications

Like it or not, the number of websites that use ASP.NET Web Forms is still larger than those based on ASP.NET MVC. With ASP.NET 4 and newer versions, Microsoft managed to streamline issues, such as limited accessibility of generated HTML, more control over the HTML being generated, mitigating the impact of viewstate, routing, and more. One issue that wasn't solved, though, was enabling Web Forms developers to quickly expose an HTTP callable endpoint.

This is not to say that in Web Forms you can't expose HTTP endpoints to be called back from client pages; you can use HTTP handlers or WCF services with freely generated JavaScript proxy classes. In the end, it works, but coding that is more and more perceived as bothersome.

Web API makes exposing an HTTP service from a Web Forms application as easy as it is to have a controller in ASP.NET MVC: just add a class and it works according to predefined routing rules. Don't like the default routing rules? Adding your own rules is easy, too!

Web API brings a huge benefit to Web Forms developers. At the same time, it represents a source of confusion for ASP.NET MVC developers. In fact, a common question is, why should I use it? What benefits does Web API offer over plain controllers?

MVC controllers vs. Web API

An ASP.NET MVC application results from the combination of multiple controller classes. Typically, each controller class exposes a number of actions that the user interface can invoke through URLs. The neat separation between the processing of the request and generation of the response makes it possible for controller classes to return any response in a variety of formats, including HTML, JSON, XML, or even plain text.

In light of this, what's the point of using Web API in an ASP.NET MVC application?

The *Controller* class does it all

If you want to return some JSON data from within an ASP.NET MVC application, all you need to do is create an ad hoc method in a new or existing *Controller* class. The sole specific requirement for the new method is returning a *JsonResult* object, as illustrated here:

```
public JsonResult LatestNews(int count)
{
    var listOfNews = _service.GetRecentNews(count);
    return Json(listOfNews, JsonRequestBehavior.AllowGet);
}
```

More than the declared return type of the method, which could also be the parent *ActionResult* class, what matters is the call to the *Json* method. The *Json* method ensures that the given object is packaged in a *JsonResult* object. After it is returned from the controller class, the *JsonResult* object is processed by the action invoker in charge of the current request.

The overall effect is that the contained object—originally calculated by the controller—is serialized to JSON and embedded in the body of the response sent back to the requesting device. Similarly, you can serve plain text, binary content, or even XML content formatted the way you like.

Feeling the difference

In ASP.NET MVC you can have HTTP services for nothing more than the cost of adding a new controller class or a specific method to an existing controller class. This has always worked since version 1 and still works today with the latest version of ASP.NET MVC. Why should you look into something else?

The Web API framework relies on a different run-time environment that is totally separated from that of ASP.NET MVC. This has been done just to enable non–ASP.NET MVC applications to use Web API. The run-time environment is inevitably largely inspired to ASP.NET MVC but overall looks simpler and more straight-to-the-point because it is expected to only serve and not markup.

From the viewpoint of an ASP.NET developer, the following three points summarize the advantages that Web API sports over ASP.NET MVC:

- **Decoupling code from serialization of results** This refers to the fact that a Web API controller requires you to simply return data from each method without dealing with the serialization of the results within the method.

- **Content negotiation** A new family of components called *formatters* take care of the serialization of the data being returned to the requesting device. More interesting, formatters are automatically selected based on the content of the Accept header of the incoming request. Built-in XML and JSON formatters are provided; replacing them is a simple matter of configuration. This feature simplifies the development of methods that might return the same raw data in a variety of formats, most typically XML and JSON.

- **Hosting outside Internet Information Services (IIS)** To some extent, content negotiation is a feature that can also be achieved in plain ASP.NET MVC. However, if you opt for implementing your HTTP services within an ASP.NET MVC application, you are bound to IIS as the web server; in other words, you can't host your API elsewhere. This is because ASP.NET MVC is inherently bound to IIS because it was primarily designed to serve as a framework for web applications. But, Web API does not require IIS, and you can self-host it in your own host process such as a Windows service or a console application. (This aspect makes Web API services close to WCF services.)

The bottom line is that Web API doesn't really add much power to ASP.NET MVC development to be considered a must-have feature as it is, for example, in Web Forms development. As usual, it depends on the requirements of the specific project and to some extent on the preferences of the team.

Building RESTful applications

If you struggled to make ASP.NET MVC controllers as RESTful as possible in the past, you'll find that you can do it in a much easier way by choosing Web API and organizing your web application accordingly. For example, you can have a mostly client-side solution (for example, a single-page application) or a bunch of server-side webpages doing most of the work via direct HTTP calls to the API to Create, Read, Update, and Delete (CRUD) data.

To build a RESTful application, you have to identify the different resources in the application and map the actions performed over them to the HTTP methods and address. With Web API, this comes for the most part naturally; all you do is define a data transfer object to return to the client and work out a class in the host ASP.NET MVC application that performs on that object the basic CRUD operations. The RESTfulness of the solution is guaranteed by Web API, which ensures that HTTP PUT requests map to the Create action, the HTTP GET requests map to the Read action, the HTTP POST requests map to the Update action, and the HTTP DELETE requests are associated with the Delete action.

Without further ado, let's proceed with some sample code.

Putting Web API to work

From Microsoft Visual Studio, you start by creating an ASP.NET MVC project of type Web API. What you get in return is an ASP.NET MVC application with two main characteristics. First, the App_Start project folder contains an initializer component for Web API that sets up an ad hoc route. Second, the Controllers folder contains two sample controller classes: the usual *HomeController* class and the Web API–specific *ValuesController* class. The latter inherits from *ApiController* instead of *Controller*.

This is a pillar of Web API. A Web API module is a collection of controller classes that inherit from predefined *ApiController* rather than *Controller*. Figure 10-1 illustrates that the Web API infrastructure and the ASP.NET MVC infrastructure are independent, with no hidden dependencies.

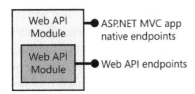

FIGURE 10-1 Web API can be hosted by different apps and is not tightly coupled to ASP.NET.

A Web API module is a stand-alone HTTP-based service that can be hosted by a number of applications, with an ASP.NET MVC application being probably the most common type of host. This is a key point: don't be fooled by seeing the term "controller" appear nearly everywhere. In the end, an ASP.NET MVC application that embeds a Web API–powered set of HTTP endpoints uses the plain *Controller* class to derive HTML-based controllers and *ApiController* to derive controller classes that return plain data to be formatted as JSON or XML. Let's see how to build a Web API module within a host ASP.NET MVC application.

Designing a RESTful interface

Web API uses conventions extensively. According to default conventions, the resulting programming style is essentially a RESTful style. This represents another relevant difference with plain ASP.NET MVC controllers, which are mostly RPC-oriented. To be precise, Web API is in no way limited to a RESTful style; as you'll see later in the chapter, you can choose to give your Web API a RESTful style or an RPC style. However, the default, and most touted, style is essentially RESTful.

Defining the resource type

REST purists argue (and with good reason) that CRUD is not even part of the REST definition. REST is defined as an *architectural style* centered on identification and manipulation of resources through web protocols, most notably HTTP. So much for abstract theory and philosophy; but when it comes to building a concrete implementation of any software that adheres to good REST principles, well... you go really close to building CRUD over HTTP.

At any rate, REST is all about giving a representation of a resource and associating server actions to common HTTP verbs when applied to those resources.

In the context of Web API, this simply means that a Web API module is a class library comprising many controller classes. These controller classes inherit from *ApiController*, which is a class defined in the new *System.Web.Http* assembly that *doesn't* inherit from the ASP.NET MVC *Controller* class. When built with the default RESTful style, Web API controller classes expose a programming interface that provide CRUD over a given resource type. Most likely, you end up having a controller class per resource type that you intend to deal with programmatically.

A resource type is commonly defined as a plain data transfer object (DTO), ultimately a plain C# class. The sample Web API controller class that the Visual Studio wizard generates for you initially doesn't have a true resource type. The sample controller just uses values in the form of plain strings.

```
public class ValuesController : ApiController
{
    public IEnumerable<string> Get()
    {
        return new [] { "value1", "value2" };
    }

    public string Get(int id)
    {
        return "value";
    }
    ...
}
```

In a more realistic example, you might want to have some *News* class defined as follows:

```
public class News
{
    public String Title { get; set; }
    public String Content { get; set; }
    public DateTime Published { get; set; }
}
```

Next, you can have a controller such as the one in the following code that deals with news entities:

```
public class NewsController : ApiController
{
    public IEnumerable<News> GetAll()
    {
        var url = ...;
        var client = new WebClient();
        var rss = client.DownloadString(url);
        var news = ParseRssInternal(rss);
        return news;
    }

    public News Get(int index)
    {
        var all = GetAll();
        return all[index];
    }
    ...
}
```

In the end, a Web API controller class is a collection of public methods. Each method just accepts and returns DTOs when not primitive data. How can a plain class like *NewsController* have its methods invoked over a URL and, for example, return values serialized to JSON or XML? That happens because of the run-time Web API pipeline (for example, routing) and the work done behind the scenes by the *ApiController* class.

The *ApiController* Class

Web API controllers do not return views; instead, they return data to *callers*. Callers are any clients that can connect to an endpoint over HTTP; for example, a webpage, C# class, or mobile app. Return values are only the most visible difference between Web API controllers and ASP.NET MVC controllers. In Web API the base controller class unifies the behavior of the action invoker and controller in ASP.NET MVC.

Chapter 1, "ASP.NET MVC controllers," demonstrates that a request captured by the ASP.NET MVC runtime is processed to a pair given by controller name and action name. The action invoker is the system component in charge of getting a fresh instance of controller class, invoking the method, and executing the expected action on the results. Executing the action on results means essentially preparing the response for the caller. Typically, this involves producing the HTML markup, serializing to JSON or configuring the *HttpResponse* ASP.NET object for a redirect.

In Web API, all these tasks are coordinated from within the *ApiController* class through the *ExecuteAsync* method. Among other things, this also means that in Web API each request is served asynchronously. Be aware, though, that this doesn't strictly mean that every potentially long-running task triggered by the request is asynchronous.

The *ApiController* class also has access to the current configuration of the Web API environment and uses that information appropriately. An instance of the new *HttpConfiguration* class, the configuration container stores the list of registered formatters for XML and JSON, routes, binding rules, and filters.

 Note The Web API infrastructure, and most notably the *ApiController* class and related classes, are hosted in the new *System.Web.Http* assembly. As mentioned, this assembly has no dependencies on *System.Web* and *System.Web.Mvc*. Any concept that sounds similar to ASP.NET MVC (for example, action filters, routing, binding) are re-implemented for the purpose of Web API.

Routing to action methods

When the Web API framework receives an HTTP request, it resolves it in terms of an action method to call on a controller class. To determine which action to invoke, the Web API framework, similar to classic ASP.NET MVC, uses a routing table. The *WebApiConfig* class in the default project template contains the following default route:

```
public static void Register(HttpConfiguration config)
{
    config.Routes.MapHttpRoute(
        name: "DefaultApi",
        routeTemplate: "api/{controller}/{id}",
        defaults: new { id = RouteParameter.Optional }
    );
}
```

As you can see, the default format of URLs recognized by Web API is one that contains the *api* token right after the server name and then the controller name. Based on the aforementioned *NewsController* class, a valid URL might be:

```
http://server/api/news/1
```

Coming from a solid ASP.NET MVC background, you should immediately spot a missing element: the action name. This is just another significant difference between Web API and ASP.NET MVC. By default, the Web API framework uses the HTTP method to select the action, not the URL. This is just the aspect that gives a touch of RESTfulness to the entire framework.

In the end, which method is called on *NewsController* when the above URL is requested?

To find the method, the Web API framework looks for a match on the HTTP method of the request. If the request comes over an HTTP GET method, Web API looks for an action whose name begins with *Get*. In the *NewsController* class shown earlier, there are two methods whose name begins with *Get*: *GetAll* and *Get*. Which one is picked up? It depends on binding rules similar to ASP.NET MVC binding rules discussed in Chapter 3, "The model-binding architecture."

According to the default route, both methods pass the test on the name. However, with the default route, methods can have an optional trailing parameter named *id*. The *GetAll* method has no parameters and thus represents a good match. The *Get* method, instead, requires a parameter named *index*. Because this parameter can't be found in the URL, the method doesn't match.

Dealing with multiple matches

It is interesting to note that little changes in the method's signature can avoid the exception depicted in Figure 10-2. For example, turn the *index* parameter of the *Get* method into a parameter with a default value, as shown here:

```
public News Get(int index=1)
{
    ...
}
```

Then, the following URL can be matched by both *Get* and *GetAll*:

```
http://server/api/news/1
```

When this happens, Web API throws an exception internally and the status code received by the caller is HTTP 500 with the JSON error message shown in Figure 10-2 embedded in the response body.

```
▼<Error>
    <Message>An error has occurred.</Message>
    ▼<ExceptionMessage>
        Multiple actions were found that match the request: Simplest.Models.Dto.News Get(Int32) on type Simplest.Api.NewsController
        System.Collections.Generic.IList`1[Simplest.Models.Dto.News] GetAll() on type Simplest.Api.NewsController
    </ExceptionMessage>
    <ExceptionType>System.InvalidOperationException</ExceptionType>
    ▼<StackTrace>
        at System.Web.Http.Controllers.ApiControllerActionSelector.ActionSelectorCacheItem.SelectAction(HttpControllerContext controllerContext) at
        System.Web.Http.Controllers.ApiControllerActionSelector.SelectAction(HttpControllerContext controllerContext) at
        System.Web.Http.ApiController.ExecuteAsync(HttpControllerContext controllerContext, CancellationToken cancellationToken) at
        System.Web.Http.Dispatcher.HttpControllerDispatcher.SendAsyncInternal(HttpRequestMessage request, CancellationToken cancellationToken) at
        System.Web.Http.Dispatcher.HttpControllerDispatcher.SendAsync(HttpRequestMessage request, CancellationToken cancellationToken)
    </StackTrace>
</Error>
```

FIGURE 10-2 The JSON error message being returned in case of multiple matches.

For a scenario in which the action name is not matched entirely, the risk of running into multiple action methods that match the request is high. A multiple action exception is also thrown if you rename the *index* parameter to *id* as in the route. In this case, because *id* is optional, any method with a single parameter whose name begins with *Get* is a candidate to serve the request.

Active naming conventions

So, it seems that you can have a hard time just finding the right names for your action methods. That's precisely the point, and it comes out of default conventions. For instance, if the request is made by using the HTTP POST verb, in order for the request to be served successfully there should be exactly one method whose name begins with Post. The same default convention applies to requests coming over GET, PUT, and DELETE verbs.

> **Note** To prevent a method from being invoked as an action, you use the *NonAction* attribute. This instructs the Web API framework that the method, even if public and matching the routing rules, should not be taken into account as an action method.

Expected method behavior

The Web API framework builds some expectation with regard to the behavior of each method as it matches HTTP verbs. As you have already seen, for an HTTP GET method, all that is required is that the method returns some serializable .NET object. For other common HTTP verbs such as PUT, POST, and DELETE, things are a little bit trickier.

Semantic of POST methods

A POST method is typically expected to add a new resource to some back-end store. The return type is *HttpResponseMessage* which represents an HTTP response message and includes both status code and actual content being returned to the caller. Here's a common signature and implementation for a POST method:

```
public HttpResponseMessage PostNews(News news)
{
    // Do something here to store the news
    var newsId = SaveNewsInSomeWay(news);
```

```
        // Build an empty response: 201 is code for Created
        var response = Request.CreateResponse<String>(HttpStatusCode.Created, "OK");

        // Store location of the new item
        var relativePath = String.Format("/api/news/{0}", newsId);
        response.Headers.Location = new Uri(Request.RequestUri, relativePath);
        return response;
    }
```

For its first task, the method should do its job of inserting or saving any received data properly. Next, it should manage to create a response object. The status code should be set to *Created* (if a new resource was actually created) and the content should be any message back for the caller. It is also recommended that the location of the newly created item be added to the collection of response headers.

Semantic of PUT methods

A PUT method is typically expected to update an existing resource in some back-end store. The return type can be void if you don't want to share feedback with the caller. To be fair, though, you should return an instance of *HttpResponseMessage* set to either HTTP 200 or HTTP 204, as is done in the following code:

```
public HttpResponseMessage PutNews(Int32 id, News news)
{
    if (id <= 0)
        throw new HttpResponseException(new HttpResponseMessage(HttpStatusCode.NotFound));

    // Do something here to update the news: consider returning HTTP 200
    var response = Request.CreateResponse<String>(HttpStatusCode.OK, "OK");
    return response;
}
```

It is also acceptable that you return a status code of HTTP 204, which indicates that the request has been successfully processed but the response is left blank intentionally. The *HttpStatusCode* value to select is *NoContent*.

Semantic of DELETE methods

A DELETE method is typically expected to delete an existing resource in some back-end store. Keeping the method void is acceptable, but as is shown in the code that follows, you should aim at returning HTTP 200 or HTTP 204. In this case, HTTP 200 or 204 will be read as the proof that the resource has been deleted successfully.

```
public HttpResponseMessage DeleteNews(Int32 id)
{
    if (id <= 0)
        throw new HttpResponseException(new HttpResponseMessage(HttpStatusCode.NotFound));

    // Do something here to delete the news

    return new HttpResponseMessage(HttpStatusCode.NoContent);   // 204
}
```

For a DELETE request, you can also opt for returning a status code HTTP 202 which would imply that the request was accepted by the server and the resource was marked for deletion. For what that matters, this gives no certainty to the caller that the resource was really removed, but at the same time it moves the responsibility of deletion to the server.

Semantic of other methods

Although GET, PUT, POST, and DELETE are the most common HTTP verbs, the list of feasible HTTP verbs doesn't end here. From the perspective of Web API, though, any other legitimate HTTP verbs except the four above don't receive special treatment from the framework. This means that no conventions apply to them. Have a look at the following code:

```
public HttpResponseMessage HeadNews(int id)
{
    var message = new HttpResponseMessage(HttpStatusCode.OK);
    message.Headers.Add("NewsId", id.ToString());
    return message;
}
```

According to the World Wide Web Consortium (W3C), a HEAD request is expected to work like a GET except that the response body is empty and only response headers are returned.

The preceding code, however, doesn't work and produces an HTTP 404. The reason is that the naming convention we discussed for most popular verbs isn't applied here. If you want the method to run for a request coming over HTTP HEAD, you should use the *AcceptVerbs* attribute.

```
[AcceptVerbs("HEAD")]
public HttpResponseMessage HeadNews(int id)
{
    ...
}
```

Again, notice that *AcceptVerbs* has the same name and behavior of the ASP.NET MVC attribute, but it is defined in a separate assembly. In the end, it's an entirely different class with the same name and largely the same behavior.

Using the Web API

A Web API module built inside an ASP.NET MVC application is hosted by the ASP.NET MVC application. To go live with the Web API module, you just need to go live with the ASP.NET MVC site. At that point, all you see are HTTP endpoints that you can reach with whatever API you have available, including a JavaScript-based API.

Invoking Web API from JavaScript

From within a web client, the Web API front end is a simple collection of HTTP endpoints. You can use jQuery facilities to place an HTTP call and perhaps use KnockoutJS facilities to render out a collection of objects. Here's the code you need to set up Web API remote data binding (this is an excerpt from a .cshtml view file):

```
<h1>Web API DEMO</h1>
<script type="text/javascript">
    function News(title) {
        this.title = title;
    }
    function NewsViewModel(listOfNews) {
        this.allNews = listOfNews;
    }
</script>
<script type="text/javascript">
    $(document).ready(function () {
        getNews(function (listOfNews) {
            ko.applyBindings(new NewsViewModel(listOfNews));
        });
    });

    function getNews(callback) {
        $.ajax({
            url: "/api/news/all",
            type: "GET",
            statusCode: {
                200: function (listOfNews) { callback(listOfNews); },
                404: function () { alert("No news found!"); }
            }
        });
    }
</script>

<div id="news-container">
    <h2>Late breaking tennis news</h2>
    <table>
        <thead><tr>
            <th>Title</th>
        </tr></thead>
        <tbody data-bind="foreach: allNews">
            <tr>
                <td data-bind="text: Title"></td>
            </tr>
        </tbody>
    </table>
</div>
```

Figure 10-3 shows the final result.

FIGURE 10-3 Downloading late-breaking tennis news by using Web API.

The *$.ajax* jQuery facility makes it possible for you to specify the HTTP verb and headers. In this way, you can easily prepare calls to invoke any sort of action on the Web API back end.

Invoking from server-side code

Because the Web API module is a plain HTTP front end, invoking it from within some .NET server-side code is in no way different from invoking any other kind of remote endpoint. From within an ASP.NET MVC application, you can have a controller method that produces HTML, as presented here:

```
public ActionResult News()
{
    var client = new WebClient();
    var content = client.DownloadString("/api/news");
    var serializer = new JavaScriptSerializer();
    var listOfNews = serializer.Deserialize<IList<News>>(content);
    return View(listOfNews);
}
```

The code downloads data as JSON and then uses the *JavaScriptSerializer* class to turn it into a .NET object—specifically, a list of *News* data objects. The list is then passed as the view model to the view engine for generating the user interface via Razor.

```
@model IList<Simplest.Models.Dto.News>
<h1>Web API DEMO</h1>
```

```
<div id="news-container">
    <h2>Late breaking tennis news</h2>
    <table>
        <thead><tr>
            <th>Title</th>
        </tr></thead>
        <tbody>
            @foreach (var n in Model)
            {
                <tr>
                    <td>@n.Title</td>
                </tr>
            }
        </tbody>
    </table>
</div>
```

The preceding code uses the simplest (but still largely effective) way of downloading and converting JSON data. In the latest versions of the .NET Framework, you have other built-in JSON converters or HTTP client classes that offer a better support for asynchronous calls. At the end of the day, though, regardless of any specific tool or technology, what's required is downloading JSON data and converting it to a .NET object.

Making the call asynchronous

We all know that the code we write must always be highly scalable. Now, I can blissfully admit that not any code lives in the context of a highly scalable application. When it comes to refactoring for scalability, though, there are two basic things you can do in both reading and writing: use caching and asynchronous logic. For a long time, writing asynchronous code was painful in .NET languages. However, starting with C# 5.0 and .NET Framework 4.5, new keywords such as *async/await* made the pill easier to swallow by adding a pinch of syntactic sugar.

As a result, although I'm still not convinced that any remote call must be asynchronous because we all need scalability, I also don't see special reasons not to write remote calls asynchronously with the advent of the *async/await* keywords, which make it possible for us to avoid non-blocking calls (especially from the user interface) and still manage to keep the code highly readable. So, here's how to rewrite a Web API method by using the *async/await* language facilities:

```
public async Task<IList<News>> GetAll()
{
    var url = ...;
    var client = new HttpClient();
    var rss = await client.GetStringAsync(url);
    var news = ParseRssInternal(rss);
    return news;
}
```

Instead of using *WebClient* to make the remote call, you can use the newest *HttpClient*, which is a revamped and richer version of the old-faithful *WebClient* client. *HttpClient* is defined in the *System.Net.Http* namespace.

The ASP.NET MVC method in charge of invoking an async-coded Web API module uses the following code:

```
public async Task<ActionResult> News()
{
    var feed = new FeedController();
    var model = await feed.GetAll();
    return View(model);
}
```

Invoking an asynchronous-coded Web API module from JavaScript doesn't require any change at all at the client code.

Designing an RPC-oriented Interface

So far, we experimented with Web API assuming a RESTful approach to the definition of the public API. All in all, for developers coming from ASP.NET MVC, just putting Web API in the right perspective is the most difficult aspect. Web API looks too similar to plain controllers that you're accustomed to, and the risk of lightly boiling it down to yet-another-weird-type-of-controller is high.

Web API is the SDK of your business domain; if used within an ASP.NET MVC application, it is the SDK on which your application is based. At the same time, though, this SDK is publicly exposed over HTTP.

CRUD-over-HTTP is just one option

Conventions enabled by default on the API tend to make developers see the API in the context of CRUD over HTTP. You define a model object and build an API controller to work on it. API methods are modeled after basic HTTP verbs performing basic operations on a given resource. This gives a flavor of RESTfulness to the design.

As seen earlier, this approach also can raise naming conflicts because you might find it hard to name a method that returns data following an unconventional scheme. The RESTful approach is not the only one that is possible: an RPC-oriented vision is fine, as well.

It's hard to say whether REST is preferable over RPC. I'd say that the largest share of apps is RPC-oriented. For example, most ASP.NET MVC sites are built on a set of methods only invoked over GET or POST. In fact, in the early years of ASP.NET MVC, many personal projects have been started to give an air of clear RESTfulness to ASP.NET MVC.

At the end of the day, though, the resolution is simple: no matter the default conventions of Web API projects in Visual Studio, you can gain total control of the API and, if you like it, give it an RPC style.

Action attributes

The key to turning the design of the Web API into RPC is using action attributes. Much like you do in ASP.NET MVC controllers, you can use attributes such as *HttpGet*, *HttpPost*, *HttpPut*, or *HttpDelete* to mark Web API methods so that, regardless of the name, they will be taken into account only if the request verb matches the attribute.

```
[HttpGet]
public IEnumerable<News> All()
{
    ...
}
```

The *All* method now is taken into account for a GET request even though its name doesn't begin with Get. The Web API libraries offer predefined attributes such *HttpGet*, *HttpPost*, *HttpPut*, or *HttpDelete*, as well as *AcceptVerbs* that you can use to bind one or more HTTP verbs to a method.

Custom routes

Action attributes alone are not enough to give you full control over the API. You might also need to change the default route defined in the standard Web API project that the Visual Studio wizard creates for you initially. The default route doesn't have a placeholder for the action name. You might want to replace the *DefaultApi* route discussed earlier in the section "Routing to action methods" with the following:

```
RouteTable.Routes.MapHttpRoute(
            name: "RpcRoute",
            routeTemplate: "api/{controller}/{action}/{id}",
            defaults: new { id = RouteParameter.Optional });
```

The key difference is that the route now reserves a placeholder for the method name—the *{action}* placeholder. This makes the process of resolving requests to methods nearly identical to ASP.NET MVC plain controllers except for the extra *api* literal in the URL.

```
http://server/api/news/all
```

The preceding URL will generate an exception in a RESTful model, but with the combined use of *HttpGet* on the *All* method and the custom *RpcRoute* route defined, it works just fine.

Attribute routing

Web API owes a large part of its design to ASP.NET MVC, even though it has no point of contact with the ASP.NET MVC runtime. In the latest version of Web API that ships with Visual Studio 2013 and ASP.NET MVC 5, you will find a feature called *attribute routing* that has no direct counterpart in ASP.NET MVC; it derives instead from old-fashioned WCF Web HTTP binding.

Classic routing is based on conventions. Any time a request comes in, the URL is matched against the template of routes registered in global.asax. If a match is found, the appropriate controller and action methods to serve the request are determined from the template. If not, the request is denied and the result is usually an HTTP 404 message. Route matching works on a first-match basis. The most immediate consequence of first-match is that the order in which routes are registered is essential. Most specific routes should appear first in the list; catch-all and most generic routes should go to the bottom of the list. Why is this so significant?

Already in medium-sized applications with a strong REST flavor, the number of routes can be quite large, easily in the order of hundreds. It can definitely become hard to determine the right order of more than 200 routes and you might find that infinite loops around regression are detected during automated tests or notified by users and testers. Attribute routing offers a smoother way to handle routing in such situations.

As the name suggests, attribute routing is all about having a route attached (as an attribute) to a specific action method, as shown in the following code:

```
[HttpGet("orders/{orderId}/show")]
public Order GetOrderById(int orderId)
{
    ...
}
```

The preceding snippet indicates that the method *GetOrderById* will be available over an HTTP GET call only if the requested URL template matches the specified pattern. The route parameter—the *orderId* token—must match one of the parameters defined in the method's signature. There are a few more details to be discussed, but the gist of attribute routes is all here. It's hard to deny that this has a close resemblance with the now-old-fashioned WCF Web HTTP programming model and the *WebGet* attribute in particular.

```
[WebGet(UriTemplate="orders/{id}/show")]
Order GetOrderById(int id);
```

Turning on attribute routing

Attribute routing is not turned on by default, but it can work side by side with conventional routing. Here's the standard way to turn it on:

```
public static class WebApiConfig
{
    public static void Setup(HttpConfiguration config)
    {
        config.MapHttpAttributeRoutes();
    }
}
```

In case you intend to use the two types of routing together, it is preferable that you give precedence to attribute routing. This means that you call *MapHttpAttributeRoutes* before you begin adding global routes into the system.

You can define a route via attribute for each method you like and also filter on the HTTP method used to call the action. In Web API, attribute classes such as *HttpGet*, *HttpPost*, *HttpDelete*, *HttpPut*, and all others have been extended with an overload that accepts a route URL template. If you prefer, you can also use the *AcceptVerbs* attribute, where the first parameter indicates the method name and the second parameter sets the route, as demonstrated here:

```
[AcceptVerbs("GET", "orders/{id}/show")]
```

You can use *AcceptVerbs* also for unsupported HTTP methods or perhaps WebDAV methods.

Attribute routing also supports constraints on parameters using a slightly different syntax than classic routing. The API has a list of predefined constraints such as *int*, *bool*, *alpha*, *min*, *max*, *length*, *minlength*, and *range*. Here's how to use them:

```
[HttpGet("orders/{id:int}/show")]
```

The goal of constraints is straightforward. For more details, you can check out some documentation at *http://www.asp.net/web-api/overview/web-api-routing-and-actions/attribute-routing-in-web-api-2*.

You can concatenate as many constraints as you wish and create custom constraints, as well.

```
[HttpGet("orders/{id:int:range(1, 100)}/show")]
```

To create a custom constraint, you create a class that implements the *IHttpRouteConstraint* interface and use the following code to register it:

```
var resolver = new DefaultInlineConstraintResolver();
resolver.ConstraintMap.Add("custom", typeof(YourCustomConstraint));
config.MapHttpAttributeRoutes(new HttpRouteBuilder(resolver));
```

The interface *IHttpRouteConstraint* has a single method named *Match*.

Security considerations

Overall, securing a web application is simpler than securing a Web API module for just one reason: there are fewer scenarios to consider. Because an ASP.NET MVC application is aimed at end users, security mostly means authenticating users and ensuring that each authenticated user is authorized to execute a given action.

Forms authentication (for example, a logon window in which to enter credentials) is the most common way to capture and verify credentials. In ASP.NET MVC, the *Authorize* attribute on action methods instructs the runtime that only authenticated users can invoke the method. Parameters on the *Authorize* attribute or plain code in the method's implementation will then perform more sophisticated checks about roles assigned to a given logged-on user. The security aspects of ASP.NET MVC applications are discussed at length in Chapter 6, "Securing your application."

When it comes to Web API, there are additional scenarios to observe. A Web API module is just an API that can be written for third-party developers to use. How would you control that the client is known and authorized?

The host takes care of security

The simplest but not necessarily most common scenario for a Web API module is when the API and host are managed by the same team. In this case, the host is responsible for authenticating the user and avoiding that any user interface where a call to the API is possible is ever displayed.

Web API, therefore, assumes that any authentication takes place in the host; for example, within IIS through HTTP modules for authentication whether built-in modules or custom modules. To address this scenario, you use the *Authorize* attribute on API controller classes or individual methods. This is nearly the same scenario you face in plain ASP.NET MVC applications.

```
[Authorize]
public IList<News> GetAll()
{
    ...
}
```

Observe that the *AuthorizeAttribute* class used here is not the same as the *AuthorizeAttribute* used in ASP.NET MVC. The programming interface is the same, but the class is defined elsewhere to avoid dependencies on the ASP.NET runtime.

You can also set the *Authorize* attribute globally so that it applies to all methods of all API controllers. If this is what you intend to do, use the following code:

```
public static SetupAuthorization(HttpConfiguration config)
{
    config.Filters.Add(new AuthorizeAttribute());
}
```

Keep in mind that in this case all methods are subject to security; however, the *AllowAnonymous* attribute lets you keep a method available for anonymous calls.

```
public class NewsController : ApiController
{
    [AllowAnonymous]
    public IList<News> GetAll() { ... }
    public HttpResponseMessage PostNews(News news) { ... }
}
```

After authentication has taken place in the body of the method, you can use the *User* property on the *ApiController* class to check details and the role of the user and deny the call if that is the case.

Using Basic authentication

Outside of the scenario in which the host provides for authentication and authorization rules, it's all about incorporating the security layer in the Web API module. The simplest approach is using the Basic authentication that is built in to the web server. Basic authentication is based on the idea that user credentials are packaged in each and every request.

Basic authentication has pros and cons. On the pros side, it is supported on major browsers; it is an Internet standard; it is simple to configure. The downside is that credentials are sent with every request and, worse yet, they are sent as clear text.

Basic authentication expects that credentials are sent to be validated on the server. The request is then accepted only if credentials are valid. If credentials are not in the request, an interactive dialog box will display. Realistically, Basic authentication also requires a custom HTTP module to check credentials against accounts stored in some custom database.

> **Note** Basic authentication is simple and quite effective if combined with a layer that does custom validation of credentials. To overcome the limitation of credentials sent as clear text, you should always implement a basic authentication solution over HTTPS.

Using access tokens

The idea here is that the Web API receives an access token (typically a GUID or an alphanumeric string), validates it, and serves the request if the token is not expired and is valid for the application. There are various ways to issue a token as well as different security solutions.

The simplest scenario for tokens is that they are issued offline when a customer contacts you to use your API. You create the token and associate it with a particular customer. From that point forward, the customer is responsible for abuse or misuse of the API.

The Web API back end needs to have a layer that checks tokens. You can add this layer as plain code to just any method or, better yet, configure it to be a message handler. In Web API, a message handler is a component that examines the HTTP request and sets the *principal* on the request so that the *User* property on *ApiController* can be properly populated.

> **Note** Similar to HTTP handlers of ASP.NET, message handlers apply only the traffic toward Web API. You can read more at *http://www.asp.net/web-api/overview/working-with-http/ http-message-handlers*.

Using OAuth

A much more complex scenario is using OAuth authentication to restrict access to a Web API module. Chapter 6 discusses how to use OAuth in conjunction with Facebook or Twitter to authenticate users of a site. The point here is to just turn your Web API module into an OAuth server similar to what Twitter or Facebook do.

In the end, OAuth is a variation of the token scenario discussed a moment ago. The difference is that you need to have a distinct component that issues tokens online after checking credentials of users. The authorization server mediates between the protected resources (the Web API) and the potential customers. Figure 10-4 shows the layout of a typical OAuth conversation.

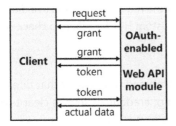

FIGURE 10-4 The typical OAuth handshake between a client and a Web API server.

How would you code this in practice?

It is mostly up to you, but it probably requires having a web back end that acts as the authorization server. It will be responsible for issuing access tokens according to the credentials provided by authenticated users (a là Facebook). Next, you want to have a message handler in the Web API layer that processes the token and sets the principal to actually authorize the call. In the message handler, you can also introduce any mechanism to invalidate the token in any way you reckon worthwhile—expiration, misuse, or because the caller exceeded the allotted quota of calls.

Using cross-origin resource sharing

Cross-origin resource sharing (CORS) is a W3C standard that defines the behavior of webpages that intend to make Ajax requests to a different domain. CORS relaxes the same-origin policy that all browsers implement which restricts calls to the sole domain of the page that makes the call.

Note Browsers implement the same-origin policy and prevent cross-domain Ajax call for security reasons. Thus, is CORS a trustworthy approach? Doesn't it weaken security, instead? The browser's same-origin policy just limits the client page to make any cross-domain calls regardless of the fact that the target site might agree to receive cross-domain calls. The CORS specification just defines a protocol through which a site can agree to receive calls from remote sites. CORS doesn't weaken security for the simple reason that cross-domain calls find both parties consenting.

You turn CORS on through a new attribute named *EnableCors*. You can set the attribute on controllers as well as methods. For the attribute to be effective, you also need to call the *EnableCors* method on the *HttpConfiguration* object in global.asax.

```
using System.Web.Http.Cors;
public static class WebApiConfig
{
    public static void Register(HttpConfiguration config)
    {
        config.EnableCors();
    }
}
```

You pass a freshly created instance of the *EnableCorsAttribute* class to the method you obtain to turn on CORS globally for all methods and all controllers. If you have CORS turned on at the controller level and want to turn it off on a particular method, you just use the *DisableCors* attribute.

Negotiating the response format

As you practiced a bit with the sample *NewsController* class, you probably noticed that by default all action methods return their data serialized as JSON strings. This is just what developers want most of the time, but it doesn't exhaust all possible scenarios. Sometimes, in fact, you want to expose the same data also through XML, as plain text or (why not) also as an iCalendar feed. Does that mean that you need to have multiple action methods for each possible output format? This is just where content negotiation in Web API fits in.

The ASP.NET MVC approach

In classic ASP.NET MVC, you address the issue by enforcing manually a neat separation in each action method between the code that produces the raw data to return and the code that formats it in a way that suits the caller.

Understanding the requested format

First and foremost, ASP.NET MVC doesn't have a default and well-defined way by which callers can specify the expected output format. A broadly accepted solution consists of using a parameter in the query string (or ad hoc routes) that bring inside the controller code the selection of the response format. Here's my favorite scheme:

```
public ActionResult All(Boolean xml = false)
{
    // Get raw data
    var listOfNews = NewsHelper.GetAllNews();

    // Serialize raw data
    if (xml)
        return new NewsXmlFormatter().Serialize(listOfNews);
    return Json(listOfNews, JsonRequestBehavior.AllowGet);
}
```

This means that by simply adding *xml=true* to the query string of the URL, you can have data back as XML. In any other case, you'll get back JSON. As for the XML scheme to format data, depending on circumstances, I resort to a generic XML formatter or a formatter specific of a particular object.

If you don't like the use of parameters, you can opt for an ad hoc route such as the following:

```
routes.MapRoute(
    name: "Xml",
    url: "xml/{controller}/{action}/{id}",
    defaults: new { controller = "Home", action = "Index", id = UrlParameter.Optional, xml =
true }
);
```

More in general, it's up to the developer to find a way to figure out the expected response format. Using routes or parameters is only a possibility. You can require that callers add a specific HTTP header or perhaps you can check some default HTTP headers such as Accept or Content-Type.

Enforcing data and format separation

As you can guess from the code earlier, the body of an ASP.NET MVC controller method is usually split in two: acquisition of action results, and processing of action results. Keeping these two phases separated is up to you. As long as you choose only between JSON and XML, this is not hard to manage. However, what if you have multiple formats to handle? And, what if you must add a new format for all methods after the service is in production?

A better strategy for negotiating the format of the response is required, and it is available in Web API.

How content negotiation works in Web API

In Web API, the term *content negotiation* refers to the process of inspecting the structure of the incoming request (typically, HTTP headers) to determine the ideal response format (or formats) that the client wants to receive.

Involved HTTP headers

In Web API, two HTTP headers play a key role in content negotiation. They are Accept and Content-Type. Of the two, the primary is Accept in the sense that Content-Type is taken into account only if the Accept header is missing or has invalid content. The following code shows how to set the Accept header in a jQuery call to a Web API endpoint to receive back some XML.

```
$.ajax({
    url: "/api/news/all",
    type: "GET",
    headers: { Accept: "text/xml; charset=utf-8" }
});
```

In C# code, you set the Accept header as shown here:

```
var client = new WebClient();
client.Headers.Add("Accept", "text/xml; charset=utf-8");
```

The *ApiController* class internally has a segment of code that processes the data being returned by each method and turns that raw data into JSON or XML as appropriate. The neat separation between production of raw results and formatting is native in Web API, and as a developer you can select XML or JSON without being exposed to the details of embedded formatter components. By using Web API, you have automatic and free serialization to JSON or XML as part of the deal.

If the Accept header is missing, or has some invalid content, Web API looks into the Content-Type header. If the header has valid content, its content is used to format results. If a valid serialization format cannot be determined either via Accept or Content-Type, Web API picks up the first formatter registered with the runtime. By default, it is the JSON formatter.

Changing default formatters

When it comes to services returning data formatted as JSON, a common issue is the case of object property names when used from within a JavaScript client and a .NET client. In .NET and JavaScript (and Java to the same extent), *camelCasing* is the default. However, in .NET, *PascalCasing* is the default. Because you write services in C#, you then likely define data transfer objects (DTOs) by using the Pascal-case. This creates a conflict when this data is received on the JavaScript end.

As an example of replacing default formatters, let's pick up one of the various community projects that contribute special flavors of formatters. I used *JsonCamelCaseFormatter*, which is available at *https://gist.github.com/rdingwall/2012642*. The class modifies the way in which JSON data is serialized, ensuring that *camelCasing* is applied to member names.

A custom formatter is an instance of a class that inherits from *MediaTypeFormatter* and overrides four key methods: *CanReadType*, *CanWriteType*, *ReadFromStreamAsync*, and *WriteToStreamAsync*. The names of these methods with respect to what they do are self-explanatory. Here's how you can register a new JSON formatter:

```
public static class WebApiConfig
{
    public static void Register(HttpConfiguration config)
    {
        var index = config.Formatters.IndexOf(config.Formatters.JsonFormatter);
        config.Formatters[index] = new JsonCamelCaseFormatter();
    }
}
```

In particular, the example shows how to replace the default JSON formatter—an instance of *JsonMediaTypeFormatter*—with an instance of *JsonCamelCaseFormatter*. If you simply want to add yet another formatter to the list, you use the *Insert* or *Add* method on the *Formatters* collection of the *HttpConfiguration* object.

Defining formatters for specific types

Another common scenario that I've run into frequently is facing the need of returning a different format for some types, in particular, a different XML schema. The aforementioned *CanReadType* and *CanWriteType* methods are of some help here. Here's a custom XML formatter for the *News* type:

```
public class NewsXmlFormatter : MediaTypeFormatter
{
    public NewsXmlFormatter()
    {
        SupportedMediaTypes.Add(new MediaTypeHeaderValue("application/xml"));
        SupportedMediaTypes.Add(new MediaTypeHeaderValue("text/xml"));
    }

    public override bool CanReadType(Type type)
    {
        return false;
    }

    public override bool CanWriteType(Type type)
    {
        var result = (type == typeof(News) || type == typeof(IList<News>));
        return result;
    }

    public override Task WriteToStreamAsync(Type type,
                                            Object value,
                                            Stream writeStream,
                                            HttpContent content,
                                            TransportContext transportContext)
    {
        return Task.Factory.StartNew(
            () =>
                {
                    var listOfNews = (IList<News>) value;
                    using (var writer = new StreamWriter(writeStream))
                    {
                        foreach (var n in listOfNews)
                        {
                            writer.WriteLine("<news>");
                            writer.WriteLine("<title>{0}</title>", n.Title);
                            writer.WriteLine("</news>");
                        }
                    }
                });
    }
}
```

The formatter handles only serialization and ignores deserialization. (See Figure 10-5.)

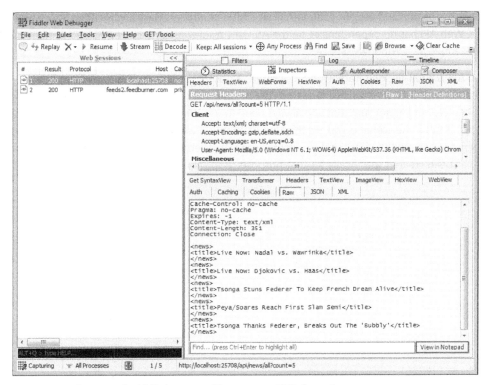

FIGURE 10-5 A request for XML data served by a custom XML formatter.

The question now becomes how you can ensure that this formatter is invoked only for the specified type and the default is used in all other cases. It's all about the order in which formatters are registered with the Web API runtime.

```
var xmlIndex = config.Formatters.IndexOf(config.Formatters.XmlFormatter);
config.Formatters.Insert(xmlIndex, new NewsXmlFormatter());
```

The code inserts the type-specific XML formatter just before the generic one. In this way, it will be invoked first.

Summary

This chapter was dedicated to a framework that plays a key role in the immediate future of web solutions. As is made clear in Chapter 12, "Making websites mobile-friendly," web solutions today are sometimes made of a mix of static HTML markup with dynamic sections generated on the fly with data coming from a remote back end. The traits of this remote back end were never defined clearly. It was first SOAP-based web services, then WCF services, and then simply a segment of an ASP.NET MVC application.

Web API is as thin and easy to code as ASP.NET MVC controllers have always been. More than this, though, Web API has no dependencies on the ASP.NET framework and can be hosted even outside IIS; for example, in a Windows service.

Web API is a full-fledged framework; it deserves a book of its own to be covered appropriately. This chapter scratched its classic surface from the perspective of an ASP.NET MVC developer. It's a design choice, but I'm not sure that you always need to use Web API if you are simply going to set up a website. If this is the scenario you are thinking of, Web API will likely be pretty much useless for you. But if you foresee multiple front ends for some core SDK, Web API is for you, for the simple reason that it has been created specifically for that purpose.

Mobile clients

CHAPTER 11

Effective JavaScript

It matters not what someone is born, but what they grow to be.

—J. K. Rowling

Developed for the web in the 1990s, JavaScript is widely used today outside the realm of web applications. For example, you find JavaScript used to write application extensions for Adobe Photoshop, Google Chrome, and Mozilla Firefox. It's also used to create native mobile applications; for example, PhoneGap or Appcelerator Titanium. JavaScript is also used for some flavors of server-side applications, most noticeably Node.js.

JavaScript's fate is curious. Born to be the language of the first web fan-boys, it has been through a series of highs and lows since the early 1990s. At some point, its use was boosted by the advent of Dynamic HTML and calmed down in only a few years with the consolidation of Java Server Pages and ASP.NET, which brought the focus of web development back to the server side. JavaScript revived and sprang back to life with Ajax and was fortified by Node.js and mobile frameworks. As the quote at the beginning of the chapter reminds us, it doesn't matter what JavaScript was born; it counts a lot more what it has grown to be.

JavaScript is a programming language that is easy to get acquainted with; at the same time, though, it is not trivial to master.

All web applications these days are required to add more and more client-side features. I'm not simply talking about client-side validation and facilities, I'm talking about full Ajax applications. A full Ajax application is a web application that reduces page swaps to a bare minimum. A full Ajax application is centered on very few core pages whose user interface changes interactively following the user's action. Obviously, you do a lot of work on the HTML Document Object Model (DOM), and you do that work by using JavaScript.

Note As an ASP.NET MVC developer, you should be ready to write more and more JavaScript code. More important, you should be ready to import more and more JavaScript code written by others. These two are not mutually exclusive options. As a matter of fact, there are nearly no websites today that are written without importing features from jQuery and a few other libraries, such as AngularJS, KnockoutJS, or Modernizr.

Revisiting the JavaScript language

JavaScript is an unusual language because it was created for non-developers; it has remarkably low barriers to entry, yet it's flexible enough that experts can use it to do nearly everything they need to, as well. As I see things, the challenge today is for average JavaScript developers to create effective content with some good design while keeping readability and maintainability at a decent level. For this reason, this section aims at refreshing some basic JavaScript facts.

Language basics

JavaScript code is interpreted, meaning that JavaScript programs need an environment in which to run. Their natural habitat is the web browser. The language syntax is driven by one solid standard: ECMA-262, which is also catalogued as ISO/IEC 16262:201. Over the years, a few JavaScript dialects have arisen based on different implementations of the standard. Sometimes, these dialects have an entirely different name such as JScript, JScript.NET, ActionScript, or EcmaScript. In the end, though, it's the result of different engines that process the JavaScript source code. Popular engines usually associated with web browsers are V8 (Google Chrome), Chakra (Microsoft Internet Explorer), Gecko (Firefox), and Opera.

Let's briefly navigate through the basics of the language and refresh concepts that, frankly, most ASP.NET developers just picked up but never studied thoroughly.

The type system

The JavaScript type system comprises primitive types and a few built-in objects. When you write JavaScript code, however, the range of types that you can work with is actually larger. In addition to using built-in objects, you can also rely on objects provided by the host. The canonical example is the window object that the most common JavaScript host—the web browser—publishes into the JavaScript engine.

Primitive types are *number, string, Boolean, null, undefined, Object,* and *function.* The built-in objects are *Array, Math, Date, Error, RegExp,* plus wrapper objects for a few primitive types: *string, Boolean,* and *number.*

The *number* type represents floating-point numbers with 0 or more decimal places. There are no separate types for integers, long, or bytes. The range of numbers is between -10^{308} and 10^{308}. You can write numbers in decimal, octal, or hexadecimal format. The special number *NaN* represents the result of a math operation that makes no sense (such as division by zero).

The *string* type represents a row of 0 or more characters; it doesn't represent an array. Individual characters are represented as strings of 1 character. Special characters in a string begin with a back slash (\), such as \n to indicate a carriage return. The content of a string is bracketed in matching pairs of single or double quotes. The primitive value is wrapped in a *string* object that adds a few methods, including *split* and *substring.*

Null vs. undefined

A JavaScript variable that doesn't contain a meaningful value can be assigned a *null* value as well as *undefined*. What's the difference? When it comes to nullness, JavaScript introduces a subtle difference that many higher-level languages such as C# and Java miss.

In particular, *undefined* is the default value that the run-time environment assigns to any variables being declared. Most remarkably, an unassigned variable contains *undefined*, not *null* or some default value as in C#. On the other hand, *null* is a value that still represents a null, empty, or non-existing reference, but it has been explicitly assigned by the developer. In a nutshell, a variable set to *undefined* has never been touched by any code; a variable that holds *null* was assigned that value via some path in your code.

If you run *typeof* on an unassigned variable, you get *undefined*—it's a distinct type by itself. If you run *typeof* on a variable assigned with *null*, you get *object*. Pay attention to the following code:

```
var x;              // hence, undefined
var y = null;
```

What happens if you compare *x* and *y*? If you use the == operator, you get *true*, meaning that *undefined* ultimately evaluates to *null*. If you compare using the === operator, you get *false*: the two variables hold the same value but are of different types.

Local and global variables

In JavaScript, a variable is a storage location that is not restricted to always storing values of a fixed type. When assigned a value, variables take on the type of the data being stored. For this reason, a JavaScript variable might change its type quite a few times during its lifespan.

```
var data = "dino";     // now data is of type string
data = 123;            // now data is of type number
```

This behavior is different from the typical behavior of C# variables, unless C# variables are defined of type dynamic in .NET 4. Variables spring into existence the first time they're used; until then, they hold a value of *undefined*.

When defining variables, you should always use the *var* keyword as a hint to the parser and yourself. The *var* keyword is not strictly required, but it's highly recommended. Variables defined within a function are scoped to the function if declared by using *var*. If not, variables are treated as global, but they remain as *undefined* until the function executes once. Variables declared in the global scope are always global regardless of whether *var* is used.

```
<script type="text/javascript">
  var rootServer = "http://www.expoware.org/";   // global
  section = "mobile";                            // global
</script>
```

```
<script>
  function doSomething() {
    var temp = 1;                        // local
    mode = 0;                            // global, but undefined until called
  }
</script>
```

The JavaScript run-time environment stores global variables as properties of hidden objects referenced through the *this* keyword. Browsers often mirror this object via the *window* object.

In any programming language, coding is (much) easier if you can use global variables. However, globals have downsides, too. A critical downside is the risk of name collisions between variables defined in different parts of your code, third-party libraries, advertising partners, and analytics libraries. A name collision combined with the dynamic typing of JavaScript variables might lead you to inadvertently modify the state of the application with unpleasant anomalies at run time.

Consider that creating globals unwillingly is easy, too: miss a *var* and you end up with a global; mistype a variable name in an assignment and you have a fresh new global. This latter feature is possible because with JavaScript you can use a variable without declaring it first. When you need to use global variables, a good technique is creating them as properties of a wrapper object. You place the following code in a JavaScript file that you link from every page:

```
var GLOBALS = (function() { return this; }());
```

Next, you use *GLOBALS.Xxx*, where *Xxx* is any global variable you might need to have. This at least ensures that your global variables will stand out.

An even better approach is to simply not use the global namespace and the *this* object and instead use a brand new global dictionary object. You initialize it as below:

```
var GLOBALS = GLOBALS || {};
```

If you have multiple JavaScript files in your application that need to reference *GLOBALS*, you place the preceding line at the top of each file. The || in the syntax ensures that the dictionary is not reinitialized every time a file is processed.

 Note JSLint (available at *http://www.jslint.com*)—an online tool for static analysis of JavaScript code—does help catch antipatterns in your code, including the lack of *var* keywords.

Variables and hoisting

Hoisting is a JavaScript feature with which developers can declare variables anywhere in the scope and use them anywhere in that scope. In JavaScript, you can first use the variable and then declare it (as *var*) later, as demonstrated here:

```
function() {       // Not allowed in C#
    mode = 1;
    ...
    var mode;
}
```

The overall behavior is as if the *var* statement was placed at the top. Historically, the feature was introduced to keep as low as possible the entry barrier to JavaScript. When you use JavaScript to write significant portions of code, however, hoisting is a clear source of confusion and becomes error prone. A good habit consists of placing all your variables at the top of each function—preferably, in a single *var* statement, as shown here:

```
function() {
    var start = 0,
        total = 10,
        sum = function (x,y) {return x+y;},
        index;
    ...
}
```

JSLint can be instructed to catch the use of multiple *var* statements in a single function and remind you about this pattern.

Objects

The primary reason for not cataloging JavaScript as an object-oriented language is that the definition of an object you get from JavaScript is different from the commonly accepted idea of an object you get out of classic object-oriented languages such as C++ or C#.

In JavaScript, an object is a dictionary of name/value pairs. The blueprint of the object is implicit, and you have no way to access it. A JavaScript object usually has only data, but you can add behavior. The (explicit) structure of an object can change at any time, with new methods and properties; the implicit structure never changes. Because of the implicit blueprint, any apparently blank object in JavaScript still has a few properties, such as *prototype*. (I'll return to *prototype* later.)

Keep in mind that variables that store objects don't actually contain the object's dictionary; they just reference the object's bag of properties. The bag of properties is distinct from the variable store, and different variables can reference the same bag of data. The *new* operator creates a new bag of properties. When you pass an object around, you just pass the reference to the bag.

Adding a member to a JavaScript object works only for that particular instance. If you want to add a new member to all instances being created of that type, you have to add the member to the object's prototype.

```
if (typeof Number.prototype.random === "undefined") {
    Number.prototype.random = function() {
        var n = Math.floor(Math.random() * 1000);
        return n;
    };
}
```

Note Augmenting the prototype of native objects is considered by some developers a bad practice (or at least, arguable) because it makes the code less predictable and can hurt maintainability. Overall, I believe this is questionable and mostly a matter of perspective. I'd say this: Be aware of potential issues and do as you feel comfortable.

You use the *Object* type to create aggregates of values and methods, which is the closest you come in JavaScript to C# objects. The direct use of the *Object*'s constructor (as shown in the following) is usually disregarded:

```
var dog = new Object();
dog.name = "Jerry Lee Esposito";
dog.getName = function() {
    return this.name;
}
```

A better approach entails using an object literal, as demonstrated here:

```
var dog = {
   name: "Jerry Lee Esposito",
   getName: function() {
      return this.name;
   }
};
```

If you use the *Object*'s constructor, the interpreter has to resolve the scope of the constructor call. In JavaScript, there's no guarantee that no local object exists in the scope with the same name as a global object. Therefore, the interpreter must walk up the stack to find the nearest definition of the constructor that applies. In addition to this performance issue, using the constructor directly also doesn't transmit the sense of objects as dictionaries, which is a key point of JavaScript programming.

Functions

In JavaScript, a function is a bit of code bundled up into a block and, optionally, given a name. If a function is not given a name, it's an anonymous function. You treat functions like objects: They can have properties, and you can pass them around and interact with them.

In JavaScript, anonymous functions are the pillar of functional programming. An anonymous function is a direct offshoot of lambda calculus or, if you prefer, a language adaptation of old-fashioned function pointers. Here's an example of an anonymous function:

```
function(x, y) {
   return x + y;
}
```

The only difference between a regular function and an anonymous function is in the name (or lack thereof).

You use functions for two main reasons: for creating custom objects and, of course, for defining repeatable behavior. Of the two reasons, the former is the most compelling in JavaScript. Consider the following code:

```
// The this object is implicitly returned
var Dog = function(name) {
  this.name = name;
  this.bark = function() {
     return "bau";
  };
};
```

To use the *Dog* object, you need to instantiate it by using the classic *new* constructor, as illustrated here:

```
var jerry = new Dog("jerry");    // OK
var hassie = Dog("hassie");      // Doesn't throw but, worse, may alter the application's state
```

The tricky thing is that if you forget the *new* operator, you won't get any exception and your code just runs, but the *this* object being used is now the global *this* object. This means that you're potentially altering the state of the application. Here's a safe countermeasure:

```
var Dog = function(name) {
   var that = {};
   that.name = name;
   that.bark = function() {
      return "bau";
   };
   return that;
};
```

The difference is that you now explicitly create and return a *new* object named *that*. This is familiarly known as the "Use-That-Not-This" pattern.

Object-orientation in JavaScript

There was a time when JavaScript code in webpages was limited to a few lines of basic manipulation of the DOM. There was no need to design this code into reusable blocks and attach it unobtrusively to page elements. Although the average level of JavaScript code complexity is nearly the same as in the recent past, the quantity of it you need to have on each page is rising dramatically. Forms of packaging are required because today, JavaScript code is like a small application on its own. You need to make gains in reusability and also (if not especially) in maintainability. Furthermore, you need to ensure that your code runs in isolation because in JavaScript, it's too easy to miss variables, spoil globals, and mistype names without a clear indication that you have done so. In this regard, JSLint is a great help, but it's not like a compiler.

To top off the discussion about the basics of the JavaScript language, let me introduce *closures* and *prototypes*—two approaches you can take to implement object-orientation in JavaScript.

Making objects look like classes

Before I get to closures and prototypes, let me say a few more words on the native *Object* type and its usage. As mentioned, you can use the *new* keyword to create a new dictionary-like object. Next, you stuff data into it and add methods by wiring functions to property names. Here's an example:

```
var person = new Object();
person.Name = "Dino";
person.LastName = "Esposito";
person.BirthDate = new Date(1979,10,17);
person.getAge = function() {
  var today = new Date();
  var thisDay = today.getDate();
  var thisMonth = today.getMonth();
  var thisYear = today.getFullYear();
  var age = thisYear-this.BirthDate.getFullYear()-1;
  if (thisMonth > this.BirthDate.getMonth())
      age = age +1;
  else
  if (thisMonth == this.BirthDate.getMonth() &&
      thisDay >= this.BirthDate.getDate())
      age = age +1;
  return age;
}
```

What you have is an object modeled after a person; you don't really have a *Person* object. As you saw earlier, this has both readability and performance issues. In addition, the object is sparsely defined over multiple lines.

Closures and prototypes offer alternate ways to define the layout of a type, and they are the native mechanisms to use for doing object-oriented programming in JavaScript.

Using closures

A closure is a general concept of programming languages. Applied to JavaScript, a closure is a function that can have variables and methods defined together within the same context. In this way, the outermost (anonymous or named) function "closes" the expression. Here's an example of the closure model for a function that represents a *Person* type:

```
var Person = function(name, lastname, birthdate) {
    this.Name = name;
    this.LastName = lastname;
    this.BirthDate = birthdate;
    this.getAge = function() {
        var today = new Date();
        var thisDay = today.getDate();
        var thisMonth = today.getMonth();
        var thisYear = today.getFullYear();
        var age = thisYear-this.BirthDate.getFullYear()-1;
        if (thisMonth > this.BirthDate.getMonth())
            age = age +1;
```

```
        else
            if (thisMonth == this.BirthDate.getMonth() &&
                thisDay >= this.BirthDate.getDate())
                age = age +1;
        return age;
    }
}
```

As you can see, the closure is nothing more than the constructor of the pseudo-class. In a closure model, the constructor contains the member declarations, and members are truly encapsulated and private to the class. In addition, members are instance based, which increases the memory used by the class. Here's how you use the object:

```
var p = new Person("Dino", "Esposito", new Date( ... ) );
alert(p.Name + " is " + p.getAge());
```

The closure model gives full encapsulation but nothing more. To compose objects, you can only resort to aggregation.

Using prototypes

The prototype model entails defining the public structure of the class through the JavaScript *prototype* object. The following code sample shows how to rewrite the preceding *Person* class to avoid a closure:

```
// Pseudo constructor
var Person = function(name, lastname, birthdate) {
    this.initialize(name, lastname, birthdate);
}

// Members
Person.prototype.initialize = function(name, lastname, birthdate)  {
    this.Name = name;
    this.LastName = lastname;
    this.BirthDate = birthdate;
}

Person.prototype.getAge = function() {
    var today = new Date();
    var thisDay = today.getDate();
    var thisMonth = today.getMonth();
    var thisYear = today.getFullYear();
    var age = thisYear-this.BirthDate.getFullYear()-1;
    if (thisMonth > this.BirthDate.getMonth())
        age = age +1;
    else
        if (thisMonth == this.BirthDate.getMonth() &&
            thisDay >= this.BirthDate.getDate())
            age = age +1;
    return age;
}
```

In the prototype model, the constructor and members are clearly separated, and a constructor is always required. As for private members, well, you just don't have them. The *var* keyword that would keep them local in a closure doesn't apply in the prototype model. So, you can define a getter/setter for what you intend to be properties, but the backing field will remain accessible from the outside. You can resort to some internal convention, such as prefixing with an underscore the name of members you intend as private. However, that's just a convention, and nothing prevents developers from accessing what the class author considers private.

By using the prototype feature, you can achieve inheritance by simply setting the prototype property of a derived object to an instance of the "parent" object.

```
Developer = function Developer(name, lastname, birthdate) {
    this.initialize(name, lastname, birthdate);
}
Developer.prototype = new Person();
```

Be aware that you always need to use this to refer to members of the prototype from within any related member function.

In the prototype model, members are shared by all instances because they are invoked on the shared prototype object. In this way, the amount of memory used by each instance is reduced, which also provides for faster object instantiation. Aside from syntax peculiarities, the prototype model makes defining classes much more similar to the classic object-oriented model than the closure model.

Plain custom objects vs. a hierarchy of classes

The choice between closure and prototype should also be guided by performance considerations and browser capabilities. Prototypes have good load times in all browsers. Closures work great in some browsers (for example, Internet Explorer) and worse in others.

Prototypes provide better support for Microsoft IntelliSense, and they accommodate tool-based statement completion when used in tools that support this feature, such as Microsoft Visual Studio. Prototypes can also help you to obtain type information by simply using reflection. You won't have to create an instance of the type to query for type information, which is unavoidable if closures are used. Finally, prototypes make it possible for you to easily view private class members when debugging.

So, you have two basic options for dealing with JavaScript objects that look like classes. Prototypes are the option chosen most often by library designers. Also, in jQuery, the *prototype* property is used extensively.

Having said that, if I had to write client code for a web front end, I'd probably go with jQuery, use a lot of anonymous functions, and not even bother about having a hierarchy of custom objects. I would certainly create custom objects, but I'd use them as plain and flat containers of data and behavior, with no inheritance or polymorphism. If, on the other hand, I had to write my own framework to support some server-side infrastructure, I'd probably opt for a more classic object-oriented approach. In that case, however, I'd probably consider using an existing library instead of creating one of my own. For that, MooTools (*http://mootools.net*) is an excellent choice.

jQuery's executive summary

Without beating around the bush, I'll say that if you're writing JavaScript code in web views today, you're likely using jQuery. If you're not, you should be; the only reasonable scenario I can think for not using jQuery is mobile sites. The jQuery library is certainly not the only JavaScript library you can pick up to save yourself quite a bit of work around DOM manipulation and event handling. However, it's the world de facto standard. I consider jQuery almost an extension to the JavaScript language, and certainly an extension to the JavaScript skills of any web developers.

This chapter is not the place where you can expect to find some sort of extensive coverage of jQuery. For that, you can pick some good books or just check out the online documentation at *http://docs.jquery.com/Main_Page*. If you're looking for online content in a more readable format than dry documentation, go to *http://jqfundamentals.com/book*.

In this chapter, I provide an overview of the key concepts in jQuery, a strong understanding of which will enable you to quickly grab programming details and features in the library.

DOM queries and wrapped sets

The main reason for the worldwide success of the jQuery library is its unique mix of functional and DOM programming. The library works by selecting DOM elements and applying functions over them, which is just what client web developers need to do most of the time.

The root object

The root of the jQuery library is the *jQuery* function. Here's the overall structure of the library:

```
(
    function( window, undefined )
    {
        var jQuery = (function() {
            // Define a local copy of jQuery
            var jQuery = function(selector, context) {
                ...
            }
            ...
            return jQuery;
        })();

        /* the rest of the library goes here */
        ...
        window.jQuery = window.$ = jQuery;
    }
) (window);
```

The nested jQuery function is mapped as an extension to the browser's window object and is aliased with the popular *$* function. The function has the following prototype:

```
function(selector, context)
```

The selector indicates the query expression to run over the DOM; the context indicates the portion of the DOM from which to run the query. If no context is specified, the jQuery function looks for DOM elements within the entire page DOM.

The jQuery function typically returns a wrapped set—namely, a collection of DOM elements. Nicely enough, this wrapped set is still a jQuery object that can be queried by using the same syntax, resulting in chained queries.

Running a query

The word query in the library's name says it all (*j* stands for JavaScript, but you knew that already)— the jQuery library is primarily designed for running (clever) queries over the DOM and executing operations over the returned items.

The query engine behind the library goes far beyond the simple search capabilities of, for instance, *document.getElementById* (and related functions) that you find natively in the DOM. The query capabilities of jQuery use the powerful CSS syntax, which gives you a surprising level of expressivity. You find similar query expressivity only in the DOM of HTML5, for which CSS syntax is widely and uniformly supported.

The result of a query is a *wrapped set*. A wrapped set is an object containing a collection of DOM elements. Elements are added to the collection in the order in which they appear in the original document.

A wrapped set is never null, even if no matching elements have been found. You check the actual size of the wrapped set by looking at the length property of the *jQuery* object, as shown here:

```
// Queries for all IMG tags in the page
var wrappedSet = new jQuery("img");
var length = wrappedSet.length;
if (length == 0)
    alert("No IMG tags found.");
```

Note that the expression just shown, through which you get the wrapped set, is fully equivalent to the more commonly used *$("img")*.

The wrapped set is not a special data container. "Wrapped set" is a jQuery-specific term that indicates the results of a query.

Enumerating the content of a wrapped set

To loop through the elements in the wrapped set, you use the *each* function. This function gets a function as a parameter and invokes that on each element:

```
// Prints out names of all images
$("img").each(function(index) {
    alert(this.src);
});
```

The callback function you pass to each receives the 0-based index of the current iteration. Nicely enough, you don't need to retrieve the corresponding DOM element yourself; you just use the keyword *this* to refer to the element currently being processed. If the callback function returns false, the iteration is stopped. Be aware that *each* is a quite generic function made available for any task for which a more specific jQuery function doesn't exist. If you find a jQuery function that already does what you intend to code through each, by all means use the native function.

You use the *length* property to read the size of the wrapped set. You can also use the *size* function, but the *length* property is slightly faster.

```
// You better use the length property
alert($("img").size());
```

The *get* function extracts the wrapped set from the jQuery object and returns it as a JavaScript array of DOM elements. If you pass an index argument, instead, it will return the DOM element found at the specified 0-based position in the wrapped set.

```
var firstImage = $("img")[0];
```

Note that the *get* function (as well as indexers) breaks the jQuery chainability because it returns a DOM object or an array of DOM objects. You can't further apply jQuery functions to the results of a *get* call.

Many more operations are available on wrapped sets, and you can add many others through plug-ins.

Selectors

A query is characterized by a selector. A selector is simply the expression that, when properly evaluated, selects one or more DOM elements. In jQuery, you have three basic types of selectors: selectors based on IDs, cascading style sheets (CSS), or tag names. In addition, a selector can result from the composition of multiple simpler selectors combined by using ad hoc operators. In this case, you have a compound selector.

Basic selectors

An ID selector picks up DOM elements by ID. An ID selector commonly selects only one element unless multiple elements in the page share the same ID—this condition violates the HTML DOM standard, but it's not too unusual in the real world. Here's the syntax of an ID selector:

```
// Select all elements in the context whose ID is Button1
$("#Button1")
```

The leading # symbol instructs jQuery how to interpret the text that follows it.

A CSS-based selector picks up all elements that share the given CSS class. The syntax is shown here:

```
// Select all elements in the context styled with the specified CSS class
$(".header")
```

In this case, the leading dot (.) symbol directs jQuery to interpret the following text as a CSS style name.

Finally, a tag-based selector picks up all elements with the specified tag, such as all <img> tags, all <div> tags, or whatever else you specify. In the following example, the selector consists of the plain tag name—no leading symbol is required:

```
// Select all IMG elements in the context
$("img")
```

As mentioned, you can also concatenate two or more selectors to form a more specific one.

Compound selectors

Concatenation is possible through a number of operators. For example, the white space picks up all elements that satisfy the second selector and are descendants of those matching the first. Here's an example:

```
// Select all anchors contained within a DIV
$("div a")
```

The selector just shown is functionally equivalent to the following jQuery expression:

```
$("div").find("a");
```

Similar to the white space, the > operator selects elements that are direct child elements (and not just descendants) of the elements matched by the first selector:

```
// All anchors direct child elements of a DIV
$("div > a")
```

The preceding selector is functionally equivalent to the following jQuery expression:

```
$("div").children("a")
```

Plain concatenation of selectors results in a logical AND of conditions. For example, consider the following query:

```
$("div.header.highlight")
```

It selects all <div> elements styled using both the class header and class highlight.

The + operator—the adjacent operator—selects sibling elements in the second selector immediately preceded by elements selected by the first selector. Here's an example:

```
// All P immediately preceded by A
$("a + p")
```

The ~ operator—the next operator—is similar to + except that it selects sibling elements just preceded by others. Here's an example:

```
// All P preceded by A
$("a ~ p")
```

By using the comma, instead, you return the union of elements queried by multiple selectors. In terms of operations, the comma represents a logical OR of selectors. The following example, picks up elements that are either A or P:

```
// All A and all P
$("a, p")
```

Beyond simple operators, you have filters. A filter is a jQuery-specific expression that contains some custom logic to further restrict the selected elements.

Predefined filters

You can further refine selectors by applying filters on position, content, attributes, and visibility. A filter is a sort of built-in function applied to the wrapped set returned by a basic selector. Table 11-1 lists positional filters in jQuery.

TABLE 11-1 Positional filters

Filter	Description
:first	Returns the first DOM element that matches
:last	Returns the last DOM element that matches
:not(selector)	Returns all DOM elements that do not match the specified selector
:even	Returns all DOM elements that occupy an even position in a 0-based indexing
:odd	Returns all DOM elements that occupy an odd position in a 0-based indexing
:eq(index)	Returns the DOM element in the wrapped set that occupies the specified 0-based position
:gt(index)	Returns all DOM elements that occupy a position in a 0-based indexing greater than the specified index
:lt(index)	Returns all DOM elements that occupy a position in a 0-based indexing less than the specified index
:header	Returns all DOM elements that are headers, such as H1, H2, and the like
:animated	Returns all DOM elements that are currently being animated via some functions in the jQuery library

Table 11-2 lists all filters through which you can select elements that are children of a parent element.

TABLE 11-2 Child filters

Filter	Description
:nth-child(expression)	Returns all child elements of any parent that match the given expression. The expression can be an index or a math sequence (for example, 3n+1), including standard sequences such as odd and even.
:first-child	Returns all elements that are the first child of their parent
:last-child	Returns all elements that are the last child of their parent
:only-child	Returns all elements that are the only child of their parent

A particularly powerful filter is *nth-child*. It supports a number of input expressions, as shown here:

```
:nth-child(index)
:nth-child(even)
:nth-child(odd)
:nth-child(expression)
```

The first format selects the nth child of all HTML elements in the source selector. All child elements placed at any odd or even position in a 0-based indexing are returned if you specify the odd or even filter, instead.

Finally, you can pass the nth-child filter a mathematical sequence expression, such as 3n to indicate all elements in a position that are a multiple of 3. The following selector picks up all rows in a table (labeled *Table1*) that are at the positions determined by the sequence 3n+1—that is, 1, 4, 7, and so forth:

```
#Table1 tr:nth-child(3n+1)
```

Table 11-3 lists expressions used to filter elements by content.

TABLE 11-3 Content Filters

Filter	Description
:contains(text)	Returns all elements that contain the specified text
:empty	Returns all elements with no children
:has(selector)	Returns all elements that contain at least one element that matches the given selector
:parent	Returns all elements that have at least one child

As far as content filters are concerned, you should note that any text in an HTML element is considered a child node. So, elements selected by the empty filter have no child nodes nor any text. An example is the <br /> tag.

A popular and powerful category of filters are attribute filters. Using attribute filters, you can select HTML elements where a given attribute is in a given relationship with a value. Table 11-4 lists all attribute filters supported in jQuery.

TABLE 11-4 Attribute filters

Filter	Description
[attribute]	Returns all elements that have the specified attribute. This filter selects the element regardless of the attribute's value.
[attribute = value]	Returns all elements where the specified attribute is set to the specified value
[attribute != value]	Returns all elements whose specified attribute has a value different from the given one
[attribute ^= value]	Returns all elements whose specified attribute has content that starts with the given value
[attribute $= value]	Returns all elements whose specified attribute has content that ends with the given value
*[attribute *= value]*	Returns all elements whose specified attribute has content that contains the given value

You can also concatenate attribute filters by simply placing two or more of them side by side, as in the following example:

```
var elems = $("td[align=right][valign=top]");
```

The returned set includes all <td> elements for which the horizontal alignment is right and the vertical alignment is top.

The next expression, which is much more sophisticated, demonstrates the power and flexibility of jQuery selectors because it combines quite a few of them:

```
#Table1 tr:nth-child(3n+1):has(td[align=right]) td:odd
```

It reads as follows:

> *Within the body of element Table1, select all <tr> elements at positions 1, 4, 7, and so forth. Next, you keep only table rows for which a <td> element exists with the attribute align equal to the value of right. Furthermore, of the remaining rows, you take only the cells on columns with an odd index.*

The result is a wrapped set made of <td> elements.

Finally, a couple more filters exist that are related to the visibility of elements. The *:visible* filter returns all elements that are currently visible. The *:hidden* filter returns all elements that are currently hidden from view. The wrapped set also includes all input elements whose type attribute equals "hidden."

Filter vs. find

To further restrict a query, you can use either the *find* or *filter* function on a wrapped set. They are not the same, of course.

The *function* filter explores the current wrapped set for matching elements and doesn't ever look into the DOM for descendants. Instead, the function *find* looks inside of each of the elements in the wrapped set for elements that match the expression. In doing so, however, the function explores the DOM of each element in the wrapped set.

Chaining operations on a wrapped set

The jQuery library offers a wide range of functions that you can apply to the content of a wrapped set. (For a complete list, you can only resort to online documentation or look for an in-depth book.) You can chain function calls because any wrapped set returned by a query is, in turn, another jQuery object that can be further queried. The following expression, for example, works just fine:

```
$(selector).hide().addClass("hiddenElement");
```

It first hides from view all matching elements and then adds a specific CSS class to each of them.

You can classify operations that you can perform on wrapped sets in a few groups, as described in Table 11-5.

TABLE 11-5 Operations on a wrapped set

Effect	Description
DOM manipulation	Creates DOM trees, adds/removes elements, or modifies existing elements
Event binding	Binds and unbinds handlers to events fired by DOM elements
Styling	Applies, removes, or toggles CSS classes to selected elements and gets or sets individual CSS properties
Visibility	Shows and hides DOM elements using transition effects (for example, fading) and duration

In addition, in jQuery you find two other groups of functionalities—cache and Ajax calls—that work with the content of wrapped sets, though they can't be strictly considered operations available on wrapped sets.

Events

Handling events is a common activity in JavaScript programming. The jQuery library provides a bunch of functions to bind and unbind handlers to events fired by DOM elements.

Binding and unbinding

The *bind* and *unbind* pair of functions are used to attach a callback function to the specified event. Here's an example in which all elements that match the selector will have the same handler attached for the *click* event:

```
$(selector).bind("click", function() {
   ...
});
```

You use the *unbind* function to detach any currently defined handler for the specified event:

```
$(selector).unbind("click");
```

Be aware that the unbind function doesn't remove handlers that have been inserted directly in the markup through any of the *onXXX* attributes.

The jQuery library also defines a number of direct functions to bind specific events. Facilities exist for events such as *click, change, blur, focus, dblclick, keyup,* and so forth. The following code shows how to bind a handler for the *click* event:

```
$(selector).click(function() {
   ...
});
```

Invoked without a callback, the same event functions produce the effect of invoking the current handler, if any are registered. For example, the following code simulates the user clicking a specific button:

```
$("#Button1").click();
```

You can achieve the same effect in a more generic way by using the trigger function:

```
$("#Button1").trigger("click");
```

Event handlers receive a jQuery internal object—the *Event* object. This object provides a unified programming interface for events that goes hand in hand with the World Wide Web Consortium (W3C) recommendation, and it resolves discrepancies in the slightly different implementations provided by some browsers:

```
$("#Button1").click(function(evt) {
    // Access information about the event
    ...

    // Return false if you intend to stop propagation
    return false;
});
```

The *Event* object features properties such as mouse coordinates, the JavaScript time of the event, which mouse button was used, and the target element of the event.

Live event binding

Live binding is a nice feature of jQuery by which you can keep track of event bindings for a given subset of DOM elements for the entire page lifetime. In other words, if you opt for live binding instead of plain binding, you are guaranteed that any new dynamically added elements that match the selector will automatically have the same handlers attached. Starting with jQuery 1.7, you should operate live binding through *on* and *off* functions. Here's an example:

```
$(document).on("click", ".specialButton ", function() {
   ...
})
```

All buttons decorated with the *specialButton* CSS style have the given function attached as the handler for the *click* event. To stop live binding for some elements, you use the *off* function:

```
$(".specialButton").off("click");
```

The difference between using *on* and *bind* (or specific event functions such as *click*) is that when the *on* function is used, any new DOM elements added to the page and decorated with the *specialButton* style automatically have the handler added. This won't happen if *bind* is used.

Note If you're using a version of jQuery older than 1.7, you use *live* and *die* methods instead of *on* and *off*. The syntax is slightly different because the *live* method doesn't take the selector as an argument. Instead, the method applies directly to the selector.

Page and DOM readiness

In the beginning of client-side development, there was just one place where you could put the initialization code of a webpage: in the *onload* event on either the window object or the <body> tag. The *onload* event fires as soon as the page has finished loading—that is, after the download of all linked images, CSS styles, and scripts is complete. However, there's no guarantee that at this time the DOM has been fully initialized and is ready to accept instructions.

The *document* root object in the DOM exposes a read-only *readyState* property just to let you know the current state of the DOM and figure out when it's OK for your page to start scripting it. Using the *readyState* property is an approach that definitely works, but it's a bit cumbersome. For this reason, jQuery offers its own *ready* event that signals when you can start making calls into the framework safely.

```
<script type="text/javascript">
$(document).ready(
   function() {
     alert("I'm ready!");
   });
</script>
```

You can have multiple calls to *ready* in a page or view. When multiple calls to ready are specified, jQuery pushes specified functions to an internal stack and serves them sequentially after the DOM is effectively ready.

The *ready* event is fired only at the document level; you can't have it defined for individual elements or any collection of elements in a wrapped set.

Note The *onload* event is called after the HTML and any auxiliary resources are loaded. The *ready* event is called after the DOM is initialized. The two events can run in any order. The *onload* event won't ensure that the page DOM is loaded; the *ready* event won't ensure that all resources (such as images) have been loaded.

Aspects of JavaScript programming

Today, you often use JavaScript for some client-side logic and input validation. You use JavaScript to download data from remote servers, to implement Windows-like effects such as drag-and-drop, for resizing, for templates, for pop-up and graphic effects, for local data caching, and to manage history and events around the page. It's used for large chunks of code that have a good level of reusability and need to be safely isolated from one another.

In other words, you want your JavaScript code to be maintainable and unobtrusive.

Unobtrusive code

For years, it has been common to write HTML pages with client buttons explicitly attached to JavaScript event handlers. Here's a typical example:

```
<input type="button" value="Click me" onclick="handleClick()" />
```

From a purely functional perspective, there's nothing wrong with this code; it works as expected, running the *handleClick* JavaScript function whenever the user clicks the button. This approach is largely acceptable when JavaScript is just used to spice up webpages; however, it becomes unwieldy when the amount of JavaScript code represents a significant portion of the page or the view.

Style the view by using code

The expression "unobtrusive JavaScript" is popular these days, and it just means that it would be desirable not to have explicit links between HTML elements and JavaScript code. In a way, unobtrusive JavaScript is the script counterpart of CSS classes.

With CSS, you write plain HTML without inline style information and add style to elements by using CSS classes. Likewise, you avoid using event handler attributes (*onclick*, *onchange*, *onblur*, and the like) and use a single JavaScript function to attach handlers when the DOM is ready. Here's a concise but effective example of unobtrusive JavaScript:

```
<script type="text/javascript">
    $(document).ready(function () {
        $("#Button1").bind("click", function () {
            var date = new Date().toDateString();
            alert(date);
        });
    });
</script>

<h2>JavaScript Patterns</h2>
<fieldset>
    <legend>#1 :: Click</legend>
    <input type="button" id="Button1" value="Today" />
</fieldset>
```

You can move the entire <script> block to a separate JavaScript file and have your view be clean and readable.

Pragmatic rules of unobtrusive JavaScript

Unobtrusive JavaScript establishes a fundamental principle—any behavior in any webpage has to be an injectable dependency and not a building block. Rich JavaScript code is made of processing logic and code that manages the user interface (UI). The UI logic needs to know about the DOM and the structure of the view. This necessarily creates a dependency. You can live with such dependencies, but you live better if you work around dependencies.

One way of limiting the impact of UI dependencies is by using templates and ad hoc libraries such as KnockoutJS to render the page. You can learn more about KnockoutJS at *http://knockoutjs.com*.

Reusable packages and dependencies

More and more pages are extensively based on JavaScript, raising the problem of componentizing more and more the structure of pages. Let's explore a widely accepted approach for packaging code in JavaScript that has no dependencies on external libraries.

The *Namespace* pattern

A golden rule of JavaScript programming is grouping related properties—including globals—into containers. When such containers are shared among multiple script files, it might be hard to decide (and enforce) which file has the responsibility of initializing containers and child objects. You just saw an example of a simple syntax that you can use to define a global container.

```
var GLOBALS = GLOBALS || {};
```

This trick works, but it's often too cumbersome to use when you have several nested objects that you need to manage. Here's where the Namespace pattern comes to the rescue.

The Namespace pattern consists of a piece of code that iterates over the tokens of a dot-separated string (for example, a C# or Java namespace) and ensures that the proper hierarchy of objects is initialized. The namespace function ensures that the code is not being destructive and skips over existing instances. Here's some sample code:

```
var GLOBALS = GLOBALS || {};

GLOBALS.namespace = function (ns) {
    var objects = ns.split("."),
            parent = GLOBALS,
            startIndex = 0,
            i;

    // You have one GLOBALS object per app. This object already exists if you
    // can call this function. So you can safely ignore the root of the namespace
    // if it matches the parent string.
    if (objects[0] === "GLOBALS")
        startIndex = 1;
```

```
    // Create missing objects in the namespace string
    for (i = startIndex; i < objects.length; i++) {
        var name = objects[startIndex];
        if (typeof parent[name] === "undefined")
            parent[name] = {};
        parent = parent[name];
    }
    return parent;
};
```

After you have referenced the namespace function, you can then place the following calls:

```
GLOBALS.namespace("Widgets");              // GLOBALS has a Widgets property
GLOBALS.namespace("GLOBALS.Widgets");      // GLOBALS has a Widgets property
```

These two calls are equivalent, and both guarantee that GLOBALS has an initialized *Widgets* property. Consider the following:

```
// GLOBALS has a Widgets property, and Widgets has a NewsBox property
GLOBALS.namespace("GLOBALS.Widgets.NewsBox");
```

The *namespace* function proceeds iteratively and also ensures that *Widgets* has an *NewsBox* property.

Important Although the implementation shown here can be considered relatively standard, I feel obliged to credit Stoyan Stefanov for inspiring this code and the section on the *Module* pattern. Stoyan is the author of the excellent book *JavaScript Patterns* (O'Reilly Media, 2010). I recommend it to anybody who wants to go beyond the content of this chapter.

The Module pattern

The Module pattern provides a way to package self-contained blocks of code that you can simply add or remove from a project. The pattern wraps a classic JavaScript function into an immediate function that guarantees privacy of data and ensures that only what you explicitly reveal as public is actually perceived as public by clients. In JavaScript, an immediate function is a function defined inline and immediately executed. The syntax is shown here:

```
(
    function(...) {
        // Body
    } (...)
);
```

Let's use the Module pattern to build a self-contained widget that grabs news from a given feed. Suppose that you save all of the following code to a JavaScript file:

```javascript
GLOBALS.namespace("Widgets.News");
GLOBALS.Widgets.News = function () {
    var localUrl = "...",
        localWidget = "",
        localBuildWidget = function (items) {
            var numOfNews = items.length;
            if (localSettings.maxNews >0)
                numOfNews = Math.min(localSettings.maxNews, numOfNews);

            var buffer = "<table rules='rows'>";
            for (var i = 0; i < numOfNews; i++) {
                buffer += "<tr><td>" + items[i].Title + "</td></tr>";
            }
            buffer += "</table>";
            localWidget = buffer;
        },
        localSettings = {
            maxNews: 5,
            autoRefreshEvery: 0
        };

    return {
        load: function (selector, settings) {
            if (settings != null)
                localSettings = settings;

            $.getJSON(localUrl)
                .done(function (data) {
                    localBuildWidget(data);
                    $(selector).html(localWidget);
                });
        },
        getHtml: function () {
            return localWidget;
        }
    };
} ();
```

The code defines a logical block that contains all the logic required to download and format a bunch of news from a feed.

With the Module pattern, you return an object that reveals the public API that you want to make visible. Here's how you use a module:

```html
<script type="text/javascript" src="@Url.Content("~/content/scripts/module-news.js")"></script>
<script type="text/javascript">
    GLOBALS.Widgets.News.load("#twitter-box", {maxNews: 10});
</script>
```

You first link the distinct file that contains the widget and then initialize it, passing settings as appropriate. The widget in this case gets the jQuery selector of the UI where it will make graphical changes—specifically, where the widget will insert the HTML table with the list of selected news.

The Namespace pattern is not necessary for the implementation of the Module pattern, but it helps a lot to have it.

Script and resource loading

More and more script in webpages means more and more script files to download. This might soon become a serious issue and needs to be addressed. When a page has several scripts, the degree of parallelism at which the browser can operate is dramatically lowered. So it is for the load time of the page. Let's see why.

The download is always synchronous

The HTTP/1.1 specification suggests that browsers download no more than two components in parallel per host name. However, that never happens for script files: browsers always download script files synchronously and one at a time. As a result, the total download time is at least the sum of times required to download individual files and, maybe worse, the browser is idle while downloading a script file. Page rendering resumes only after the script files have been downloaded, parsed, and executed.

Browsers implement synchronous downloads mostly to stay on the safe side. In fact, there's always the possibility that script files include instructions such as JavaScript immediate functions or *document.write* that could modify the status of the current DOM.

Scripts at the bottom

To improve the page-loading performance, you can use a simple trick that consists of moving all links to script files to the bottom of the page just before the </body> tag. When you do this, browsers don't need to interrupt the page rendering process to load scripts. Browsers can then do their best to display an early view of the page.

Although placing manual scripts at the bottom is the safest approach, another option exists that you can set up declaratively and without resorting to writing or importing ad hoc JavaScript code: the *defer* attribute.

```
<script src="..." defer="defer"></script>
```

Introduced with the HTML 4 specification, the *defer* attribute instructs the browser whether loading the script can be deferred to the end of the page processing. A <script> tag decorated with the *defer* attribute implicitly states that it's not doing any direct document writing and it's safe for it to be loaded at the end. The purpose of the *defer* attribute is similar to the *async* attribute you find in the HTML5 specification.

Dealing with static files

A golden rule of web development states that after you've neutralized the performance hit of static files such as scripts, style sheets, and images, you're pretty much done with optimization. There are two main ways to minimize the download time of static resources, and one doesn't exclude the other.

The most obvious trick is reducing the size of the files being downloaded. The second most obvious trick consists of not downloading them at all. Before I get into the details, let me state up front that these optimization tricks should be played when you're done with development. If they're applied at development time, most of them only add frustration and slow down your progress.

Reducing the size of downloadable files means compressing their content. Browsers inform the web server about the type of compression they support through the *Accept-Encoding* header. Chapter 8, "Customizing ASP.NET MVC controllers," demonstrates that in ASP.NET MVC you can add a proper response header to any controller action and instruct the web server to use any of the supported encodings for the response. Compression can also be turned on for static resources directly at the web-server level. It should be noted that you should not use GZIP compression (or perhaps the deflate compression) on files (and responses) that are already compressed on their own. For example, you don't want to use GZIP for a JPEG image. Although GZIP compression can cut the size by 50 percent or so, it gives you much less impressive results on sources that are already compressed and at the cost of more CPU work.

The second aspect to consider is browser caching. Static resources are said to be static just because they don't change frequently. So, why should you download them over and over again? By assigning your static resources a very long duration (through the Expires response header), you save the browser from downloading these resources frequently. Again, you can do that at the web-server level for static resources and programmatically via the *Response* object for dynamically served resources.

In this regard, a content delivery network (CDN) is beneficial because it increases the likelihood that the browser cache already contains a resource that might have been referenced by using the same URL by other sites using the same CDN. Be aware that you won't benefit much from placing on a CDN files that only one application uses.

 Note Yet another option to neutralize the costs of static resources is putting those resources on a different server that is optimized to return static content. Or, perhaps you can use a reverse proxy tool such as Varnish (*http://www.varnish-cache.org*) to collect images from various servers and return them as if they originated from the proxy. By having a reverse proxy in front of the CDN or the website, you can get significant benefits in terms of reduced requests for static files.

Using sprites

To improve the serving of images, you can consider using sprites. A sprite is a single image that results from the composition of multiple images. Constituent images are saved side by side in the process of forming a new image, as shown in Figure 11-1.

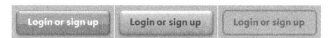

FIGURE 11-1 A composed image served as a sprite.

In pages, you use the <img> tag to reference the total image and resort to using a specific CSS style to select the portion of it in which you're interested. For example, here's the CSS you need to use for the segments of the image just shown to render a clickable button:

```
.signup-link
{
    width: 175px;
    height: 56px;
    background-image: url(/images/loginsprite.png);
    background-position: -0px 0px;
    background-repeat: no-repeat;
}

.signup-link:hover
{
    background-position: -177px 0px;
}

.signup-link:active
{
    background-position: -354px 0px;
}
```

The background-position indicates the relative position at which to start rendering the image. For example, when the mouse hovers over the image, the browsers begins rendering skipping the initial 177 pixels. This means that the first button is not displayed and the section of the sprite that is rendered coincides with the highlighted button. (As you can see in Figure 11-1, for clarity, I added a blank line of pixels, which is why you have to skip one pixel when counting positions.) The net effect is that you have just one image, just one download, a cached image, and a cool effect for users. (See Figure 11-2.)

FIGURE 11-2 Sprites in action.

Bundling and minification

As webpages continue to offer ever-richer visual content, the cost of downloading related resources such as CSS, scripts, and images grows significantly. Surely, for the most part these resources might be cached locally by the browser; yet the initial footprint can really be hard to sustain. For script and CSS files, GZIP compression can be combined with *bundling* and *minification*.

Bundling is the process of rolling up a number of distinct resources together into a single downloadable resource. For example, a bundle might consist of multiple JavaScript or CSS files. Minification is a transformation applied to an individual resource. In particular, minification consists of removing all unnecessary characters from a text-based resource in a way that doesn't alter the expected functionality. This means removing comments, white space characters and new lines; in general all characters that are usually added for readability but take up space and do not really serve any functional purposes.

You can apply bundling and minification together, but they remain independent processes. Depending on the needs, you can decide to only create bundles or minify individual files. Usually, however, there are no reasons on production sites not to bundle and minify all CSS and JavaScript files. At debug time, though, it's an entirely different story: a minified or bundled resource is quite hard to read and step through, so you just don't want bundling and minification enabled.

There are a lot of frameworks out there that provide bundling and minification services with slightly different levels of extensibility and different feature sets. I dare say that for the most part they all offer the same capabilities; so, picking one over the other is purely a matter of preference. If you're writing an ASP.NET MVC application, the natural choice for bundling and minification is the Microsoft ASP.NET Web Optimization framework, available through a NuGet package.

Bundling related resources

Typically, you create bundles programmatically in global.asax. In accordance with the ASP.NET MVC conventions, you create a *BundleConfig* class in the *App_Start* folder and expose a static initialization method out of it, as shown here:

```
BundleConfig.RegisterBundles(BundleTable.Bundles);
```

A bundle is simply a collection of files (typically style sheets or script files). Here's the code you need to group two CSS files into a single download:

```
public class BundleConfig
{
    public static void RegisterBundles(BundleCollection bundles)
    {
        bundles.Add(new Bundle("~/all-css").Include(
                "~/content/styles/site1.css",
                "~/content/styles/site2.css"));

        BundleTable.EnableOptimizations = true;
    }
}
```

You create a new *Bundle* class and pass to the constructor the virtual path that will be used to reference the bundle from within a view. To associate CSS files with the bundle, you use the *Include* method. The method takes an array of strings representing virtual paths. You can indicate CSS files explicitly, as in the preceding example, or you can indicate a pattern string, as demonstrated in the following:

```
bundles.Add(new Bundle("~/all-css").Include("~/content/styles/*.css");
```

Bundling is a form of optimization; as such, it mostly makes sense when the site is in production. The *EnableOptimization* property is a convenient way to set up bundling as it should work in production. Be aware that until it is turned on explicitly, bundling is not active.

Bundling script files

Bundle classes can work with CSS or JavaScript files without difference. However, the *BundleCollection* class has a couple of features that are mostly useful when bundling script files: ordering and ignore lists.

The *BundleCollection* class has a property named *Orderer* of type *IBundleOrderer*. As obvious as it might seem, an orderer is a component responsible for determining the actual order in which you want files to be bundled for download. The default orderer is the *DefaultBundleOrderer* class. This class bundles files in the order that results from the settings set through the *FileSetOrderList* property, which is another property of *BundleCollection*. The *FileSetOrderList* property is designed to be a collection of *BundleFileSetOrdering* classes. Each of these classes defines a pattern for files (for example, *jquery-**) and the order of *BundleFileSetOrdering* instances determines the actual order of files in the bundle. For example, given the default configuration, all jQuery files are always bundled before Modernizr files. Orderings for common groups of files (such as jQuery, jQuery UI and Modernizr) are predefined; you can programmatically reset and update orderings at will.

 Note The impact of the *DefaultBundleOrderer* class on CSS files is more limited but not null. If you have a *reset.css* and/or a *normalize.css* file in your website, these files are automatically bundled before any of your other CSS files, and *reset.css* always precedes *normalize.css*. The goal of having reset/normalize style sheets is to provide a standard set of style attributes for all HTML (reset) and HTML5 (normalize) elements so that your pages don't inherit browser-specific settings such as fonts, sizes, margins. Although some recommended content exists for both CSS files, the actual content is up to you. If you have files with these names in your project, ASP.NET MVC makes an extra effort to ensure that they are bundled before anything else.

If you want to override the default orderer and ignore predefined bundle file set orderings, you have two options. First, you can create your own orderer which works on a per-bundle basis. Here's an example that just ignores predefined orderings:

```
public class SimpleOrderer : IBundleOrderer
{
    public IEnumerable<FileInfo> OrderFiles(
            BundleContext context, IEnumerable<FileInfo> files)
    {
        return files;
    }
}
```

You use it as illustrated here:

```
var bundle = new Bundle("~/all-css");
bundle.Orderer = new SimpleOrderer();
```

In addition, you can reset all orderings by using the following code:

```
bundles.ResetAll();
```

In this case, the effect of using the default orderer or the simple orderer shown earlier is the same. However, be aware that *ResetAll* also resets all current script orderings.

The second noteworthy feature is the ignore list. Defined through the *IgnoreList* property of the *BundleCollection* class, it defines the pattern matching strings for files that were selected for inclusion in the bundle, but should be ignored instead. The major benefit of ignore lists is you can specify **.js* in the bundle, but you can use them to skip over, for instance, **.vsdoc.js* files. The default configuration for *IgnoreList* takes care of most common scenarios (including **.vsdoc.js* files) while giving you a chance to customize.

Adding minification

The *Bundle* class is only concerned with packing multiple resources together so that they are captured in a single download and cached. However, both style sheets and script files are padded with blanks and newline characters for readability purposes. Readability is important for humans (and then at debug time) but is never an issue for browsers. The string below is a sample minified version CSS perfectly acceptable for a browser. As you can see, it doesn't include any extra characters.

```
html,body{font-family:'segoe ui';font-size:1.5em;}html,body{background-color:#111;color:#48d1cc}
```

How would you add minification to CSS and JavaScript files? It is as simple as changing the *Bundle* class with *StyleBundle* or *ScriptBundle* class. Both classes are surprisingly simple: They inherit from *Bundle* and just consist of a different constructor.

```
public ScriptBundle(string virtualPath)
        : base(virtualPath, new IBundleTransform[] { new JsMinify() })
{
}
```

The *Bundle* class has a constructor that accepts a list of *IBundleTransform* objects. These transforms are just applied one after the next to the content. The *ScriptBundle* class just adds the *JsMinify* transformer. The *StyleBundle* class adds instead the *CssMinify* transformer. *CssMinify* and *JsMinify* are the default minifiers for ASP.NET MVC 4 and are based on the WebGrease framework. Needless to say, if you want to switch to a different minifier, all you need to do is to create the class—an implementation of *IBundleTransform*—and pass it via the constructor.

Summary

People like to consume interactive applications through the web. For various reasons, the most common way of writing these applications is still JavaScript. A die-hard language, JavaScript happily survived the advent of Adobe Flash and Microsoft Silverlight. Although Flash and Silverlight are still used in some web applications, they currently have no chance to cannibalize JavaScript.

JavaScript was originally introduced to give web authors the ability to incorporate some simple logic and action in HTML pages. JavaScript was not designed to be a cutting-edge programming language. The design of JavaScript was influenced by many languages, but the predominant factor was simplicity. It needs extra facilities to support the development of any functionality that goes beyond changing the attribute of a DOM element, which is where libraries such as the de facto standard jQuery as well as KnockoutJS and AngularJS fit in.

In Chapter 12, "Making websites mobile-friendly," we step into the development of a type of client-side, JavaScript-intensive application: single page applications.

Making websites mobile-friendly

Don't walk in front of me, I may not follow. Don't walk behind me, I may not lead.
Walk beside me and be my friend.

—A. Camus

When referring to software, the term *mobile* is usually associated with native applications for a particular platform such as Apple's iOS, Windows Phone, or Android. A common vision in fact is that you should aim at having apps for some platforms and just ensure that the website can be comfortably viewed on smartphones and (mini) tablets. Most recent devices can comfortably display nearly any website. This leads many executives to address mobile with just a few native apps, thus completely ignoring the subtler issues of mobile web.

My vision is different. I don't argue with having (or not having) mobile apps, because that is an aspect that is too business-specific to be addressed in general terms. But, I do argue that providing a mobile-friendly website is indeed quite important. More precisely, I argue that although any company can content itself with a website that just shows up and can be read on a smartphone, the user experience (UX) that you can provide with a mobile-optimized design of the site is incomparably better than just pinch-and-zoom to fill forms and read news.

In this chapter, you'll first review some of the technologies that help you to make a website mobile-friendly. Of course, the list includes HTML5, but it also extends to Responsive Web Design (RWD) and touches on some specific JavaScript frameworks such as jQuery Mobile. Next, you'll learn about the concrete challenges you face when you're called to action. You will see how to link together two distinct sites (desktop and mobile) so that they appear to be just one to users. Chapter 13, "Building sites for multiple devices," takes the discussion one step further and addresses the entire point of multidevice website design.

Technologies for enabling mobile on sites

Mobile users have high expectations in terms of UX; they expect the application to provide an overall user interface (UI) similar to that of popular devices (for example, iPhone), touch-based, and populated by common widgets such as pick-lists and the iPhone-ish toggle-switch. These widgets don't exist (yet?) as native elements of HTML and must be simulated by using server-side controls that output a mix of JavaScript and markup every time.

The bottom line is that it is one thing to create a plain site making the best possible use of HTML, cascading style sheets (CSS), and JavaScript; it is quite another to make a compelling mobile site that looks like a native application or, at the very minimum, behaves like that.

On the average, mobile browsers offer good support for HTML5 elements. This means that at least on devices that fall under the umbrella of "smartphones" or "tablets," you can default to HTML5 elements without worrying about workarounds and shims. So, let's summarize the key facts of HTML5.

HTML5 for the busy developer

HTML5 marks the beginning of the third age of the web in which HTML advances at a brisk pace toward becoming a true and fully-fledged application delivery format. HTML5 is not limited to presentation; rather, it also provides a slew of new functionalities for web and other types of applications. The big change is that HTML5 is about client-side programming and about building applications that can run within the browser with limited (or no) interaction with the back end.

Compared to its predecessor (which was defined more than a decade ago), HTML5 is a significantly richer markup language. One could say that all these years have not passed in vain as HTML5 now incorporates in the standard syntax many common practices that developers and designers employed in thousands of websites. In doing so, HTML5 issues specific rules on how to structure HTML elements and deprecates tags that were introduced in the past in favor of style elements. The new message is that you should use CSS to style elements and use specific (new) tags to define the structure of the document.

Semantic markup

Most all websites share a common layout that includes a header and footer as well as a navigation bar on the left of the page. More often than not, these results are achieved by using <div> elements styled to align to the left or the right. Most pages today end up with the following template that we also used in the samples throughout this book:

```
<div id="page">
   <div id="header">
      ...
   </div>
   <div id="navbar">
      <ul>
         <li> ... </li>
         <li> ... </li>
         <li> ... </li>
      </ul>
   </div>
      <div id="container">
         <div id="left-sidebar">
            ...
            <ul>
               <li> ... </li>
               <li> ... </li>
               <li> ... </li>
            </ul>
```

```
      </div>
      <div id="content">
        ...
      </div>
      <div id="right-sidebar">
        ...
      </div>
    </div>
    <div id="footer">
      ...
    </div>
</div>
```

This template includes header, navigation bar, footer, and a three-column layout between. The preceding markup alone, however, doesn't produce the expected results. For that, you need to add ad hoc CSS styles to individual <div> elements and make them float and anchor to the left or right edge.

What's different in HTML5?

First off, using HTML5 doesn't mean that you stop using CSS to transform a layout into a nice looking page. You still need to use the same bit of CSS to make the page look compelling and place segments where they belong. However, you can now describe the page in a much cleaner way that is also easier to read for a designer working on CSS stylesheets. Essentially, with HTML5 you replace generic <div> elements with more semantically meaningful elements such as <header>, <footer>, and <article>. Here's how you can rewrite the preceding template by using the newest HTML tags.

```
<header> ... </header>
<nav> ... </nav>
<article>
    <aside>
        ...
    </aside>
    <section> ... </section>
    <section> ... </section>
    <section> ... </section>
    <aside>
        ...
    </aside>
</article>
<footer> ... </footer>
```

The <nav> element logically groups links that would go in a navigation bar. The <article> element represents the container of any content for the page and incorporates <aside> elements and <section> elements.

All of these are *block elements* which must be styled properly to form a presentable page. Other new elements complete the list of enhancements such as <figure> and <details>. The <figure> element is designed to include figures with caption, whereas <details> replaces the canonical hidden <div> that developers use to hide optional content and display it via JavaScript.

A native collapsible element

The new <details> element is functionally equivalent to a <div> but its internal content is interpreted by the browser and used to implement a collapsible panel. Here's an example of the new element:

```
<details open="true">
   <summary>Drill down</summary>
   <div id="details_inside">
        This text was initially kept hidden from view
   </div>
 </details>
```

The *open* attribute indicates whether you want the content to be initially displayed or not (see Figure 12-1). The <summary> element designates the text for the clickable placeholder, whereas the remaining content is hidden or shown on demand. As of this writing, Google Chrome and Apple Safari are among the few browsers that support this feature. Internet Explorer 11 doesn't support it.

FIGURE 12-1 The new <details> element in action in Google Chrome.

Note If you want to support HTML5-compliant browsers while remaining compatible with old browsers, too, you should use both new HTML5 tags and replacement tags; older browsers will just ignore the new HTML5 tags.

The icon you see in the figure is provided by the browser. The <details> element requires a bit of CSS to look nice. Here's the CSS used for the element in Figure 12-1:

```
<style>
summary {
    padding: 5px;
    font-weight: bold;
    color: #708090;
}
#details_inside {
    font-style: italic;
}
</style>
```

Note HTML5 removes a few elements of little use whose presence would only increase redundancy. The list of elements no longer supported most notably includes the <frame> (the IFRAME element remains, however) and <font> elements. In addition, a few style elements such as <center>, <u> and <big> are removed. The reason is that this functionality can be easily achieved through CSS. For some reason, the current draft maintains analogous elements such as <b> and <i>.

New input types

Currently, HTML (and subsequently browsers) supports only plain text as input. There's quite a bit of difference between dates, numbers, or even email addresses, not to mention predefined values. Today, developers are responsible for preventing users from typing unwanted characters by implementing client-side validation of the entered text. The jQuery library has several plugins that simplify the task, but this just reinforces the point—input is a delicate matter.

HTML5 comes with a plethora of new values for the attribute type of the <input> element. In addition the <input> counts several new attributes mostly related to these new input types. Here are a few examples:

```
<input type="date" />
<input type="time" />
<input type="range" />
<input type="number" />
<input type="search" />
<input type="color" />
<input type="email" />
<input type="url" />
<input type="tel" />
```

What's the real effect of these new input types? The intended effect, although not completely standardized yet, is that browsers provide an ad hoc UI with which users can comfortably enter a date, time, or number. Some of these new input types specifically address the need of mobile site users. In particular, *email*, *url*, and *tel* types push mobile browsers on smartphones (for example, iPhone, Android, Windows Phone) to automatically adjust the input scope of the keyboard. Figure 13-2 shows the effect of typing on a *tel* input field on an iPhone: the keyboard defaults to numbers and phone-related symbols.

FIGURE 12-2 The *tel* input field on Safari for iPhone. You will find a similar implementation on Android and Windows Phone.

Today, not all browsers provide the same experience, and although they mostly agree on the UI associated with the various input types, still some key differences exist that might require developers to add script-based custom polyfills. As an example, let's consider the *date* type. As of this writing, the interface provided by Opera is different from what you see in Chrome (see Figure 12-3); Internet Explorer 11 doesn't offer any special support for dates.

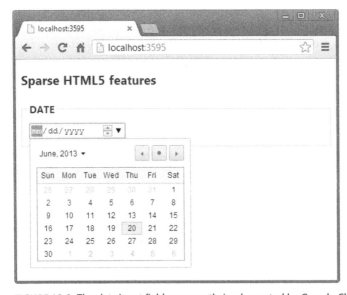

FIGURE 12-3 The *date* input field as currently implemented by Google Chrome.

In general, mobile browsers on recent smartphones are quite respectful of HTML5 elements. Still, as a mobile site developer, you might want to be very careful when using new input elements for *email*, *number*, *url*, *date*, *tel*—well, for just about everything!

Finally, it's worth noting that for the *placeholder* attribute that implements the long-awaited ability to display a hint in a text box wherever possible, hint text is not displayed for *range* and *date/time* input fields.

Note In the end, until browsers willfully and uniformly support the new input fields, developers have still a bit of work to do with JavaScript polyfills to ensure that correct data is posted to the server and that the users are properly informed about what is wrong. Mobile pages, much more than desktop pages, benefit from HTML5-compliant browsers.

The <datalist> element

Another nice improvement in HTML5 forms is the <datalist> element. The element is a specialized version of the popular <select> element. It provides the same behavior except that the drop-down list applies to a text input field. Here's an example:

```
<input list="countries" />
<datalist id="countries">
    <option value="Italy">
    <option value="Austria">
    <option value="Australia">
    <option value="Albania">
    <option value="Sweden">
    <option value="Denmark">
</datalist>
```

The net effect is that when the input field receives the focus, the menu displays and the user can either enter free text or pick up one of the predefined options. Figure 12-4 presents the feature as you would find it in Google Chrome.

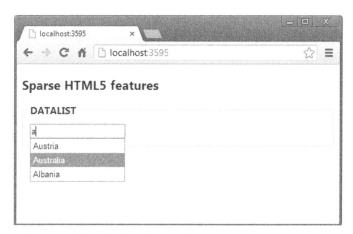

FIGURE 12-4 The <datalist> element in action.

Local storage

HTML5 provides a standard API that makes saving data on the user's device more affordable and represents an effective replacement for cookies. The average size of local storage is around 5 MB, which is much more than a cookie.

You access the local storage through the *localStorage* property exposed by the browser's window object. The *localStorage* property offers a dictionary-based programming interface similar to that of cookies. You have methods to add and remove items, to count the number of items in the store, to get the value of a particular item, and to empty the store. Here's how you can save a value and retrieve it later:

```
<script type="text/javascript">
function save() {
    window.localStorage["message"] = "hello";
}
function init() {
    document.getElementById("message").innerHTML = window.localStorage["message"];
}
</script>
```

Upon loading, the page retrieves and displays data from the local storage (if any). Data is saved to the storage through a function invoked interactively. Data saved to the local storage remains on the user's device indefinitely unless you programmatically empty it. The storage is specific for the application.

In addition to *localStorage*, HTML5 provides a *sessionStorage* object with the same programming interface but saving to the browser's memory, instead. The *sessionStorage* object is emptied at the end of the current browser session. Web storage accepts primitive types (the specification is not restrictive on this point, so any JavaScript type is acceptable), but you can save complex objects, as well, if serialized to the JavaScript Object Notation (JSON) format.

Audio and video

One of the biggest gains of HTML5 is saying farewell (but really?) to external plugins such as Flash and Silverlight for just playing audio and video. HTML5 brings two new elements, <audio> and <video>, that point to a URL and play any content. The browser implementation of these tags is also expected to provide a control bar for the user to pause and resume the playback. Here's how to link an audio resource.

```
<audio poster="init.png" controls="controls">
    <source src="nicestory.wav" />
</audio>
```

The sore point of multimedia elements (mostly, video) is the format of files, both file format and codecs. The HTML5 standard won't make an official call about codecs, so deciding about the format to support will remain up to the vendors. From a developer's perspective this is not exactly great news because it represents a breaking point; different browsers support different formats, and you should detect the browser or provide multiple files for the browser to choose. Here's the syntax to indicate a selection of video formats:

```
<video poster="init.png" controls="controls">
    <source src="tiger.mp4" type="video/mp4" />
    <source src="tiger.webm" type="video/ogg" />
    Oops, it seems that your browser doesn't support video.
</video>
```

Observe that you use the *controls* attribute to display the control bar and the *poster* attribute to specify an image to use as a splash-screen until the media is ready to play.

Popular codecs are MP4, MOV, and AVI. You should plan to have an MP4-encoded video for Internet Explorer and Safari, and OGG/Theora for all the others. At present, this seems to be the perfect solution to avoid external plugins. But, because this is a matter that changes frequently, look before you leap.

RWD

Most developers and technical managers remember very well the nightmare it was to build websites for a variety of browsers a mere decade ago. There was a time at which, for example, Internet Explorer had a different set of features compared to Firefox or perhaps Safari, or even just an earlier version of itself. That really made authoring markup for pages a mess. It is said that about 70 percent of the code that makes up jQuery today deals with quirks for older browsers, most notably Safari and Internet Explorer. I'd even say that developers started forgetting the "browser wars" as jQuery conquered ground; at the same time, the browser wars were definitely one of the factors for jQuery's rapid adoption.

In the mobile space, the order of magnitude of different devices is thousands, not units as with desktop browsers a while back. If the browsers fragmentation of a decade ago scared you, what about the vastly larger fragmentation of mobile devices today? This can be a real torment. Mindful of that, developers learned to focus on effective capabilities rather than pointing out a generic behavior associated with a browser's brand and name. This principle, however, is simple in understanding but quite hard in adoption. This is the starting point of RWD.

Feature detection

RWD sprung to life from the following example of lateral thinking. Detecting devices is hard? Well, then don't do that. You grab a few snippets of basic information available on the client side (for example, the size of the browser window), set up ad hoc style sheets, and let the browser reflow content in the page accordingly.

You stop detecting the capabilities of the requesting device and decide what to display based on what you can detect programmatically on the device. This approach relies extensively on a number of browser technologies—primarily CSS media queries—and offers the significant plus that you as a developer have just one site to design and maintain. The burden of adapting content responsively is pushed to graphical designers or to ad hoc libraries such as Twitter Bootstrap.

The major strength of feature detection, which we can summarize as "one *site* fits all," is also likely to be the major weakness, though. Is just one site what you really want? Do you really want to serve the "same" site to smartphones, tablets, laptops, and smart TVs? The answer to this question invariably is specific to each business. In general terms, it can only be a resounding, "It depends."

Let's first see the essence of RWD and then move to its possible shortcomings.

CSS media queries

The magic potion that gave life to RWD is CSS media queries. Introduced with CSS 3, media queries is syntax for developers to define conditional CSS style sheets that the browser will load dynamically any time the window is resized or some other system event takes place. CSS media queries make it possible for developers to easily create multiview pages that can be consumed through devices of different screen sizes ranging from the 24 inches of a desktop monitor to the 3-inch screen of most smartphones.

 Note It is crucial to note that CSS media queries are not specifically a technology for mobile development. However, the inherent power and flexibility of the solution makes it suitable for use in the building of a mobile site, too.

The key benefit of CSS media queries for developers is obvious. Developers write one set of pages and one back end. The set of pages targets the widest possible screen you intend to support—typically the desktop size—and stores as many elements as possible. Next, designers come up with multiple CSS files, one for each intermediate screen size to support. An intermediate screen size is referred to as a *layout breakpoint*. Most commonly, you have a break point placed at 480 pixels and another at 800 pixels, and possibly more. As the user resizes the browser window and width falls below 480 pixels, the browser automatically selects the CSS for 480 pixels. The same happens when the window is between 480 and 800 pixels; in this case, the CSS for 800 pixels is picked up. When the same page is viewed with a smartphone, the CSS for small screens (480 pixels) is automatically applied; for tablets you'll likely get the 800-pixel layout. Simple and effective.

By adding another break point and related CSS file, you can create an ad hoc view when the screen size is between 480 and 800 pixels. In this way, you address minitablets, as well. Do you need to support large screens such as smart TVs? No problem. You just add another CSS file. It is really easy and it works great, even though setting up an RWD solution for a realistically complex set of pages might not exactly be a walk in the park.

CSS media queries in action

How many different screen resolutions do you want to support? The answer depends on the expected audience and also on the content to render. However, there's a huge difference between a desktop browser resized to a width of 400 pixels and a smartphone screen of the same size. A laptop is one thing; a smartphone is quite another, as far as computing power and resources are concerned. CSS media queries, though, are unable to distinguish on a per-device basis.

Let's assume that this is not going to be an issue for now and further assume that it is acceptable from a business viewpoint to focus only on the size of the viewport. First, you need to decide for how many resolutions you intend to have a different layout. A sample classification might consist of the following breakpoints:

- Up to 480 pixels

- Up to 800 pixels

- Beyond 800 pixels

For each breakpoint, you create a distinct CSS file that takes care of styling elements, including flowing them toward the bottom of the screen or hiding some. In doing so, you can also decide to reference smaller images, if your pages link static images.

You reference such CSS files by using a slight variation of the classic syntax for the <link> element:

```
<link type="text/css"
      rel="stylesheet"
      href="view480.css"
      media="only screen and (max-width: 480px)">
```

In this case, the file view480.css will be used only when the page is rendering on a screen and when the browser window is no larger than 480 pixels. When media queries are used and no match can be found, quite simply no style sheet will be applied to the page.

 Note Historically the *media* attribute indicates the medium for which the CSS is intended—screen, printer, TV, video terminals, and more. In modern browsers that support the full CSS 3 standard, the value of the media attribute can include a query that selects the medium as well as some run-time conditions. You can find the full documentation about media queries at *http://www.w3.org/TR/css3-mediaqueries*.

The CSS media query language is based on a pair of Boolean operators—*and* and *not*—and a few browser properties. Table 12-1 lists the browser properties that you can use to select the most appropriate style sheet.

TABLE 12-1 Properties to build CSS media queries.

Browser property	Description
device-width, device-height	Width and height of the physical device screen.
width, height	Width and height of the rendering viewport; for example, the browser's window.
orientation	Returns portrait when height is greater or equal than width. Otherwise, it returns landscape.
aspect-ratio	Indicates the ratio between width and height; an example is "16/9".
device-aspect-ratio	Indicates the ratio between *device-width* and *device-height*; an example is "16/9".

Keep in mind that *device-width* and *device-height,* as well as the *width* and *height* properties, also support *min/max* prefixes.

You often find the keyword *only* at the beginning of media query expressions, but it doesn't really play a functional role. This keyword is added for the sole purpose of keeping older browsers away from the media query statements; older browsers don't understand the media type when it is pre-fixed with *only* and blissfully ignore the statement.

You can use the media query expression within the <link> element of the host page as shown ear-lier. In this way, you end up with one distinct CSS file for each breakpoint. You can also create a single CSS file that contains multiple media sections, as demonstrated in the following code:

```
@media screen and (min-width: 480px) {
    body {
        background: yellow;
    }
    ...
}
@media screen and (min-width: 800px) {
    body {
        background: blue;
    }
    ...
}
```

Note Whether you create a single file or multiple files, consider that in an RWD solution, you deal with a ton of CSS settings, repetitive for the most part. For this reason, it might be worth taking a look at dynamic stylesheet frameworks such as LESS (*http://lesscss.org*). Using these type of frameworks, you can create the CSS settings programmatically by using programmer-friendly constructs such as variables and functions.

In Table 12-1, there are two similar-looking properties: *width* and *device-width.* As mentioned, the former refers to the browser's width, whereas the latter indicates the device's screen width. For adaptive rendering, you should always be using *width.* However, on mobile devices (smartphones and tablets), any application is always available in full-screen mode, so there's really no actual difference between the two. In this regard, Windows 8 tablets are a notable exception because applications can run in snapped and filled mode, not just in full-screen mode.

Note In CSS Media Queries Level 4 (*http://dev.w3.org/csswg/mediaqueries4*), the next ver-sion of the standard, a few new properties will be added to make it simpler to distinguish between a mobile and a desktop device. It doesn't seem, however, to be the set of device capabilities that developers need to arrange really mobile-oriented views.

Fluid layout

CSS media queries alone don't really make the layout responsive, but it surely helps responding in some way to dynamically changing conditions. If your design caters only for a few preset breakpoints, users will get the same layout whenever their browser's width falls between two breakpoints. For example, suppose you have the following:

```
@media screen and (min-width: 480px) {
    body {
        background: yellow;
    }
    #container {
        width: 480px;
    }
    ...
}
@media screen and (min-width: 800px) {
    body {
        background: blue;
    }
    #container {
        width: 800px;
    }
    ...
}
```

You have one breakpoint set when the browser width reaches 480 pixels—at that point, the background becomes yellow and the container element is set to 480 pixels. You can enlarge the browser window but you won't notice any change until the width reaches 800 pixels. Figure 12-5 depicts a screen captured at 600 pixels.

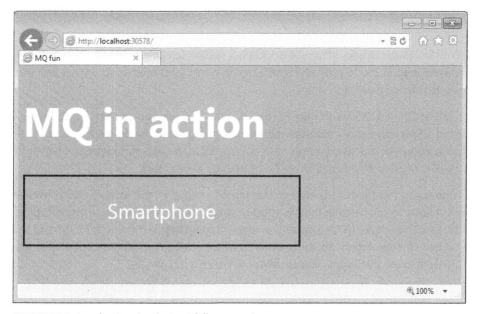

FIGURE 12-5 An adaptive view but not fully responsive.

Because the layout uses fixed measures, we end up with some empty and unused space. The impact of unused space can be mitigated by adding more breakpoints and then by authoring and maintaining more CSS files. However, for non-toy sites you can't realistically deal with more than three or four breakpoints.

A truly responsive layout is a layout that adapts to any change in the width and/or height of the browser window. To achieve this, you need to build your layout using CSS measures based on *em*s or percentages. In this way, your design can scale up and down with nearly no limits. This is also sometimes referred to as a *fluid* or *proportional layout*.

In CSS, you can use a number of units to set width, height, and font sizes. A unit that is becoming more and more popular is *em*. One "em" equals the current font size; subsequently, "1.2 em" increases the current font size by 20 percent. Pixels and points are both fixed unit and can't scale with the size of the window. However, percentage and em are both relative measures—although relative to different things. The unit "em" is always relative to font size, whereas percentage is relative to the containing block (for example, <body> or <div>). You can also apply a percentage to a font size. In this case, it indicates a variance related to the parent font size. In general, I'd say that using percentages to express dimensions of web elements (blocks and text) is more reliable and consistent across browsers.

Having said that, a fluid layout results primarily from expressing whatever is in the layout through relative measurements.

When RWD meets mobile

RWD is definitely a powerful approach to web design. It helps you in two ways: It makes your site look better, whatever the browser's size is, and, through frameworks such as Twitter Bootstrap, it also makes it possible for non-designers to quickly create nice templates. RWD, however, was not devised to serve mobile devices specifically, but it is so powerful and flexible that it can be used to adapt views of pages on nearly any mobile device.

One of the key characteristics of mobile devices is a smaller screen—around 400 pixels for a smartphone and around 800 to 1000 pixels for a tablet. When RWD renders your views well on those screen sizes, you should be all set—right?

RWD requires CSS and CSS media queries to work. With CSS, you can do a lot, but CSS is not about programming. CSS media query properties tell you something about the device, but not all that you might need to know. For example, you still have no clue about the operating system, whether the device is mobile, whether it's a tablet, smart TV, or perhaps a web robot.

RWD informs you that the page is currently hosted on a viewport, for instance, 800 pixels wide. But, it can't indicate to you whether that viewport belongs to tablet or a resized Internet Explorer desktop window. Sometimes, this is a detail that makes a considerable difference for the end user; and subsequently for developers. So, the question is where exactly does RWD fit in a mobile scenario? Is it really reliable to use RWD when you are about to create a mobile site?

A mobile device is different from a classic personal computer. It has a smaller screen—sometimes a significantly smaller screen. It doesn't have the same computing horsepower and storage; it doesn't have the same power source; and it is always touch-enabled (the same can't be said for desktops, although newer models might use a touchscreen monitor). Furthermore, a mobile device is often used on-the-go and to do things quickly and immediately. Because of this, connectivity might come and go at any time and might sometimes be slow and unreliable.

When users are on a mobile device they want to find options and actions one or two taps away; they likely don't need a lot of functions and information. They sometimes need information or aggregates of information different from those that work well for full sites. Mobile users might need a different metaphor of work and definitely need you to carefully devise the use-cases of the application.

RWD is an excellent approach to take a site devised for the desktop and make it render well on a variety of mobile devices. But even with it, you won't *necessarily* end up with a site that is optimized for mobile devices. Many developers sometimes claim to design in a *mobile-first* way, but all they are really doing is designing for desktop and then simply adapting to mobile. I'm not sure this is really a *mobile-first* approach!

Note RWD works well for some websites such as portals. It doesn't work the same way for sites that are highly interactive, implement workflows (for example, a booking site) and are full of forms that the user must fill in.

jQuery Mobile's executive summary

Working on top of the popular jQuery library, jQuery Mobile (jQM) is built from the ground up to be a comprehensive platform for building mobile sites. You code your way through the library and the library takes care of rendering the markup in the best possible way on the browser. By using jQM, you don't have (necessarily) to worry about device detection and capabilities. The library guarantees that the output works also on down-level browsers; whether the obtained output is really what you want... well, that's quite another story.

ASP.NET MVC developers can find the jQM library featured in the mobile project template that comes with Microsoft Visual Studio. This fact seems to push the vision that jQM is sort of a must for enabling mobile support in websites. As usual, it depends.

The quick answer is that jQM is simply a rendering JavaScript library that knows how to turn plain HTML markup into a mobile view. This means that buttons and input fields you might have in pages are rendered in a way that mimics the look-and-feel (and partly the behavior) of analogous visual elements of popular mobile platforms such as iOS. The simple adoption of jQM lends a mobile look-and-feel to your pages. It doesn't necessarily mean that your site has suddenly become a well-crafted mobile site.

Important You can use jQM (or even other vendor-specific frameworks such as Kendo UI or Sencha) and be happy. However, you'll keep your customers happy primarily if you design the site to be easily and comfortably used from mobile devices. This is also a matter of reworking use-cases and data aggregations. No libraries will help with this.

The official site of jQM is *http://www.jquerymobile.com*. You can also get the latest version from NuGet or directly at *http://code.jquery.com*.

Themes and styles

The jQM library is nearly unusable without a companion CSS file. The library does a lot of work on any page and transforms it from a plain collection of <div> tags into a pleasing, usable, and mobile-friendly document. For this to happen, a slew of styles and images must be created that follow strict standards. The library comes with a predefined CSS file to include. Like many other things, themes are of course customizable by developers.

The jQM library comes with a few predefined themes identified with the first letters of the alphabet: a, b, c, and so forth. Each theme consists of a number of CSS styles being uniformly applied to various HTML elements. Most of the time, you just pick up the theme you prefer; and the choice is based on colors. Here's how to set a theme.

```
<div data-role="page" data-theme="b">
   ...
</div>
```

You can apply a different theme to different parts of the page by using the *data-theme* attribute. (More on *data-** attributes in a moment.) Themes are applied by default; however, you can override their settings by using plain CSS commands on particular elements, as shown here:

```
<div data-role="footer" class="my-footer center">
   ...
</div>
```

The preceding <div> element has been given the role of the footer. As such, it gets a particular style from the library depending on the current theme. However, the *class* attribute is used to override some properties (colors, borders, font, and so on). The *class* attribute will hardly replace settings completely; if that's your purpose, you are probably better off creating your own custom theme by using the ThemeRoller tool of jQM.

*Data-** attributes

In HTML5, *data-xxx* attributes are custom attributes that you can use to better define the semantic of an element. Such attributes are forced to have a name in the form of data-xxx, but any framework (or page) is responsible for specifying the *xxx* variable part and, more important, for its interpretation. A *data-xxx* attribute always returns and accepts a string.

The jQM library recognizes quite a few *data-xxx* attributes and uses them to decorate HTML elements and give them a special meaning. The semantic expressed by the attributes determines the graphical output.

One of the most important *data-** attributes in jQM is the *data-role* attribute. It indicates the role played by that specific element in the context of the page. The attribute is commonly used to decorate <div> tags and make them pass as very specific semantic components such as the header, footer, or content.

Pages in jQM

In jQM, a page can either be a single HTML file or an internal section of an existing page. In the library jargon, the two scenarios are referred to as *single-page template* and *multi-page template*. Nicely enough, the library makes it possible for you to navigate to pages regardless of their nature, whether physical pages (distinct HTML file) or logical sections of an existing HTML file. Here's the typical page definition:

```
<div id="homePage" data-role="page" data-theme="a" class="my-bkgnd">
    ...
</div>
```

A page is identified by a <div> element decorated with the *data-role* attribute set to the *page* value. The page can have its own ID and can use the *class* attribute to override style settings. You can select the theme for the entire page by using the *data-theme* attribute. A jQM page often comprises a header, footer, and content. It should be noted, however, that this is just a convention; the page can contain any valid markup. An HTML file can contain multiple elements marked as logical pages, such as those presented here:

```
<div id="homePage" data-role="page" data-theme="a">
    ...
</div>
<div id="aboutPage" data-role="page" data-theme="b">
    ...
</div>
```

When multiple logical pages are used, you might want to use unique IDs for each of them in order to enable navigation and also initialization.

jQuery developers are very familiar with the *ready* event. This event is fired as soon as the page DOM is fully initialized and the page author can safely complete the initialization of the page elements. In jQM, you don't use the *ready* event; instead, you use the new *pageinit* event.

```
<div id="homePage" data-role="page">
    <script type="text/javascript">
        $("#homePage").bind("pageinit", function () { alert("home");  });
    </script>
    ...
</div>
```

The difference is that in jQM, Ajax calls are used to silently download requested pages and set up animations and page transitions. This means that the display of the page (whether a real page or a virtual page container) follows different rules than in classic jQuery.

In a nutshell, all you need to do is to add a <script> tag within the page element and bind the <div> that represents the page with the *pageinit* event. This code is guaranteed to be invoked every time that page is loaded, whether it was requested following a link or an Ajax call. In *pageinit*, you typically register your jQuery plugins and do your initialization work (apply localized strings, set up controls, and the like). Similar events exist for page display and unload.

Header and footer

Two commonly used values for the *data-role* attribute are *header* and *footer*. The header bar contains the page title and a couple of optional buttons to the left and right (mimicking the iPhone template). The header role receives a special style by the framework and undergoes some default manipulation. As a developer, you can completely customize both the header template and text and target of the buttons. Here's a sample header bar:

```
<div data-role="header">
    <h1>Home page</h1>
</div>
```

In particular, the first heading element (h1 through h6) is used to title the bar; if the content is not empty, that text also becomes the page title, overriding any value assigned to the <title> element. The heading element you use to title the header bar doesn't matter as long as it is an *Hx* element—the style applied is the same. If you want to give the page its own title distinct from the header text, you use the *data-title* attribute on the page container. The first link found in the header bar is automatically styled as a button and moved to the left.

```
<div data-role="header">
    <h1>ASP.NET MVC</h1>
    <a href="..." data-icon="gear">Login</a>
</div>
```

The second link, instead, is placed to the right. If you want just one button to the right, you add an extra class attribute, as illustrated in the following:

```
<div data-role="header">
    <h1>ASP.NET MVC</h1>
    <a href="..." data-icon="back">Back</a>
    <a href="..." data-icon="gear" class="ui-btn-right">Login</a>
</div>
```

The *data-icon* attribute selects one of the predefined icons in the jQM themes; the *ui-btn-right* value moves the button to the right (in the example, it is not strictly needed because the button to the right is the second.) It is interesting to note that if you use ASP.NET MVC and HTML helpers, the preceding anchors must be rewritten as demonstrated here (the names of the methods and controllers might change):

```
@Html.ActionLink("Back", "index", "home", null, new {data_icon = "back"})
@Html.ActionLink("Save", "login", "account", null, new {data_icon="gear", @class="ui-btn-right"})
```

ASP.NET MVC will automatically expand the underscore (_) to the dash (-) symbol and the @ symbol escapes the word class, which would otherwise have another meaning to the Razor compiler.

Unlike the header, the footer is not designed to simplify a given markup template. However, any link you place in the footer area is automatically turned into a button and any markup, including form markup, is acceptable in the footer. In this way, you can place an application bar in the footer or even a drop-down list to let the user choose, for instance, the language. Note that jQM manages the actual position of the footer bar. By using the *data-position* attribute you can keep the position constant to the bottom of the page, as illustrated here:

```
<div data-role="footer" data-position="fixed" data-id="about">
    ...
</div>
```

When the user follows links between pages, jQM applies transitions to the entire page. Sometimes, you get a smoother effect by keeping the footer still. For this to happen, the footer must be fixed in both pages making the transition, and in addition, both footers must have the *data-id* attribute set to the same (unique) identifier. Figure 12-6 shows a sample page with header, footer, and a placeholder for the body.

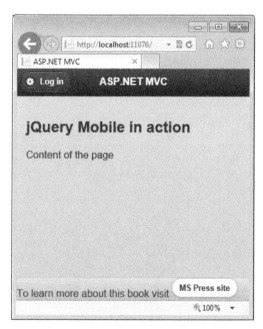

FIGURE 12-6 Header and footer in a jQM template.

To customize the header template entirely, you add a child <div> to the header block and populate it at will. Keep in mind that in this case you lose automatic manipulation; for example, links display as plain links. You need the *data-role=button* attribute to make the transformation.

```
<div data-role="header">
    <div>
        <img src="@Url.Content("~/content/images/mobile.png")" alt="">
        <h3>Custom templates</h3>
        @Html.ActionLink("Back", "index", "home", null,
                new {data_icon = "back", data_role="button", @class="ui-btn-right"})
    </div>
</div>
```

Lists, lists, and lists

The home page of most mobile sites should simply provide a list of actions like the classic main menu of applications of some thirty years ago. You can render the items of the menu in a number of ways; you can have them form a navigation bar, a button bar, a collection of tiles, or a plain list of nice-looking links. jQM supports nearly any scenario, but in particular, it is works great with navigation bars and list views.

The *listview* role provides the most common UI on mobile devices these days—very close to iPhone and Android picklists. The following plain HTML code, massaged by jQM, produces the output of Figure 12-7.

```
<ul data-role="listview" data-inset="true" data-theme="c" data-dividertheme="a">
    <li data-role="list-divider">Chapter 12</li>
    <li>@Html.ActionLink("Read content", "Content", "Home")</li>
    <li>@Html.ActionLink("Run samples", "Samples", "Home")</li>
    <li data-role="list-divider">General</li>
    <li>@Html.ActionLink("About the author", "About", "Home")</li>
    <li>@Html.ActionLink("About the publisher", "About", "Home")</li>
    <li>@Html.ActionLink("Related books", "About", "Home")</li>
</ul>
```

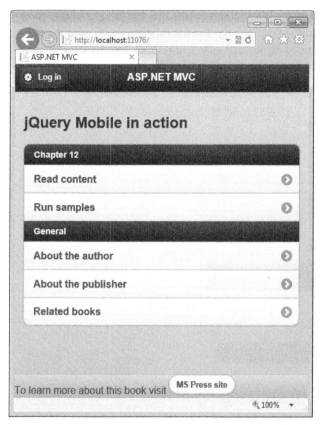

FIGURE 12-7 A jQM list view.

By using variations of the <ul> and <ol> elements you can create numbered lists as well as nested lists. Graphical variations include the *data-inset* attribute responsible for the rounded corners and nice scaffolding displayed in Figure 12-7 and *data-filter* to add a search bar with autocompletion of the list items statically added to the page. (This autocompletion doesn't entail connecting to a remote service to download dynamic data.)

You can add icons and images to the list items. Here's how to add a small icon to the left of the list item:

```
<li><a href="...">
    <img alt="" class="ui-li-icon" src="..." />
    <span>Run samples</span>
</a></li>
```

The class *ui-li-icon* ensures that the image is left-aligned; note that the image element must be a child of the anchor. Similarly, you can add text to the right of the list item. If you want the text to be automatically rendered within a bubble, as demonstrated in Figure 12-8, you mark the text with the *ui-li-count* class; otherwise, use the *ui-li-aside* class.

```
<li>
    @Html.ActionLink("Related books", "Related", "Home")
    <span class="ui-li-count">3</span>
</li>
```

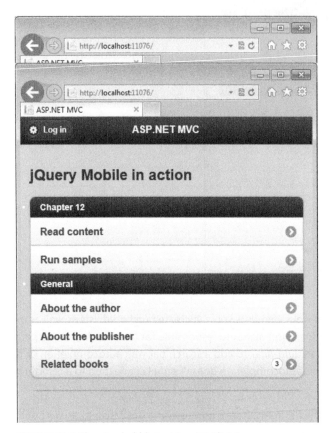

FIGURE 12-8 Showing bubble text in a jQM listview.

Fluid layout

Although having multiple columns in the layout is hardly a great idea in a mobile site, having an easy way to place a few elements side by side would be really nice. In jQM, you find a very basic but effective implementation of CSS grids and fluid layouts that automatically adapt to the screen.

The library makes available two main CSS classes: *ui-grid* and *ui-block*. The former marks a <div> (or a <fieldset>) as the container grid, whereas the latter marks a <div> as a child element. The main CSS classes, however, need a progressive letter to indicate number of cells and position, respectively. For example, the *ui-grid-a* class splits each row evenly into two blocks. The first is assigned to the content referenced by *ui-block-a*; the second goes to *ui-block-b*. Here's an example:

```
<fieldset class="ui-grid-a">
    <div class="ui-block-a"> First block </div>
    <div class="ui-block-b"> Second block </div>
    <div class="ui-block-c"> Third block </div>
</fieldset>
```

In this case, we also have a third cell assigned to a grid that can't host more than two (it splits 50/50 the row width). The net effect is that the third <div> styled as *ui-block-c* wraps to a second row. To keep the three child blocks on the same row, you change the grid style to *ui-grid-b*, which splits into three even parts (see Figure 12-9). Likewise, *ui-grid-c* splits into four parts, and *ui-grid-d* into five parts.

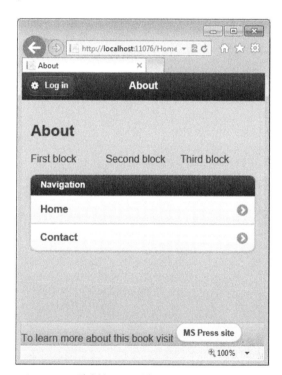

FIGURE 12-9 Fluid layout with jQM.

Collapsible panels

Collapsible panels are easy, too, as the following code snippet shows:

```
<div data-role="collapsible" data-theme="a" data-collapsed="true" data-content-theme="e">
    <h3>See navigation options</h3>
    <div>
        <ul>
          ...
        </ul>
    </div>
</div>
```

Assigned to a container element, the collapsible role uses the first <H*n*> child element to title the panel and makes everything else collapsible. You can use *data-collapsed* to decide whether the content is initially hidden. You use *data-content-theme* to style the content of the panel and *data-theme* to style the header, as depicted in Figure 12-10.

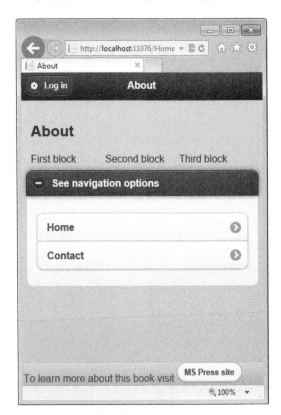

FIGURE 12-10 Collapsible panels with jQM.

By simply surrounding an array of collapsible panels with an outermost container, you can obtain an accordion widget.

```
<div data-role="collapsible-set">
    <div data-role="collapsible">
      ...
    </div>
    <div data-role="collapsible">
      ...
    </div>
      ...
</div>
```

By placing style attributes on the parent container, all panels are styled the same. Otherwise, you can style each panel individually.

Mobile frameworks

The jQM library has been the first framework for mobile programming to appear. At first, it gained the reputation of being slow, and this caused developers to explore other options and vendors to propose new frameworks. Over the course of a few versions, jQM has become more usable and just represents one option.

The fact is, even though vanilla JavaScript is always an option—and likely the most compact and fastest option—you probably need to look around for some framework to keep users happy with a nicer UI and UX. If you don't use jQM, where else can you turn?

An interesting option is Twitter Bootstrap. Even though this framework is not specifically designed for mobile scenarios, it offers excellent capabilities when it comes to fluid layouts and incorporates several jQuery plugins to implement quickly many of the jQM features. On the other hand, Bootstrap has an overall nimbler structure.

By contrast, Kendo UI is a fully-fledged framework for mobile devices developed based on HTML5 and designed from the ground up to produce high-quality and nifty UIs for different classes of devices. Similar in these goals is Sencha. And, the list of new frameworks grows bigger every day.

If you're a bit confused, don't worry: you're not alone. In general there's no clear winner here. If you find that a given framework works well for you, just stick with it. On the other hand, if the framework you're using doesn't work that well, you can easily find a better one just waiting for you to download it.

Twitter Bootstrap at a glance

All websites today are expected to be responsive—at least responsive to changes in the width of the host screen. As a member of a development team, you can achieve this in two main ways: You can just order an HTML responsive template from a vendor (and be transparent to implementation details), or you can do in-house development of the template. In the latter case, which framework would you use? Bootstrap is probably the first framework that you should consider, but it's not the only one.

Other equally popular and effective responsive frameworks are Foundation (*http://foundation.zurb.com*), Skeleton (*http://getskeleton.com*), and Gumby (*http://www.gumbyframework.com*). You can find a quick guide to CSS responsive frameworks and custom development approaches at *http://mashable.com/2013/04/26/css-boilerplates-frameworks*.

Bootstrap is quickly becoming the de facto standard in modern web development, especially now that Visual Studio 2013 incorporates it in the default template for ASP.NET MVC applications. With Bootstrap, you can easily arrange the UI of webpages, make them responsive, and provide advanced navigation and graphical features. Bootstrap essentially consists of a CSS file and an optional JavaScript file. Applied to HTML page elements, Bootstrap's CSS classes change the appearance of the current DOM and, more than everything else, your code will still look like plain HTML. As an added bonus, for most tasks you don't even need additional JavaScript.

Setting up Bootstrap

Bootstrap is articulated in modules and was originally developed as a collection of LESS files. You have essentially a LESS file for each module the Bootstrap framework is made of: forms, buttons, navigation, dialogs, and so forth. A LESS file is an abstraction over plain CSS syntax that makes it possible for you to declare how a CSS file will ultimately be. You can consider LESS as a programming language that when compiled, produces CSS. For this reason, with LESS, you can use variables, functions, and operators—wildly streamlining the process of creating large and complex CSS stylesheets.

By making changes to the original LESS file, as a developer you can customize Bootstrap at will. If you don't feel comfortable with the LESS syntax, you can still apply light forms of customization to Bootstrap by using a configuration engine. If you're OK with the Bootstrap internals and only want to minimize the download, you can pick up the CSS file from the central GitHub repository, selecting just the modules in which you're interested. You can download Bootstrap from *http://getbootstrap.com*.

Recently, Twitter released version 3.0 of Bootstrap, which introduces some new elements but also changed the behavior of existing styles. If you have a Bootstrap 2.x site, have a look at the migration guide on *http://getbootstrap.com* before you leap; in general you might expect some breaking changes.

To begin with Bootstrap, you just add the following to the <head> section of an empty HTML page:

```
<meta name="viewport" content="width=device-width, initial-scale=1.0">
<link href="bootstrap.min.css" rel="stylesheet" media="screen">
```

The *viewport* meta tag sets the width of the browser viewport to the actual device width and sets zoom level to normal. The <link> element just brings in the minified version of the Bootstrap style sheet. You are expected to download the Bootstrap CSS files from *http://getbootstrap.com* or link it from a known content delivery network (CDN).

```
<link rel="stylesheet"
    href="//netdna.bootstrapcdn.com/bootstrap/3.0.0/css/bootstrap.min.css">
```

You also need to link the jQuery library. This is enough for having a responsive template with no additional features such as drop-down menus or pop-up dialog boxes. If you intend to bring in some of the most advanced features that require client-side scripting, you should also add the Bootstrap.js file that you can find in the download. If you picked up a special Bootstrap theme, add the CSS file to the page, too. You can find free Bootstrap themes at *http://wrapbootstrap.com/themes*.

Keep in mind that Bootstrap is not supported in the old Internet Explorer compatibility mode. The best way to ensure that your pages are being viewed in the best possible rendering mode under Internet Explorer is to add the following <meta> tag in your pages:

```
<meta http-equiv="X-UA-Compatible" content="IE=edge">
```

CSS classes of Bootstrap make use of the latest CSS features (such as rounded corners) that might not be available on older browsers. A good example of an older browser that is partially supported by Bootstrap is Internet Explorer 8.

The grid system

Responsiveness in Bootstrap is achieved through a few breakpoints. The first breakpoint is placed at 480 pixels, which is considered the default. Other breakpoints are at 768 pixels (mostly tablets), at 992 pixels for desktops, and over 1,200 pixels for large screens. Any content in Bootstrap is usually laid out according to the following schema:

```
container > row > span
```

Each of the words above refers to a Bootstrap class name you typically apply to a <div> element. In particular, *container* manages the width of the page and padding. The *row* style ensures that the content is placed within the same row and multiple rows are stacked up vertically. Without a *row* element, any content within the container will flow horizontally and wrap to the next line when the end of the screen is reached. Finally, the *span* style identifies monolithic blocks of content within a row. In general, if you choose a combination different from *container-row-span*, results might be unpredictable. However, if you can manage to get exactly what you want, don't be worried if it doesn't fit the suggested relationship.

```
<div class="container">
    <div class="row">
        ...
    </div>
    <div class="row">
        ...
    </div>
</div>
```

The content of a row is subject to a fluid grid system that scales up to 12 columns as the device size grows. You use the *col-md*-N style for a row cell, where N is the number of cells in the grid to be used. In addition, you can use columns of different sizes using styles such as *col-lg*-N (large screens), *col-sm*-N (tablets), and *col-xs*-N (smartphones). Here's an example:

```
<div class="container">
   <div class="row">
       <div class="col-md-3">
       </div>
       <div class="col-md-3">
       </div>
       <div class="col-md-3">
       </div>
   </div>
</div>
```

The preceding code snippet creates a block element with three <div> elements laid out horizontally to take up evenly the entire space. Content within each <div> is centered in the available space.

Navigation bars

You can easily turn a <div> element into a navigational bar by using the *nav* base class followed by more specific styles. Here's how to create a top-level tab menu.

```
<ul class="nav nav-tabs">
  <li class="active"><a href="#">One</a></li>
  <li><a href="#">Two</a></li>
  <li><a href="#">Three</a></li>
</ul>
```

Accessory styles are *nav-tabs*, *nav-pills*, *nav-stacked*, and *nav-justified*. They end up producing graphical effects such as pills (equally spaced buttons), vertically stacked blocks, and horizontally centered blocks.

The *navbar* style generates a responsive navigation header for the website—something very similar to the classic toolbar. Quite interesting, Bootstrap *navbars* are initially displayed in a collapsed state in small views and stretch horizontally when there's enough room and the viewport size increases. All of this behavior is automatic and built in to the Bootstrap CSS. If you're not convinced yet, consider that this style gives you (for free) the typical behavior of a horizontal menu that collapses to a few vertical lines and expands back when the size of the host windows can accommodate that. Likewise, you can easily fix the position of the *navbar* at the top or bottom of the page by simply using the additional *navbar-fixed-top* or *navbar-fixed-bottom* styles.

Sometimes, the navigation bar is used to host the logical path of the page within the application's tree. This is called a breadcrumb in Bootstrap. Here's the code you need:

```
<ol class="breadcrumb">
  <li><a href="#">One</a></li>
  <li class="active"><a href="#">Two</a></li>
  <li>Three</li>
</ol>
```

The final output is a string of markup that automatically includes links and separators. You don't have to spend a line of script or markup to complete the rendering.

Finally, as far as the top of the page is concerned, you can also use the *page-header* style. It is a basic wrapper for the <h1> markup element and recognizes the <small> element within the content. The nice effect is that the child small text is automatically styled differently to reflect a lower-level heading.

Embellishing the UI with icons and images

The zipped file that contains the Bootstrap files also includes a directory full of glyph icons licensed free from *http://glyphicons.com*. You can use these icons in any place where markup is expected; you don't need an <img> element. Most typically, you wrap glyphs in a <span> tag set and combine that with some free text, as shown here:

```
<span class="glyphicon glyphicon-wrench"></span> Tools
```

The effect of the markup is to show the wrench glyphs followed by the text "Tools". You can use that within a <div> element and easily style the container as a button. It is important to notice that you need to specify two classes: the base *glyphicon* class followed by the specific class that identifies just the icon you want.

In a responsive template, images are a bottleneck in the sense that they might be too large for some screen sizes and hit the bandwidth. In addition, when too large, images can be cut off the screen and provide a poor UI. In Bootstrap 3, you can easily make an <img> tag responsive by doing nothing more than adding the *img-responsive* class.

```
<img src="..." class="img-responsive">
```

The effect is that the following styles are added:

```
max-width: 100%;
height: auto;
```

In this way, the image scales nicely to the size of the parent element. Be aware that this trick is not helpful with the download. It only ensures that the images are rendered nicely and properly shrunk; however, the size of the downloaded image is always the same.

Drop-down menus

Drop-down menus are nothing new in computer UIs, but they only recently started becoming common in webpages. HTML—and not even the latest HTML5—has no syntax element that can be used to produce drop-down menus when buttons are clicked. You can accomplish this by using a mix of everything: CSS, ad hoc markup, and jQuery plugins. With Bootstrap 3, all of these nitty-gritty details are completely hidden from view. The code that follows shows the markup you need in a webpage to place a button and attach a drop-down menu to it.

```
<div class="dropdown">
  <button data-toggle="dropdown">Actions</button>
  <ul class="dropdown-menu" role="menu">
    <li role="presentation">
        <a role="menuitem" tabindex="-1" href="#">One</a></li>
    <li role="presentation">
        <a role="menuitem" tabindex="-1" href="#">Two</a></li>
    <li role="presentation">
        <a role="menuitem" tabindex="-1" href="#">Three</a></li>
    <li role="presentation" class="divider"></li>
    <li role="presentation">
        <a role="menuitem" tabindex="-1" href="#">Four/a></li>
  </ul>
</div>
```

As you can see, all of the markup is wrapped in a <div> element styled by the *dropdown* class. Defined in the Bootstrap CSS file, the class prepares the ground for actual UI and associated behavior. In a way, you could rewrite the entire preceding HTML markup by using some pseudo-markup, as illustrated in the following:

```
<dropdown>
    <trigger>Actions</trigger>
    <dropdown-menu>
        <menuitem href="#">One</menuitem>
        <menuitem href="#">Two</menuitem>
        <menuitem href="#">Three</menuitem>
        <menudivider />
        <menuitem href="#">Four</menuitem>
    </dropdown-menu>
</dropdown>
```

All a developer needs to do is to define the target URLs and the code behind them. It can be a hash tag to some internal HTML element or it can be a pointer to some JavaScript code or external URL. Figure 12-11 shows the effect of the drop-down markup.

FIGURE 12-11 A drop-down menu associated with a button.

There are many other aspects of the drop-down menu that you can customize. For example, you can add a sort of comment line between clickable menu items. All you need to do is define a regular <li> element and assign it the *dropdown-header* class.

```
<li role="presentation" class="dropdown-header">Special actions</li>
```

You can disable a menu item by styling the corresponding <li> element with the disabled class, as demonstrated here:

```
<li role="presentation" class="disabled">
    <a role="menuitem" tabindex="-1" href="#">Four/a>
</li>
```

To trigger the menu, you need a <button> or an <a> element configured with the *data-toggle* attribute set to the *dropdown* value. In Bootstrap, you use the *data-toggle* attribute for requesting click behavior on some elements. The value of the attribute is one of a few predefined keywords that basically instruct the framework to select a particular jQuery plugin which will actually do the dirty work. You use the keyword "dropdown" if you want a drop-down behavior accomplished through the *dropdown* jQuery plugin.

Button groups

More often than not, a webpage needs to display several buttons that are somewhat related. You can certainly treat buttons individually and style them as you prefer. However, a few years ago, the iOS UI introduced the concept of segmented buttons; now, segmented buttons are, if not a must, a feature that's desirable to have on board. A segmented button is essentially a group of buttons acting individually but rendered as a single strip of buttons. The nicest effect is that the first and last button of the strip have rounded corners, whereas middle buttons are fully squared. In Bootstrap, you use the following HTML-based markup:

```
<div class="btn-group">
  <button type="button" class="btn btn-success">Agree</button>
  <button type="button" class="btn btn-default">Not sure</button>
  <button type="button" class="btn btn-danger">Disagree</button>
</div>
```

As you can see, there's really little more than just a few distinct buttons, each with its own click handler added either explicitly through the *onclick* attribute or unobtrusively via jQuery. To have a button group, all you need to do is wrap the list of buttons with a <div> element styled as *btn-group*. Figure 12-12 shows the effect.

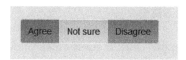

FIGURE 12-12 The HTML counterpart of iOS segmented buttons.

Each button is styled individually through the *btn* class; you can add additional attributes through the *btn-xxx* classes that affect the background color: *success*, *danger*, *warning*, *info*. You can control the size of buttons in the group with an additional class: *btn-group-lg*, *btn-group-sm* or *btn-group-xs*. By default, buttons are stacked horizontally. To stack them vertically, you just use the *btn-group-vertical* class. You can place multiple groups side by side by wrapping them in a button toolbar:

```
<div class="btn-toolbar">
  <div class="btn-group">...</div>
  <div class="btn-group">...</div>
  <div class="btn-group">...</div>
</div>
```

Finally, you can nest button groups. Nesting makes particular sense when one group is rendered as a drop-down list. Here's an example:

```
<div class="btn-group">
  <button type="button" class="btn btn-default">One</button>
  <button type="button" class="btn btn-default">Two</button>
  <div class="btn-group">
    <button type="button" class="btn dropdown-toggle" data-toggle="dropdown">
      Numbers
      <span class="caret"></span>
    </button>
    <ul class="dropdown-menu">
      <li><a href="#">1</a></li>
      <li><a href="#">2</a></li>
      <li><a href="#">3</a></li>
    </ul>
  </div>
</div>
```

The first two items in the group are plains buttons, followed by a nested group. The button group is made of a button with an attached drop-down menu. Of interest, the button features a caret segment that visually implies the message that there are more options to see. The class *caret* assigned to a <span> element within a button renders a down arrow similar to that of classic Windows drop-down arrows.

 Note Bootstrap has many more features than discussed here. To find out more, visit *http://getbootstrap.com*.

Adding mobile capabilities to an existing site

The most important task when planning a mobile site is selecting use-cases. It doesn't mean, however, that use-case selection is unimportant when developing full sites or other types of applications. It's just that a mobile application and site are structurally built around a few (and well-chosen) use-cases. Sometimes, even if you simply pick up a use-case from the existing desktop site, the way in which you implement it for a mobile audience might require significant changes—possibly a different UI and perhaps even a different workflow. RWD is not always as powerful as you need it to be when it comes to serving completely different views to mobile users.

So, more often than many seem to think, it turns out that you need to have one set of pages for full browsers and then multiple sets of pages for each class of mobile devices that you support. Really, the desktop becomes the special case. How would you manage to make these multiple sets of pages look like a single site? In Chapter 13, I discuss the native tools that ASP.NET MVC makes available to route users to specific views depending on the requesting device.

Sometimes, though, it is simpler to build a separate website designed from the ground up for a mobile audience and then link the two sites together by using HTTP modules and cookies.

Routing users to the correct site

Because you now have two distinct sites, you now need an automatic mechanism to switch users to the appropriate site based on the capabilities of the requesting device. If the host name belongs to the desktop site and the requesting browser is detected to be a desktop browser, everything works as expected. Otherwise, the user should be presented with a landing page on which she will be informed that she's trying to access a desktop site with a mobile device. The user is given a chance to save her preference for future similar situations. The preference is stored to a cookie and checked next.

The routing algorithm

If the request refers to a URL in the mobile site and the user seems to have a desktop browser, consider showing another landing page rather than simply letting the request go as usual. Finally, if a request is placed from a mobile device to the mobile site, it will be served as expected; namely, by looking into the device capabilities and determining the most appropriate view. Figure 12-13 presents a diagram of the algorithm.

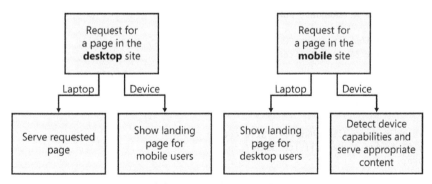

FIGURE 12-13 The desktop/mobile view switcher algorithm.

Note It's always a mistake to assume a one-to-one correspondence between desktop and mobile pages. This might happen, but it should not be considered a common occurrence. By saying "page correspondence," I simply mean that both applications can serve the same URL; I'm not implying anything about what each page will actually serve.

How would you implement the algorithm depicted in Figure 12-13?

Implementing the routing algorithm

In ASP.NET, the natural tool to implement this routing algorithm is by using an HTTP module that is active on both sites and capturing the *BeginRequest* event. The module will use plain redirection or, if possible, URL rewriting to change the target page, as appropriate.

Here's some code that implements the aforementioned algorithm in the desktop site:

```
public class MobileRouter : IHttpModule
{
    private const String FullSiteModeCookie = "FullSiteMode";
    public void Dispose()
    {
    }
    public void Init(HttpApplication context)
    {
        context.BeginRequest += OnBeginRequest;
    }

    private static void OnBeginRequest(Object sender, EventArgs e)
    {
        var app = sender as HttpApplication;
        if (app == null)
            throw new ArgumentNullException("sender");

        var isMobileDevice = IsRequestingBrowserMobile(app);

        // Mobile on desktop site, but FULL-SITE flag on the query string
        if (isMobileDevice && HasFullSiteFlag(app))
        {
            app.Response.AppendCookie(new HttpCookie(FullSiteModeCookie));
            return;
        }

        // Mobile on desktop site, but FULL-SITE cookie
        if (isMobileDevice && HasFullSiteCookie(app))
            return;
```

```
        // Mobile on desktop site => landing page
        if (isMobileDevice)
            ToMobileLandingPage(app);
    }

    #region Helpers
    private static Boolean IsRequestingBrowserMobile(HttpApplication app)
    {
        return app.Context.Request.IsMobileDevice();
    }

    private static Boolean HasFullSiteFlag(HttpApplication app)
    {
        var fullSiteFlag = app.Context.Request.QueryString["m"];
        if (!String.IsNullOrEmpty(fullSiteFlag))
            return String.Equals(fullSiteFlag, "f", StringComparison.
                                  InvariantCultureIgnoreCase);
        return false;
    }

    private static Boolean HasFullSiteCookie(HttpApplication app)
    {
        var cookie = app.Context.Request.Cookies[FullSiteModeCookie];
        return cookie != null;
    }

    private static void ToMobileLandingPage(HttpApplication app)
    {
        var landingPage = ConfigurationManager.AppSettings["MobileLandingPage"];
        if (!String.IsNullOrEmpty(landingPage))
            app.Context.Response.Redirect(landingPage);
    }
    #endregion
}
```

After it is installed on the desktop site, the HTTP module captures every request and checks the requesting browser. If the browser runs within a mobile device, the module redirects to the specified landing page. The landing page will be a mobile-optimized page that basically offers a couple of links to the home of the desktop site and to the home of the mobile site. Figure 12-14 shows a sample landing page as viewed on an old Android 2.2 device.

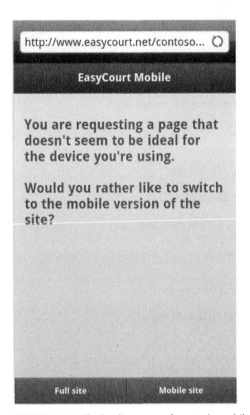

FIGURE 12-14 The landing page of a sample mobile site, viewed on an Android 2.2 device.

Tracking the chosen route

If the user insists on viewing the full site, you can't simply redirect to the plain home page. By its nature, the HTTP module will intercept the new request and redirect again to the mobile landing page. From the landing page, you can simply add a specific query string parameter that the HTTP module will detect on the successive request. Here's the actual link that results in Figure 12-14:

```
<a href="http://.../?m=f">Full site</a>
```

You are responsible for defining the query string syntax; in this case, *m* stands for mode and *f* for full. The task is not finished yet, though. At this point, users navigate to the home page of the site. What about any other requests? Those requests, in fact, will be intercepted by the HTTP module. By adding a cookie, you can provide additional information to the HTTP module about requests deliberately sent to the desktop site from a mobile device.

How can the user switch back to the mobile site? Ideally, any desktop site with a sister mobile site should offer a clearly visible link to switch to the mobile version (and vice versa when the full site is viewed on a mobile device). If not, the user won't be offered a chance to choose the full or mobile site until the cookie expires or is cleared. To clear cookies, users deal with the Settings page of the mobile browser.

Tweaking the configuration files

Where do you place the landing page? Is it on the desktop or on the mobile site? In general, it doesn't matter; however, if you put it on the mobile site, you really can enable a scenario in which you deploy a mobile site with all the required routing logic without touching the codebase of the existing desktop site.

However, the desktop site needs some changes in its configuration. In particular, you edit the web.config file of the desktop site and deploy a library with the HTTP module in the Bin folder. No changes should be made to the source code. Here's the configuration script to add a router HTTP module to the desktop site:

```
<system.webServer>
    <modules>
        <add name="MobileRouter" type="..." />
    </modules>
    ...
</system.webServer>
```

Keep in mind that the welcome page should always be visible, and it never should need authentication. Depending on how you deploy the mobile site—a distinct root site/application or a child application/directory—you might need to tweak the web.config file of the mobile site to turn off the HTTP module. If the mobile site is a distinct application, it needs its own web.config file that has been fully configured with the HTTP module. However, if the mobile site is hosted as a child directory in the desktop site, it inherits the configuration settings of the parent site (the desktop site), including the HTTP module. To speed up requests, you might want to disable the HTTP module in the mobile site.

Following is the configuration script that you need in the mobile site's web.config file. The script clears the list of HTTP modules required by the mobile site.

```
<system.webServer>
    <modules>
        <clear />
    </modules>
    ...
</system.webServer>
```

In addition, you need to instruct the parent application/site explicitly to stop the default inheritance chain of settings. Here's what you need:

```
<location path="." inheritInChildApplications="false">
<system.webServer>
    <modules>
        <add name="MobileRouter" type="..." />
    </modules>
    ...
</system.webServer>
</location>
```

Also, notice that when the mobile site is a child application/directory, it inherits a bunch of settings (for the section where inheritance is not turned off) that don't need to be repeated (for example, connection strings and membership providers).

 Note This example is based on the default Internet Information Services (IIS) 7.5 configuration, integrated pipeline mode. If you're using the classic pipeline mode, instead of *system. webServer/modules*, you should operate on the *system.web/httpModules* section.

From mobile to devices

Until a couple of years ago, websites were for desktop browsers or mobile browsers. The term "mobile," however, is progressively losing focus. Does mobile refers to smartphones or tablets, or both? And, what about minipads or large smartphones? How about regular cell phones? Smart TVs? The point is that you really need to start thinking in terms of multiple devices and decide whether your RWD gives you all that you need or you need to look elsewhere for more powerful device detection. In light of this, adding a single "mobile" site to an existing desktop site tastes like a temporary or just patched solution.

Reasonably, you should split the term "mobile" at least into two categories: smartphones and tablets. Having other categories such as large screens (for instance, smart TVs) and legacy, old-fashioned phones is also recommended but not strictly needed in just any application.

If you opted for a mobile site bolted on an existing desktop site, does this mean that you need to have two or three additional sites? When support for multiple classes of devices cannot be further delayed, you should look into multidevice design. Conceptually, it shares some aspects with RWD; in particular, it pushes the idea of a single back end and a single URL to invoke. Yet, at a deeper look, multidevice design is different from RWD because it pushes the use of different views for different classes of devices. A view is not simply a different CSS file, but it encompasses different markup and script, as well.

Multidevice doesn't mean you are going to create a different UI for each device; and it doesn't mean that you must be responsible for the identification of a given device. Classes of devices (smartphones, tablets, large screens) are nearly the same as the breakpoints in RWD. Feature detection needs to happen, but on the server side with some help from ad hoc tools such as device description repositories (DDR). Chapter 13 covers this in greater detail.

Summary

The challenge I see these days is how we can find a programming paradigm that weds mobile needs with desktop needs. Many efforts are focused on making mobile look and behave like the desktop. I'm not sure this is the right way of approaching mobile development.

Let's even assume that in, say, five years, we end up with even more powerful devices than today; this won't change the basic characteristics of a mobile device, though, which will likely remain smaller and less powerful than a laptop. In addition, businesswise, there's the problem of the long-tail to address. How many devices do you lose along the way (possibly leaving them to your competitors) by addressing only the high-end devices?

Although several solutions are possible to make a website device-friendly, the main route passes through an architecture that serves different views for different classes of devices. Sometimes, different views can be simply obtained by changing a CSS file; sometimes this is not sufficient, and different markup and script is required. In the former case, RWD and client-side feature detection is a great option. Otherwise, you need to implement server-side feature detection, but possibly by using smart tools and not handmade code.

In this chapter, we covered the basics of what you need to make your webpages responsive to different browser window sizes. We covered HTML5, the foundation of responsive web design, and Twitter Bootstrap as one of the most common ways to create a responsive experience on websites. Furthermore, we looked into jQuery Mobile as a sample JavaScript framework for mobile views.

CHAPTER 13

Building sites for multiple devices

The future belongs to those who prepare for it today.

—Malcolm X

I predict that within a couple of years any website that is not easy to consume by mainstream devices will suffer a significant drop in traffic. I deliberately used the term "mainstream device" here instead of a more specific term like tablet or smartphone just to give a measure of how fluid the situation is: nobody knows exactly which devices might show up and enjoy widespread adoption in a couple of years.

Beyond predictions, however, one thing is a certainty: Cell phones are a thing of the past. They're as modern as a dinosaur can be. The definition of smartphones is changing, too, and devices only two years old are already significantly different in terms of capabilities and power from the latest generation. In this context, nobody can reasonably afford to stick to Web Forms websites that are stretched into the device viewport and that require users to zoom in and out to read and follow links.

How should you approach the task of creating websites that look great and are highly usable on a broad range of devices?

There are two main schools of thought. Some claim that you should always focus on the features that the device actually exposes. Called *feature-detection*, this approach is inherently client-side and uses cascading style sheets (CSS)/JavaScript frameworks to decide which layout is more appropriate for the requested page. Also related to client-side feature detection is Responsive Web Design (RWD), a popular design methodology that pushes liquid layouts which take advantage of advanced CSS capabilities to flow pieces of content into the available space.

At the other extreme of the scale, there are server-side folks. They prefer to sniff the user agent string sent by the device's browser and figure out statically some of the capabilities the detected device is *known* to have. Then, based on this information a server-side solution can intelligently serve ad hoc markup, tailor-made for the requesting device.

RWD is a good approach; server-side is a good approach. You can use both to work out solutions; sometimes a mix of the two is even more powerful. Supporters of the client-side solution definitely scream louder than supporters of the server-side approach. This has attracted more and more people who seem to have bought the argument that feature-detection is smarter and quicker than any search in an unmaintainable mess of weird user agent strings.

Overall, I believe that the pros of RWD are well understood and cons of RWD are being mitigated by additional frameworks that show up every day. However, I also believe that the pros of server-side solutions are not really understood and the alleged cons are children of a previous and completely bygone software age—the age of the desktop-browser wars.

In this chapter, I aim at presenting the pros and cons of a server-side feature-detection approach and the additional (and not free of charge) tools you might need to use to implement it.

Understanding display modes in ASP.NET MVC

For years a webpage has always been just a webpage. If, for instance, a user requested default. aspx, she just got the content computed for default.aspx, usually regardless of the capabilities of the requesting browser. This more or less worked as long as requesting browsers were all fitting into the same class: desktop browsers. There might be slight (and annoying) rendering differences between different versions of desktop browsers, but by using a bit of jQuery and some forks in the HTML, we all worked around it for years. The advent of HTML5 added another level of differences beyond markup: functionality. Thankfully, libraries such as Modernizr came to the rescue, helping with the detection of some functionality and providing an infrastructure for shims.

Supporting multiple devices (and not just desktop browsers) is a different problem, though.

Multiple devices mean that requesting browsers can be of significantly different types because they might be mounted on smartphones, tablets, smart TVs, very large screens, or very small screens. It's not simply a matter of adapting the same content to render in the best possible way; it becomes a matter of adapting both content *and* behavior to completely different types of devices and possibly implementing a different set of use-cases.

In a multidevice scenario, the aforementioned default.aspx page explodes into a slew of pages such as default.smartphone.aspx, default.tablet.aspx, and so forth. Each logical page might therefore display in several ways according to user-defined rules.

Display modes form the infrastructure in ASP.NET MVC to effectively address multiple views for a single logical page.

Separated mobile and desktop views

Even though I'm a firm believer that there can't be any magic in software, I have to say that I faced some terrible doubts when I went through the following steps and met ASP.NET MVC display modes.

Built-in support for mobile views

In ASP.NET MVC, you now experience an interesting feature that apparently works as a result of pure magic. Suppose that you have a *HomeController* class with a plain simple *Index* method, such as that shown here:

```
public class HomeController : Controller
{
    public ActionResult Index()
    {
        var model = ProcessRequestAndGetData();
        return View(model);
    }
}
```

Chapter 2, "ASP.NET MVC views," points out that a file named index.cshtml located in the Views/Home folder in the project provides the HTML for the browser to render.

You now add a view file to the Views/Home folder and name it index.mobile.cshtml. You can give this file any content you like; just ensure that the content is different from the aforementioned index.cshtml. Now, launch the sample site and visit it with a regular desktop browser (for example, Microsoft Internet Explorer) and a mobile browser. You can use the Windows Phone emulator or perhaps Opera Emulator. Quite surprisingly, the view you get for the *home/index* URL is the mobile view as coded in the file index.mobile.cshtml.

> **Note** Overall, the simplest thing you can do to test the feature without much pain is to press F12 in Internet Explorer to bring up the Developer Tools window. From there, you set a fake user agent that matches a mobile device. If you are not sure about what to enter, here's a suggestion that matches an iPhone running iPhone OS 6: *Mozilla/5.0 (iPhone; CPU iPhone OS 6_0 like Mac OS X) AppleWebKit/536.26 (KHTML, like Gecko)*.

What's going on here? How is all this possible?

Default configuration for mobile views

Let's step through the code of ASP.NET MVC. From the *View* method invoked in the controller's method, the code flow reaches the *RazorViewEngine* class in all cases in which CSHTML views are used. In ASP.NET MVC, all predefined view engines inherit from the same class: *VirtualPathProviderViewEngine*. This class has a protected property named *DisplayModeProvider* of type *DisplayModeProvider*. The view engine receives the name of the view as set at the controller level: it can be a name such as "index" or it can be the empty string, as in the preceding example. If no view name is provided, the view engine assumes that it is the name of the action.

In the *VirtualPathProviderViewEngine* base class, from which both *WebFormsViewEngine* and *RazorViewEngine* inherit, during the resolution of the view name, the view engine queries the *DisplayModeProvider* object to see if any of the registered display modes can be applied to the requested view.

Each display mode is characterized by a suffix string, such as "mobile". If a match is found between the suffix string and an existing view name, the original view name is changed to point to the CSHTML file that represents the match. So, for instance, it can happen that "index" becomes "index.mobile" if such a view file exists in the project.

It turns out that by default *DisplayModeProvider* holds two predefined display modes: default and mobile. The default display mode is characterized by the empty string; the mobile display mode is characterized by the "mobile" string. These strings basically identify the suffix appended to the view name. This is where the file name index.mobile.cshtml comes from.

Rules for selecting the display mode

At the end of the day, the display mode provider is the internal component that decides about the actual view that the view engine needs to render. It receives the view name set at the controller level and decides whether to replace it with the name of a device-specific view, if any. The question is: which logic is driving the choice? By default, the display mode provider can choose between the regular desktop view and the mobile view. But, what determines the best choice?

Naming a display mode

In ASP.NET MVC, a display mode is represented by an instance of a class named *DefaultDisplayMode*. Here's the definition of the mobile display mode:

```
var mobileMode = new DefaultDisplayMode("mobile") {
    ContextCondition = context => context.GetOverriddenBrowser().IsMobileDevice
};
```

A display mode class is built around two main pieces of information: suffix name and matching rule. In the preceding code snippet, a new display mode class is created with the suffix of "mobile" and a matching rule assigned to the *ContextCondition* property.

The display mode name can be any string that uniquely identifies the particular view you want your site to support. By convention, the empty string identifies the default view—mostly, but not necessarily the desktop view. By default, the mobile view identifies any other requesting browser whose user agent string can be matched to a mobile device by using some internal ASP.NET logic.

It should be noted that under the umbrella of the mobile display mode fall any sort of non-desktop device, including old-fashioned legacy cell phones, the newest smartphones, tablets, mini-pads, and so forth. Also, the mobile display mode doesn't distinguish between operating systems. In this regard, an iPhone device is completely indistinguishable from an Android device, and a device with Android 2.1 is treated the same as an Android 5.0 device.

This is precisely the area where you want to intervene with some deep customization to tailor-make the markup being served to devices.

The matching rule

The *DefaultDisplayMode* class has a property named *ContextCondition* that you use to examine the context of the request and match it to one of the supported display modes. The *ContextCondition* property is a delegate defined as shown in the following:

```
Func<HttpContextBase, Boolean>
```

The purpose of the delegate is to analyze the HTTP context of the current request and return a Boolean answer to the following question: should this display mode be used to serve the current request? How the Boolean response is found is entirely up to the implementation of the matching rule.

In ASP.NET MVC, the default implementation of the mobile display mode parses the user agent string that comes with the request and seeks to find known keywords that would mark the request originator as a mobile device.

> **Note** In the end, it turns out that the name of the *DefaultDisplayMode* class is a bit misleading. That's just the class that defines a display mode. As I see things, the "Default" prefix in the name is just out of place.

Adding custom display modes

Display modes are a truly powerful feature, but you get the most out of it only when you wipe out the default configuration and create your own. To begin, and to become familiar with the API, let's first see how you list existing display modes.

Listing current display modes

You hardly have the need to do this in code, but I encourage you to try it out for pure fun. Here's the code that reads and displays the currently available modes:

```
<ul>
    @{
        foreach(var d in DisplayModeProvider.Instance.Modes)
        {
            <li>@(String.IsNullOrEmpty(d.DisplayModeId) ?"default" :d.DisplayModeId)</li>
        }
    }
</ul>
```

You use the *Instance* static member to access the singleton instance of the *DisplayModeProvider* class and flip through the *Modes* property. Figure 13-1 shows the sample page when a mobile and desktop user agent string is selected through the Internet Explorer Developer's toolbar.

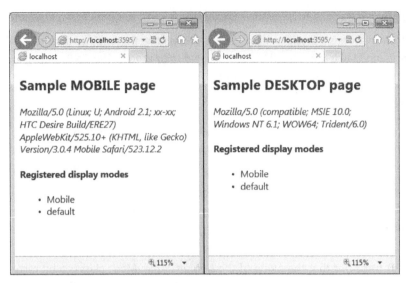

FIGURE 13-1 The sample ASP.NET MVC application choosing between desktop and mobile views of a given page.

Modern websites need more than just a mobile/desktop dichotomy for selecting views. Most likely, you will want to distinguish tablets, smartphones, legacy phones, and perhaps smart TVs. Sometimes, a simple CSS manipulation is enough to give you the output you need. This is where RWD is up to the task. Sometimes, however, you need to do server-side detection of the device via its provided user-agent string.

Going beyond the default configuration

Even if a plain desktop/mobile dichotomy works for your site, you should note that the logic behind the default mobile context condition is weak and flaky. It has good chances to work with iPhone and BlackBerry devices, but it might not even work with Windows Phone and Android devices, let alone with older and simpler devices. The *IsMobileDevice* method that you saw referenced a while back does sniffing of the user agent string based on the information it can find in the .browser files that are installed with ASP.NET, which are illustrated in Figure 13-2.

The model is clearly extensible and you can add more information at any time; but writing a .browser file might not be easy, and the burden of testing, checking, and further extending the database is entirely on your shoulders.

If you compare the content of Figure 13-2 with the content of the same folder you might have on your Internet Information Services (IIS) computer, you might notice some differences. In particular, the folder in the figure includes a fairly large (18 MB) browser file—an XML file actually—named mobile.browser. That file comes from an old, discontinued Microsoft project and contains a reasonable amount of devices as of the summer of 2013. (See *mdbf.codeplex.com*.) All devices and browsers which came next are not correctly detected.

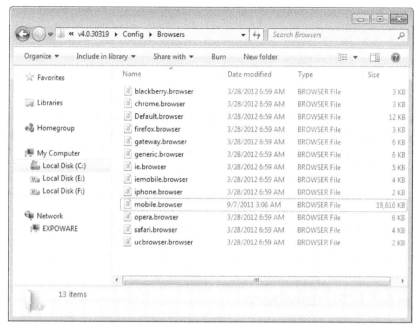

FIGURE 13-2 The list of browser configuration files you get out of the box with a clean installation of ASP.NET on a server computer.

Curiously, no changes occurred to the ASP.NET MVC infrastructure to address this point more specifically. In the end, display modes are an excellent piece of infrastructure but require a bit of work on your end for configuration and additional tools to carry out view routing work effectively. More important, to make ASP.NET MVC sites mobile-friendly, you need to pick up an external framework to help with device detection. (I'll return to this point in a moment.)

Defining custom display modes

You use display modes to give your site multiple views in front of the same URL. More concretely, this mostly means defining a display mode for each device or class of devices in which you're interested. You could create an *iphone* display mode, for example. Likewise, you could create a *tablet* display mode. In general, display modes are incredibly useful to create mobile-specific views, but they are just a tool to create specific views to be applied whenever a Boolean condition applied to the HTTP context evaluates to true. Here's some code that defines some custom display modes and replaces the default configuration:

```
var modeTablet = new DefaultDisplayMode("tablet")
{
    ContextCondition = (c => IsTablet(c.Request))
};
```

```
var modeDesktop = new DefaultDisplayMode("desktop")
{
    ContextCondition = (c => return true)
};
displayModes.Clear();
displayModes.Add(modeTablet);
displayModes.Add(modeDesktop);
```

Run from *Application_Start*, the code drops default display modes and defines two new modes: tablet and desktop. The tablet mode is added first and will be checked first. In fact, the internal logic that finds the appropriate display mode stops at first match. If the HTTP request is not matched to a tablet, it is then treated by default with a view optimized for a desktop device.

Be aware that because the desktop mode is associated with a specific non-empty string (desktop), each view needs to have the proper suffix to be recognized. In other words, standing the configuration above an index.cshtml view file won't be used. You need to have view files named index.desktop.cshtml and index.tablet.cshtml, instead.

Introducing the WURFL database

The key question now becomes the following: how could you reliably determine whether a given request comes from a tablet?

The simple answer is that it is all about sniffing the user agent string. But wait: wasn't sniffing the user agent string just the type of nightmare that brought developers to blissfully embrace RWD and client-side feature detection? And then, wasn't client-side feature detection insufficient to detect, for example, the operating system of the device as well as many other device-specific capabilities?

Server-side feature detection is not simply a long list of branches in an endless *switch* statement— one for each possible and known agent. More important, you are not expected to code user-agent sniffing yourself. If you do so, you will likely be reinventing the wheel and giving yourself a very hard time of crazy development and maintenance. For server-side feature detection to be affordable and effective, you need a professional tool for user-agent sniffing: a Device Description Repository (DDR) framework. A DDR is the component that works like an oracle, revealing all (the known) truth about the mobile browser that is viewing your page so that you can intelligently decide about the markup to serve as a response.

WURFL (see *http://wurfl.sourceforge.net/*) is the most widely used DDR today, but certainly it is not the only one. Large organizations such as Facebook and Google use WURFL for their mobile sites. It is also free for open-source projects and has a partially-free cloud version. For commercial use, though, you likely need to buy a license. For more information, refer to *http://www.scientiamobile.com*.

Note Whether you opt for WURFL or other products such as 51degrees.mobi, the key point is that you should not spend a second on crafting your own solution for sniffing user-agent strings. Not only because it takes a lot of time, but also given the high fragmentation of mobile browsers, it will also likely produce a flaky solution.

Structure of the repository

The WURFL DDR consists in an XML file that is about 1.5 MB in size when compressed, and just under 20 MB expanded. You can download the latest snapshot of the file from *http://wurfl.sourceforge.net*.

Note Upon downloading the WURFL database, you must agree explicitly to some terms and conditions. Basically, you are authorized to use the WURFL file without modification and only through one of the standard WURFL APIs as provided by ScientiaMobile. For ASP.NET, you can find a NuGet package to download and install the latest WURFL API and database.

The overall XML schema

The WURFL data file consists of a flat list of <device> elements. Here's the overall skeleton of the database:

```
<devices>
  <device id="..." user_agent="..." fall_back="...">
    <group id="...">
       <capability name="..." value="..." />
       ...
    </group>
    ...
  <device>
  ...
</devices>
```

The *id* attribute uniquely identifies a device by name. The *user_agent* attribute indicates a specific user agent string to be matched.

The key attribute is *fall_back*, which refers by name to other <device> elements. The *fall_back* attribute indicates the device from which missing capabilities of the present device will be inherited. Put another way, each device section describes just the delta between the current device and its parent device. All devices refer directly or indirectly to a root generic device, which ensures that any capabilities supported always have a default value and no exceptions will be thrown during queries. WURFL supports a number of root generic devices, one for each category of devices recognized: mobile phones, tablets, smart TVs, and possibly more in the future.

Groups of capabilities

Each device is associated with a list of capabilities. A capability is described as a name/value pair in which the value is always considered to be a string. This means that the WURFL API will always return capability values as plain strings with no attempt to match the value to a specific type such as a Boolean or integer.

This choice has been made to privilege extensibility and performance of the API over everything else. In fact, quite a few capabilities take values from an enumeration of values. For example, the *pointing_method* capability indicates how links are activated on the device. Possible values are *stylus*, *joystick*, *touchscreen*, *clickwheel*, or the empty string. All these options could comfortably be expressed as an *enum* type in Java and .NET languages. However, in this case any extension to the data file to add a new possible pointing method would also require a change to the API with the potential of breaking existing applications.

To keep things manageable, capabilities are split into groups. Table 13-1 lists the currently recognized groups. Groups, however, have no role in the API, in the sense that you don't need group information to retrieve the value of a capability.

TABLE 13-1 Groups of browser and device capabilities in WURFL

Group	Description
ajax	In spite of the name, this group defines capabilities that also go beyond plain Ajax programming. It informs you as to whether Ajax is supported but also whether DOM and CSS manipulation are allowed and geolocation.
bearer	Capabilities regarding networking aspects such as support for radio, Wi-Fi, virtual private network (VPN), and maximum reachable bandwidth.
cache	Capabilities related to the configuration of the cache of the embedded browser.
chtml_ui	Capabilities related to Compact HTML markup.
chips	Capabilities related to features available through extra chips installed on the device such as FM radio and a near-field communication (NFC) facility.
css	Capabilities related to CSS features such as sprites, borders, rounded corners, and gradients.
display	Capabilities related to screen size (both pixels and millimeters) and orientation.
drm	Boolean capabilities related to the support of a few DRM standards.
flash_lite	Capabilities about built-in support for Flash application types and version.
html_ui	Capabilities related to content served with the HTML MIME type. The group includes properties about viewports, HTML5 canvas, inline images, and preferred Document Type Description (DTD).
image_format	Boolean capabilities related to the support of a few image formats.
j2me	Capabilities that inform developers as to which Java features are available for midlets in the J2ME runtime—location, screen size, sockets, images, multimedia, and more.
markup	Boolean capabilities related to the variety of markup types being supported including XHTML, Wireless Markup Language (WML), and HTML.
mms	Capabilities that are relevant for MMS such as images supported, videos, and maximum frame rate.
object_download	Capabilities related to downloadable objects such as video-clips, images, wallpapers, screensavers, and ringtones.

Group	Description
pdf	Capabilities related to native support for PDF content.
playback	Capabilities related to supported video formats and codecs for content downloaded from websites.
product_info	Capabilities related to the device such as brand and model name, whether it is a mobile device, phone or tablet, operating system, keyboard, and browser.
rss	Capabilities related to native support for RSS feeds.
security	Capabilities related to HTTPS support and IMEI visibility.
sound_format	Boolean capabilities related to a variety of different sound formats.
smarttv	Capabilities that are relevant for Smart TVs.
sms	Capabilities that are relevant for SMS, EMS (rich-text SMS), and ringtones, including those specific of some vendors such as Nokia and Panasonic.
storage	Capabilities related to the size of the pages the device can manage.
streaming	Capabilities related to supported video formats and codecs for content streamed from websites.
transcoding	Capabilities aimed at identifying the request as coming from a transcoder—a piece of software that can act as a gateway and hide real device information. These capabilities are offered in case you need to handle such requests in a special way.
wap_push	Capabilities aimed at detecting effective Wireless Application Protocol (WAP) features.
wml_ui	Capabilities related to WML markup.
xhtml_ui	Capabilities related to XHTML markup.

The following listing shows an excerpt illustrating the CSS capabilities of the generic device—the root of WURFL devices:

```
<group id="css">
    <capability name="css_gradient" value="none" />
    <capability name="css_border_image" value="none" />
    <capability name="css_rounded_corners" value="none" />
    <capability name="css_spriting" value="false" />
    <capability name="css_supports_width_as_percentage" value="true" />
</group>
```

By contrast, the following example shows the same group for a generic Android device:

```
<group id="css">
    <capability name="css_border_image" value="webkit"/>
    <capability name="css_rounded_corners" value="webkit"/>
    <capability name="css_spriting" value="true"/>
    <capability name="css_supports_width_as_percentage" value="true"/>
</group>
```

As you can see, some properties are overridden.

WURFL patch files

The WURFL repository comes with two or more files (arbitrarily named): one is the XML file that represents the repository itself (usually named *wurfl.xml*); the others are patch files that are usually named using the pattern *xxx_patch.xml*. Patch files are optional.

> **Note** The WURFL API is based on a configuration module through which you point to the repository and optional patch files. In ASP.NET, you can do that either programmatically through a fluent interface or via a custom section in the *web.config* file.

Using a patch file, you can make changes to some capabilities within the default repository without physically tweaking the original file (which would break the license anyway, even if you did it on your legally acquired copy). In other words, a patch file is the provided way to override some content within the WURFL database. If any patch is found when the WURFL file is parsed, its content is imported to build a modified version of the repository. Here's an excerpt from a patch file that adds support for Firefox 10 (in case it is not supported in the latest update of the repository):

```
<device user_agent="Firefox" fall_back="generic_web_browser" id="firefox">
    <group id="product_info">
        <capability name="brand_name" value="firefox" />
    </group>
</device>
<device user_agent="Mozilla/5.0 (Windows NT 5.1; rv:10.0) Gecko/20100101 Firefox/10.0"
        fall_back="firefox" id="firefox_10_0">
    <group id="product_info">
        <capability name="model_name" value="10.0"/>
    </group>
</device>
```

Why would you want to use a patch file?

Overall, the primary reason for using a patch file is that you have your own good reasons to assign certain capabilities a different value. For example, suppose that you custom-tailored a website for tablet devices. Next, you run across a particular device whose screen is large enough to accommodate the tablet user interface that you designed. Unfortunately, though, WURFL continues to consider that particular device as something other than a tablet. You then create a new patch file (or edit an existing one) and override the *is_tablet* capability, for that particular user agent only. Here's an example:

```
<device user_agent="your nice tablet device that WURFL doesn't consider a tablet"
        fall_back="generic_mobile" id="mytablet">
    <group id="product_info">
        <capability name="is_tablet" value="true" />
    </group>
</device>
```

Another scenario for which patch files are useful is when you need a capability that is not natively supported in WURFL either because it is too specific for your application or because nobody ever thought of it before. Finally, a patch file can come to the rescue when some wrong data is found to exist in the original WURFL database. For more information and examples of patch files, visit *http://wurfl.sourceforge.net/patchfile.php*.

Essential WURFL capabilities

Let's take a closer look at some of the WURFL capabilities to get a precise idea of the level of control over the content being served that you can gain through WURFL. What follows is just a very small selection of the over 600 capabilities available. You can find full documentation about capabilities at *http://wurfl.sourceforge.net/help_doc.php*.

Identifying the current device

The most common type of information you want to know about the requesting device is its identity. Table 13-2 lists some very handy capabilities that describe the device being used to carry the current request. The table shows the name of the capability, its WURFL group, its description, and possible values for it.

TABLE 13-2 Device-related capabilities

Capability	WURFL group	Value	Description
is_wireless_device	product_info	true/false	The device is wireless.
is_tablet	product_info	true/false	The device is a tablet.
is_smarttv	smarttv	true/false	The device is a smart TV.
device_os device_os_version	product_info	string	The name and version of the current device (for instance, Android 2.2).
resolution_width resolution_height	display	integer	The screen width and height in pixels.
max_image_width	display	integer	The maximum width, in pixels, of images as they can be viewed on the device.
can_assign_phone_number	product_info	true/false	The device can be associated with a phone number. This is used to distinguish devices using a SIM only to browse the web.
pointing_method	product_info	joystick, stylus, touchscreen, clickwheel, ""	The method used to select links. Note that the empty string indicates classic four-way navigation on devices with top-left-right-bottom buttons to navigate links.
brand_name model_name marketing_name	product_info	string	The brand (for example, HTC), model name (for example, HTC A8181), and even marketing name of the device (for example, HTC Desire).

Some of these properties make it possible for you to catalog the device very precisely. For example, you can check whether the incoming request comes from a browser hosted on a wireless device. The *is_wireless_device* capability returns true for any user agent string matched to mobile devices such as cell phones, PDAs, and tablets (but not laptops and smart TVs such as AppleTV). If all you need to do is detect a mobile device, this property is all you need. For a more detailed analysis, you can also check *is_tablet* which returns true on iPads and *can_assign_phone_number* which returns true on cell phones (which can have a phone number assigned) but not on, for instance, iPods. Another similar capability is *has_cellular_radio* (in the *bearer* group): This capability indicates whether the device can mount a SIM for whatever reason. You can have a SIM on an iPad but not, for example, on an iPod Touch.

If you need to distinguish iOS from Android or Windows Phone devices, you can use the *device_os* and *device_os_version* capabilities. If you then need to know the exact device (manufacturer and product name), you can go with *model_name* and *brand_name*.

The known size of the actual screen is returned by *resolution_width* and *resolution_height*. Finally, information about touch capabilities is returned by the *pointing_method* capability when the value equals *touchscreen*.

 Note Any information about the operating system is implied by the user agent. When a newer version of the operating system is installed on a device, it should also update the browser, and the browser should reflect the version of the operating system in the sent user-agent string. However, this is only the expected way of working. On old devices, it might not be surprising to have, for example, version 2.2 of Android but a browser that still refers to version 2.1.

Serving browser-specific content

Table 13-3 lists a few capabilities that can help you to fine-tune the markup that you serve to the browser. WURFL is full of capabilities for fine-tuning the markup being served. The capabilities below are representative of scenarios in which you will want to use different markup templates on the server to generate the view.

TABLE 13-3 Capabilities for serving ad-hoc content

Capability	WURFL Group	Value	Description
viewport_supported	*html_ui*	*true/false*	The browser supports the <viewport> meta tag.
image_inlining	*html_ui*	*true/false*	The browser can display images embedded via the data Uniform Resource Identifier (URI) scheme.
full_flash_support	*flash_lite*	*true/false*	The browser fully supports Flash.
cookie_support	*xhtml_ui*	*true/false*	The browser supports cookies.
preferred_markup	*markup*	*string*	The preferred type of markup to serve to the browser.
png, jpg, gif, tiff, greyscale	*image_format*	*true/false*	The browser can display images of a given type.

Some mobile browsers assume that they can render every page, so they shrink the page to the actual screen size and let users zoom in and out to view a section of the page in a convenient manner. The HTML <viewport> meta attribute has been introduced to enable the developer to indicate which size the virtual screen—the viewport—actually should have. However, the <viewport> meta tag is not standard, and it is safer if you check before you emit it. The *viewport_supported* capability simply indicates to you as its name suggests.

Browsers treat images as separate resources and trigger an additional request to download them (if not cached locally). For mobile devices, HTTP requests carry a much higher cost than they do for desktop browsers, so any techniques are welcomed that reduce the number of HTTP requests necessary to finalize a page. A common technique consists of embedding small images as Base64-encoded text within the HTML page. This technique is known as image inlining and is not supported on several older devices, just the category of devices for which minimizing downloads is more critical.

With the *image_inlining* capability, you can know in advance whether the requesting browser will be able to show correctly an image embedded in this way. If you fail this check, though, the worst problem you can run into is that the image is replaced by the browser's specific placeholder for missing images. Image inlining is just one of those features that is simply impossible to check from within the browser via some smart piece of JavaScript.

In mobile web, there are two types of markup languages, which are only apparently similar:

- **XHTML MP**   This is a mobile-optimized markup format that browsers can parse and render extremely fast. In addition, by simply seeing the Multipurpose Internet Mail Extensions (MIME) type, any browser can reasonably perceive that the page is a mobile page. Unfortunately, the markup language is not as powerful as plain HTML, and support for DOM manipulation, CSS, and JavaScript is not really advanced—at least not in a cross-browser manner.

- **HTML/viewport**   This is plain HTML markup with the addition of the <viewport> meta tag. HTML/viewport was essentially introduced by iPhone and Safari for mobile. Because the MIME type is the same as for a full webpage, Apple added the <viewport> meta tag as a clue to the browser about the page being mobile.

In WURFL, the *preferred_markup* capability indicates which type of markup is ideal for a given browser. If the capability returns *html_wi_oma_xhtmlmp_1_0*, you should serve XHTML MP markup; if the returned value is *html_web_4_0*, you'd better go with plain HTML and use the <viewport> meta tag to mark the page as mobile.

Knowing in advance that the page is mobile helps the browser to arrange an optimal rendering, avoiding shrunken pages and the need to zoom in to interact effectively.

Using WURFL with ASP.NET MVC display modes

As mentioned, the WURFL library is available for ASP.NET through a NuGet package. Along with binaries, the NuGet package downloads a sample WURFL database file. Keep in mind that the WURFL database file you get through the package might not be the most up-to-date file. To get the latest public chunk of the WURFL database, visit *http://wurfl.sourceforge.net*.

Configuring the WURFL framework

Using WURFL requires a few simple steps such as getting hold of the binaries and referencing them through the project and initializing the WURFL runtime.

Installing the NuGet package

The simplest way to add WURFL to an ASP.NET project is via NuGet. The package name is WURFL_Official_API. (See Figure 13-3.) Among other things, the package installs the WURFL database (a zipped file) in the *App_Data* folder. You don't need to unzip the file; the API can also handle it when zipped.

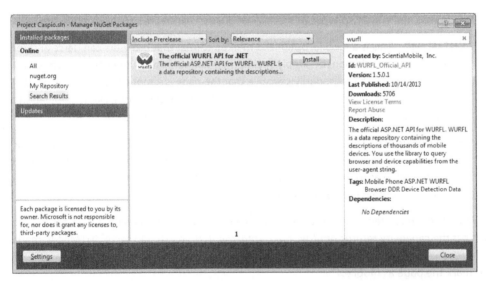

FIGURE 13-3 Installing the WURFL API NuGet package.

The package also copies some documentation and an introspector tool (basically, an HTTP handler) that when placed online facilitates querying remotely the WURFL database for debugging purposes. You can safely remove it from the project because it doesn't play any role in the regular functioning of the API. The package also makes some changes to the web.config file. In particular, the package adds the following new section:

```
<configSections>
    <section name="wurfl" requirePermission="false"
            type="WURFL.Aspnet.Extensions.Config.WURFLConfigurationSection,
                  Wurfl.Aspnet.Extensions, Version=1.5 ..." />
</configSections>
```

It also provides some content for it.

```
<wurfl mode="Accuracy">
    <mainFile path="~/App_Data/wurfl-latest.zip" />
</wurfl>
```

The *wurfl* section is not strictly necessary, and the configuration you get from NuGet only represents a possible way of configuring WURFL. The *wurfl* section mainly lets you set the location of the WURFL database and optionally patch files to apply. You can use the ASP.NET root operator (~) to refer to a virtual path. However, you can also set source and patch files outside configuration programmatically by using the native API.

Referencing the device database

You can point the WURFL library to the source database in either of two ways by using a *configurer* object. You use the *ApplicationConfigurer* object if you intend to specify the database path through the web.config file. You add the following line to *Application_Start*:

```
WURFLManagerBuilder.Build(new ApplicationConfigurer());
```

The *ApplicationConfigurer* class reads path information from the web.config file. You use the *InMemoryConfigurer* object, instead, if you intend to specify the location of the WURFL database and optional patch files programmatically.

```
var configurer = new InMemoryConfigurer()
            .MainFile(wurflDataFile)
            .PatchFile(yourWurflPatchFile1)
            .PatchFile(yourWurflPatchFile2);
```

In case of need, you can also create your own *configurer* class by implementing the *IWURFLConfigurer* interface. The interface is fairly simple and only counts a single method, as illustrated here:

```
public interface IWURFLConfigurer
{
    Configuration Build();
}
```

The *Configuration* object is also part of the public WURFL API. For more details, you can read the documentation at *http://wurfl.sourceforge.net/docs/dotnet* or download its source code.

Initializing the WURFL runtime

The WURFL library works by loading the content of the database in global memory and serving responses on demand to callers. Any returned response is cached indefinitely so that it won't be recalculated on subsequent requests until the application restarts. The initial loading of the database takes place on application startup; if at some point you replace the WURFL database on your server you also need to restart the application for changes to take effect.

The entry point into the WURFL library is the WURFL manager object returned by the *Build* method on the aforementioned *WURFLManagerBuilder* type. The builder does just one main thing: it locates the WURFL database and loads its content into a memory data structure. Because the WURFL database is essentially an XML file, the process of loading consists of reading the entire document and parsing it out to proper bits and pieces.

The memory data structure that ends up containing parsed WURFL data acts as an internal cache privately owned by the WURFL manager. This data structure takes up most of the run-time memory required by WURFL. In the end, when you hold an instance to the WURFL manager, you hold both the actual WURFL data and a tool to read it. WURFL data should be considered global in the context of an ASP.NET application.

Now, the question becomes how can you reference the single instance of the WURFL manager being created at startup from any other places within the application? Internally, the WURFL manager is built like a singleton. The instance of the WURFL manager class created (and then returned) by the builder is assigned to a public static member of the builder class named *Instance*. In any place where you need to make a WURFL query, you refer to the manager, as demonstrated here:

```
var deviceInfo = WURFLManagerBuilder.Instance.GetDeviceForRequest(userAgent);
```

Be aware that the WURFL manager is never reset internally. If you correctly initialize it at the start of the application, there's no way for the manager to become null; except, of course, that your code has a path where the manager variable is assigned a potentially null reference.

Detecting device capabilities

Let's now see what it takes to process a user-agent string and learn as much as possible about the calling device.

Processing the HTTP request

The WURFL manager object has a method called *GetDeviceForRequest*, which is the primary tool you'll use to learn about the calling device.

```
var deviceInfo = WURFLManagerBuilder.Instance.GetDeviceForRequest(userAgent);
```

The *GetDeviceForRequest* method has a few overloads and can be called passing in the user-agent string as well as the ASP.NET *HttpRequest* object or perhaps a WURFL-specific *WURFLRequest* object. The overload accepting the *WURFLRequest* type is the easiest and most flexible to mock up for testing purposes because you can also use it to list HTTP headers as well as the user-agent string.

The *GetDeviceForRequest* method returns an internal object that implements the public *IDevice* interface. Of all the members on the interface, the most important and most frequently used is *GetCapability*. The method accepts the name of the capability as a string and returns the value for the identified device as a string. Here's how you know about the operating system (if any) of the current device:

```
String os = deviceInfo.GetCapability("device_os");
```

Each call to *GetCapability* first checks an internal cache and then proceeds to read through the in-memory database. Any computed results are cached for further use. The WURFL manager holds its own private cache for obvious performance reasons. You can measure that the startup of the WURFL library usually takes a few seconds (only once, when *Application_Start* is invoked), but each request is served in a matter of milliseconds, and often instantaneously. The WURFL internal cache uses a Least-Recently-Used (LRU) algorithm and automatically refills device information that might have been discarded.

For this reason, you can repeatedly call *GetCapability* to read multiple properties. However, you also have available a *GetAllCapabilities* method, and only in version 1.5 of the .NET API can you rely on API filters that restrict the capabilities managed by the API for performance reasons.

Important WURFL capabilities always return a string value. It is a developer's responsibility to turn any returned string into a more manageable data type such as integer or Boolean, as applicable. You might want to check the documentation carefully to ensure that you are not missing some possible response strings in the conversion to a basic .NET type.

Virtual capabilities

A common scenario for using WURFL in an ASP.NET website is to serve different markup to different classes of devices. For this to happen, you should be able to quickly classify a device from its user agent string and determine if it's a smartphone, a tablet, or perhaps a legacy phone. WURFL also provides a few virtual capabilities just for this purpose.

Virtual capabilities are processed in the same way as regular capabilities; they're just called *virtual* because they don't specifically refer to an individual and specific attribute of the device. The canonical example is the capability named *is_smartphone*. The capability indicates whether the user agent can be associated with a smartphone device. The algorithm to recognize a smartphone from the capabilities associated with the user agent is internal to WURFL and basically checks the version of the operating system, touch capabilities, and screen width. Table 13-4 shows the full list of WURFL virtual capabilities.

TABLE 13-4 WURFL virtual capabilities

Virtual capability	Description
is_android	True if the device runs any version of Android.
is_ios	True if the device runs any version iOS.
is_windows_phone	True if the device runs Windows Phone 6.5 or higher. Note that this does not include Windows Mobile or Windows CE.
is_app	True if the requests come from a native app. This typically is when the request comes from a WebView component or native app making a REST API call.
is_full_desktop	True if the requesting device has a full desktop experience.
is_largescreen	True if the requesting device's screen is of a high resolution (over 480 pixels in width and height).
is_mobile	True if the device is mobile, like a phone, tablet, media player, portable game console, and so on.
is_robot	True if the request is from a robot, crawler, or some other automated HTTP client.
is_smartphone	True if the device is a smartphone. Internally, the matcher checks the operating system, screen width, pointing method, and a few other capabilities.
is_touchscreen	True if the primary pointing method is a touchscreen.
is_wml_preferred	True if the requesting device should be served with WML markup.
is_xhtmlmp_preferred	True if the requesting device should be served with XHTML-MP markup.
is_html_preferred	True if the requesting device should be served with HTML markup.
advertised_device_os	Returns the operating system name of the requesting device. This works for mobile and desktop devices (for example: "Windows", "Mac OS X").
advertised_device_os_ version	Returns the operating system version of the requesting device. This works for mobile and desktop devices (for example: "XP", "10.2.1").
advertised_browser	Returns the browser name of the requesting device. This works for mobile and desktop devices (for example: "Internet Explorer", "Chrome").

To work with virtual capabilities, you use a slightly different API, as shown in the following:

```
String response = deviceInfo.GetVirtualCapability("is_smartphone");
```

At any rate, you can override any user agent to be a smartphone through a patch file.

Accuracy vs. performance

The WURFL engine that matches a user agent to a set of capabilities has two working modes: accuracy and performance. You typically set the working mode through the *configurer*. If you grab configuration from the web.config file, you specify the working mode through the *mode* attribute of the *wurfl* node, as demonstrated here:

```
<wurfl mode="Accuracy">
   <mainFile path="~/App_Data/wurfl-latest.zip" />
</wurfl>
```

Possible values for the *mode* attribute are *Accuracy* and *Performance*. Alternatively, you can use the *SetMatchMode* on the *InMemoryConfigurer* object and configure the working mode programmatically.

```
WURFLManagerBuilder.Build(
        new InMemoryConfigurer()
                .MainFile(...)
                .SetMatchMode(MatchMode.Accuracy));
```

What's the difference between the two working modes? The difference exists only for desktop user agents. As far as mobile devices are concerned—those with the *is_wireless_device* capability set to *true*—the working mode is not relevant, and there's no difference in the overall behavior. For other types of devices, the *Performance* mode represents a shortcut and delivers a less accurate response in a much faster way. The effect of the *Performance* mode is that if the user agent is a desktop browser, you won't get effective capabilities values for the particular user agent, only the description associated with a generic desktop browser.

Put another way, the *Performance* mode is an option only if you need to quickly rule out (or in) a desktop browser without distinguishing between, for instance, versions of Internet Explorer or Chrome or Opera. For mobile devices, *Accuracy* or *Performance* always delivers the same service and returns the most accurate response possible.

Keep in mind that you can specify the working mode globally (as explained earlier), but you can also do that on a per-call basis by using the following overload of the *GetDeviceForRequest* method on the WURFL manager object:

```
public IDevice GetDeviceForRequest(WURFLRequest wurflRequest, MatchMode matchMode)
```

Using WURFL-based display modes

Earlier in the chapter, we discussed ASP.NET MVC display modes as the ideal way to route controllers to pick up a specific view. In general, display modes are not device-specific modes, in the sense that you can also use display modes to simply switch to a grayscale version of the site or to optimize for particular browsers such as Windows 8.

In any case, with display modes, the logic to route to a given view is always up to the coder. If you intend to build a single website for multiple devices, you just arrange multiple set of views—one for each class of device that you support. Each class of device then gets its own display mode. WURFL helps to ensure that the requesting device is mapped to the proper display mode. This means that a tablet will get the tablet view of a given page (if any) and a smartphone will get its own view, as well.

Important How does this approach ensure that you actually set up multidevice sites? After you have device-specific home pages, you're mostly done. From the device-specific home page, you can point to pages common to all views or just to pages implementing use-cases specific of a device. You can also decide to have a device-specific controller (for example, a *TabletXxxController*) to process use-cases particular to a device class and keep common actions in any *XxxController* class that you might have.

Selecting display modes

To effectively plan a multidevice site, regardless of the implementation techniques and patterns that you intend to use, the first step is always to have a clear idea of the classes of devices you propose to support. If you want to rely only on CSS, this leads to defining RWD breakpoints (see Chapter 12, "Making websites mobile-friendly"). Or, if you anticipate setting up a server-side engine and serving ad hoc markup to requesting devices, it leads to defining display modes.

In global.asax, you place a call to some *DisplayConfig* class that defines and registers all display modes that your website supports.

```
DisplayConfig.RegisterDisplayModes(DisplayModeProvider.Instance.Modes);
```

Here's the code for the *RegisterDisplayModes* method:

```
public class DisplayConfig
{
    public static void RegisterDisplayModes(IList<IDisplayMode> displayModes)
    {
        var modeDesktop = new DefaultDisplayMode("")
        {
            ContextCondition = (c => c.Request.IsDesktop())
        };
        var modeSmartphone = new DefaultDisplayMode("smartphone")
        {
            ContextCondition = (c => c.Request.IsSmartphone())
        };
        var modeTablet = new DefaultDisplayMode("tablet")
        {
            ContextCondition = (c => c.Request.IsTablet())
        };
        var modeLegacy = new DefaultDisplayMode("legacy")
        {
            ContextCondition = (c => c.Request.IsLegacy())
        };

        displayModes.Clear();
        displayModes.Add(modeSmartphone);
        displayModes.Add(modeTablet);
        displayModes.Add(modeLegacy);
        displayModes.Add(modeDesktop);
    }
}
```

The method first clears all default modes and then adds four modes: smartphones, tablets, desktop browsers, and legacy phones. This means that any devices used to access the site will be mapped to any of these modes.

In the preceding code, *IsLegacy, IsTablet,* and other methods on the HTTP *Request* object are plain .NET extension methods that receive the HTTP context and return a Boolean answer to the question *"is this request coming from given type of device?"*

Defining matching rules

Beyond tailoring the content of a given view, you can also use WURFL capabilities effectively to determine whether a user agent belongs to a particular type of device. The extension methods you see in the source code of the *RegisterDisplayModes* method implement matching rules for user agent strings by using WURFL capabilities. Here's some code that you can use to detect a smartphone:

```
public static Boolean IsSmartphone(this HttpRequestBase request)
{
    return IsSmartPhoneInternal(request.UserAgent);
}
private static Boolean IsSmartPhoneInternal(String userAgent)
{
    var device = WURFLManagerBuilder.Instance.GetDeviceForRequest(userAgent);
    return device.IsWireless() && !device.IsTablet() &&
            device.IsTouch() &&
            device.Width() > 240 &&
            (device.HasOs("android", new Version(2, 1)) ||
            device.HasOs("iphone os", new Version(3, 2)) ||
            device.HasOs("windows phone os", new Version(7, 1)) ||
            device.HasOs("rim os", new Version(6, 0)));
}
```

IsTouch, Width, and *HasOs,* as well as other methods in the listing are themselves extension methods defined on the WURFL *IDevice* interface. Here's the code:

```
public static class DeviceExtensions
{
    public static Boolean IsWireless(this IDevice device)
    {
        return device.GetCapability("is_wireless_device").ToBool();
    }

    public static Boolean IsTablet(this IDevice device)
    {
        return device.GetCapability("is_tablet").ToBool();
    }

    public static Boolean IsTouch(this IDevice device)
    {
        return device.GetCapability("pointing_method").Equals("touchscreen");
    }
```

```
public static Int32 Width(this IDevice device)
{
    return device.GetCapability("resolution_width").ToInt();
}

public static Boolean HasOs(this IDevice device, String os, Version version)
{
    // Check OS
    var deviceOs = device.GetCapability("device_os");
    if (!deviceOs.Equals(os, StringComparison.InvariantCultureIgnoreCase))
        return false;

    // Check OS version
    var deviceOsVersion = device.GetCapability("device_os_version");
    if (!deviceOsVersion.Contains("."))
        deviceOsVersion = String.Format("{0}.0", deviceOsVersion);

    Version detectedVersion;
    var success = Version.TryParse(deviceOsVersion, out detectedVersion);
    if (!success)
        return false;

    return detectedVersion.CompareTo(version) >= 0;
}
}
```

Likewise, *ToInt* and *ToBool* are also utility extensions methods that just parse strings to numbers or Booleans. I used extension methods in the example mostly for the purposes of clarity. You can definitely achieve the same without using them.

A multidevice site in action

The net effect of display modes is that when the request comes from, for instance, a tablet, the view engine subsystem routes the controller to pick up the tablet version of the view, if any. Given the previous configuration the selected view matches up to a Razor file named xxx.tablet.cshtml. (See Figure 13-4.)

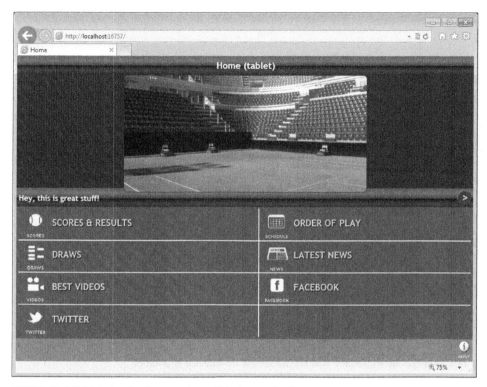

FIGURE 13-4 Tablet view for the sample multidevice application.

The same page will look different on a smartphone and on a legacy device, as depicted in Figure 13-5.

FIGURE 13-5 Smartphone and legacy view for the sample multidevice application.

All you need to do is have multiple Razor files, one for each view you want to be different from default. The default view is often (but not necessarily) the desktop view. Consider that display modes are selected on a first-match basis; the order in which you add display modes determines the fallback mechanism of views you actually have. You are not forced to have a smartphone or tablet file for each view of the application; for example, if the desktop view doesn't pose any issue on tablets, you don't need to have a xxx.tablet.cshtml file.

The WURFL cloud API

In the example just discussed, we used an on-premises version of WURFL, which requires that you manage the database yourself, ensuring that you always have an up-to-date repository and can patch the database properly in case of troubles. However, WURFL also comes as a cloud version.

Not surprisingly, the WURFL cloud offers ranges from a free but restricted plan up to a nearly unlimited access option for a flat monthly rate. You can find details at *http://www.scientiamobile.com/cloud*. The free plan is limited to two capabilities of choice, one IP address and one domain, and no more than 5,000 detections per month.

Setting up the API

After you've set up a subscription, you'll have the credentials to access the administrator panel and define the capabilities in which you're interested. At that point, you can use code similar to the following:

```
var config = new DefaultCloudClientConfig
{
    ApiKey = "267026:ZpXrnoY3JOhfzMBd7CEyRS2acuqOH6NU"
};
var manager = new CloudClientManager(config);
var info = manager.GetDeviceInfo(httpContext, new[] { "is_wireless_device", "is_tablet" });
```

The *GetDeviceInfo* method takes the HTTP context of the ASP.NET request and an array with the capabilities properties that you want to receive. For performance reasons, you can also request a smaller number of capabilities than those to which you are enabled.

The object that is returned to you contains a dictionary named *Capabilities* with all the values for the requested capabilities. For more information and details, go to *http://www.scientiamobile.com/wurflCloud/gettingStarted*.

Cloud API vs. on-premises API

When it comes to WURFL (and more generally, using a DDR), is the cloud a better option than storing everything on premises? The trade-off that you need to make is fairly simple to understand.

On one end of the scale you have the performance of a single WURFL request, which is significantly faster if it happens within your web server. On the other end, though, you have the cost of ownership and maintenance. The cost of an on-premises license and the pace at which you can amortize it is a variable to consider. Another variable is the cost of updating the WURFL database regularly—downloading the weekly update, restarting the application, and checking patch files. Finally, in an on-premises scenario you are responsible for any scalability issue that might be tracked down to the WURFL database.

In a cloud scenario, you just pay for a service, as little as you might need. Each request, though, is subject to the terms of service and is generally slower. Finally, with the cloud you have no control over the database and its update cycle.

As usual, the best option will vary depending on the particular situation.

Why you should consider server-side solutions

In web development, you can achieve *multivision*—that is, content that is intended to be viewed on different devices such as tablets, laptops, and smartphones—in either of two ways. You can have a single set of pages and multiple auxiliary resources such as CSS, images, and script files, or you can have multiple sets of pages and related resources. In both cases, the backend of the site is the same and the business logic is nearly the same.

But do you want it to be "nearly the same" or "exactly the same"?

This is one of the key points that might influence your decision process. If the experience you want *must* be the same across tablets, smartphones, and laptops, RWD and a client solution is the ideal approach. RWD is a technique that creates a single website that automatically adapts and renders differently to fit the size of the screen on which it displays, whether that screen belongs to a smartphone, tablet, desktop computer, or perhaps a smart TV. The work of detecting the screen size and applying the correct stylesheet is performed by the web browser.

Does this sound like the perfect solution? Should you stop here or give it more thought? Let's see what might come out of a second pass.

A common complaint about RWD is that it doesn't really distinguish devices, but only screen sizes. Subsequently, it might be sending a lot of content to small devices connected via a slow 3G network. Put another way, RWD is a methodology for effectively handling multiple screen sizes but not necessarily multiple devices with different characteristics, including different screen sizes. A point that you can hardly address with RWD is how to handle situations in which you want to offer different functions, layout, and use-cases to users connecting through a particular device.

To cut a long story short, the key question you must answer to make an informed decision is whether you want to provide a unique and device-specific experience. Do you want to make different analysis and design for tablets, smartphones, and laptops? Is one design good for you? If so, proceed with RWD and use implementation tricks to minimize download and performance issues. If not, focus on technologies and products to do server-side analysis of the user agent to recognize the class of the requesting device.

A client solution can work when you're OK with a single design/project to be adapted to any device. A server solution is appropriate when you want to have a specific design/project for each class of device in the context of a single website.

Summary

There aren't many websites that really need to resort to server-side device detection. For most sites, a client solution based on RWD principles is more than acceptable. But, this doesn't mean that a client-side solution is always preferable to a server-side solution.

A server-side solution is inherently much more flexible than a purely client-side, RWD-based solution.

To overcome some of the structural limitations of RWD solutions, you need to add some server-side logic. This means that you identify the requesting device, figure out its capabilities, and then serve ad hoc markup. This guarantees that an 800-pixel tablet will receive content tailor-made for a mobile audience, whereas users who connect through an 800-pixel browser window will receive desktop-specific content. With client-side logic, you can't determine if the browser viewing the page is hosted on a mobile device or in a small browser window.

This chapter offered a powerful perspective of server-side detection; use it to match a class of device (smartphone, tablet, smart TV, laptop, and whatever else you can think of) and serve the site you have in mind for those devices. The display mode feature of ASP.NET MVC makes it so easy to create a single website with as many faces (and groups of functionality) that you might need.

Index

Symbols

51degrees.mobi, 447
200 response code (HTTP), 347
202 response code (HTTP), 348
204 response code (HTTP), 347
301 response code (HTTP), 152–153, 155
302 response code (HTTP), 8, 113, 152, 172
400 response code (HTTP), 163
403 response code (HTTP), 172, 286
404 response code (HTTP), 8, 172–173
500 response code (HTTP), 163, 345
$ function, 377
, (comma), 381
{ } curly brackets, 10
. (dot), 380
/ (forward slash), 10, 13
+ operator, 380
== operator, 369
=== operator, 369
> operator, 380
| (pipe symbol), 370
@ symbol, 44, 55–56, 58
~ (tilde), 177, 381, 455

A

AAA (arrange, act, assert), 311
acceptance tests, 322
Accept-Encoding header, 269, 270, 392
Accept header, 360
AcceptVerbs attribute, 19, 348, 353, 355
access tokens
    social authorization, 221–223
    Web API, 357
Account controller, 218

Accuracy mode, 459
action attributes, 353
ActionFilterAttribute class, 267, 272
action filters
    built-in, 266
    custom
        adding response header, 267–268
        compressing response, 268–271
        view selector, 271–275
    defined, 255, 263
    dynamic loader filter
        adding action filter using fluent code, 280
        customizing action invoker, 280–282
        enabling via filter provider, 282–285
        interception points, 279–280
        registering custom invoker, 282
    embedded, 263–264
    external, 263–264
    global, 266–267
    implementing as attribute, 264
    types of, 265–266
Action HTML helper, 72
action invoker
    defined, 79
    replaceable components, 256, 258
    view engine and, 37–38
ActionLink HTML helper, 18, 43, 47, 53
action links, 46–47
action methods
    controller classes, 20–22
    example of proper, 236
    keeping lean, 231–236
    restricting, 190–191
    routing to
        REST, 344–346
        RPC, 353

E

S

U

X

Y

About the author

DINO ESPOSITO is CTO and cofounder of *e-tennis.net*, a startup providing software and IT services to professional tennis and sports companies. Dino still does a lot of training and writing and is the author of several books on web development and .NET design. His most recent books are *Architecting Mobile Solutions for the Enterprise* and *Microsoft .NET: Architecting Applications for the Enterprise,* both from Microsoft Press. Dino speaks regularly at industry conferences (including DevConnections) and premier European events such as Software Architect, DevWeek, and BASTA. A technical evangelist covering Android and Kotlin development for JetBrains, Dino is also on the development team of WURFL—the ScientiaMobile database of mobile device capabilities that is used by large organizations such as Facebook.

You can follow Dino on Twitter at *@despos* and through his blog (*http://software2cents. wordpress.com*).

Now that you've read the book...

Tell us what you think!

Was it useful?
Did it teach you what you wanted to learn?
Was there room for improvement?

Let us know at http://aka.ms/tellpress

Your feedback goes directly to the staff at Microsoft Press,
and we read every one of your responses. Thanks in advance!

 Microsoft

DISCARD

CPSIA information can be obtained at www.ICGtesting.com
Printed in the USA
LVOW03s0704140214

373709LV00006B/16/P